Arthur Wright

Some New Testament Problems

Arthur Wright

Some New Testament Problems

ISBN/EAN: 9783337118143

Printed in Europe, USA, Canada, Australia, Japan

Cover: Foto ©ninafisch / pixelio.de

More available books at **www.hansebooks.com**

SOME
NEW TESTAMENT
PROBLEMS

BY

REV. ARTHUR WRIGHT, M.A.

FELLOW AND TUTOR OF QUEENS' COLLEGE, CAMBRIDGE

METHUEN & CO.
36, ESSEX STREET, STRAND
LONDON
1898

CONTENTS

		PAGE
I.	First, Second and Third Editions of S. Mark's Gospel	1
II.	S. Mark's Order	11
III.	S. Matthew's "Logia"	16
IV.	S. Luke's "Travel Narrative"	23
V.	Identical Passages	30
VI.	Conflations	40
VII.	On the Proper Names in S. Mark's Gospel	56
VIII.	On the Proper Names in S. Luke's Writings	74
IX.	On Oral Teaching	91
X.	On the Precept to Sell your Cloak and Buy a Sword	104
XI.	S. Mark's Testimony to the Resurrection	115
XII.	The Camel and the Needle's Eye	125
XIII.	The Origin of the Lord's Supper	134
XIV.	On the Date of the Crucifixion	147
XV.	Mr. Halcombe's Strictures on Modern Criticism	195
XVI.	Theories of Messrs. Badham and Jolley	243
XVII.	Papias on S. Matthew	265
XVIII.	The Gift of Tongues	277
XIX.	The Beautiful Gate of the Temple	303
XX.	Apollos	309
XXI.	That Prophecy is Conditional	323
XXII.	The Authorship of the Epistle to the Hebrews	331

PREFACE

THE chief use of the New Testament is, and always should be, devotional. We approach it best in the sanctuary, when our minds have been prepared by confession, prayer, and adoration to learn of Him who has said, "Whosoever shall not receive the kingdom of God as a little child, will not enter therein."

But when we have come to love the book as the revelation of JESUS CHRIST, we find that it appeals to our intellect as well as to our affections. The proper preparation for the pulpit is conscientious work in the study, and even laymen will find that their apprehension of Scripture truth is assisted by some acquaintance with the history of the first century and its immediate precursors, with the geography of the Holy Land, and with Semitic modes of thought and expression. Grammar is the first essential in exegesis. Textual criticism is indispensable. Historical criticism, with which the present volume chiefly deals, is still more fundamental. Without it the commentator is at fault and the apologist loses his most effective weapons. Destructive it may be—like every other weapon—if unfairly used; but as it is a true science, it must in the long run prove the supporter of truth.

It is impossible that "the higher criticism," as it is called, should so rapidly gain ground in the domain of the Old Testament, and yet the New Testament remain in the grasp of mediæval harmonists. They served their time and served it well, but their methods will not suffice for ever. We must keep pace with the age, if we would hand down the truth to future generations.

It is in the hope of contributing something to that end that the present work is written. No attempt has been made to cover the whole ground. The problems which are discussed arise, with one exception, out of the Synoptic Gospels and the Acts of the Apostles. Not that S. Paul's writings or S. John's yield no problems, but in these days it is impossible for one man to deal adequately with the whole range of New Testament study. I, at any rate, have found it better to concentrate my attention on one or two small departments.

I have recently published a Synopsis of the Gospels, and I am now engaged on a critical edition of S. Luke's Gospel for use in the lecture-room.

PREFACE

The work of preparing these volumes has suggested many of the problems which are here propounded, and, at the same time, has made it possible to collect the statistics which have facilitated their solution.

I have added some expository papers for the purpose of showing how criticism may assist in interpretation and apologetics. I have also at times defended my own position against opponents of various kinds, not from any love of controversy, but in the hope of contributing towards the settlement of many questions which in the infancy of the new science are necessarily debated.

What I have written in defence of the oral hypothesis may be read in connexion with the Introduction to my *Synopsis*, in which I have summarised the arguments, some of which are produced at length here—some, but not all; the argument from the assimilation of doublets, which I think the most convincing of all, has been deemed to be sufficiently expressed there. Yet, as I have some misgivings on that point, perhaps I may be pardoned for lingering on it a moment now.

The term "doublets" is used in the widest sense to include all similar passages. My contention is that in oral teaching, owing to a well-known trick of the memory, similar passages are sure to become more similar; whereas, if documents were slavishly copied the original differences would in all probability be maintained.

Now it seems to me that in the Gospels according to S. Matthew and S. Luke the process of unconscious assimilation is very frequently to be observed. We may take as an illustration the Feeding of the Five Thousand and the Feeding of the Four Thousand. Many critics have held these to be mere doublets, *i.e.*, two records of one and the same event. For is it conceivable (they ask) that the Twelve, after witnessing the former miracle, should have been totally unprepared for the latter? Should have felt the same difficulties, asked the same questions, and reported the occurrence on the same lines?

There would be force in these objections if we held that the conversations in the Gospels are *verbatim* reports. But if they are only summaries of what was really said, and if gaps in the narrator's recollections were supplied from conjecture or by conflation, then we must remember the biblical method, which is so strongly marked in Amos and other Old Testament writers, of telling similar things in similar language. And when this had once been done, the effect of oral repetition (if there was such a thing) would be to make the two narratives still more alike. S. Mark's accounts of these two parallel events, although originally sufficiently resembling each other, have probably been still further assimilated to some extent; S. Matthew's unquestionably to a very much greater extent, for in the latter part of the sections he makes the words practically identical. Another case in which he has done the same thing is given on page 48, but there are scores of passages in which this process, which we would attribute to unconscious cerebration, may be perceived. S. Luke exhibits it to a less degree, but a striking example of it in his Gospel is pointed out on page 111. No dull copyist with documents before him would, I maintain, be at all likely to produce these effects; no oral teaching could be carried on for forty years without them.

These arguments, I believe, will have to be reckoned with. It is of little help for the supporters of the documentary hypothesis to admit that oral teaching is a *vera causa*, as they now frequently do, and then to pronounce in favour of documents without removing one of the objections which have been shown to lie against them. That is not the way to advance the cause of truth, which is what we all alike desire.

The papers on the Acts of the Apostles deal with hermeneutics. I do not as yet feel prepared to analyse that book into its sources. The materials for doing so are insufficient. We have four Gospels, which can be compared with each other, but we have only one Acts of the Apostles. The comparative method cannot be directly applied to the book. Certain broad outlines are plain, but I reserve discussion of them for a future occasion.

The paper on the Epistle to the Hebrews is tentative and suggestive rather than exhaustive. Perhaps it may stir up others to pursue a fascinating study.

A correct theory of the Scriptures is an immense aid to their interpretation, but it does not supply the inward illumination, which makes them the salvation of our souls. And therefore I invite all students of Holy Writ to join with me in using the ancient prayer :—

>Veni, Creator Spiritus,
>Mentes tuorum visita,
>Imple superna gratia
>Quae Tu creasti pectora.

NEW TESTAMENT PROBLEMS

I.

FIRST, SECOND AND THIRD EDITIONS OF S. MARK'S GOSPEL

THE priority of S. Mark's Gospel is an axiom with the great majority of critics. Those who accept the documentary hypothesis respecting the origin of the Gospels are forced, sooner or later, to admit that not our S. Mark, but an earlier *Ur-Marcus* lies at the basis of the synoptic records. We who hold to the oral hypothesis have a much freer hand. We are not bound to postulate the existence of one, or indeed several, primitive and priceless records, which had once a wide circulation, but nevertheless were permitted by the supposed carelessness of the early Christians to perish. We know of one S. Mark, and only one. But we believe that the written S. Mark was preceded by an oral S. Mark, and that the oral S. Mark took many years in forming. We are not tied to a document beginning with John the Baptist and ending with ἐφοβοῦντο γάρ, or any other formula. We believe that a single lesson, perhaps connected with the Passion, was the first small origin of the book, and that other lessons, one at a time, collected round that centre, the whole record expanding by degrees, sometimes in one chapter sometimes in another, till it reached its present dimensions.

What I want to insist upon in the present paper is that we may still trace three stages in the formation of S. Mark, and that they may be said to constitute a first edition, a second, and a third.

In S. Luke's Gospel we shall find, embedded amongst other matter, the first edition; in S. Matthew's the second; while S. Mark himself may be said to have written the third.

If these three editions had all proceeded direct from S. Mark's pen, the problem would be simple. The first edition would have been—as far as it went—the nearest to the primitive oral teaching; the second and third, though useful for corroboration, would have been chiefly valued for their new matter. At present the case is different. S. Luke's edition, though the first, had been modified before it reached him, by passing through the minds and memories of perhaps a dozen teachers, all of whom were men of mature age, who had lost the freshness of verbal memory. Although they learned the lessons by heart, and so did not materially or consciously change them, they unconsciously—especially at the first—substituted synonyms, omitted details, occasionally improved the diction. And so, before the Gospel reached S. Luke, its wording had been a good deal modified, as we may see by comparing his edition of it with S. Mark. Not only so, but nearly forty years passed between his first undertaking to teach and his final resolution to write. And during these forty years a certain amount of change in his own teaching also must be allowed for.

The second edition, embedded in S. Matthew, exhibits the same process. Verbally it is more in agreement with S. Mark, but the desire for brevity has often led to great curtailment. And so the third edition—S. Mark's own—as a rule best represents the original oral teaching. Except when the other Evangelists are agreed against it in the choice or addition of a word, we rightly prefer S. Mark's testimony.

But in one important particular S. Luke's evidence is of the greatest value. It helps us, I maintain, to fix the relative date at which S. Mark's sections were produced. If S. Luke contains a section of Marcan matter, we may feel sure that that section belonged to the first edition of S. Mark; if he omits it, there is a strong presumption that it did not.

I therefore append a list of those sections of S. Mark which are absent from S. Luke. In the margin I give such scraps of them as S. Luke has nevertheless preserved. For in some cases, which it is most important to distinguish, the section is omitted from S. Luke, but a small fragment, or scrap, of it is given. This curious phenomenon will be explained afterwards. At first it seems fatal to our theory, but in the end it will be seen to yield the strongest confirmation.

	Sections belonging to the later, or second, edition of S. Mark.	S. MARK.	Scraps of them found in S. LUKE.
{	1. The Baptist's clothing and dress	i. 6	...
	2. The Baptist's preaching (?)	i. 7–8	iii. 16
	3. The calling of SS. Simon, Andrew, James and John	i. 16–20	v. 10–11
{	4.*"He is mad."	iii. 19b–21	...
	5. "He hath Beelzebub."	iii. 22–27	xi. 14–15, 17–18, 21–22
	6. Blasphemy against the Holy Spirit	iii. 28–30	xii. 10b
	7. "Who is my mother?" (?)	iii. 31–35	viii. 19–21
{	8.*The seed growing secretly	iv. 26–29	...
	9. The grain of mustard seed	iv. 30–32	xiii. 18–19
	10. Nothing without a parable	iv. 33–34	...
	11. A visit to Nazareth	vi. 1–6a	iv. 16, 22, 24
	12. The death of John the Baptist	vi. 17–29	iii. 19–20 (?)
	13. The walking on the sea	vi. 45–52	...
	14. The landing at Gennesaret	vi. 53–56	...
	15. Eating with unwashed hands	vii. 1–23	xi. 38 (?)
	16. The Syrophenician woman's daughter	vii. 24–30	...
{	17.*The deaf man who had an impediment in his speech	vii. 31–37	...
	18. The feeding of the four thousand	viii. 1–10	...
	19. A sign from heaven demanded	viii. 11–13	xi. 16, 29
	20. The leaven of the Pharisees	viii. 14–21	xii. 1
	21.*The blind man of Bethsaida	viii. 22–26	...
	22. S. Peter rebukes our Lord	viii. 32–33	...
	23. Descent from the Mount of Transfiguration	ix. 9–13	ix. 36b
{	24. The cup of cold water in the name of a disciple	ix. 41	...
	25. Of causing scandals	ix. 42–49	xvii. 2
	26. Salt is good	ix. 50	xiv. 34
	27. On the question of divorce	x. 1–12	xvi. 18
	28. The ambitious request	x. 35–45	xxii. 25–26
	29. The fruitless fig tree	xi. 12–14, 20–25	...
	30. The question put by the scribe	xii. 28–34	x. 25–27
	31. "Lest He find you sleeping"	xiii. 34–37	...
	32. The anointing at Bethany	xiv. 3–9	vii. 36–38, 40 (?)
	33. "I will smite the shepherd"	xiv. 27–28	...

EDITIONS OF S. MARK'S GOSPEL

S. MARK.

34. "I will destroy this temple" .	xiv. 55-61	...
35. Mockery by the soldiers .	xv. 16-20ª	...
36. Elahi, Elahi, lᵉma sᵉbhaqtani .	xv. 34-36	...

Cases about which there is some doubt are marked thus (?)
Sections which are found in the third edition only are marked thus *
To the above should probably be added a few words, lines, or paragraphs embedded in other sections, *e.g.* S. Mark xiv. 38ᵇ—42.

I will now produce some reasons for believing that the sections here catalogued are of later date than the rest of S. Mark's Gospel, so that we may reasonably speak of them as belonging to the second edition.

And first this supposition corresponds with certain facts which are narrated in the Acts of the Apostles and in the earliest Fathers of the Church.

We are told by Papias* that S. Mark's Gospel is S. Peter's work, which S. Mark translated (from Aramaic into Greek). We accept this statement as generally true and therefore believe that both S. Peter's and S. Mark's presence were necessary for the production of a Gospel section in Greek. Now S. Peter—except during certain missionary journeys —lived and laboured in Jerusalem from the great day of Pentecost until he took up his residence in Joppa (Acts ix. 43). During this period we believe the first edition of S. Mark's oral Gospel to have been composed. Then came a considerable gap, during which S. Mark also left the Holy City and became S. Paul's companion to teach the Gospel to the Gentiles (Acts xii. 25, xiii. 5). But S. Mark

* EUSEBIUS, *Hist. Eccl.*, iii., xxxix. 15.

gave up this work and returned to Jerusalem (Acts xiii. 13). Other catechists had to be found for S. Paul's Gentile Churches, and undoubtedly they were brought from Jerusalem, like the prophets and evangelists, for so only can we account for the rapid Judaising of S. Paul's converts. My point is that the oral Gospel, which was carried to the West and became the basis of all subsequent teaching there, must have been S. Mark's Gospel at this particular stage of its growth, which I have called the first edition.

When S. Mark returned to Jerusalem (Acts xiii. 13) he either found S. Peter there or was soon joined by him (Acts xv. 7). How long the pair remained in Jerusalem we do not know; but probably long enough for the completion of the second edition.

As for the third edition we need not feel troubled, because it only added four new sections and these may be of very much later growth. At any rate S. Peter in his first epistle, which is generally admitted to belong to the closing period of his life, calls S. Mark "his son" (1 Pet. v. 13), and sends a salutation from him, showing that the early associates were once more united and may even then have composed these four sections.

Secondly, by our hypothesis we sweep away at a single stroke the stupendous difficulty which beset the question of S. Luke's omissions. Few people face that difficulty as they ought; to me it was a stumbling block for many years, but it has been removed. S. Luke is seen to have omitted little or even nothing. We thus make him a reasonable man and

EDITIONS OF S. MARK'S GOSPEL 7

a conscientious worker. The gain in this respect can hardly be exaggerated.

Thirdly, internal evidence supports our contention. It will be seen that many of the new sections fall together so as to form a group. I have bracketed five such groups, one a particularly long one. Now we see from the parallel case of the "Travel Narrative" in S. Luke (paper iv.) that new materials are apt to be aggregated together. When once a gap is made, it has a tendency to increase in size. The huge addition, Mark vi. 45—viii. 26, is only a striking illustration of this tendency.

Fourthly, we must notice the eighteen scraps. The first thing to observe is that they are short; they are scraps and not sections. Next, they are put by S. Luke into a different context from that which they occupy in S. Mark. Lastly, they are always taken from what I have called S. Mark's second edition, and therefore frequently agree with S. Matthew against S. Mark.

From these facts we conclude that they reached S. Luke in the same way in which we shall see (paper iii.) that S. Matthew's *Logia* reached him. That is to say, they were sent to him by correspondents, who quoted them because of their intrinsic value, but did not at the same time give the necessary information about the occasions on which they were spoken. S. Luke, therefore, misplaced them through imperfect knowledge.

If we are right in supposing that all S. Paul's churches, and many others, possessed an oral Gospel, which was jealously guarded by the authorities,* none

* See *Critical Review* (T. and T. Clark), vol. i. p. 370 f.

but experts would know which portions of it were S. Peter's work, which S. Matthew's, and which were supplied from other sources. S. Luke, therefore, would often receive from his various correspondents some sayings which he possessed already. And although the great majority of new sayings came from S. Matthew's *logia*, a few would be sure to belong to the earlier cycle. If, then, no Marcan scraps had been utilised by S. Luke, we should have had to explain why it was so. At present the simple fact that he misplaces them is an indication that our explanation is correct.

S. Mark's Gospel—if reckoned without the last twelve verses which textual critics reject—contains 666 verses. The second edition adds 192 verses, and the third edition 18. The first edition, therefore, contained 456 verses; probably, however, a good many words, lines, and paragraphs which now figure in these 456 verses were really absent from the first edition, being later expansions.

Now, if we may look to S. Matthew's Gospel for the second edition of S. Mark, we notice, as has been said already, that S. Matthew presents it in an abbreviated form, much curtailed by riddling out words which were not essential. The same process, perhaps, has sometimes been carried a little farther, and has swept away sections as well as lines. At any rate the following sections, though present in S. Luke and reappearing in S. Mark, are absent from S. Matthew :—

(1) The healing of the demoniac in the synagogue at Capernaum (Mark i. 23-28 = Luke iv. 33-37);

EDITIONS OF S. MARK'S GOSPEL

(2) The stranger who exorcised in Jesus' name (Mark ix. 38-40 = Luke ix. 49-50);

(3) The widow's mites (Mark xii. 41-44 = Luke xxi. 1-4).

The third edition contains four new sections which according to our hypothesis are the latest additions to S. Mark :—

(1) The suspicion that our Lord was mad (Mark iii. 19^b–21);

(2) The parable of the seed growing secretly (Mark iv. 26-29);

(3) The healing of the deaf man who had an impediment in his speech (Mark vii. 31-37);

(4) The healing of the blind man of Bethsaida (Mark viii. 22-26).

One more topic deserves consideration. S. Mark's wealth of words has long been noticed. The more closely we test it, the more convinced we are that it is characteristic of his style, derived in part perhaps from S. Peter's oriental redundancy. The longest phrases with him, the most graphic and picturesque, give the oldest form of the narrative. Even when S. Matthew and S. Luke agree in omitting a word or a line, and S. Mark gives it, S. Mark is generally original.

Nevertheless there may be some exceptions to this. S. Mark, during forty years of oral teaching, may have gathered new information from divers quarters and used it to expand his already long expressions.

When words which are not merely picturesque, but convey additional information, are found in S. Mark, but not in the parallel passages in the other Gospels, we may allow that they belong to the third edition. For example, in a few cases S. Mark agrees with S. John, while the others are silent ("200 denarii," Mark vi. 37 = John vi. 7; "Pistic nard" Mark xiv. 3 = John xii. 3). If S. John's oral teaching at Ephesus preceded the writing of the fourth Gospel by many years, as we believe it to have done, there is no difficulty in supposing that S. Mark during visits to Ephesus derived something from it. On the oral hypothesis we are perfectly free to think so if the facts require.

Let no one suppose that the minute examination to which we have subjected the synoptic Gospels in this and in the following chapters is unprofitable. Anything which throws light upon their genesis is valuable to the apologist. We accept the Gospels because they speak direct to our hearts as no other books do. We know them to be living, to be the work of the Holy Spirit, and to reveal Him who is the Life; but they have a human side as well as a divine; they appeal to our intellect as well as to our heart, and anything which will make them more real to us, or will uphold them in the presence of objectors, demands our earnest consideration.

In the papers which follow we shall find many places where the hypothesis of S. Mark's second edition will explain serious difficulties. It has all the advantages of an Ur-Marcus, without any of the improbability.

II.

S. MARK'S ORDER

IN the last paper we saw reason to believe that S. Mark's Gospel admits of analysis. To a certain extent, we can distinguish between its earliest sections, its later additions, and its final touches.

Papias complains that it is not written "in order." If we carefully examine his indictment in the light which his own words immediately throw upon it, we shall see it to be a very serious one. The chronology of S. Mark's Gospel (he says) is in a more or less chaotic state, because S. Peter did not attempt to write history, but to supply a few lessons for the immediate need of the Church.

Now the Church stood in need of teaching, and we believe this teaching, in accordance with the custom of the day in the East, to have consisted in *learning* by heart. In that way the lessons would become a permanent possession; in that way we can account for the strange variations and stranger similarity of identical sections in the synoptic Gospels. Those Gospels were the work of experienced teachers or "catechists," who were highly proficient in their lessons, yet did not copy a document, but derived their information from the more fluctuating processes of tradition.

But while we place the genesis of our Gospels in the schoolroom rather than in the congregation, we think it highly probable that Gospel sections were recited in public worship as well as in the classes of catechumens. It was so in the earliest times of which we have record (Justin Martyr, *Apology*, i. § 67), and it may well have been so much earlier than that, yea, even in Apostolic days.

The Christians inherited from the Jews a division of time into weeks of seven days each. At first Christian assemblies met in the synagogue, and on the Saturday (James ii. 2; Acts ix. 20, etc.). When the Christians separated themselves from the Jews they met on Sunday (Acts xx. 7). And although week-day services were not unknown, and Good Friday with other holy days became sacred, the "Lord's Day" retained its peculiar pre-eminence, and Easter Day was the greatest of all Sundays in the year.

Can we doubt that on Easter Day, Good Friday,* Palm Sunday, and Passion Sunday (to use modern terms), those Gospel sections which narrated the events which all Christians were thinking of, were selected for repetition?

In the warmth of their first love services were held every day, celebrations of the Eucharist at every meal, and catechetical classes were always at work. But as time went on daily business demanded attention, and the religious standard of the synagogue became the religious standard of the Church. Catechizing would gradually be confined

* The name Quartodeciman proves this. See page 172.

to the young, and the recitation of Gospel sections in public worship would meet the wants of the old.

Now in the synagogue the Law was divided into sections, one for every Sabbath in a cycle of three years. The Christians, whether they adopted the Jewish table of lessons or not, certainly read the Old Testament in public worship. At whatever date they began to recite the Gospel sections also—and I think it must have been at a very early date—there would be a tendency to take them in regular course; in fact, sooner or later every Sunday would be provided with what we call a "Gospel" of its own.

Greek lectionaries provide a Gospel for every day in the year. Western liturgies provide one for every Sunday and high-day. The practice of doing this goes back, as far as we can trace, into the unknown past. It may have extended a good deal further back than the time at which our four Gospels were received as canonical, into the older period, when every church had an oral Gospel of its own.

If this were so, we should expect to see some traces of the old divisions in our present Gospels. It ought to be possible to divide them easily and naturally into fifty or fifty-one lessons; for a lunar year consists of about $354\frac{1}{3}$ days, and therefore contained fifty or oftener fifty-one Sundays.*

Now it is remarkable that S. Mark's Gospel in the Westcott and Hort text is divided into forty-eight paragraphs, two or three of which are long and readily admit of division.

* Intercalated months (see page 168) would be provided for by repetition.

In the case of S. Matthew and S. Luke those editors have divided the Gospels into a large number of paragraphs, some of which consist of a single verse, and could not have formed a lesson. But if we turn to the revised Table of Lessons now used in the Church of England, we find S. Matthew's Gospel divided into fifty-one lessons, S. Luke's into forty-seven. As far as S. Matthew goes, nothing could be more satisfactory. With S. Luke the case is not so favourable. His is the longest Gospel of the four, and I have for some time contended that chapters i., ii., iii. 23-38 are comparatively late additions to it, which never formed part of the primitive oral teaching. It would, however, be quite easy to divide this Gospel somewhat differently from the way adopted by the revisers of the Table of Lessons, whose design was to serve the present age, and not to discover the ancient landmarks.

If it be true that at a comparatively early date S. Luke's Gospel was already divided into fifty-one lessons, each of which was connected with a particular Sunday of the year, it is plain that whatever additions were subsequently made in his work, must have been done by lengthening some of the lessons. And as this could obviously only be permitted within narrow limits, he would be compelled to distribute any new *logia* which reached him, over a large number of the lessons. And this consideration will help to explain their present position in his Gospel, which, as we shall shortly see, is so different from that which they occupy in S. Matthew.

If there really was an attempt to provide every

Sunday with a Gospel of its own, we shall understand why the formation of Gospel sections proceeded rapidly at first and then ceased; we shall understand why all our Gospels are so short and contain so little which is not essential; we shall understand how S. Mark's order became fixed. And although I am very far from insisting that the idea is more than a speculation, I claim that it should not be dismissed as unworthy of consideration. We must not allow our own prejudices to obscure our perception of truth.

If the Gospels for the day in the English Book of Common Prayer, from Christmas to Ascension Day, were put together into one volume, with the aid of a few editorial notes, they would present the reader with a work which would be very similar to what Papias declares S. Mark's Gospel to be. It would give a rough approximation to the true sequence of events in the main particulars, but it would not be chronological in detail. The bulk of it would be arranged for edification, rather than for history.

How completely unchronological S. Mark's Gospel is, I have shown in the introduction to my Synopsis of the Gospels. I need not, therefore, pursue the subject now, save only to impress on the reader the supreme importance of this fundamental question. The ordinary commentator assumes that our Gospels are arranged chronologically, and in his endeavours to harmonize one with the other, produces so many tortuous explanations as to do violence to the faith of the simple. Once admit that our Gospels are arranged on a different plan, and all these difficulties cease.

III.

S. MATTHEW'S *LOGIA*

THE recent discovery and publication of the papyrus containing "Sayings of Jesus," if it had done nothing else, would have been useful as an object lesson in the meaning of the word *logion*.* S. Matthew's *logia*, of which Papias speaks, were probably similar in form to those on the papyrus. There is good reason to think that they possessed no more clue to the occasion of utterance than the simple preface "Jesus saith," which is there used. And they were probably often as little connected with each other in subject-matter or sequence of thought, as are these sayings.

S. Matthew (Papias writes, according to the well-attested Vulgate reading) "procured their compilation" (συνετάξατο). That is to say, he superintended the work, rather than produced it. Multitudes of eye and ear witnesses contributed their recollections. He sifted and arranged them, tested them from what he personally remembered, and authorised their reception into the body of Church teaching.

If the various reading συνεγράψατο be correct, Papias will have committed himself to the assertion that S. Matthew caused them to be *written*. This,

---

* On this question see below, page 270.

according to my belief, is less probable; and Papias, if he really said that, may have been mistaken. For there was a prejudice against writing in Jerusalem, and the variations between S. Matthew and S. Luke, both in wording and in order, are best explained by oral teaching.

As to the general scope and contents of these *logia*, I see no reason to doubt that they correspond to what I have put into the second division of my Synopsis, where they can be conveniently studied. At the same time I fully admit that the lines which separate my fourth division from the second are very faint. In no case can we feel certain that any particular *logion* belonged to the one division rather than the other.

Papias continues, that "each man translated S. Matthew's *logia* as he was able." This important statement need not imply that the *logia* were read aloud in Aramaic during divine service, and rendered into Greek by a *viva voce* translator, like the Old Testament lessons in the Hebrew synagogue. Nor need it imply that many translations of varying merit were in use. The verb is in the singular, and "each man" does not necessarily imply very many. Papias means that several persons essayed the task. To me his curious wording conveyed the idea that he himself, in his younger days, had been one of them. His great work in five books, consisted, I understand him to say, of translations of these *logia*, accompanied by a running commentary, and interspersed with numerous, and often apocryphal additions, which he obtained from oral sources. But

C

there is nothing in what Papias says to prevent us from supposing that in or about 50 A.D., an oral Greek version of the *logia* was in use at Jerusalem in Hellenic circles.

Translation implies a certain amount of sacrifice. The precise meaning of the original words can never be reproduced. And if the two oral editions—the Aramaic and the Greek—circulated side by side for nearly twenty years in Jerusalem, it is certain that modifications and corrections would be made. Generally the Greek would be corrected from the Aramaic, but sometimes the Aramaic would be influenced by the Greek. All these complications must be taken into account by anyone who would understand the formation of our Gospels.

Certain *logia*, notably those connected with John the Baptist, our Lord's baptism, and His temptation, required some historical setting to make them intelligible. And it is not surprising that they borrowed from S. Mark's oral Gospel a few words for that purpose. But whether the *logia* in the Church of Jerusalem were ever combined with S. Mark's oral Gospel so as to form one body of teaching, we cannot say. There is much to incline us to believe that to the last they circulated there as a separate cycle of oral teaching. All that we can see our way at present to affirm, is that in S. Matthew and S. Luke they are blended with other matter into one history, yet in such a way that the process of blending has been done by, or for, these evangelists independently and quite differently.

Let us take S. Luke first. He at any rate had no

personal knowledge of the sequence of events to guide or hamper him. Unless a *logion* contained internal evidence which settled its date, he could not decide of himself to which period of our Lord's ministry it belonged.

Now, judging from their present condition, and from the degree of their verbal agreement with S. Matthew, I infer that the *logia* reached S. Luke a few at a time, and in different ways. (1) Some came overland through Asia Minor, as S. Mark's Gospel had done. These would pass from church to church. The process would take several years, and the words would be a good deal disturbed. (2) Others came by sea, being either (*a*) brought by a Christian passenger from Palestine; or (*b*) sent by letter. The majority of them came in Greek, but certainly (*c*) a few in the original Aramaic.*

These various modes of transport will account for the fact that some *logia* of great length are almost *verbatim* the same in two Gospels, others vary, sometimes considerably, while a few are clearly new translations of the same original.

Now if these *logia* had come all at once, S. Luke might have felt overwhelmed by them and might have written to Jerusalem for further information about their chronology. But receiving them, as he probably did, a few at a time, he would be the more likely to deal with them on his own responsibility.

He was in this dilemma; either he must omit them from his teaching, or he must find a place

---

* For examples see Introduction to the *Synopsis of the Gospels*, page viii.

for them in his lessons. The facts indicate that he chose the latter course. A certain number of them were sufficiently ear-marked by their subject and were put into their proper places, but the great mass were crowded into that "Travel Narrative," which we shall examine in the next paper. Suffice it now to say that the "Travel Narrative" is, in my opinion, simply a collection of undated materials, arranged roughly for convenience of teaching.

S. Luke was a Gentile and worked for Gentiles. More literary methods were in favour with his pupils than were tolerated in Palestine. Writing materials were not tabooed; and so, though he can hardly have finally written his Gospel before 80 A.D., his materials once received were well preserved. His edition of the *logia*, though very incomplete, seems in many cases to be more original than S. Matthew's. In S. Matthew the sentences are smoother and more rotund, the effect of oral repetition during a much longer period. Thus belief in the oral hypothesis gives us freedom in the face of facts. We have to consider (1) at what stage in its formation and after what amount of attrition an evangelist received a section; (2) what further modification it underwent in his hands. A period of thirty or forty years, during which the records were in a more or less fluid state, will account for the facts. In one particular S. Matthew may be nearer the original, in another S. Luke, and that in the same *logion*. They both remain reasonable men and honest workers.

We do not know in what Church S. Matthew's

Gospel was formed. A community of Greek-speaking Jews is demanded, at some distance from Palestine, for geographical details were not familiar to the compilers. Alexandria satisfies the conditions; and there are some things—such as the flight into Egypt, and the prophecy, "Out of Egypt did I call My Son"—which favour that direction. More than this we cannot say.

The second edition of S. Mark forms the groundwork of S. Matthew's oral Gospel, and indicates the date at which the Church was founded which used it, considerably later than the foundation of the Church at Philippi in which S. Luke laboured.

The same difficulty which had confronted S. Luke about arranging the *logia* into the Marcan framework, appears to have confronted the authorities at Alexandria (or whatever other place is the true one); but they settled it in a different way. Instead of one great gap into which they accumulated undated materials, they had five smaller gaps, viz., (1) the Sermon on the Mount; (2) the Charge to the Twelve; (3) the Parables in Matthew xiii.; (4) the woes on the Pharisees; (5) the eschatological discourses. Amongst these most of the *logia* have been distributed.

We cannot undertake to say whether S. Luke or S. Matthew comes nearest to the truth in these arrangements. We only warn the reader against the common assumption that one or other of them, if not both, has always, or even usually, given us the real occasion of utterance.

Our reason for believing in a literary rather than a chronological setting, will be given further in the papers which follow. They arise from a comparison of the order in S. Matthew and S. Luke. Enormous difficulties will be overcome by the frank acceptance of the fact that imperfect knowledge has led to its natural consequences. Modern commentators admit this grudgingly and in a few cases. But if the principle is conceded, there is no reason why its extension should not be carried as far as the facts demand.

IV.

S. LUKE'S "TRAVEL NARRATIVE"

(S. LUKE ix. 51—xviii. 14.)

S. LUKE'S Gospel consists, roughly speaking, of four parts, viz.:
Preliminary matter, chapter i., ii.
First Marcan portion, chapters iii.—ix. 50.
"Travel Narrative," chapters ix. 51—xviii. 14.
Second Marcan portion, chapters xviii. 15—xxiv.

In the Marcan portions I do not mean to imply that all the materials are derived from S. Mark. Much non-Marcan matter is interspersed. But S. Mark furnishes the groundwork. His history and chronology are S. Luke's guide.

But in the great "Travel Narrative" this is no longer the case. Here at last S. Mark is entirely deserted. Except an occasional brief "scrap" nothing is taken from him, and S. Luke, I hold, is left without a guide.

The facts are startling, and should be fully appreciated. This huge slice—consisting of nearly nine chapters, or more than one-third of the whole Gospel—is inserted between what probably were in the first edition of S. Mark two consecutive verses.

For S. Luke ix. 50 corresponds to S. Mark ix. 40 and Luke xviii. 15 to S. Mark x. 13. The twenty-two verses of S. Mark which intervene have every mark of belonging to the second edition of his Gospel. S. Luke, therefore, having closely followed S. Mark for seven chapters, abruptly abandons him. Nine chapters later on he abruptly returns to him at the very point of severance, and never leaves him again for any length of time.

Harmonists account for the facts in the following way: These nine chapters of S. Luke narrate, they say, a ministry in Peræa, which S. Mark for some reason omitted to notice, but S. Luke has recorded at great length. The Peræan ministry (they continue) lasted about six months, and included one or probably several visits to Jerusalem prior to that last journey which is described by S. Mark.* This explanation, I submit, satisfies none of the conditions of the problem.

The nine chapters are introduced by the remarkable words, "And it came to pass that as the days of His assumption were being fulfilled He hardened His face to go to Jerusalem." No one questions that "His assumption" means His ascension into heaven. The phrase, "the days were being fulfilled" occurs again in S. Luke, "When the day of Pentecost was being fulfilled" (Acts ii. 1), the only difference being that "day" there is in the singular, "days" here is in the plural. Admitting fully the vagueness of the Hebraic use of the word "days," I nevertheless ask any candid reader whether a space of six months is sug-

* Ellicott's *Lectures on the Life of our Lord*, p. 236 ff.

gested, or indeed is to be tolerated by the expression. No; a space of time not greatly exceeding a fortnight is in S. Luke's mind, and the journey of which he makes so much is certainly the final departure from Galilee. On that point we can hardly be mistaken.

S. Luke, in short, has crowded into one brief fortnight a whole mass of the most weighty teaching. His conception is that as our Lord approached the end of His ministry, His greatest wisdom was poured forth, His perfect love was manifested, and the approaching departure colours everything which intervened.

This is a noble conception. S. Luke was a great artist and a consummate historian. But his personal knowledge of the events which he describes was small, and his informants generally spoke at second-hand. Let us consider whether his arrangement is chronological.

The division consists of discourse matter. For although it contains three miracles and two other historical incidents, these are all subordinated to the discourse which accompanies them.

In the division there are 20 scraps from S. Mark belonging to the first division in my Synopsis, 58 *logia* from S. Matthew belonging to the second division, 15 Lucan narratives belonging to the third division, 35 fragments from anonymous sources (whereof six are common to S. Matthew and S. Luke; of the rest, three are historical and 26 are sayings). These belong to my fourth division. The whole is blended together by about 50 editorial notes, of which 14 are something more than mere literary connecting links.

It is important to collect all the notices of time and place which these nine chapters contain subsequent to the introductory verse, which has already been considered.

And first, those of place:

(1) "They come to a village of Samaritans." (ix. 52.)
(2) "They went to another village." (ix. 56.)
(3) "And as they went, He entered into a certain village." (x. 38.)
(4) "And it came to pass, as He was in a certain place." (xi. 1.)
(5) "And He was journeying through cities and villages, teaching, and making journey to Jerusalem." (xiii. 22.)
(6) "And it came to pass, as He was journeying to Jerusalem, that He passed between Samaria and Galilee." (xvii. 11.)

Peræa, the supposed scene of this hypothetical six months' ministry, is neither mentioned nor hinted at. Jerusalem is the only city, Galilee and Samaria the only countries named. S. Luke, who in the Acts of the Apostles shows a perfect passion for geographical details, and gives the name of nearly every city and village through which S. Paul passes, does nothing of the kind here. "A certain place," "a certain village," is the reiterated formula. A certain village! Every schoolboy knows that one of those villages was Bethany (S. Luke x. 38), and that it was within two miles of Jerusalem. But S. Luke, it would seem, does not know, and the harmonists are obliged to assume visits to Jerusalem, of which he makes no mention, to account for what he says.

Now consider his notices of time:
(1) "After these things." (x. 1.)
(2) "At that very hour." (x. 21.)
(3) "And it came to pass, while He was saying these things." (xi. 27.)
(4) "While He spake"* (xi. 37.)
(5) "Meanwhile." (xii. 1.)
(6) "At that very time." (xiii. 1.)
(7) "At that very hour." (xiii. 31.)

There are thirty-two sections in the division, twenty-five of which have no note of time or place, except an occasional "after these things," "at that very hour," which, like S. Mark's "and immediately," are, I maintain, only literary connecting links. When section after section is introduced by the simple phrase "And He said," to one who can read between the lines S. Luke is professing that he does not know the date. My contention is, that both S. Luke and the writer of the Gospel according to S. Matthew, had S. Mark's oral Gospel as their groundwork and their guide to arrangement. I will

---

* I cannot agree with Dr. Plummer (*Commentary on S. Luke*, iii. 21) that this must be translated "After He had spoken." Except in the Indicative or the Participle, and in oblique narration the Infinitive or Optative, where these stand for the Indicative of direct, the Greek tenses are timeless; in fact they are not tenses, strictly speaking, but moods, for they indicate the quality of the action, whether it is momentary and complete, or continuous and repeated; time is more frequently expressed by the mood. The difference between ἐν τῷ λαλεῖν and ἐν τῷ λαλῆσαι I take to be hardly more than that between "while He was speaking" and "while He spake," of which the former is the more natural expression, though S. Luke is fond of the latter. See Professor Burton's excellent manual, *The New Testament Moods and Tenses*, § 109.

not say to chronology, for it is very slightly chronological. But, besides this, they had a large quantity of undated materials, chiefly *logia*, the great mass of which contained nothing which to that age would indicate the date or the occasion on which the words were spoken. Their task was to blend the two sources of information into one narrative. S. Matthew chose one plan for arrangement, S. Luke another. If S. Mark furnished a convenient peg on which to hang materials, S. Matthew availed himself of it. Every *logion* which at all corresponded to it in thought was put there. And thus in his Gospel the non-Marcan matter is, for the most part, grouped into five great discourses:—(1) The Sermon on the Mount; (2) the Charge to the Twelve; (3) the seven parables (chapter xiii.); (4) the woes against the Pharisees; (5) the eschatological discourses; every one of which we shall hereafter show to be conflations.

S. Luke did not, as a rule, care to avail himself of the opportunities which S. Mark gave him. He had one great gap at the end of his ninth chapter, and into this he gradually collected most of the non-Marcan sections which he decided to accept.

Hence, this "Travel Narrative" teems with teaching which really belonged to every stage in our Lord's ministry. If we are capable of judging from internal evidence, much of the discourse which is there accumulated appertained to the earliest days. S. Luke has put it there, not because he thought, much less knew, this to be its real occasion of speaking, but because he did not know.

That this is the true view is shown by the fact

that S. Luke differs so widely from S. Matthew in his arrangement of these sections; but with this subject and the questions which it involves we shall deal in the next two papers. Only I would warn the reader against making the common but unwarranted assumption that, whereas the materials which are common to S. Matthew and S. Luke are, to a great extent at least, misplaced, those materials which are peculiar to S. Luke are always in the correct place. If S. Luke adopted a literary arrangement in the one case, it is reasonable to suppose that he has done the same in the other. To speak of a great trilogy of parables, and suppose that they were all uttered at the same sitting, seems to me to be a fatal misapprehension. If the parables of the Prodigal Son, the Unjust Steward, the Rich Man and Lazarus, were spoken on the same day to the same audience, the utterance of one would surely have the effect of checking meditation on the others, that is to say of defeating the very purpose for which a parable was spoken.

V.

IDENTICAL PASSAGES

I PROPOSE in the present paper to compare S. Matthew vi. 25–33 with S. Luke xii. 22–31. I shall give the results in English where possible, but for facility of comparison I shall use my own *Synopsis of the Gospels*, in which the passages are arranged side by side in thirty parallel lines on pages 108, 109.

Eight out of these thirty parallels are verbally identical, but the remaining twenty-two present certain differences which may be classified thus:

(1) Five times the order of the words within a line is not quite the same. (2) Seventeen lines are somewhat shorter in one Gospel than in the other, S. Matthew presenting the longer recension in twelve cases, S. Luke in five. For example, S. Luke writes, "If ye therefore are not even capable of that which is least," but S. Matthew reduces this line to the single monosyllable "and." Again, S. Luke gives "Who have no *storehouse nor* barn," where S. Matthew has "Nor gather into barns." On the contrary, S. Matthew's twice-repeated "Your *heavenly* Father," becomes in S. Luke on one occasion "God," on another "Your Father." For

S. Matthew's "Be not anxious for *your* life what ye must eat *or what ye must drink*," S. Luke gives "Be not anxious for life what ye must eat." In the twenty-ninth verse, however, he alludes to drinking as well as eating. S. Matthew mentions "the lilies *of the field*" when S. Luke has "the lilies," but S. Matthew speaks of "the nations," S. Luke "the nations *of the world*." (3) Twice S. Matthew puts a sentence into the form of a rhetorical question, where S. Luke is content with an assertion. S. Matthew bids us "*Look at* the fowls," "*Learn the lesson of* the lilies." S. Luke, with better effect, repeats the same verb "consider." (4) Instead of S. Matthew's vague expression, "the fowls of the heaven," S. Luke specifies "the ravens." S. Matthew, however, makes the whole argument turn on three definite necessaries of life—food, drink, raiment—recurring to these again and again; S. Luke is more discursive: "Why are ye anxious about *the other things?*" "Do not *live in a state of suspense*." (5) In the twenty-seventh verse S. Luke has written singular verbs after the neuter plural subject according to Greek rule; S. Matthew puts the verbs into the plural in accordance with the sense. (6) Lastly, S. Matthew has the classical form ἀμφιέννυσιν, while S. Luke gives the Hellenistic form ἀμφιάζει.

Such are the principal variations. Lest the reader should carry away an exaggerated notion of their number, I have deemed it desirable to count the words as well as the lines. I find that S. Matthew has used 169 words and S. Luke 156. Of these 124 are the same in both Gospels, while only twenty-two are different. S. Matthew, however, has added twenty-three words which have no parallels in S. Luke, and S. Luke ten words which have no parallels in S. Matthew.

It is important to observe that the general sense is the same in both Gospels. Such divergences as occur touch only its expression. Nor are these divergences greater than is usual in the Synoptists. On the contrary, it may be safely affirmed, that wherever three Gospels narrate what all commentators admit to be the same event, greater discrepancies in the wording are to be found than exist in these verses. I have therefore selected this as a test case for the comparison of the critical with the harmonistic view of the structure of the Gospels. However widely critics differ from each other in detail, they would unite with me in maintaining that the passage of S. Matthew which we are considering is identical with that in S. Luke, that it came from the same original source, and from the same Greek version of that source; but harmonists are constrained by their principles to assert that our Lord repeated His words, and that S. Matthew has given us what He said upon one occasion, S. Luke what He said upon another.

Our task is to discover which of these rival views is true. And the matter is one of serious importance, because this is a typical case. The same question arises in scores of other cases, and it must be decided one way or other by every one who undertakes to expound the Gospels.

The divergence between S. Matthew and S. Luke

respecting the occasion on which this *logion* was spoken is almost as great as it can be; for S. Matthew puts it into the Sermon on the Mount, close to the beginning of our Lord's ministry, S. Luke puts it into the "Travel Narrative," which he assigns to the close of His ministry. According to the common view a period of about three years intervened between these two dates.

Now when two evangelists differ respecting the time and place of one of our Lord's utterances, three alternatives present themselves. (1) Our Lord may, as the harmonists assume, have repeated His words, and one evangelist has recorded the first occasion, the other the second. (2) One evangelist has placed the saying into its historical setting, the other has arranged it on some different plan. (3) Neither evangelist has given the true chronology, but both have adopted (presumably for lack of better information) a literary arrangement.

Of these hypotheses the first appears at the outset to be the simplest and most probable. That our Lord repeated many of His sayings is almost certain. Why, therefore, should we hesitate to accept that solution of the difficulty in the present case?

We should have to believe that a complex utterance, thirty lines in length, was spoken twice with, at any rate, a long interval between the times of speaking. Our Lord was perfect man, and spoke to us as man. Such a feat is possible for man under either of two conditions; (1) if he write down his sermons and read them from the manuscript; (2) if he learn them by heart and repeat them frequently. No one claims that our Lord used either of these devices. Yet it would seem to be a denial of the Incarnation to think that during His earthly sojourn He could, or at any rate would, reproduce long speeches without them.

But in arguing about our Lord's knowledge as man and His state of subjection and obedience when He wore our flesh upon earth, we are out of our depth, and dare not pronounce with confidence. Granted, therefore, that He *may* have willed to speak the same words twice after so long an interval, the further question arises about the recollection and preservation of His utterances. How was that effected? There is good reason to think that he spoke in Aramaic; how comes it that the Greek of these *logia* is the same? and how could two spectators recall so long and elaborate a speech, years after it was uttered, with so few variations? If they were supernaturally helped to do so, why are there any variations at all? The extreme advocates of verbal inspiration would say: Because when our Lord repeated His sayings He deliberately made certain changes, and these have been faithfully reproduced in the Gospels. But few now would care to plead for such a Judaic and mechanical theory of inspiration, against which every page of Scripture appears to most of us to protest.

This case does not stand alone. It must be considered in connexion with others. For in the non-Marcan sections of S. Luke there are seventy-five passages which are parallel to passages in S.

IDENTICAL PASSAGES

Matthew, and I have deemed it important to give a complete list of them, following S. Matthew's order, that the reader may see for himself at a glance how systematically S. Luke diverges from it. Indeed, it may be said that unless a *logion* is very definitely fixed to a particular date by its subject-matter, S. Luke invariably arranges it in a way quite different from S. Matthew's.

S. MATTHEW.		S. LUKE.
iii. 7-10, 12	=	iii. 7-9, 17
iv. 2-11	=	iv. 2-13
v. 3-12	=	vi. 20-23
v. 13	=	xiv. 34-35
v. 15	=	viii. 16 (doublets) / ix. 33
v. 18	=	xvi. 17
v. 25-26	=	xii. 57-59
v. 32	=	xvi. 18
v. 39-42	=	vi. 29-30
v. 42-48	=	vi. 27-28, 32-33, 35-36
vi. 9-13	=	xi. 2-4
vi. 19-21	=	xii. 33-34
vi. 22-23	=	xi. 34-35
vi. 24	=	xvi. 13
vi. 25-33	=	xii. 22-31
vii. 1-2	=	vi. 37-38
vii. 3-5	=	vi. 41-42
vii. 7-11	=	xi. 9-13
vii. 12	=	vi. 31
vii. 13	=	xiii. 24
vii. 16-18 / xii. 33-35 (doublets)	=	vi. 43-45
vii. 21-23	=	vi. 46 / xiii. 26-27
vii. 24-27	=	vi. 47-49
viii. 5-10, 13	=	vii. 1-10
viii. 11-12	=	xiii. 28-30

S. Matthew.	S. Luke.
viii. 18-22	= ix. 57-60
ix. 37-38	= x. 2
x. 7	= { ix. 2 / x. 9 }
x. 10	= x. 7
x. 12-13	= x. 5-6
x. 15	= x. 12
x. 16	= x. 3
x. 24-25	= vi. 40
x. 27-33	= xii. 3-9
x. 34-35	= xii. 51-53
x. 37-39	= xiv. 26-27
x. 40	= ix. 48
xi. 2-11	= vii. 18-28
xi. 12-13	= xvi. 16
xi. 16-19	= vii. 31-35
xi. 20-24	= x. 13-15
xi. 25-27	= x. 21-22
xii. 11-12	= xiv. 5
xii. 27-28	= xi. 19-20
xii. 30	= xi. 23
xii. 32	= xii. 10
xii. 38-40	= xi. 29-30
xii. 41	= xi. 32
xii. 42	= xi. 31
xii. 43-45	= xi. 24-26
xiii. 16-17	= x. 23-24
xiii. 33	= xiii. 20-21
xv. 14	= vi. 39
xvii. 20	= xvii. 5-6
xviii. 7	= xvii. 1
xviii. 12-14	= xv. 3-7
xviii. 15, 21-22	= xvii. 3-4
xix. 28	= xxii. 28-30
xxii. 1-14	= xiv. 15-24
xxiii. 4	= xi. 46
xxiii. 11	= xxii. 26
xxiii. 12	= { xiv. 11 / xviii. 14 } (doublets)

IDENTICAL PASSAGES

S. Matthew.				S. Luke.
xxiii. 14	.	.	=	xi. 52
xxiii. 23	.	.	=	xi. 42
xxiii. 25–26	.	.	=	xi. 39–41
xxiii. 27	.	.	=	xi. 44
xxiii. 29–36	.	.	=	xi. 47–51
xxiii. 37–39	.	.	=	xiii. 34–35
xxiv. 26–27	.	.	=	xvii. 23–24
xxiv. 28	.	.	=	xvii. 37
xxiv. 37–39	.	.	=	xvii. 26–27, 30
xxiv. 40–41	.	.	=	xvii. 34–35
xxiv. 43–44	.	.	=	xii. 39–40
xxiv. 45–51	.	.	=	xii. 42–46
xxv. 14–30	.	.	=	xix. 12–27

When the reader has examined this list, and formed from it some conception of the extraordinarily different grouping adopted by these two evangelists, I would ask him to consider these questions: If the variations in order are due to the fact that our Lord repeated very many of His sayings, as harmonists maintain, how comes it that S. Matthew's informant always recollected one occasion, S. Luke's another? Why did not they at times recollect the same occasion? or one informant recollect both? The idea of repetition—though so popular and convenient when the reader's attention is fixed on an isolated case—breaks down when applied to seventy-five cases, particularly when we keep in mind the infirmities of the human memory, the necessary variations made in translating from Aramaic into Greek, and the long period which elapsed between the time when our Lord spoke and the Gospels were finally committed to writing.

Nor is it probable that when evangelists differ,

one of them always gives the historical occasion, the other departs from it. As long as our first Gospel was believed to proceed from the pen of S. Matthew, it was naturally thought that he, an eye-witness, had a special claim to be heard; but when it was perceived* that our first Gospel is a composite work, and that neither internal evidence, nor external testimony, permit it in its present form to be attributed to one of the Twelve, the case is altered. If the *logia* circulated in the Church as "Sayings of our Lord," apart from dates, persons, and places, we have no reason to think that the editor of the first Gospel was in a better position than S. Luke to discover their true chronology. If the evangelists were more anxious to record, in a readable and convenient form, the utterances of our Lord, than to discover lost dates and occasions, we must accept what they have given us. To be wise above that which is written is mere folly. Our Gospels are not formal histories but Gospels.

The harmonistic view is not the ancient view. Tatian, Ammonius, and Eusebius identify similar passages as fearlessly as a modern critic. We are only sweeping away some mediæval traditionalism when we invite the reader to do the same. Too long have our commentators wasted their strength in harmonizing. The first step towards better work is to recognise the impossibility of their task. Nor is it enough to admit, as modern commentators generally do, that a few speeches in S. Luke or S. Matthew may possibly be misplaced. The harmonists

* *Composition of the Four Gospels*, p. 61.

have too long had their way. It is time that the critic superseded them on entirely different lines.

The synoptic Gospels, I hold, are seldom arranged chronologically. Their divergences from each other abundantly prove that. And even when they agree, they do so by following S. Mark's order, which is unchronological. We have in the synoptists a series of "recollections" rather than a formal biography. Further illustration of this will be given in the next paper.

VI.

CONFLATIONS

LET the reader compare S. Mark i. 7-8 with S. Matthew iii. 7-12 and S. Luke iii. 7-17, in which passages we are presented with the Synoptic account of John the Baptist's preaching. S. Mark has devoted two verses to it, S. Matthew six, and S. Luke eleven.

That S. Mark's record is the primitive *nucleus*, round which the later additions circulated, is proved (1) from the well-established priority of S. Mark in general; (2) from the brevity of S. Mark's narrative here; (3) from the fact that it figures not only in three Gospels, but (with a few variations) in the fourth; nay, quotations of it are found in several passages of the Acts of the Apostles. The non-Marcan portions, on the other hand, are found in one Gospel or in two at the most; clearly they were not so widely known.

At a later date in the Church of Jerusalem S. Mark's record was supplemented by the addition of two *logia*, and in the Western Church by the further addition of a third. It is reasonable to suppose that the two earlier *logia* (which are found in S. Matthew and S. Luke) were collected under

S. Matthew's guidance, and are therefore rightly classed under my second division. But, of course, they may be of later date, and so belong to my fourth. In any case, all three *logia* may with some confidence be assumed to proceed from some disciple or disciples of John the Baptist. The two, which are found in two Gospels, are unusually alike in both. Nine out of the fourteen lines are *verbatim* the same. The order of the words is maintained. One line reads "fruits" instead of "fruit," another "begin" instead of "think," a third adds "also," and the two remaining lines use infinitives instead of the future indicative; so slight and immaterial are the variations. Plainly S. Luke received the passage in writing, or by an express messenger, and not after passing through many minds and memories.

It is to be noticed further that the close resemblance between S. Matthew and S. Luke in these *logia* extends also into the Marcan portion, in which these evangelists agree with one another against S. Mark in the order of the lines and in the wording, except in one remarkable instance, in which S. Matthew differs from S. Mark, S. Luke, S. John, and the Acts of the Apostles in writing "Whose shoes I am not worthy *to carry*" instead of "the latchet of whose shoes I am not worthy to stoop down and untie."

We are presented therefore with a case of "mixture" possessing much interest. Some critics have proclaimed that S. Matthew's account must be primary and S. Mark's secondary, but we are by no means compelled to admit that; indeed the weakened metaphor about the shoes seems to me to be fatal to such an assumption. Under the oral hypothesis it is easy to urge (1) that S. Mark himself, during forty years of oral teaching, sometimes unconsciously altered his original wording, so that one of the other Gospels occasionally retain the older reading; and indeed, when they both unite against him, there is a presumption that this is the case; (2) in several instances S. Luke, upon receiving a fuller account, has discarded S. Mark in favour of the later teaching. For the friend who sent him these new *logia* sent the whole section in which they were embedded, and not the new portions only, and S. Luke has adopted it entire; (3) it is probable that Mark i. 7–8 was no part of the first edition of S. Mark's oral Gospel, but, like the account of the Baptist's food and clothing, first appeared in the second edition with which, as we have seen, S. Luke was not acquainted. We are, therefore, at full liberty to gather from the passages themselves the lessons which they teach respecting their origin, being in no way fettered to the idea of S. Matthew's priority.

S. Luke, in the course of his travels, must have come in contact with some of John the Baptist's disciples. There was Apollos, and the twelve men at Ephesus, "who had been baptized into John's baptism." Doubtless there were many others, and all would preserve recollections of their martyred leader's teaching.

Probably from one of them S. Luke obtained the further *logion* which he has incorporated into his Gospel. It runs thus:

"And the multitudes asked him, saying, What must we do? And he said, Let him that hath two tunics impart one of them to the poor man, and let him that is rich in food do likewise. And taxgatherers also came to be baptized, and said to him, Teacher, what must we do? And he said to them, Collect no more than that which is appointed you. And soldiers on service asked him, And what must we do? And he said, Buffet no man, nor play the informer, and make both ends meet with your pay." *

This *logion* S. Luke inserted in the midst of the others. But as he dislocated the speech in doing so, he pieced it together again by an editorial note, after his habitual manner, viz.: "And as the people were expecting, and all men were reasoning in their hearts concerning John, whether he was the Messiah, John answered them all, saying—."

There is one other point to be noticed. We have drawn attention to the close verbal correspondence between S. Matthew and S. Luke in the *logia*: it is important to show how widely they differ in the historical fact. S. Matthew says that John's outburst of denunciation was occasioned by the advent of certain Pharisees and Sadducees, and that it was

* The translation, "Be content with your wages," is wrong. Contentment is not a Christian virtue, but a Mahommedan vice. No man should be satisfied with his attainments, temporal, intellectual, or spiritual. Progress is our watchword. S. John bids the soldiers not to get into debt. Similarly S. Paul did not mean "I have learned in whatsoever state I am therewith to be content," but "I have learned to make the best of things, to live within my income, however small it be." This meaning alone satisfies the context, as well as is required by the word. (Phil. iv. 11.)

addressed to them; S. Luke says that it was spoken to the multitudes, and this he supports in another editorial note when he reverts to the history of John. "All the people when they heard it, *and the taxgatherers*,* justified God, having been baptized with John's baptism; but the Pharisees and the lawyers rejected the counsel of God towards themselves, *having not been baptized by him.*" (vii. 29-30.)

Now S. Matthew's narrative is a "conflation," for the primitive account has been welded with two new *logia*, until the whole forms one complete section. Still more is S. Luke's narrative a conflation, for the primitive account has been welded with three new *logia*, by the aid of a long editorial note, which solders them together.

The result of this welding is that fragments cease to be fragmentary. As flints can be fitted together and with the help of mortar make a solid wall, so isolated *logia* were compacted into a Gospel section. S. Luke shows considerable artistic skill in piecing his materials together, and uses plenty of cement when there is need for it. But in the case which we are now considering no one is deceived by the process. No one supposes that these speeches of the Baptist were all spoken to the same audience, and on the same day. It is clear that they are fragments, mere samples of addresses which were delivered daily for many weeks or months.

So far we have explained what a conflation is, and we have shown that there are conflations in at least two of our Gospels: now let us see whether there is

* S. Luke iii. 12.

CONFLATIONS

reason to think that any of the speeches attributed to our Lord are conflations.

In Luke xi. 14-28 we have a Gospel section. It begins with the cure of a demonized mute. The spectators are divided. Some admire the miracle, others attribute it to Satan. Our Lord replies to the latter, maintaining that it was improbable that Satan should cast out Satan; nay, rather the exorcism was an indication that Messiah was stronger than Satan. Some of the people were convinced by this appeal to their reason, but many wavered and suspended their judgement. To them our Lord addresses a warning. Neutrality, in this case (He said) was impossible. Anyone who attempted it would become Satan's slave more than he was before. A woman from the audience thereupon congratulates the Teacher's mother on the possession of such a son, but our Lord makes light of mere human ties. True happiness is to be sought, He affirms, in finding out and doing God's will.

Who can deny that the whole section, as S. Luke presents it, coheres most closely? The sequence of thought could hardly be more natural; the actors seem to stand before us. And yet when we examine the other Gospels, we are forced to the dilemma that either our Lord has repeated His words in the way which was discredited in the last chapter, or else S. Luke has welded together a number of isolated utterances into one conflation. For the saying about Satan casting out Satan is found in S. Mark (*Synopsis*, pages 16, 17); not, however, in the first edition of S. Mark which S. Luke used. The order of the sections in S. Luke is decisive on that point, still more so is the wording, in which S. Luke agrees with S. Matthew against S. Mark.

S. Mark, as usual, has given us the earliest form of this saying, which afterwards was expanded at Jerusalem, under S. Matthew's superintendence, by the addition of some new matter, for which room was made by the curtailment of the original narrative. Then the section in its Matthæan form was carried to S. Luke without information about its date, and he put it into a niche in his oral Gospel quite different from that which it occupies in S. Mark or S. Matthew. At a later date he expanded it by conflation with new materials.

S. Mark's historical setting, which is obscured in the other Gospels, is of the highest importance, for it explains the process of that loss of popularity which undoubtedly befell our Lord and enabled His enemies ultimately to effect the crucifixion. He cannot be a good man (it was argued) because He breaks the Sabbath. His miracles, therefore, are not the works of God. There remains but one other way to account for them. He has sold Himself to Satan and has received power from him.

In an age which firmly believed Satan to be second only to God in wisdom, power, and ubiquity this argument would come with a force which we can hardly realise. We should infer from S. Luke that it was casually made by one of the spectators; from S. Matthew that a local Galilean Pharisee brought it; it is only from S. Mark that we hear of a special delegation from the Pharisees at

Jerusalem. They, the trusted leaders of the people, the divinely appointed guides of the blind, took upon themselves to pronounce our Lord to be Satan's vassal; and we can understand the effect which their words had. Thousands of simple folk would, sooner or later, believe that you could only accept healing from Christ at the price of losing your soul.

S. Mark says nothing about the cure of the mute demoniac, nor can we feel at all sure that it really happened on this occasion. It somewhat helps the narrative. The sinister accusation would be more pointed if made when an exorcism had just excited popular feeling; but this, of course, does not settle the question. If the text be genuine, S. Matthew by a doublet says that the speech about the prince of the demons helping to cast out demons was made twice (ix. 34 = xii. 24); but Westcott and Hort bracket it in the former case, and its removal would much reduce complexity.

S. Matthew adds two *logia* which treat of the same subject, but need not necessarily on that account have been spoken at this time. "If I by Beelzebub cast out demons, by whom do your pupils cast them out?" And, "He that is not with Me is against Me." These additions were made before the sections were carried to S. Luke, for they appear also in his Gospel in the same relative order, and with nearly the same wording. One other *logion* reached him afterwards in an isolated form, for S. Matthew gives it as a fragment in a different context (Matt. xii. 43-45) very slightly welded with what precedes. S. Luke has found a much more suitable place for it here, for it speaks of the exorcized demon seeking rest and finding none, but returning to the house from which he had departed; but, of course, its suitability does not prove that S. Luke has given it in its real position.

Probably at a later date, S. Luke made three other changes in his narrative. First he inserted the sixteenth verse, "And others, tempting, sought from Him a sign from heaven." This scrap comes from S. Mark viii. 11 = Matt. xvi. 1, and has a complex history which may be unravelled thus: On one occasion our Lord was asked for a sign from heaven, *i.e.* a clap of thunder or a voice from the sky; this He positively refused to grant, as S. Mark tells us. On another occasion He was asked for a sign, *i.e.* a miracle, and He replied enigmatically that He would give them the sign of Jonah. S. Mark narrates the former occasion with the positive refusal. S. Luke gives both cases (xi. 16, 29). S. Matthew gives both, but confuses them by a doublet, for he intrudes the words, "except the sign of Jonah," from the second into the first also (xvi. 4; xii. 39) by a not unusual mixture, produced unconsciously by the assimilation of doublets.

Next S. Luke remodels verses 21, 22. Whether he has done so on his own responsibility, to put them into better literary form, or whether he has received information from other spectators who had heard them spoken, we need not now pronounce. The general sense is the same, but the wording is quite different from S. Matthew's, though S. Matthew's order is observed.

Thirdly, S. Luke appends the incident of the woman from the multitude exclaiming on the happiness of His earthly mother. This he obtains from some private source. There is no trace of it in the other Gospels, though its general meaning is paralleled in Mark iii. 33-35 = Matt. xii. 48-50 = Luke viii. 21.

Such is a conflation. It is a literary expedient, justified by the lack of historical knowledge. If S. Luke had been an eye-witness and had recollected the exact occasion on which every utterance of our Lord was published, he would not have resorted to conflations, for historical veracity had much greater attraction for him than dramatic suitability. But his knowledge being imperfect, and a heap of undated *logia* lying before him, he was induced to take refuge in conflation as the nearest approach to the truth which was possible for him.

We felt no difficulty when we saw that John the Baptist's speech was a conflation. We must recognise the same principle in our Lord's utterances also.

For this is not an isolated case. If it were, we might be content to account for it by supposing that there was a repetition of the same sayings. But, if we set aside the longer parables, which form complete discourses in themselves, we shall find that all the other sayings of our Lord in S. Luke (except those which He obtains from S. Mark) are worked up into conflations. There are in this Gospel just twenty of these conflations. Sometimes they are very loosely strung together, as in xvi. 13-18, xvii. 1-10; sometimes they are most elaborately compacted, as in xiv. 1-24. But conflations they are, admirably adapted for oral teaching or public recitation, but not to be pressed in the matter of chronology. It is on comparing them with the other Gospels that we discover their present form to be due to independent editorial work. As the subject is fundamental, and has not been pointed out before, I append a detailed analysis of these twenty discourses.

1. A VISIT TO NAZARETH (Luke iv. 16-30).— Here much new material has been welded with a few sentences from S. Mark (Mark vi. 1-4 = Matt. xiii. 53-57).

2. THE CALL OF SS. SIMON (ANDREW), JAMES, AND JOHN (Luke v. 1-11). — Here some new material containing the "draught of fishes" has been welded with Mark i. 16-20 = Matt. iv. 18-22.

3. THE SERMON ON THE MOUNT (Luke vi. 20ᵇ-49).—One Marcan scrap (Mark iv. 24ᵇ) is welded with eleven *logia* from S. Matthew, and two from other sources. Of the eleven Matthæan *logia* nine come from S. Matthew's "Sermon on the Mount," one of them is a doublet (Matt. vii. 16-18 = Matt. xii. 33-35), one comes from the Charge to the Twelve (Matt. x. 24-25), and one from a fragment (Matt. xv. 14). How completely both Sermons are conflations is shown by the fact that S. Matthew's contains 107 verses, of which only fifty-eight have parallels in S. Luke. Of these fifty-eight, however, only twenty-six have parallels in S. Luke's "Sermon on the Mount," the remaining thirty-two are scattered over seven other chapters of S. Luke.

4. DISCOURSE AT THE ANOINTING OF OUR LORD'S FEET (Luke vii. 36-50). (*Synopsis*, pages 82, 83.)—Two explanations of this very difficult section compete for our acceptance. The former is simpler, and is supported by Tatian's *Dia Tessarôn;* the latter is on the whole more probable, and has the sanction of the Ammonian sections. (1) There were two anointings, one of our Lord's head, the other of His feet; the one in love, the other in penitence; and S. John has confused the two. (2) There was only one anointing, and S. John has deliberately corrected, as well as supplemented, the Synoptic account of it, which first appeared in S. Mark's second edition, and therefore was not carried westwards at first; but came, as far as it did come, in a fragment afterwards. Here S. Luke has entirely misplaced it, putting it far too early. He has likewise blended it with much new discourse. S. Luke on the latter supposition has borrowed the name of Simon from S. Mark, but the details of anointing from S. John, misplacing the whole as usual.

5. THE CHARGE TO THE SEVENTY (Luke x. 2-16).—Here one saying from S. Mark (Mark vi. 11 = Matt. x. 14) and some scraps are worked up with ten Matthæan *logia*, of which one is put by S. Matthew independently (Matt. xi. 20-24); the others form part of the "Charge to the Twelve," which itself is a great conflation. Only one scrap (Luke x. 4^b) is new, but there are four doublets, viz., Luke x. 4^a = ix. 3^a; x. 5^a, 7^a = ix. 4; x. 10-11 = ix. 5; x. 16 = ix. 48, and some editorial additions in x. 7-11. Some critics have concluded that the Mission of

the Seventy is therefore unhistorical, but it is more scientific to insist on S. Matthew's "Charge to the Twelve" being a conflation. Doubtless S. Luke had excellent authority for the appointment of the Seventy, however uncertain he was left about the limits of the Charges addressed to them and to the Twelve.

6. EXULTATION AND CONGRATULATIONS (Luke x. 21-24).—A conflation of three *logia* (Matt. xi. 25-26, 27; xiii. 16-17) which S. Matthew arranges differently.

7. THE STORY OF THE GOOD SAMARITAN (Luke x. 25-37).—A conflation of Lucan matter with fragments borrowed from S. Mark. (Mark xii. 28-33.)

8. PRAYER (Luke xi. 1-13).—A conflation of two Matthæan *logia* (Matt. vi. 9-13; vii. 7-11) with one Lucan section. S. Matthew has put these *logia* into different chapters of the Sermon on the Mount, but in doing so has broken the sequence of thought. The editorial note with which S. Luke introduces the section shows how S. Luke collected information from all quarters. Apollos or any other of John the Baptist's disciples may have furnished the information which it contains.

9. ON CASTING OUT DEMONS (Luke xi. 14-28).—A conflation which we have fully unravelled already.

10. THIS IS AN EVIL GENERATION (Luke xi. 29-36).—A conflation of five *logia*, and one Lucan saying. One of the *logia* is a doublet occurring also in S. Luke viii. 16, which is parallel to S. Mark iv. 21. The first three *logia* cohere closely together, and are found together, but in inverted order, in

Matthew xii. 38–42. The next *two* have no real connexion with what precedes, nor with each other (Matt. v. 15; vi. 22–23). S. Luke's new *logion* (xi. 36) coheres closely with what precedes, and welds the whole collection into one speech.

11. DISCOURSE AT A PHARISEE'S BREAKFAST-TABLE (Luke xi. 37–53).—This should be compared with the discourse at the Pharisee's dinner-table. (Luke xiv. 1–24.) S. Luke stands alone in telling us that our Lord on three occasions accepted hospitality from Pharisees. We may feel sure that he had excellent authority for this, and yet doubt whether the speeches which he connects with these visits were always spoken on the occasion. The machinery of the breakfast-table is not much used, and S. Matthew gives the whole discourse in his twenty-third chapter with a different setting and in inverted order, with frequent diversity in wording.

12. AN ADDRESS TO THE TWELVE IN PRESENCE OF A MULTITUDE, WITH TWO APOSTROPHES TO THE CROWD (Luke xii. 1–59).—A conflation of twenty sayings, of which six are peculiar to S. Luke, fourteen are taken from S. Matthew's *logia*, but two of the latter have certain parallels with S. Mark. S. Matthew has distributed the *logia* thus: (1) Three in the Sermon on the Mount; (2) six in the Charge to the Twelve; (3) three in the eschatological discourse; (4) two in other chapters. S. Luke binds the conflation together by six editorial notes, five of which demand notice; but none indicates special information. There is no conclusion. Verses 35–51 appear to be an expansion of Mark xiii.

33-37, but from another eye-witness, and in another translation.

13. THE MISERIES OF THE LOST (Luke xiii. 22-30).—A conflation of three *logia* with a Lucan scrap and a refrain. S. Matthew puts one of these *logia* into the midst of the healing of the centurion's servant. (Matt. viii. 11.)

14. JERUSALEM THE CITY OF MARTYRDOMS (Luke xiii. 31-35).—A conflation of a *logion*, which occupies a more suitable position in S. Matthew, with some new matter.

15. DISCOURSES AT THE DINNER-TABLE OF A PHARISEE (Luke xiv. 1-24).—Three *logia*, including a parable, are welded with three new fragments.

16. WE MUST GIVE UP ALL IF WE WOULD FOLLOW CHRIST (Luke xiv. 25-35).—A conflation of two *logia* with some new matter.

17. FIVE DISCONNECTED APOPHTHEGMS (Luke xvi. 13-18)—A conflation of four *logia* with one new scrap. S. Matthew gives the *logia* in widely different contexts, and each with an appropriate setting.

18. FOUR DISCONNECTED APOPHTHEGMS (Luke xvii. 1-10).—Four *logia*, two of which are found in the second edition of S. Mark, are followed by a new section. The five sayings are worked up with some editorial notes into four apophthegms.

19. DISCOURSE ABOUT THE LAST DAYS (Luke xvii. 20-37).—Our Lord's sayings about the last days were probably uttered on many different occasions scattered over His ministry. He also spoke parables on this subject. S. Matthew, after his usual manner,

has massed the sayings into chapters xxiv., xxv., except that a few of them are inserted strangely into the Sermon on the Mount and the Charge to the Twelve. S. Luke has divided them into four speeches. The first of these (Luke xii. 35-48) forms part of a longer discourse. The other three are Luke xiii. 22-30, xvii. 20-37, xxi. 7-38. The last of these is taken from Mark xiii., the other three were either *logia* or doublets. S. Matthew's arrangement is much more effective for reading aloud in church, S. Luke's is better adapted for oral teaching. This discourse consists of four new scraps, three doublets, and five *logia* welded together by three editorial notes into nine sentences, three of which have parallels in S. Mark.

20. THE COMING OF THE SON OF MAN (Luke xxi. 7-38).—This discourse has been already described. Its basis is Marcan, but it has a few new scraps.

VII.

ON THE PROPER NAMES IN S. MARK'S GOSPEL

HITHERTO I have assumed the truth of the oral hypothesis. I have assumed, that is, that S. Matthew and S. Luke did not copy from S. Mark's written Gospel, nor from any other Ur-Marcus, but that they derived their knowledge of his teaching from oral tradition.

Any other hypothesis so fetters the critic that it does not leave him the necessary freedom to explain the existing state of things in the synoptic Gospels. In this and the next two papers I propose to bring forward some arguments in defence of the oral hypothesis. And in this paper I deal with the proper names in S. Mark, comparing S. Mark's list of them with the lists preserved in the parallel passages of S. Matthew and S. Luke.

I have not reckoned as proper names *God, Lord, Son of Man, Son of God*, or *Holy Spirit*. Neither have I admitted *Satan, the devil*, or *Beelzebub*. The name *Jesus* occurs so frequently, and its repetition in many passages is so much a matter of literary feeling, that I have given the numbers first with, then without it.

PROPER NAMES IN S. MARK

I find that in S. Mark's Gospel eighty-six[*] proper names occur, many of which are repeatedly given until the sum total amounts to 341. In the Marcan sections of S. Matthew they amount to 270, and in the Marcan sections of S. Luke to 175.

Excluding the name *Jesus*, we find in S. Mark 261 proper names, in S. Matthew's parallel passages 194, and in S. Luke's 128.

Further details are shown in the following tables:

	S. MARK.	S. MATTHEW.	S. LUKE.
Common to all three Gospels	105	105	105
Common to S. Mark and S. Matthew	111	111	
Common to S. Mark and S. Luke	35		35
In one Gospel only	90	54	35
	341	270	175

Omitting the name *Jesus*:

	S. MARK.	S. MATTHEW.	S. LUKE.
Common to all three Gospels	85	85	85
Common to S. Mark and S. Matthew	82	82	
Common to S. Mark and S. Luke	21		21
In one Gospel only	73	27	22
	261	194	128

It must, however, be remembered that S. Matthew omits five of S. Mark's sections containing in all 7 proper names, and S. Luke omits 14 sections containing 36 proper names. The corrected proportion, therefore, will be for S. Mark, 341; for S. Matthew, 275; and for S. Luke, 196.

It is evident, however, on examination that, as we should have expected, the 54 names peculiar to S. Matthew, and the 35 peculiar to S. Luke are,

---

[*] I reckon Jacob and Israel, Simon and Peter, Levi and Matthew, James, John, and Boanerges as distinct names. I allow three Maries, four Jameses, and two each of Joses and Judas.

except in one instance, editorial additions possessing no claim to be considered part of the Petrine Memoirs. We may deduct them all but one, and the result will then be, S. Mark, 341; S. Matthew, 222; S. Luke, 162.

The first thing that strikes us on inspecting these figures is the large proportion of proper names (105 out of 341) which have resisted all the attrition of years of catechizing, and all the changes of widely diverging literary styles, and still keep their place in three Gospels. Secondly, we notice that more than double the number (216, *i.e.*, 105+111) are found in the two Gospels S. Mark and S. Matthew; but when we come to the other pair, S. Mark and S. Luke, there is a great falling off. Only 140 (105+35) are common to these.

As with the proper names, so fared it with the other words generally. The catechists of Jerusalem, who were responsible for the safe keeping of the Marcan portions of S. Matthew's Gospel, were, as their oriental training and sympathies inclined them to be, very jealous for the precise wording of the narratives which they taught. They abbreviated them, sometimes considerably; but they did not often change them. The Gentile catechists, inheriting a Greek love of liberty, were not so closely tied to their original. As long as the general sense was retained, the words were altered with no little freedom. S. Luke supports S. Mark in only 35 cases beyond those which are common to three evangelists, and several of these are where S. Matthew has omitted the section.

PROPER NAMES IN S. MARK

Lastly, in only one case—exclusive of "editorial notes"—does S. Matthew support S. Luke against S. Mark. For in Mark i. 5 the word *Jordan*, according to the united testimony of S. Matthew and S. Luke, ought to have been written twice instead of once. In all other cases in which S. Matthew and S. Luke agree S. Mark agrees with them. Even in this case the meaning is not affected. Whether the word should be given once or twice is a question of literary propriety.

It is of course theoretically possible, if the documentary hypothesis be true, that S. Mark wrote later than S. Matthew and S. Luke, and diligently incorporated into his work the whole of the proper names which he found in them, adding many more from external sources. But it seems to me very much simpler and more probable to hold that S. Mark gives us S. Peter's teaching in its fullest form, the other Gospels in a curtailed form. The priority of S. Mark is generally admitted by all classes of critics, and the facts which we have just stated most strongly confirm it.*

Professors Sanday† and Marshall‡ have recently been calling upon us to abandon the oral theory of the origin of the Gospels, and to recur to the hypothesis of written documents (which have un-

---

* In Matthew xxvi. 50-52 = Luke xxii. 48-51, the word *Jesus* is twice inserted on the united authority of S. Matthew and S. Luke only. But the clauses in which it occurs, though they have Petrine words embedded in them, are, both of them, "editorial notes." They have no real resemblance with each other, nor is there anything corresponding to them in S. Mark. They come from other sources.

† *Expositor*, vol. iii. p. 180. ‡ *Ibid.*, p. 17.

accountably perished and left no trace behind) as the foundation of the common matter in the synoptic Gospels. Professor Sanday's reasons for urging this are different from Professor Marshall's. Professor Sanday holds fast to the unity of S. Mark, and accepts his Gospel as the historical framework of the other two. He believes, as I do, that S. Matthew's *Logia*, or "utterances of the Lord," were unknown to S. Mark, or, at least, not used by him.

Professor Marshall, on the other hand, requires us to believe that S. Mark had before him, and deliberately rejected from his Gospel, the Lord's Prayer, the Sermon on the Mount, the longer parables and discourses. In fact, on Professor Marshall's showing, S. Mark becomes a mere editor of other people's work, and one who had so decided a preference for what I had almost called the chaff to the wheat, that the comparative neglect into which his Gospel has fallen is excusable.

Professor Marshall also asks us to believe that with Aramæan scribes writing was so uncertain an art that one letter was constantly misread for another. In a single line of three words he would have us maintain that six letters were confused and one dropped altogether!* Now I admit that the square "Hebrew" characters in which Aramaic was written in the time of our Lord, being without vowel points and having no spaces between the words, did often, in spite of final letters, lead to misreading. But writing would have been of little use in trade

* *Expositor*, vol. iii., p. 387.

if it had not been tolerably trustworthy. The scribes knew which letters were liable to be mistaken, and shaped them with corresponding care. A modern teacher has no difficulty in writing Hebrew letters distinctly. It is one thing for mistakes to have been made in deciphering a manuscript of the Old Testament, which might be centuries old with many letters frayed or rubbed away; it is quite another thing to blunder in reading a manuscript which, according to Professor Marshall, can hardly have been ten years old.

Moreover, if it be true—as it surely must be—that S. Peter's Memoirs as well as S. Matthew's *Logia* were originally composed in Aramaic, and continued to circulate in that language amongst the "Hebrews" of the Church at Jerusalem; if also both the Memoirs and the *Logia* were translated into Greek (as Professor Marshall allows the *Logia* to have been), and freely circulated amongst the "Hellenists," how can his linguistic test distinguish between them? The most that it can do is to discover the places where the oral Greek of either the one or the other has been revised through changes in the oral Aramaic. And thus Professor Marshall's main contention falls to the ground.

Professor Marshall himself is obliged at last to admit* the fact of a Greek oral version existing side by side with his supposed Aramaic documents. And this amounts practically to a surrender of his position, for the existence of such a version would

---

* *Expositor*, vol. vi. p. 93.

inevitably prevent the numerous corruptions and mistakes which his theory requires. And if the version was oral, why should not the original have been oral also? And why should not S. Peter's Memoirs have been current in both languages, as well as S. Matthew's *Logia?* S. Peter spoke Aramaic: his knowledge of at least literary Greek was small: else why did he use S. Mark or Silvanus to translate his words into Greek? But if both cycles existed in both languages, what becomes of the linguistic test?

Professor Stanton appears to agree with me in holding that the documentary hypothesis entirely fails to account for the multitude of minute discrepancies in the identical portions of the synoptic Gospels. Nothing but years of oral teaching can have produced them. Oral teaching also alone can account for the present state of the *Logia*. He has done excellent service in insisting on these important points. Nevertheless, certain minute resemblances in language and in order seem to him to make it probable that the authors of the first and third Gospels had a copy of S. Mark before them when they wrote, though pressure of local opinion in the Churches for which they wrote prevented them from using it except in unimportant details. This assumes that *two* men treated an almost apostolic document with equal timidity, and that S. Mark's Gospel had a wider circulation in early times than the loss of the last verses indicates. But our present paper points to what I consider a more serious difficulty.

If S. Matthew and S. Luke had had before them, as Professor Stanton supposes, a written copy of S. Mark's Gospel or of its prototype, is it credible that they would have treated the proper names in it as they have done?

S. Luke, in his Gospel and in the Acts of the Apostles (as we shall show in the next paper), writes as an historian. In his "editorial notes" he masses proper names as an historian would. He knows the importance of giving dates, places, and persons. Is it conceivable that with S. Mark's 341 proper names in front of him he should have omitted all but 175? Or if he had only a mutilated copy of S. Mark, from which passages containing 36 proper names were absent, still the reduction of even 305 to 175 is impossible to account for, and, as we have seen, the reduction really is to 140.

Grant, however, that S. Luke was a catechist, engaged for many years in teaching "the facts concerning Jesus"* to the Christians at Philippi, and is it not certain that with ordinary prudence and kindness he would avoid burdening the memory of his pupils with obscure and unfamiliar foreign names? Such places as Jerusalem, Nazareth, Capernaum; such persons as S. Peter, Mary of Magdala, Judas Iscariot, were essential to his narrative, and must be learned: but Cæsarea Philippi, Magadan, Decapolis, Bartimæus, Herod Philip, and the Herodians, had either disappeared from the oral teaching before S. Luke received it, or

* Acts xviii. 25.

slipped out of his lessons at an early date. When, therefore, he came to write his Gospel, he did not produce them, because he was no longer able to do so, though, if I understand his aims aright, he would have given almost anything for the recovery of just such proper names as these.

Our belief in the oral theory is greatly strengthened when we find that new investigations so decidedly confirm it. It has enabled me, in the simplest way,* to account for S. Luke's omissions, which had puzzled me for twenty years; it has forced upon me an easy answer to the question about the day of the Crucifixion† which was becoming a difficulty of the first magnitude. And while supporters of the documentary hypothesis sooner or later speak of disappointment, despair, and insoluble problems, those who adopt the oral hypothesis are full of hope.

Professor Sanday, for example, confesses‡ his inability to account for the extraordinary discrepancies which exist between S. Luke's preface to the Sermon on the Mount and S. Matthew's (Luke vi. 17-26 = Matt. v. 1-12), when compared with the close resemblance between them in the later sections of the same sermon. To me the explanation is easy. S. Luke was a diligent collector of evangelical facts and sayings. During his long residence at Philippi, his wanderings over S. Paul's churches, or his visit to Palestine, he received by word of mouth or by letter—in Greek or Aramaic§

---

* See above, p. 3 ff.   † See below, p. 179.
‡ *Expositor*, vol. iii. p. 311 ff.
§ This will account for some of the traces of translation which Professor Marshall observes.

—not merely the important contributions which make up the third cycle, but an abundance of words or works of Christ collected by many private Christians.

Some of these were parts of the second cycle, which was being slowly compiled at Jerusalem; more were sent by independent witnesses. Most of them reached S. Luke without note of time or place. He found room for them in his oral lessons one by one as they came, to the best of his ability. Often he arranged them according to subject-matter rather than by their true chronology. The present state of his Gospel confirms what I say. Only thus can we account for the many boulders in it, deposited in places which are certainly not their own.

Now some of these private contributions S. Luke actually preferred to S. Peter's Memoirs. In chapters xxii. and xxiii. he has substituted several of them for S. Peter's records. What more natural than that one of the spectators should have furnished him with an independent account of the opening words of the Sermon on the Mount? His edition of these opening words, besides showing signs of literary polish, differs from S. Matthew's account, as S. John's feeding of the five thousand, or S. John's and S. Luke's version of S. Peter's denials differs from S. Mark's. There are some additions and much change, but the same scene is plainly described. It is possible, of course, that S. Luke never received S. Matthew v. 1–12: it is more probable that he set it aside in favour of his private information.

The argument from the order of the narratives in

the three Gospels, which Mr. F. H. Woods* has worked out in detail, so far from being fatal to the oral hypothesis, as Professor Stanton and many others suppose, appears to me to be a strong support of it. For experience shows that if you are to learn by heart a large quantity of loosely connected matter with a view to daily repetition, you must be as careful in preserving the order as in preserving the words. You must even resort to artificial means to assist you in doing this. For memory is so constituted that a variation in order would lead to the loss of matter. Every system of mnemonics is based on association and order. The catechists could only perform their duty by dividing their subject into lessons, and taking each lesson in its proper sequence.† The addition from time to time of new matter would not disturb the order of the old sections. A few minor changes would be made, as they have been, in the several Churches on first starting, for each considerable Church must have had its own oral Gospel; but when once the order was fixed in any Church, it would remain.

Lastly, the contention that the first cycle, if published in Jerusalem, must have contained a Judæan ministry,‡ does not appear to me decisive. In the first place more than a third—three-eighths—of S. Mark's Gospel is taken up with events which happened and discourses which were delivered in

---

* *Studia Biblica*, series ii. pp. 59-104. For further development of this subject see my *Synopsis of the Gospels*, Preface xi.-xiii.

† See above, p. 14.

‡ *Expositor*, vol. iii. p. 187.

Jerusalem. Several of these, I maintain, though placed in Holy Week by S. Mark, belong really to the earlier years of our Lord's ministry.* And if, as becomes increasingly probable, a Johannine course of oral teaching was extant in comparatively early times, it is not strange that, as S. John dealt chiefly with the Judæan ministry, S. Peter should have refused to intrude into his brother Apostle's domain. They may have agreed at the outset to divide the work thus between them.

"Mr. Wright," Professor Sanday writes,† "knows the ins and outs of his friends the catechists' proceedings more intimately than most of us." I admit that I have collected for the first time and put together the obscure hints scattered over the New Testament, which indicate the existence and work of a noble band of men who have been hitherto strangely neglected, but to whom the Church is under infinite obligation. And in filling up the picture I have no doubt made some use of the historical imagination, as every one must do who would present a vivid picture of bygone ages; and to a certain extent at least I have been successful. The existence of the catechists is no longer denied. An effort is sometimes made to belittle them and minimise their work. Not so did the learned author of the Clementine homilies estimate them when he called the catechist of the Apostolic age the officer in command at the prow of the ecclesiastical ship. That was a post of dignity and responsibility second

---

* See *Synopsis of the Gospels*, Preface xi.
† *Expositor*, vol. iii. p. 83.

only to the position of the Bishop in the poop. And the catechists, if I mistake not, are regaining it. We have seen how Professor Marshall flies for refuge to them from a serious difficulty. Even Professor Sanday is forced to admit* that the catechists lived and laboured in all parts of the Christian world. The contention between us is reduced to this, whether they taught (as Apollos, who was one of them, taught) "the facts concerning Jesus,"† which facts alone their pupils would be willing to learn, or only moral precepts and "the two ways," which belong, I contend, to the less earnest times of the second century, when the Gospels were a written possession. Theophilus, at any rate, had been catechized in the very facts about which S. Luke wrote in his Gospel.

But, to return to the proper names, the first cycle speaks of the exercise of miraculous power on twenty-eight occasions. Four times it tells us generally that many were healed, twice definite numbers—5000 and 4000—were fed. Eight miracles concerned our Lord Himself. The recipients of the remaining fourteen were individuals. Now it is very remarkable that only one of these individuals is mentioned by name—Bartimæus, the son of Timæus—and that by S. Mark only. S. Peter's mother-in-law and Jairus's daughter are designated by the name of a relative. Eleven are anonymous.

If S. Peter had been writing history for the refutation of adversaries, he would have taken pains

---

* *Expositor*, vol. iii. p. 84.
† Acts xviii. 25.   ‡ Luke i. 4.

to discover (if he had forgotten or never known) the names of these eleven persons, and he would have appealed to them as witnesses in his support. But S. Peter was teaching Christians who accepted his testimony. They wanted information, not proof. They were little disposed to burden their memory with proper names of persons whom they did not know. They expected the end of the dispensation very shortly, and knew nothing of the claims of posterity.

On the other hand, S. Peter's knowledge of places might be expected to be fuller. And we find that he fixes the locality of fourteen miracles. Four others are said to have been wrought "in the desert," "in a desert spot," "on a lofty mountain," or at its foot. The remaining ten have no local clue.

Seven Old Testament saints are mentioned—Abraham, Isaac, Jacob or Israel, Moses, David, Elijah, Isaiah. S. Mark adds Abiathar, and S. Matthew Jeremiah and Daniel, in what are probably "editorial notes." It is noteworthy that the seven are mentioned in all the three Gospels. The common idea that Gentile Christians took little interest in the Old Testament is not supported. S. Luke's quotations from the Old Testament in the Acts of the Apostles completely refute it.

The name of Jesus is mentioned 80 times in S. Mark, John the Baptist 16 times, the Boanerges and Pilate 10 times, Peter and Herod (Antipas) 8 times. So truly is the first cycle described as "the facts concerning Jesus."*

* Acts xviii. 25.

Something is told concerning nine faithful men of that age, John the Baptist, Simon Peter, the sons of Zebedee, Matthew (if indeed he is identical with Levi, which is more than doubtful), Jairus, Bartimæus, Joseph of Arimathæa, Simon the Cyrenian; and of three holy women, the Virgin Mary,* Mary of Magdala, Salome. Then come four unbelieving men—Herod, Pilate, Barabbas, Judas Iscariot, and one unbelieving woman, Herodias.

Very little is recorded of the above persons. If it were not for the dramatic vividness of S. John's Gospel, we should be singularly in the dark about the Apostles and leaders of the Church. Except in the one tragic scene of the Baptist's murder, our Lord is the central figure in every section of the first cycle. Other characters are entirely subordinate to Him.

Names and nothing more are given of twenty-three other persons, of whom seven were Apostles and four "brethren of the Lord." The rest are Alphæus, Zebedee, James the Little and his brother Joses, Simon the leper, Timæus, Alexander and Rufus (these two I regard as an editorial addition of S. Mark's), Mary (who is once described as the mother of James the Little and Joses, on another as the mother of Joses, and on a third as the mother of James), (Tiberius) Cæsar, Herod Philip (in Cæsarea Philippi), and apparently another Herod Philip in the narrative of the Baptist's murder.

* Nothing more is said of her than that our Lord spoke slightingly of earthly relationships. It is only S. John who tells us that she was present at the crucifixion.

PROPER NAMES IN S. MARK

Geographical details are scanty. Five countries are mentioned—Judæa, Galilee, Gennesaret, Beyond Jordan, and Decapolis. Eleven cities or villages—Jerusalem, Capernaum, Nazareth, Bethsaida, Cæsarea Philippi, Jericho, Bethphage, Bethany, Magadan, Tyre and Sidon. I might have given Dalmanutha instead of Magadan, but, as Professor Rendel Harris has shown,* it is probably a "primitive error," in which S. Matthew has preserved the true Petrine word. If, as I have long suspected, Bethphage and Bethany are two names of the same village, all difficulty about them disappears. Captain Conder does not admit the existence of two Bethsaidas on the shore of the same lake. And such a thing is hardly credible in itself. Either, therefore, S. Luke† has unwittingly transposed the name from the end of the narrative to the beginning, or some private informant has told him the locality of the feeding of the four thousand—for which Bethsaida is singularly well suited—and he, knowing nothing of that event, has transferred the word to the feeding of the five thousand. S. Mark‡ only knows of a "desert spot" as the scene of the miracle, and S. John's narrative does not at all suit the north end of the lake. It is true that S. John in another place§

---

* On the *Codex Bezæ*, p. 178. † Luke ix. 10. *Cf.* Mark vi. 45.

‡ Harmonists require us to believe that 5,000 men, women, and children crossed the Jordan at a place where no ford nor bridge existed, in the month of April when the river would be in flood. It is to be remarked that "the city Bethsaida" is clearly a late addition to S. Luke's narrative, for in the sequel the disciples propose to send the people for food, not to the city, but to the villages and homesteads round about them.

§ xii. 21.

speaks of a "Bethsaida in Galilee," whereas the only Bethsaida of which we know was on the east shore of the Jordan, and therefore just out of Galilee in Gaulanitis. But S. Luke has once interchanged Gaulanitis* with Galilee, and it may well be that the word Galilee had a wider application in addition to its strict geographical use.

S. Mark tells us that Nazareth was in Galilee,† S. Matthew that Capernaum was by the sea-side,‡ and S. Luke that Tyre was on the shores of the Mediterranean,§ and that Capernaum was a city in Galilee.|| But all these additions seem to be "editorial notes." Knowledge on the part of the reader is generally assumed.

Five other places are mentioned—the river Jordan, the Sea of Galilee, the Mount of Olives, the Garden of Gethsemane, Golgotha. S. Luke omits Gethsemane, and translates Golgotha "a skull."¶ So he translates Cananæan "Zealot."** To prevent mistake he calls the Sea of Galilee the Lake of Gennesaret. He defines the "two disciples" (Mark xi. 1 = Matt. xxi. 1) to be Peter and John. He describes John as "the son of Zechariah." (iii. 2.) For Thaddæus he puts "Judas the (son) of James." (Luke vi. 16; cf. Acts i. 13, John xiv. 22.) He adds Joanna (xxiv. 10) to the list of women who visited the sepulchre.

Again, twelve adjectives derived from proper names are found—Jews, Pharisees, Sadducees, Galilæans, Jerusalemites, Herodians, Gerasenes,

* Acts v. 37. † i. 9. ‡ iv. 13. § iv. 17.
|| iv. 31. ¶ xxiii. 33. ** vi. 15.

Idumæans, Nazarene, Cyrenian, Greek, Syrophœnician. S. Matthew, at least in the present text, changes Gerasenes into Gadarenes.

Finally, we may observe that of the eighty-six proper names which occur in the first cycle, the following twenty-five are absent from S. Luke's parallels: Abiathar, Thaddæus, Boanerges, the names of the four brethren of the Lord, James the Little, Joses, Bartimæus, Timæus, Alexander, Rufus, Salome, both the Herods Philip (if indeed there were two), the Herodians, Jerusalemites, Greek woman, Syrophœnician, Gennesaret, Beyond Jordan, Decapolis, Cæsarea Philippi, Magadan. These names, I submit, are exactly the kind of names which we should expect to be riddled out of the tradition in forty years of catechetical teaching amongst persons who were not resident in Palestine. But if we look at the proper names in the non-Petrine portions of S. Luke's Gospel, or at the remarkably rich array of famous and obscure persons and places mentioned in the Acts of the Apostles, they will be seen to be just the kind of names which S. Luke would have wished to record in a written Gospel.

VIII.

ON THE PROPER NAMES IN S. LUKE'S WRITINGS

OF the three synoptists, the second writes as a catechist, the first as a theologian, the third as an historian. S. Mark's aim is to record what he had been daily teaching, as nearly as possible in the form in which he had learned it from S. Peter. The writer of the Gospel "according to S. Matthew" gives us the same record as S. Mark, with large additions, which tend to explain and justify the ways of God to men, especially in the mystery of the Incarnation, the Messiahship, and the teaching of Jesus. S. Luke desires to connect his Divine revelation with the ordinary course of this world; to show that the record was true and would bear scrutiny; to satisfy the demands of the intellect as well as the cravings of the heart.

It is of S. Luke's right to be considered an historian that we propose to treat in this paper. Not only is he seen to be such by the care with which he prefixes to his sections an introductory sketch to describe the historical situation, or concludes them with a few remarks to point out the historical result, though these "editorial notes" of

PROPER NAMES IN S. LUKE 75

his form quite a feature of his Gospel; but he essays to arrange the narratives in chronological order, and inserts a number of dates. He is also at pains to substantiate the record with the names of the persons who are described, and of the places where the events happened.

I. Let us glance first at his dates. It was not till the sixth century of our era that the convenient practice of naming the year by its numerical distance from the birth of Christ was first invented. Before that period there was no system of chronology universally accepted, but every nation had a method of its own. The Greeks reckoned by Olympiads; the Latins, from the building of Rome; the Syrians, from the victory of Seleucus Nicator; while many cities had one, and sometimes two or three epochs of their own. Not only is it necessary to discover and distinguish between all these, but we must find whether the year was solar or lunar, or a mixture of both, and whether it began in January or March, or at any other season. Indeed, the facts are so obscure and complex that precision in dates is often unattainable.

In the time of Christ, however, even these reforms had not been generally adopted. The vulgar did not reckon the years numerically, but by the names of their annual magistrates—by the archon of Athens, the ephor at Sparta, the consuls at Rome, the high priest at Jerusalem; while for cosmopolitan purposes, emperors, kings, proconsuls, and propraetors were freely made use of.

S. Luke, therefore, is giving dates after the common

practice of his time, when he states that John the Baptist was born "in the days of Herod the king of Judæa"; that Christ's birth took place "when Quirinius was proprætor of Syria"; that His ministry began "in the fifteenth year of the Emperor Tiberius, when Pontius Pilate was procurator of Judæa, and Herod tetrarch of Galilee, his brother Philip tetrarch of Ituræa and Trachonitis, Lysanias tetrarch of Abilene, in the high priesthood of Annas or Caiaphas"; that S. James was martyred under Herod Agrippa I.; that a famine took place in the time of Claudius; and that various parts of S. Paul's history fell under the proconsulship of Gallio, or the procuratorship of Felix or Festus. These, as well as the name of Ananias the high priest, are so many dates, and would be reckoned as such by the readers of the day. Compared with the other New Testament writers, who seldom give a date at all, S. Luke is seen to be the true historian. We could wish that he had told us more clearly whether our Lord's ministry lasted one year, as he seems to have held,* or several; what was the date of S. Paul's birth, the duration of his first missionary journey, and one or two other details. But speaking generally, S. Luke gives us very important help towards determining the chronology; the other New Testament writers seldom do so.

II. With respect to the arrangement of the narratives in the true chronological order, we must distinguish between those periods, like S. Paul's

* See below, page 185.

journeys, in which S. Luke accompanied the apostle or obtained information directly* from him, and those other periods, especially our Lord's ministry, where he depended upon second-hand information. In the former case, his arrangement, as far as we can test it, is perfect; in the latter case, I am convinced that it is not so. The Gospel begins, indeed, and ends with the true sequence, just so far as the events narrated indicate their own order; in other parts S. Luke simply follows S. Mark, whose order Papias rightly declares to have been made for the convenience of teaching, and not as the facts occurred. In the unique section, chs. ix. 51–xviii. 14, where S. Luke has no one to guide him, the sections are massed together on no discovered principle. In the first half of the Acts of the Apostles there appears also to be some misplacement. Not only does ch. xi. 19 ff. resume the history left off at ch. viii. 1, but the Acts of the Seven (chs. vi.–viii.) are grouped together for unity of subject, it would seem, rather than proximity of events. At any rate, the conversion of the Ethiopian eunuch (chs. viii. 26 ff.) must have happened subsequently to the conversion of Cornelius (chs. x., xi.), for the religious status of the two men was exactly the same,† and the fact is repeatedly emphasized that Cornelius was the first Gentile to receive baptism.

Partly, therefore, for artistic reasons, but oftener, I

---

* That he did this for the first journey is shown by Professor Ramsay, *The Church in the Roman Empire.*

† The eunuch cannot have been a full proselyte (Deut. xxiii. 1).

think, from inability to recover the true order, S. Luke's arrangement is defective. We have no reason to think that inspiration was a guide in matters chronological. Many incidents reached him without any clue to the time of their occurrence. His authorities also were not, like himself, Gentiles—Greek students of Herodotus and Thucydides *—but Orientals to whom "in those days" or "after these things" were satisfactory connecting links. S. Luke had seldom the means of testing their arrangement, even if it were desirable to raise doubts by disturbing the stereotyped order of catechetical teaching.

S. Luke promised, in his preface, to write "in order," and it is simplest to suppose that he meant "in chronological order," as his historical instinct would direct. But harmonists have been too ready to assume that he succeeded in accomplishing his purpose. Recent investigations make it daily more clear that he did not. His Gospel is by far the least orderly of the three. He had not the opportunities to recover the true sequence of events, and it is most important to admit this.†

III. In examining S. Luke's list of proper names, I set aside those which belong to ancient days, whether obtained from the Old Testament or from family genealogies, and consider only the names of contemporary persons, of which fifty are introduced to us in the Gospel, and ninety-five in the Acts of

---

* Many coincidences of expression indicate S. Luke's acquaintance with these authors.

† See above, page 40 ff.

the Apostles. Eighteen out of the fifty are not mentioned by the other synoptists; sixty-two out of the ninety-five are not mentioned by any other New Testament writer.

A religious teacher speaks but seldom of those whom the world considers great. To him S. Paul is a more important person than Tiberius, Dorcas than Drusilla. But the historian is obliged to take note of temporal rulers, and accordingly a large number of unbelievers find a place in S. Luke's chronicles. He names four Cæsars — Augustus, Tiberius, Claudius, and Nero*; five Herods—Herod the Great, Antipas, Philip, Agrippa I., and Agrippa II.; three royal ladies, Candace, Berenice, and Drusilla; seven Roman governors—Quirinius, Gallio, Pilate, Felix, Festus, Sergius Paulus, and Publius; three officers of the army — Lysias, Julius, and Cornelius; three high priests—Annas, Caiaphas, and Ananias. Besides these, we have Lysanias the tetrarch, Chuzas the house steward of Antipas, Blastus the keeper of Agrippa's harem, Gamaliel the doctor of the Law, Tertullus the advocate, Demetrius the coppersmith, Theudas the Zealot, and Elymas the sorcerer.

Some of these are mentioned cursorily to fix a date or brighten a page. Some play no mean part in the sacred drama. But there is a singular historical calmness in dealing with them. There is no raking up the foul deeds of their past lives, none of the sensational stories about Tiberius or Berenice,

---

* He calls Nero simply Cæsar. Caius is the only emperor of the time that he omits.

in which the modern commentator delights. Full justice is done to the political fairness of Gallio, and the honest purpose of Festus. No censure is pronounced on the weakness of Pilate or the meanness of Felix. The facts are stated, and the reader is left to draw what conclusions he pleases. Thucydides himself is not more impartial. "Those that are without God judgeth."

Far more interesting to us are the names of the faithful whom S. Luke enumerates. "Not many rich, not many noble, are called." Of that class, however, are Sergius Paulus, Barnabas, Dionysius, Theophilus, and Joanna. "But the weak things of this world hath God chosen to confound the mighty." Many who were honourable in the Church were unknown outside of it. It is in dealing with them that S. Luke writes with the hopefulness which is so painfully absent from the pages of contemporary heathen authors. How much poorer should we be without his pictures of Zacharias and Elizabeth, Simeon and Anna, Martha and Mary, Zacchæus, Cleopas, S. Matthias, S. Stephen and S. Philip, Cornelius, Dorcas, Lydia, Rhoda! What tragedies centre round the names of Simon Magus or of Ananias and Sapphira! How frequently, too, S. Luke fills in the gaps left by S. Paul! How little should we know about Aquila and Priscilla, Apollos, Timothy, Barnabas, and Silas, if we depended upon the great apostle only!

The names in the Gospel are as follows. An asterisk is prefixed to names not mentioned by S. Mark or S. Matthew:—

PROPER NAMES IN S. LUKE

A. UNBELIEVERS.

(a) *Men.*

- *Augustus Cæsar
- *Tiberius Cæsar
- Herod the Great
- Herod Antipas
- Herod Philip
- *Lysanias
- *Quirinius

- Pontius Pilate
- *Annas
- Caiaphas
- *Simon the Pharisee
- Barabbas
- *Chuzas

(b) *Women.*

- Herodias

B. BELIEVERS.

(a) *Men.*

JESUS CHRIST

Apostles—
- Simon Peter
- Andrew
- James
- John
- Philip
- Bartholomew
- Matthew
- Thomas
- James the son of Alphæus
- Simon the Zealot
- *Judas the son of James
- Judas Iscariot

Before Christ—
- *Zacharias
- *Simeon
- *Phanuel
- Joseph
- John the Baptist

During the Ministry—
- Zebedee

- Alphæus
- Levi
- Jairus
- *Zacchæus
- Simon the Cyrenian
- Joseph of Arimathæa
- *Cleopas

After Christ—
- *Theophilus

(b) *Women.*

Before Christ—
- Mary the mother of Jesus
- Elisabeth
- Anna

During the Ministry—
- Mary the mother of James
- Mary of Magdala
- *Mary the sister of Lazarus
- *Martha
- *Joanna
- *Susanna

The names in the Acts of the Apostles are as follows. An asterisk is prefixed to those who are not mentioned by other sacred writers:—

A. Unbelievers.

(a) Men.

*Claudius Cæsar
*(Nero) Cæsar
Herod Antipas
*Herod Agrippa I.
*Herod Agrippa II.
*Gallio
Pontius Pilate
*Felix
*Festus
*Ananias, high priest
*Alexander, chief priest
*John, chief priest
*Gamaliel
*Claudius Lysias

*Julius
*Blastus
*Bar-Jesus
*Dionysius
*Alexander
*Demetrius
*Scevas
*Elymas
*Judas of Galilee
*Theudas

(b) Women.

*Candace
*Berenice
*Drusilla

B. Believers.

(a) Men.

JESUS CHRIST

The Twelve Apostles—

Simon Peter
John
James
Andrew
Philip
Thomas
Bartholomew
Matthew
James son of Alphæus
Simon the Zealot
Judas son of James
*Matthias

Apostles—

Paul (Saul)
Barnabas

Church workers of various grades—

James the Lord's brother
Apollos
Silas
Timothy
John Mark
Sosthenes
*Agabus (prophet)
*Joseph Barsabas
*Judas Barsabas
Lucius
*Symeon Niger
*Manaen
Aquila

Delegates of the Churches—

*Sopater
Aristarchus
*Secundus
*Gaius of Derbe
Tychicus
Trophimus

PROPER NAMES IN S. LUKE 83

The Seven—
 *Stephen (prophet)
 *Philip (evangelist)
 *Prochorus
 *Nicanor
 *Timon
 *Parmenas
 *Nicolaus

Connected with S. Peter—
 *Æneas
 *Simon the tanner
 *Cornelius
 *Ananias
 *Simon Magus

Connected with S. Paul—
 *Ananias of Damascus
 *Judas of Damascus
 *Sergius Paulus
 *Mnason

*Gaius of Macedonia
*Tyrannus
*Titius Justus
 Crispus
 Jason
*Eutychus
 Erastus
 Alphæus
*Pyrrhus
*Theophilus

(*b*) *Women.*
 Mary the mother of Jesus
*Mary the mother of S. Mark
*Tabitha (Dorcas)
*Rhoda
*Lydia
*Damaris
 Priscilla (Prisca)
*Sapphira

Still more remarkable is the geographical knowledge exhibited by S. Luke. From Babylon in the east to Rome in the west, from Bithynia in the north to Ethiopia in the south, he takes us at pleasure. In the Acts of the Apostles alone he mentions thirty-two countries, fifty-four cities, and nine of the Mediterranean islands. At a time when there were no maps deserving the name, no systematic geography except Strabo's, which is incomplete, few books of travel or of reference, he takes us over no inconsiderable part of the inhabited world. We need not suppose that he had anything beyond a vague idea of the situation of Parthia, Persia, or the Soudan. He probably would not have set Ur of the Chaldees where modern geographers have discovered it; but his knowledge of the places which he describes is correct and minute. The more his statements are tested, the more their accuracy is seen.

Mr. Smith, of Jordanhill, spent years in investigating the shipwreck. Subsequent workers have followed on his lines, with the result that S. Luke's account is seen to be as true as it is graphic. Professor Ramsay has devoted a large part of his active life to the study of Asia Minor. He corrects the German commentators, and finds mistakes even in Bishop Lightfoot, but not in S. Luke.

In the Gospel the sweep is, of course, much more confined. Our Lord's work was carried on within the province of Syria, and, except the incidental mention of Cyrene as the home of Simon, no place outside of Syria is alluded to. S. Luke adds from his own researches three countries—Abilene, Ituræa, Trachonitis—and four places—Sarepta, Nain, Emmaus, Siloam—which are not in the other synoptists. But his authorities had cared little for geography. Seven cities in Galilee and nine in Judæa are all that he could collect. At the time when he wrote it was not easy to recover the neglected facts. The poverty of the Gospel in topography is as remarkable as the wealth of the Acts of the Apostles.

The following is the list of places mentioned in S. Luke's Gospel. An asterisk is prefixed to the names of places which are not mentioned by the other synoptists. Adjectives are given only when the corresponding noun does not occur:—

A. Names of Countries.

In Syria—
  *Abilene
  *Ituræa
  *Trachonitis
  Syria

In the Holy Land—
  Judæa
  Samaria
  Galilee

In Africa—
  Cyrenian

B. Names of Towns.

In Syria—
  Tyre
  Sidon
  *Sarepta

In Galilee—
  Nazareth
  Capernaum
  Bethsaida
  *Nain
  Gerasene
  Magdalene

Chorazin

In Judæa—
  Jerusalem
  Bethlehem
  { Bethany
  { Bethphage
  Jericho
  *Emmaus
  *Siloam
  Arimathæa
  Sodom

C. Names of Lakes and Rivers.

Lake of Gennesaret | Jordan

The following is the list of places mentioned in the Acts of the Apostles. An asterisk is prefixed to the names of places which are not mentioned by any other New Testament writer. Adjectives are given only when the corresponding noun does not occur:—

A. Names of Countries.

(a) In Europe.
  Italy
  Achaia
  *Greece
  Macedonia

(b) In Asia Minor.
  Roman Provinces—
    Asia
    Galatia
    Cappadocia

Cilicia
*{Lycia
*{Pamphylia
{Bithynia
{Pontus

Districts—
*Phrygia
*Pisidia
*Lycaonia
*Mysia

(c) *In Syria and the East.*
*Elamites
*Medes
*Chaldees
*Mesopotamia
*Parthians
*Chanaan
Galilee
Samaria

Judæa
Syria
*Phœnicia
*Midian
Arabians

(d) *In Africa.*
*Libya
Egypt
*Ethiopian

(e) *Islands.*
*Cyprus
*Rhodes
*Cos
*Samos
*Chios
*Samothrace
Crete
*Cauda
*Melita

B. NAMES OF TOWNS.

(a) *In Europe.*
Rome
*Tres Tabernæ
*Appii Forum
*Puteoli
*Rhegium
Corinth
Cenchreæ
Athens
*Berœa
Thessalonica
*Apollonia
*Amphipolis
Philippi
*Neapolis

(b) *In Asia Minor.*
Troas
*Assos

*Adramyttium
Thyatira
Ephesus
Miletus
*Patara
*Myra
*Attalia
*Perga
Antioch
Iconium
Lystra
*Derbe
*Tarsus

(c) *In Syria and the East.*
In the Holy Land—
Jerusalem
*Gaza
*Azotus

*Lydda
*Joppa
*Cæsarea
Ptolemais
*Antipatris
*Sychem
Nazareth

*Haran
Babylon

(d) *In Africa.*

Cyrene
*Alexandrian

(e) *In Islands.*

*Salamis
*Paphos
*Lasea
*Phœnix
*Mitylene
*Syracuse

Outside the Holy Land—
Tyre
Sidonian
*Seleucia
Antioch
Damascus

C. Seas, Harbours, Promontories.

Red Sea
*Adriatic
*Fair Havens

*The Syrtis
*Salmone
*Cnidus

D. Local Names.

*Aceldama | *Areopagus

About three-fourths of S. Mark's Gospel is found embedded in a considerably altered form in S. Luke's, and it is a burning question of the day how it came there. Had S. Luke a copy of S. Mark's Gospel before him when he wrote, or did both evangelists obtain their information from oral tradition?

Our present subject will throw some light on that exceedingly dark question. We have seen S. Luke's enthusiasm for proper names. His Gentile birth, his Greek education, his literary models, his historical insight, had taught him their importance. He cannot but have noticed the extraordinary lack of proper names in the Gospel, for he draws upon his own knowledge to increase the stock upon every available opportunity.

How, then, has he treated S. Mark? S. Mark (as we saw in the last paper) gives eighty-six proper names of persons and places—a miserably small number indeed, but S. Luke reduces it by omitting twenty-five of them. Had he possessed a written copy of S. Mark, I cannot but think that he would carefully have made full use of every one of them. But in oral tradition amongst Gentiles, who were unfamiliar with the localities or the people, proper names would inevitably disappear. Important places, like Bethlehem, Nazareth, Jerusalem, would remain; but Bartimæus, Salome, Decapolis, Magadan, Cæsarea Philippi, would one by one be left out. In a written book these names would be both useful and ornamental; when the lesson was learned by heart, they would needlessly cumber the memory.

We notice next the evidential value of proper names, especially in the Acts of the Apostles. We consider them the strongest proof of the authenticity of the book. A man who would venture to introduce ninety-five persons and a hundred and three places into a history of his own times must have been pretty sure of his ground. The majority of those persons were still living when he wrote; into every one of these places his volume shortly penetrated. If the story was not substantially true, could it possibly have survived? If he had misrepresented a single person or misplaced a single village, would not the whole neighbourhood have denounced him? The magnitude of the interests at stake, the eternal value of the doctrines proclaimed, would have made men insist upon a scrupulous adherence to the truth. To him it might with good reason have been said—

> "Incedis per ignes
> Suppositos cineri doloso."
> (HOR., *Odes*, ii., 1, 7.)

The only way to deal successfully with geography is to travel, and either S. Luke himself or his informants had visited the places and been present at the scenes which are described. The correctness of his geography upholds the truth of his history.

The Gospel, as we have seen, has but little of this external confirmation. God's ways are not as our ways. The less important work of the apostles is abundantly attested, the infinitely more important work of the Master stands alone.

It might easily have been otherwise. If only S. Luke had been one of the Twelve, and had accompanied them as their chronicler, in what a different way would the Gospel have been written! We should not have been left in doubt whether the ministry lasted one year, two, three, or as many as ten. Our Lord's journeys would have been as clearly defined as S. Paul's. Every incident would have been set in its proper surroundings. The miracles would have been confirmed by the name and abode of the recipient; the parables would have been illustrated by their geographical surroundings. The gain to the student would have been enormous; to the faith of the Church, perhaps very little.

Our Lord's words speak to the heart and the

conscience. It is not well that our attention should be drawn from them by the picturesqueness of the scenery. Have we ears to hear? Then it matters little to us who first received the message, or in what place or at what time it first was spoken. The words are for us.

IX.

ON ORAL TEACHING

WE propose in this paper to attempt to remove some of the objections which many men feel to the oral hypothesis, objections which, we believe, arise chiefly from the imagination, through the difficulty which all men feel in picturing a state of things which is widely different from anything existing now. The objections to the use of documents appear to me to be much more serious.

When a man copies from a written document, he may easily omit words or verses through carelessness or design. He may easily add an occasional comment of his own, or a few verses from another source. He may correct the grammar, polish the style, and remove barbarisms. But he cannot readily invert the order, still less can he habitually change from thirty to forty per cent. of the words, where he gains nothing by doing so, but rather blunts the sharpness of the original narrative. This last, as a literary feat, we may fairly pronounce to be impossible. It would require an almost infinite effort. And for what conceivable purpose should that effort have been made? To give a semblance of originality? But by these multitudinous variations the author irritates those who are familiar with the original document, and wastes his labour on those who are not. That one evangelist should have been guilty of this petty conceit is a shock to our moral sense. That two men, working independently in different parts of the world, should have hit on the same preposterous expedient for magnifying their task and diminishing its credit, is surely inconceivable. But with the oral hypothesis this stupendous difficulty disappears. The very changes which one man, copying direct from a document, could not have sufficient versatility to make, are made naturally and unconsciously by an army of catechists during thirty or forty years of oral tradition. This is the chief argument for the oral hypothesis, and the upholders of the documentary hypothesis are, as a rule, very reluctant to face it.

It is often assumed that S. Luke asserts in the preface to his Gospel that he had read and was making use of those narratives which "many" of his contemporaries had "undertaken to draw up." It seems to me that his language, when carefully examined, decidedly favours the opposite conclusion. He asserts that both they and he derived their information through tradition handed down by the regular catechists from the original eye-witnesses. He does not affirm that his precursors had actually published anything, but rather implies that they undertook the task of writing, and abandoned it. If, however, they did publish Gospels, his own was intended to supersede theirs, not so much by its greater comprehensiveness, as by its stricter accuracy

—a result which he could not have attained if he had copied from them.

Again, it is often tacitly assumed that the twelve apostles were all engaged in narrating their recollections of the words and deeds of Christ. But this cannot have been done officially to any great extent, or a diversity of tradition would have arisen instead of the one stereotyped record which we possess. S. Peter is the only member of the Twelve who is recorded in the Acts of the Apostles to have originated anything. The activity of S. John we gather from his own writings, that of S. Matthew from tradition. And these three are the only eye-witnesses who are said to have produced Gospel history. A number of anonymous authors, some of whom may have been apostles, contributed chapters or verses in S. Matthew and S. Luke, notably the great section Luke ix. 51–xviii. 14; but the other members of the Twelve have left no known record.

Again, it is essential to distinguish sharply between S. Peter the preacher and S. Peter the teacher. In the former capacity he dealt with the fulfilment of prophecy, exhorted his converts to live up to their high calling, or reproved them for their failings; in the latter it has long been my contention that he made them commit to memory a Gospel section, repeat it every day, with the addition of new sections, until a considerable body of teaching was acquired, which was frequently recited, and always in the same order, until the order became as much fixed as the subject-matter.

In assuming this, I only assume that S. Peter was

wise in his generation, and acted as everyone in his circumstances and in that time and place must have acted. He had several thousands of converts to educate, who were all ignorant, and many of them eager to learn. Preaching would not satisfy them nor supply their need. The fashion of the day was to store the memory. There was an unreasoning prejudice against religious books. "Commit nothing to writing" was a maxim with the Rabbis. Neither S. Peter nor his fellows had any literary instincts. Believing that the end of the age was at hand, they had no sense of duty to posterity.

In the unchanging East the habit of committing to memory is still strong, and it may confirm what I have written if I produce some examples from ancient and modern times in illustration of the practice.

The first quotation is taken from *A Buddhist Catechism*, published by Messrs. Redway, in London, 1890.

"151. *Were these holy books composed and written by the Buddha himself?*

"Neither by him nor by any of the brethren who were the Buddha's first disciples. It was not the custom in India in those times to set in writing any religious or philosophic truths. They were taught by word of mouth from master to pupil, and impressed on the memory by incessant repetition of words and whole passages. In this way they were handed down from one generation to another."

The next quotation is from Professor Max Müller, in the *Christian Commonwealth* for October 4th,

ON ORAL TEACHING

1894. It was kindly furnished to me by the Rev. Joseph Twidale.

"At a time when writing did not exist the human memory was infinitely superior to what it is now. People could remember an enormous amount of what we call poetry, and even prose; nay, they could compose without any writing materials. This is very difficult for us to believe, but we have in Sanskrit literature an accurate description of how a man who was being educated had to learn every day so many lines, and how he learned them and repeated them, going on day after day, always repeating what he had learned, and adding to it. That system is described in books of the fourth century B.C. I have had people in this room who knew by heart the whole of the Rig-Veda, which consists of more than a thousand hymns of about ten lines each, and who could take it up at any point. That is not at all an uncommon thing among educated men in India, but women are not usually educated up to the point. I have had, however, staying here a lady, Rámabhai, who had committed to memory pretty well what would correspond in extent to our Bible. Her father, evidently an enlightened man, had allowed her to be present at the lessons of her brother, and in that way she learned all that he learned. When she was staying with us I asked some of my friends, professors in the university, who are always somewhat sceptical about this faculty of memory, to come and test this young lady, who was only twenty-two. I gave them the Rig-Veda, the Bhagavad-gêtâ, and other books, telling them they might open them where they liked, and she would go on till they were tired. And so she did, never hesitating for a word."

The third witness is the Ven. Archdeacon Moule, of Mid-China, who said, at a public meeting in Chelmsford, that there is a school at Ning-po to which orphans are taken when twelve years old and taught. He was asked to examine it, and promised to give an hour. "That will not do," was the answer; "it must be a morning." So he gave a morning. He discovered that the children knew the whole of the four Gospels by heart. They could be put on anywhere, and would go straight away, the beginning, middle, or end of a chapter, or the beginning, middle, or end of a verse. And it was no mere parrot-learning. They could explain in their way what they had been taught.

These examples, which I could easily multiply, will show that the memory is capable of the work which I have attributed to it, and that the men of that time and century would be likely to make use of it. But if the teaching was to be carried into distant lands, a band of teachers must have been prepared and set forth, taking S. Peter's Memoirs with them. These, I maintain, were the catechists, about whose existence and work so much incredulity has been expressed in certain quarters. The Provost of Trinity College, Dublin, Dr. Salmon, objects that I use the word "catechist" in an unusual sense, to signify an instructor of the baptized, whereas, in the third century and afterwards, the catechist instructed the catechumens who were candidates for baptism.

Dr. Salmon, however, admits that in the first century neophytes were baptized immediately on their profession of faith in Christ, without either instruction or probation. Does it not follow from this that a catechumen, in the apostolic age, was a newly baptized person? And must not his education have been in accordance with the pressing necessities of the time? When no written Gospel existed, a knowledge of the words and works of Christ was the one thing which was indispensable, and the one thing, therefore, which the catechists may be supposed to have taught.

But neither the catechists nor their work are inventions of mine. I have good warrant for what I have written about them. (1) S. Paul says, "Let him that is catechized in the Word give a share in all good things to him that catechizeth." (Gal. vi. 6.) From this verse it is clear that the catechist was an unpaid agent, engaged in a highly important work, and that he taught "the Word," by which I understand the Gospel sections; for (2) S. Luke states that Theophilus had been catechized in that very Gospel history which S. Luke himself proposed to reduce to writing (Luke i. 4); and (3) Apollos "taught with precision the facts concerning Jesus." (Acts xviii. 25.)

Many, like Professor Sanday, feel a strong objection to the oral hypothesis, not only in the order of the narratives (which we have already explained), but in the fact that so many insignificant words, such as conjunctions, remain unaltered in all the three Gospels. Surely, they say, such trivial words as these would be the first to disappear in oral teaching. Have we, however, any reason to think that it would be so? The human memory is particularly tenacious of connecting links. A man who recites poetry would break down if he neglected them. When once he has thoroughly mastered his lesson, they become as fixed as the weightier words. It is only during the process of learning, as the records passed from catechist to catechist, or by deliberate effort, as often in S. Luke's Gospel, that they would be changed. Quite enough of them have been changed to make us suspicious about the use of documents.

If my view of the whole matter is right, the proper persons to write Gospels were the catechists, and the natural thing for them to write was that particular form of oral Gospel which had gradually grown up in their own Church, and which they had long been in the habit of frequently repeating to their pupils. To such persons the labour of writing a Gospel would be small. And we may well believe, as S. Luke tells us, that many of them attempted the task. Why they did not complete it, or why, if they did, their work never gained general acceptance, we are no longer in a position to examine.

S. Mark was a primitive catechist of the earliest type, a pupil of S. Peter, and the translator into Greek of his Aramaic sections. He has given us in his Gospel S. Peter's Memoirs, with a very few remarks and additions of his own. Historical criticism has brought to light the extreme value of his Gospel, as being the nearest approach to S. Peter's actual teaching.

Our first Gospel must have been written by a catechist also. It is called the Gospel "according to S. Matthew," because its distinctive feature is S. Matthew's "utterances of our Lord," which, however, are not given as S. Matthew taught them, but massed together into long discourses or collections of parables for the greater convenience of teaching.*
S. Peter's Memoirs, however, are the backbone of this Gospel also. And a considerable number of fragments from other sources are embedded in the narrative, but there is very little comment or explanation. It is usual to say that this Gospel was intended for Jewish readers: it would be truer to say that it had been formed in a Jewish Church. Where that Church was situated I do not venture to assert. Not in Judæa, for there is no local colouring, no additional geographical knowledge, such as a Palestinian must surely have contributed. Moreover, the Rev. Thomas Barns points out to me that the Holy Land is called "Syria" (Matt. iv. 24), which is the name of the Roman province of which it formed part. I infer that some Greek-speaking community within the Roman empire is indicated. Alexandria answers to the conditions, but I cannot at present pronounce anything definite.† The cradle of this Gospel was Jerusalem, but it grew to maturity elsewhere.

S. Luke was both a catechist and an historian. The earlier part of his Christian life was spent at Philippi, and it is there that he must have formed

---

* See above, p. 21. † See above, p. 20.

the main part of his Gospel, though he had rare opportunities for collecting new matter while he waited on S. Paul for two years at Cæsarea. His first two chapters are direct translations from a written document, the original of which my colleague, the Rev. R. H. Kennett, lecturer in Aramaic to the University of Cambridge, suggests was in New Hebrew rather than Aramaic. They can be retranslated into Hebrew much more readily than into Aramaic, and Hebrew was used by the learned as Latin is still used in University life. The Rev. Prof. J. Armitage Robinson contends that they were originally composed in Greek to imitate the style of the Septuagint. Certainly a tendency to follow the Septuagint is perceptible wherever S. Luke has a free hand in writing his Gospel. Biblical facts were naturally expressed in Biblical language, and the Septuagint was his only Bible. The original narrator, however, must surely have told the story in Aramaic, not, however, perhaps reduced to literary form. S. Luke was taught the Memoirs of S. Peter when about two-thirds of them only had been composed, and thus his omissions are easily accounted for. Into them he inserted such portions of S. Matthew's "utterances of our Lord" as reached him piecemeal in his distant home, finding places for them according to their subject-matter rather than by their strict chronology, which he had not the means of discovering. His arrangement of them, therefore, differs widely from that of the first Gospel, and is probably even further removed from the true order. The "third cycle" he inserted for the most part bodily into the middle of his work, without any attempt at chronological arrangement. Finally, he interspersed throughout his work a large number of comments and historical notes, thus making his book more complete as a work of art than either of the other Gospels.

Such, according to the oral hypothesis, was the genesis of our three Gospels. It was strictly in accordance with the habits of the time and the place of their birth. All the overwhelming difficulties about omissions and variations in order and language which beset the documentary hypothesis disappear. The Gospels were written for local use; in God's providence they were fitted for universal acceptance. They were written for the need of one generation; they have satisfied the requirements of sixty. They were published anonymously; the authors' names we gather from tradition. They rapidly pushed their way over the Christian world, not by an apostolic edict or Church Council, but because they commended themselves as faithful records to the universal Christian conscience. Out of weakness they became strong.

The oral hypothesis receives very strong confirmation from the writings of the earlier Christian Fathers. These writings teem with quotations from the Gospel history, but it is the rarest exception for such quotations to agree *verbatim* with any one of our Gospels. No doubt the Fathers quoted from memory, but even that will not account for the facts. We hold that they found it easier to quote that oral Gospel which they had learned in their childhood, rather than these written Gospels which had become the treasure of their old age. Even though they read our four Gospels aloud in the Church services, their sermons and writings were embellished with the older reminiscences.* For every considerable Church must, under the oral hypothesis, have had a tradition of its own, differing both in contents and wording from that of other Churches, and in particular exhibiting much mixture and many sayings of Christ which are not in our Gospels at all.

Now, contrast with this simplicity the difficulties which beset the documentary hypothesis. And first its advocates, as far as they venture upon any definite statements, are at variance between themselves. One school repudiates the catechists, the other gladly avails itself of their teaching. The former school is compelled to hold, either that the discourses in S. Matthew are free inventions, based on a few scanty reminiscences, in which case they could hardly have gained the sanction of the Church Catholic; or else that certain documents, which have perished, were written within a few years or even months of the Ascension, while the recollection of our Lord's teaching was still fresh. In either case they do not account for the divergence in wording between S. Matthew and S. Luke, nor for the still wider varieties in patristic quotations, nor for the loss of these pristine documents.

The other school holds, either that a hypothetical batch of documents based on oral tradition sprang

---

* Where the English Revised Version is read in Churches, *ex tempore* preachers continue to quote the old Authorised Version, because from youth they have been familiar with it.

ON ORAL TEACHING

into existence about A.D. 70, rapidly spread over the world so as to reach all our evangelists, were used as sources of our three Gospels, and then perished, leaving no trace behind; or else that S. Mark's Gospel alone was used as a source by S. Matthew and S. Luke, oral tradition doing the rest.

It is here that the problem becomes so complex as to be the despair of the most able and clear-headed thinkers.

To suppose that some of the documents were in Aramaic will not do, unless, as Professor Marshall holds, an oral Greek version accompanied them. The multitudinous varieties in wording are inexplicable unless we hold, with Dr. Stanton, that, if the evangelists had documents, they dared not use them. The circumstances of the time compelled them to prefer the oral tradition which was stored in their own memory to the most venerable records by apostolic men. And if so, why should we postulate the existence of these documents at all? If the memory of the catechist supplied so much, why should it not have been equal to everything?

Lastly, the reluctance to use the name of God, which is a remarkable feature of S. Matthew's Gospel, and may be noticed also in S. Mark, will be appreciated if we realise the irreverence of a large class of thoughtless boys shouting out the sacred name after the oriental way of learning by heart.

Let no one think that this is a barren controversy. Much depends upon it in establishing the truth, the trustworthiness, and the inspiration of God's precious gift to the Church.

X.

ON THE PRECEPT TO SELL YOUR CLOAK AND BUY A SWORD

CRITICISM is not only essential to establish the historic truth of the Gospels, but it is of practical importance for their exegesis and in apologetics. I shall attempt to illustrate this in the present and following papers.

I propose to examine here one of the most interesting sections of those which are peculiar to S. Luke. It runs thus: "And He said, When I sent you forth without purse, or wallet, or shoes, lacked ye anything? And they said, Nothing. And He said to them, But now let him that hath a purse take it, likewise also a wallet; and let him that hath no money sell his cloak and buy a sword; for I say unto you that this which is written must be fulfilled in Me, And He was numbered with lawless men; for my course is drawing to a close. And they said, Sir, behold, here are two swords. And He said, It is enough." (Luke xxii. 35–38.)

I. The section is introduced by the phrase, "And He said," not "Then said He," nor "After these things said He," nor by any of those longer prefaces which form quite a feature in S. Luke's Gospel.

I infer from this that S. Luke wished us to understand that he was not quite sure that the paragraph belonged to the place where he has put it.

S. Luke, I hold, began to work as a catechist—probably at Philippi—at so early a date, that his first lessons did not contain even the whole of S. Peter's Memoirs. Indeed, the greater part of the latest portion of these Memoirs, lying chiefly between S. Mark vi. 14 and viii. 10, never reached him at all. And the second cycle of oral teaching, commonly called S. Matthew's *Logia*, was as yet scarcely begun. In his distant Gentile home S. Luke received from time to time, either by letters from friends or by word of mouth from travellers, detached parts of it, as well as a few narratives like this, which were no part of it, but he seldom had any other clue to the chronology of these new sections than was contained in the passages themselves. It was S. Luke's task, I maintain, upon receiving a contribution to find a suitable place for it in that ever-expanding course of oral instruction which he gave to his pupils and finally stereotyped in his written Gospel. By this simple explanation, and by no other, we can account for the extraordinary difference between S. Luke's arrangement of conversations and S. Matthew's. The conversations are the same, though with varying degrees of divergence, according to the precision with which they were reported, but the context is widely different. And S. Luke's chronology is far less likely to be correct than S. Matthew's.

Suppose then that this paragraph is one of those jewels, if I may so call them, which came to S. Luke broken loose from its original setting. He must make a new setting for it, if it was to add its lustre to his Gospel. And on proceeding to examine it, he could have little doubt to which part of our Lord's ministry it belonged. A time of persecution is indicated. Hospitable homes were no longer open to Christ's emissaries. Henceforth the disciples must take with them a purse to buy bread and a wallet to carry it. A sadness pervades the passage, a melancholy, almost a despair. The shadow of the cross rests upon it. The evangelist, therefore, has put it between the prediction of S. Peter's denials and the account of the agony in Gethsemane. In no other place would its meaning have been so heightened.

To us, however, who have four Gospels before us, teeming with words spoken and deeds done on that last overwhelming night, it is a task of no small difficulty to piece them harmoniously together, and find the right place for each. And it is a relief to the historical critic to find that he is under no obligation to do so. The Gospel narratives are seldom presented to us in their true order. Even "straightway," "then," or "after these things," cannot always be pressed. Much less can a plain "And He said" be decisive of the date. Many words assigned by one or other of the evangelists to that supreme night may have been spoken at some other time during the preceding week. S. Luke's paragraph would suit any stage in the last journey. From its mournful tone we are disposed to refer it to that time of anxiety when our Lord first set out for Jerusalem.

The student of the Gospels will be saved many hours of anxious labour if he learns how unchronological the synoptic Gospels are. How could S. Luke, arranging detached narratives at Philippi for the immediate need of his pupils, have discovered the true order? Why should he have thought it of any great importance to do so?

II. "When I sent you forth without purse, or wallet, or shoes, lacked ye anything?" There is an allusion to the first mission of the Twelve, when Christ "sent them forth two by two into every city and village into which He himself would come." An account of this mission was given in S. Peter's Memoirs, for it was an important epoch in that apostle's life. And as S. Peter's narrative is reproduced in each of the synoptic Gospels, it is interesting to observe the variations which have been made in it by the catechists. These variations are so curious, that no hypothesis of copying from a written document, whether Greek or Aramaic, can account for them. The changes must be due to the unconscious working of human memory during a long period of oral transmission.

S. Mark, preserving as usual S. Peter's words with much precision, writes, "Take nothing for your journey save a staff only, not bread, not a wallet, not copper for your belt, but be shod with sandals, and do not put on two tunics." (vi. 8.) S. Matthew, with more than his customary changes, gives, "Provide no gold nor silver nor copper for your belts, not a wallet for the road, nor two tunics, nor shoes, nor a staff." (x. 9, 10.) St. Luke, with unwonted brevity, has, "Take nothing for your journey, neither staff nor wallet, nor bread, nor silver coin, nor two tunics to wear." (ix. 3.)

The only coins minted in Palestine during the Roman period were of copper. Being of small value, and free from idolatrous symbols, they circulated freely amongst the poor. S. Mark's "Take no copper" is probably the original precept. But to prevent mistake, S. Matthew has expanded it into "no gold nor silver nor copper." S. Luke has altered it into "no silver coin," because silver in imperial times was the only legal tender at Rome, until "silver," like the Scotch "siller," became the ordinary expression for "money."

Here then we have examples of changes made by the catechists in the wording of S. Peter's Memoirs, either to prevent misunderstanding or to suit the different environment of their pupils.

A more serious difficulty arises about the shoes and the staff. S. Mark enjoins the use of both, S. Matthew prohibits both, S. Luke prohibits the staff, and says nothing about the shoes. In his instructions, however, to the Seventy in the next chapter, he bids them go forth "without purse or wallet or shoes." (x. 4.)

This discrepancy was observed in very early times. The first harmonist with whose works we are acquainted is Tatian, who wrote about A.D. 160. In his *Dia Tessarôn*, written in Syriac, but translated into Arabic, of which version a copy has been recently discovered, he undertook to construct a complete Life of Christ by piecing our four Gospels together into

SELL YOUR CLOAK, ETC.

one continuous narrative. In this way he produced a book of considerable interest, but dull and heavy, overloaded with words, and possessing none of the literary charm which characterizes our Gospels. It became, however, so popular that the Bishop Theodoret was obliged to prohibit its use in the churches of his diocese, because it was actually superseding the Gospels.

Tatian deals with the passage thus: "Provide not gold nor silver nor copper for your belts, not a wallet for the road, not bread, nor shoes, nor a staff but a cane only; be shod with sandals, and do not put on two tunics." Tatian evidently assumes (as later commentators have strangely done) that there was such a difference between sandals and shoes that the one must be forbidden as a luxury, the other enjoined as necessary; and although the Greek word for a "staff" (ῥάβδος) is the same, he seems to think that the original Aramaic must have been different. A staff to walk with would be an unwarranted indulgence to the flesh, a stick to chase away the dogs which encompass the traveller's path in an Eastern village must be conceded.

All honour to Tatian for his conscientious attempt to serve his day and generation, but when a Scotch writer of the present time, working on similar lines, suggests that ῥάβδος in S. Mark means a "staff," but in S. Matthew a "tent-pole," we must protest against such trifling with sacred records. It is true that ῥάβδος, like "stick," may have many meanings, but, as in English, if you told a man who was setting out on a journey to take a stick, he could only understand you to mean a walking-stick, so also in Greek the context is decisive. It would be absurd to speak of a tent-pole without mention of a tent. And the divergence in narrative could only be accounted for in this way, if S. Peter's Memoirs had originally a double sentence, "Go shod with sandals, but not with shoes, and take a cane, but not a staff," of which S. Mark in each case has preserved the first member and the other evangelists the second. Such a supposition is altogether improbable. Rather, therefore, must we admit that oral tradition is not always to be trusted in preserving these complex regulations. There is a tendency towards severity. The priests in the temple went bare-foot when performing their sacred duties, why should not Christ's servants do the same? Mankind are fond of imposing irksome rules on those who are engaged in specially sacred work.

III. It is further to be noticed as an indication of the light esteem in which S. Luke held verbal precision that, although he has exactly reproduced the three words, "purse, wallet, shoes," from his own Gospel, he has not taken them from our Lord's instructions to the Twelve, but from His instructions to the Seventy.

S. Luke could easily have turned back his own pages and verified the reference, correcting either the one passage or the other until he made them agree, but he has not done so. The self-contradiction remains, as in several passages in the Acts of the Apostles (ix. 3–9 = xxii. 6–11 = xxvi. 12–18; x. 1–48 = xi. 1–18).

SELL YOUR CLOAK, ETC.

If what we have advanced above is a true account of the matter, it evidently follows that the two words, "or shoes," were no authentic part of our Lord's saying on this occasion, but arose from that assimilation of doublets which is a necessary feature of oral tradition. That this is so is seen on a close examination of the passage; for not only do these two words destroy the balance of the sentence, but there is nothing corresponding to them in the next clause, which is constructed with precise parallelism: "But now let him that hath a purse take it, likewise also a wallet."

Lastly, the word "purse" is another adaptation to local requirements. S. Peter had said, "Take no copper for your *belt*," a phrase which S. Mark and S. Matthew retain, because the tunic of a Jew was fastened round the body with a belt (Acts xii. 8), which, whether made of leather or raw hide (Mark i. 6), was doubled and stitched till the hollow thus produced formed an excellent purse. But this custom, though known to Roman soldiers (Hor. *Ep.* ii. 2. 40), does not seem to have prevailed in the civil life of Gentiles. They carried their coins (which were of silver) in their mouth or in a pouch. Hence S. Luke's alteration.

I venture to press these facts upon the student, because most commentators take pains to obscure them. Yet surely they are full of significance. They teach us to value the general sense more than the words, the spiritual lesson more than the picturesque surroundings.

IV. "And let him that hath no money sell his

cloak and buy a sword." No doubt this precept means that every Christian missionary must provide himself with a sword, even though it be at the cost of parting with his cloak.

The extreme urgency of the order will be seen if we remember how important a part the cloak played in the dress of a Jew. It was not indeed a necessity. It was laid aside during the hours of work. But if the climate of Palestine, a country the main ridge of which on an average is 2500 feet above the sea-level, made it necessary for the aged and infirm to wear two tunics in cold weather ("Then the high priest rent his tunics," Mark xiv. 63), much more was a cloak needful for everyone in the winter evenings. By the poor it was also used as a blanket. And the humane legislation of the Old Testament enjoined upon even the money-lender that he should in any case restore it at sunset when it had been given as a pledge, for else "wherein was its owner to sleep?" (Ex. xxii. 26, 28.)

But Christ's messengers must not think of bodily comfort. "If they have no money, they must sell their cloak and buy a sword."

Three notable interpretations are offered of this startling paradox—the mystical, the allegorical, the literal. The mystics said that the "two swords" which the disciples produced in reply are the temporal and the spiritual power, without which the Church is not perfect. According to this explanation, our Lord's rejoinder, "It is enough," signifies His approval, whereas any other explanation requires that it should signify disapproval, as though He had said, "I will say no more: you have not understood Me."

SELL YOUR CLOAK, ETC.

Mystical interpretation was once universal in dealing with the Old Testament and common in dealing with the New. It is the glory of our age to have thrown discredit on so fanciful and phantastic a device, which we would not tolerate in the interpretation of any except sacred books. Few persons now would admit it here.

The allegorizer says that the sword in Christ's thought was not of steel, but referred rather to intellectual weapons. The missionary of the future would have to face antagonists, and must be prepared to do battle with them on their own ground. Education was henceforth essential for him. Rhetoric, oratory, philosophy, could not be dispensed with. A S. Paul would succeed where a S. Peter might fail to secure a hearing.

This is true, and contains a useful lesson for those who are preparing for holy orders. Let them as a matter of duty do their utmost to acquire the best possible training. Especially let them investigate the pressing questions of the day.

But this interpretation does not lie on the surface. It is an extension rather than the original meaning. We come therefore to the literal sense.

In the quiet easy times of prosperity Christ's messengers had had a simple task. Their glad tidings had found a way to ready minds and hearts. Loving disciples had vied with one another in supplying their bodily needs. But a different day was dawning now. The 53rd chapter of Isaiah, which says of the Messiah, " He was numbered with lawless men," and goes on to speak of death and burial, would soon be fulfilled. And " if they persecute Me, they will also persecute you." You must take nothing from them. You must earn your own money and provide your own food. You will be brought before kings and rulers. You will encounter brigands and assassins. For your defence you must learn to wield a sword.

This is the only interpretation which satisfies the context. It was when the disciples understood Him too literally that He cut them short. Oriental figures of speech were not to be taken in their strict sense. No servant of Christ could really go forth with a sword. "They that take the sword shall perish by the sword." Rather he must go expecting opposition, with the martyr spirit, but as a good soldier of the cross.

Does anyone think it impossible that Christ could thus positively have made a command and then immediately on second thoughts explained it away by a kind of recantation? Let him beware of denying the reality of the Incarnation. That our Lord should have had a human mind is an essential part of that inexplicable mystery. And impossible though it be for us to understand the union of so finite and limited a thing with the fulness of the Godhead, we must not on that account deny it. And we have at least one, and that a more striking example of its presence, when Christ said, "It is easier for a camel to go through the eye of a needle than for a rich man to enter into the kingdom of God," that is, "It is absolutely impossible for a rich man to be saved," and yet presently added, "With men this is impossible, but not with God; for with God all things are possible." (Mark x. 27.)

XI.

S. MARK'S TESTIMONY TO THE RESURRECTION

THE present paper shows the importance of criticism in apologetics.

In our own day the witness of S. Mark to the Resurrection has been thought to be somewhat impaired by the rapid growth of the doubt which has always rested upon the last twelve verses of his Gospel.

Many persons have upheld the genuineness of these verses, chiefly from a conviction that they are genuine, but partly, perhaps, from a fear that if we surrender them we should be doing violence to our idea of what Holy Scripture is and ought to be, should be opening the door to the adversary, and giving occasion for stumbling to those who are timid and weak in the faith.

To the former feeling we would wish to do full justice, against the latter we would enter a protest. If the Church is the custodian of Holy Writ, those of her members who by education or official position have the responsibility of guiding opinion are bound to face the facts, and not yield to their wishes or fears.

If internal evidence is—as we believe it to be—decisive against the said verses, and external evidence, when properly examined, is almost equally fatal, it is our duty fearlessly to proclaim the state of things. We need not tremble lest the truth should suffer by the avowal of truth. Our own ideas about the canon may have to be readjusted. But it is better to stand upon a foundation which cannot be moved, than to insist on holding ground which in the day of struggle will crumble away beneath our feet.

If, however, we take this view about these verses, it becomes our duty to examine the real extent of our loss. And therefore in this paper I propose to say something about S. Mark's witness to the Resurrection apart from these twelve verses, for some persons have hastily assumed that if these verses are set aside the Resurrection itself might be allowed to disappear from the Christian creed.

In the first half of S. Mark's Gospel, immediately after S. Peter's confession of the Messiahship of Christ, stand these words: "And He began to teach them, that the Son of Man must suffer many things, and be rejected by the elders, and the chief priests, and the scribes, and be killed, and after three days rise again." (Mark viii. 31.)

These words, in the same context, and with no alterations of any consequence, were transferred from S. Mark's oral teaching into S. Luke's, and at a somewhat later date into S. Matthew's also. They therefore, we have good reason to believe, must have formed part of the earliest edition of S. Mark's oral Gospel. They must have been taught in the Church of Jerusalem before S. Paul's first missionary journey began, within at least seventeen years after the crucifixion; nay, probably within twelve years, before S. Peter took up his residence at Joppa. They were, therefore, most firmly believed in the very place where the events had happened, and while hundreds of Christians were living who knew what could be known about it. They were accepted in Judæa, Samaria, Antioch, and all other churches in which S. Mark's Gospel, in its oral form, was the sole exponent of the faith.

In the next chapter we read that as the disciples descended from the Mount of Transfiguration Jesus "charged them that they should tell no man what things they had seen, save when the Son of Man should have risen again from the dead." (Mark ix. 9.)

These words did not pass into S. Luke's Gospel, but they did into S. Matthew's. (xvii. 9.) We infer that they were not yet part of S. Mark's Gospel when that Gospel was first carried westward. They belong to what we have called the second edition of S. Mark, *i.e.*, to those sections which were added to the oral teaching at Jerusalem after the year 47 A.D.

In the early stages of Christianity the apostles had been popular with the masses; but as time went on a change came over the public feeling. "Herod the king slew S. James with the sword. And when he saw *that it pleased the Jews*, he proceeded further to take S. Peter also." (Acts xii. 3.) Persecution became the rule. To profess Christ was not only to be excommunicated from the synagogue, but was to incur the wrath of the civil ruler. The officers of the Church were men whose lives were in danger. Did that make them untrue to their trust? Did they give up or conceal their principles? On the contrary, they only sought occasion for further avowing them. Instead of removing the prediction of our Lord that He would rise again from the dead, they recalled to memory other occasions on which He had foretold it; and thus this paragraph was added to the cycle of teaching.

Further on in the same chapter we read, "Jesus taught His disciples, and said unto them, The Son of Man is delivered up into the hands of men, and they shall kill Him; and when He is killed, after three days He shall rise again." (Mark ix. 31.)

This, the second prediction of the Passion, is found also in S. Matthew (xvii. 23); but in S. Luke (ix. 44) the last clause about rising again is not found. Either, therefore, that clause is a later addition, made, when the love of many was growing cold, to strengthen those who remained, or it has dropped out of S. Luke because it was regarded by him as superfluous. S. Luke's Gospel was used in Pauline churches; and wherever S. Paul taught, belief in the Resurrection was so foremost an article of the creed, that the constant assertion of it was unnecessary.

In the tenth chapter we read the third prediction of the Passion, and this time all three Gospels unite in their witness to the Resurrection. For S. Mark writes, in words of unusual solemnity, "And they were in the way going up to Jerusalem; and Jesus was going before them: and they were amazed; and they that followed were afraid. And He took again the twelve, and began to tell them the things that were to happen unto Him, saying, Behold, we go up to Jerusalem; and the Son of Man shall be delivered unto the chief priests and the scribes; and they shall condemn Him to death, and shall deliver Him unto the Gentiles: and they shall mock Him, and shall spit upon Him, and shall scourge Him, and shall kill Him; and after three days He shall rise again." (x. 32-34.)

The unique solemnity of the opening words not only indicates the effect upon our Lord's human mind of the truths which He was announcing, but also the abiding impression which they made upon those who heard Him; for though at the time "they understood not the saying," it is abundantly plain that they were awe-stricken by our Lord's manner.

Lastly, on the Mount of Olives, after the last supper, Jesus said to His disciples, "Howbeit, after I am raised up, I will go before you into Galilee." (xiv. 28.)

Now is it possible, I ask, that if S. Mark had denied or doubted the Resurrection, he would have preserved these sayings—five times repeated—of his Lord concerning it? Would he not have forgotten them, or kept them back? He had abundance of time to reflect on this question, for he can hardly have finally committed his teaching to writing before the destruction of Jerusalem, and yet all five of the predictions are deliberately recorded in it.

It is certain from the whole tone of his Gospel that he was writing an account of One whom he regarded as an altogether supernatural Being. It will not suffice to say that S. Mark held our Lord to be superior to Moses, or to Elijah, or to John the Baptist. It is as clear as he can make it that he regarded Him as *the Son of God*, in the highest sense in which those words can be understood. He is second to none in thus bearing witness.

Why, then, should he five times put into our Lord's mouth the prediction that He would rise from the dead, unless he was as firmly convinced, as Christians always have been, that the Resurrection was an actual fact?

If the whole of his last chapter had been lost, and not merely the concluding verses, we should have felt sure that S. Mark agreed with S. Peter, S. Paul, S. John, S. Matthew, S. James, and every other New Testament writer, that Christ was proved to be the Son of God with power by the Resurrection from the dead.

We now come to his last chapter. "And when the Sabbath was passed" (*i.e.*, about seven o'clock on Saturday night), "Mary Magdalene, and Mary the mother of James, and Salome, brought spices, that they might come and anoint Him."

Then, after the night's rest, "very early on the first day of the week" (*i.e.*, about four o'clock on Sunday morning), "they come to the tomb *when the sun had risen*"—such is the MSS. reading; and that it has stood so long, in face of the assertion of S. John that it was still dark, is a proof of the fidelity of scribes. But assuredly a negative (μήπω) must be inserted: "When the sun had *not yet* risen." Not so much to bring S. Mark into agreement with the testimony of all the other Gospels—for discrepancies of this kind are frequent in the New Testament—but to reconcile him with himself; for by "very early in the morning" no ancient writer could mean after sunrise. This, we may feel confident, should be added to the list of primitive errors.

"And they were saying among themselves, Who shall roll us away the stone from the door of the tomb? and looking up, they see that the stone is rolled away: for it was exceeding great. And entering into the tomb, they saw a young man" (S. Luke and S. John say TWO *angels*) "sitting on the right side, arrayed in a white robe; and they were amazed. And he saith unto them, Be not amazed: ye seek Jesus, the Nazarene, which hath been crucified: He is risen; He is not here: behold, the place where they laid Him! But go, tell His disciples and Peter that He goeth before you into Galilee: there shall ye see Him, as He said unto you. And they went out, and fled from the tomb; for trembling and astonishment had come upon them; and they said nothing to any one; for they were afraid."

Does any candid student of this passage doubt that S. Mark believed in the Resurrection? Observe how he draws attention to our Lord's prediction of it. Observe how he repeats the order that the Twelve should go into Galilee. But because he stops there, and does not record any appearance of Christ, therefore we are told by certain persons that S. Mark knew of no such appearance—the disciples were put off with prophecies and promises; they never beheld their risen Lord.

But can any one really suppose that S. Mark stopped here? Is it not certain that his last sentences have been obliterated? And, if so, what did they contain?

We can have very little doubt on that question. Throughout his Gospel S. Matthew has adhered most closely to S. Mark. He has many discourses, parables, and sayings which are not found in S. Mark, but only on the rarest occasions does he omit any historical narratives which S. Mark has given. It is to S. Matthew, therefore, and not to S. Luke (as some contend), that we must turn if we would supply the lost verses. S. Luke says nothing from beginning to end about the returning to Galilee, but S. Mark has made this a feature in the story, and most certainly must have told us how the disciples went there and were met by their Lord.

In S. Matthew, therefore, we find this continuation: "They ran to bring His disciples word. And behold, Jesus met them, saying, All hail! And they came and took Him by His feet, and worshipped Him. Then saith Jesus unto them, Fear not: go tell My brethren that they depart into Galilee, and there shall they see Me."

Then after a few verses from another source, S. Matthew continues: "But the eleven disciples went into Galilee, unto the mountain where Jesus had appointed them. And when they saw Him, they worshipped Him: but some doubted. And Jesus came to them and spake unto them, saying, All authority hath been given unto Me in heaven and on earth. Go ye therefore, and make disciples of all the nations, baptizing them into the name of the Father and of the Son and of the Holy Ghost: teaching them to observe all things whatsoever I commanded you: and lo, I am with you alway, even unto the end of the world."

Such, in substance, must have been the last verses of S. Mark's Gospel.

We have five accounts of the Resurrection. First, that which is common to S. Mark and S. Matthew; then S. Paul's; next, some facts peculiar to S. Matthew; after that S. Luke's; and, finally, S. John's. These accounts differ considerably from one another, and are so difficult to piece together, that some persons condemn them as unhistorical, and declare that they must be given up.

Entirely different from this is the verdict of scientific criticism. The more divergent narratives are, and the more difficult to reconcile, so long as they are not absolutely contradictory, the more valuable is their testimony; for the differences prove that they are independent, and not mere repetitions from the same source.

From the very earliest Christian times, as recorded in the Acts of the Apostles, to the latest the Resurrection is the chief fact attested. Indeed, Christianity is built upon it. The existence of the Church during all the centuries is an expression of the confidence in its truth. History, as well as criticism, leaves us no room to question this. On so sure a foundation is our most holy faith erected.

But the best witness to the Resurrection is its power over the hearts of those who believe it. "If ye then be risen with Christ," S. Paul writes, "seek those things which are above, where Christ sitteth on the right hand of God. Set your affections on things above, and not on things upon the earth. Mortify your affections which are upon the earth. For ye are dead, and your life is hid with Christ in God. When Christ, who is our life, shall appear, then shall ye also appear with Him in glory." (Col. iii. 1-4.)

XII.

THE CAMEL AND THE NEEDLE'S EYE

FEW of our Lord's sayings obtained an earlier or a wider recognition than this. It was freely circulated in the first days of the Church, or it would not have appeared in S. Mark's Gospel. It retained its hold on the memory of the Church at Jerusalem when S. James, the Lord's brother, succeeded to S. Peter's chair, or it would not be found in S. Matthew. It spread among the Gentiles, and was often on the lips of S. Paul, or we should not read it in S. Luke.

If it is lawful to look for earthly reasons to account for this triple attestation, we may surmise that its place in S. Mark is due to its startling nature; for in the earliest days the chief endeavour of the new teachers was to arrest attention. Its place in S. Matthew may be due to its Rabbinical form. The Jews would be attracted by the oriental hyperbole. Its place in S. Luke may be assigned to its philosophical depth. The "Greeks sought wisdom," and might find it here.

But who shall say with what different feelings the words have been repeated through the ages by different men? At one time the rich man may have found in them an excuse for gainsaying, while with no real earnestness he muses, as Shakespeare represents:

> "My thoughts of things divine are intermixed
> With scruples, and do set the Word itself
> Against the Word:
> As thus, 'Come, little ones,' and then again,
> 'It is as hard to come, as for a camel
> To thread the postern of a small needle's eye.'"
>
> (*Richard II.*, Act V., Scene 5.)

At another time the poor man may have repeated the verse with unholy satisfaction. Let us make every allowance for him. He had a hard lot, and felt its bitterness. He was filled with envy and malice and wrath, not knowing that these were the works of the evil one. He grasped at the words because their outer form gratified his excited feelings; but he knew not—he could not fathom—the depth of sorrow in the Saviour's heart, of which they were the sad expression.

And a similar want of sympathy with Christ may lie at the root of those numerous attempts to soften down the severity of the saying which have been made in different ages by the scribe, the critic, the commentator.

First came the scribe, who, with that wanton boldness which happily expired at the end of the second century, presumed to alter the words of the evangelist.

According to the true text, S. Mark's narrative ran thus: "And Jesus looked round about and saith unto His disciples, How hardly shall they that have riches enter into the kingdom of God! And the disciples were amazed at His words. But Jesus answereth again, and saith unto them, Children, how hard a thing it is to enter into the kingdom of God!" Then follows the saying.

But this simple and striking sentence, "How hard a thing it is to enter into the kingdom of God!" was altered by a very early scribe through an interpretation of his own, "How hard a thing it is *for them that trust in riches* to enter into the kingdom of God"; and this false reading has obtained gradual currency, because it seems at first sight to sustain the argument and to explain it, though on closer examination it will be found to spoil it.

Still less happy was the work of the critic. Theophylact tells us that one such conjectured that κάμηλος, *a camel*, should be altered into κάμιλος, *a cable*, because a camel has nothing to do with a needle, but a cable might be threaded, if it were not too thick, and the pronunciation of the two words would be almost identical in the first century. I pass over the question whether the word κάμιλος was invented for the occasion; it is certainly of doubtful authority. But surely the close resemblance between κάμηλος and κάμιλος exists only in Greek, whereas our Lord spoke in Aramaic, in which the saying must have been a proverbial one, for the Talmud reproduces it in a slightly altered form: "It is easier for an elephant to go through a needle's eye."

It has been reserved for the commentator to suggest a more plausible explanation.

In the description of a journey through Hebron, Lord Nugent wrote: "We were proceeding through a double gateway .... there was one *wide*-arched road, and another narrow one for foot passengers by its side. We met a caravan of loaded camels. The drivers cried out to us to betake ourselves for safety .... to the smaller arch. They called it the *hole*, or *eye of the needle*. If .... this name is applied, not only to this gate at Hebron, but to all similar gates, it may give an easy solution of what has appeared to some the strained metaphor 'of the camel going through the needle's eye.' A camel could not be made to pass through the smaller gate except with great difficulty, and stripped of the encumbrances of its load, its trappings, and its merchandise."*

Many people have gladly adopted this suggestion. In the Revised Version you will find that the words "the eye of a needle" have in each case been altered to "the needle's eye," out of deference, no doubt, to this interpretation.

The explanation, however, appears not to be a new one. It is thought that Shakespeare was acquainted with it when he wrote in the passage which I have just quoted, "To thread the *postern* of a small needle's eye"; for a "postern" is a little back door, or back entrance, of a castle. And although the language is reduced to chaos by the combination of the literal meaning with the figurative, it is difficult to account in any other way for the poet's words.

Now it is notorious in the East that whenever the Arabs discover that European travellers are on the look-out for certain words or names, no opportunity is lost of repeating them. Whatever you want to

* *Lands Classical and Sacred*, i. 326.

hear you will hear. And therefore it is no argument to say that the phrase "needle's eye" is *now* universally current in the Holy Land for a postern gate unless you can show that the phrase is really ancient, and was not first suggested by a too simple traveller.

And this interpretation is not so probable as at first sight it appears; certainly it removes all exaggeration from our Lord's words, reducing them indeed to a feeble commonplace. But are there no other sayings of His which are exaggerated? Did He never say that the Pharisees *devoured* widows' houses? that a man cannot add one cubit (half a yard) to his stature, as if half an inch were not enough? Is it possible literally to have a *beam* in the eye? Can you strain out the intrusive gnat and then *swallow the camel?*

In all these cases our Lord spoke to Orientals in an oriental manner. Western logic may think the language unnatural; but a poet's fancy feels little difficulty about it. Southey, at any rate, seems to have caught the spirit of the passage when he wrote:

> " I would ride the camel,
> Yea, leap him flying, through the needle's eye,
> As easily as such a pampered soul
> Could pass the narrow gate."

But, the reader may object, there is something more than hyperbole here. Explain the words as you will, they cannot amount to less than this, that " it is impossible for a rich man to enter the kingdom."

That, I maintain, is precisely what they do mean. They were wrung from the Saviour's human heart by the smart of a great disappointment. The young man over whom He had yearned had gone away sorrowful, because he had great possessions. And in the first blow of this grief our Lord exclaimed, "A rich man cannot enter the kingdom." Immediately afterwards He modified the expression. It was hard for anyone, it was inexpressibly hard for a rich man, to enter. But God's grace could enable him to do so. "For the things which are impossible with men, are possible with God."

Thus interpreted, the text will be a good example of the reality of our Lord's human mind, for we see second thoughts correcting a too sweeping expression.

So far we have dwelt on the *form* of the saying. Now let us add something to the teaching itself, that it is peculiarly hard for a rich man to enter the kingdom of God.

There is a passage in Plato* where Socrates is represented as asking a rich old man what he had found to be the chief advantage of wealth. And the man replies: "I am getting old, and I am forced to think about death and the coming world. Riches have enabled me to offer to the gods an unusual abundance of sacrifices; I have also had no temptation to steal from my fellow-men. And so I can contemplate the future with complacency."

Whether Plato himself meant any irony here may be matter of opinion, but it is certain that the mass of his readers would detect none, for he was but giving expression to the common opinion.

* *Republic*, i. cap. v.

THE CAMEL AND NEEDLE'S EYE 131

The Jewish system of sacrifices had inevitably fostered the same belief. Sacrifices were costly, and the rich alone could offer them properly. In vain had the prophets extolled the piety of the poor. In vain had our Lord said, "Blessed are ye poor, for yours is the kingdom of heaven." Such teaching had already been forgotten by the disciples. If the *rich* could not be saved, who then could?

It was necessary to teach in a more incisive manner; and our Lord did so when He spake the parable of the rich fool and the rich man and Lazarus, when He declared that the poor widow with her two mites had cast into the treasury more than all, but not least when He pronounced the paradox, "It is easier for a camel to go through the needle's eye than for a rich man to enter into the kingdom of God."

But *why* was it specially difficult for the rich to follow Christ? Because their whole education had taught them to value what He considered unimportant. Gold with them is the measure of all things, but it will not purchase heaven. The almighty, omnipotent God is altogether superior to bribery.

In that single sentence the whole fabric of false religion is overthrown; the righteousness of God is vindicated. Nothing will avail with Him but a broken heart, a consecrated life, a perfect self-surrender. No wonder that it is hard to enter the kingdom!

Happy they who enter it in infancy, who carry out their baptismal vows as fast as their childish intellect develops, who learn to love God before they discover the attractions of the world or know the worth of money.

For them riches, like everything else, may be made a means of grace. For with Christ "all things are ours." Riches as well as poverty may become a blessing. S. Paul expressly says, "Charge them that are rich in this world, that they be ready to give and glad to distribute . . . *laying up in store for themselves a good foundation against the time to come, that they may lay hold on eternal life.*" *

Christ has made this possible. He has shown that there is a Gospel for the rich as well as for the poor. Was not Barnabas rich? † Was not Zacchæus rich? ‡ Did not Joseph of Arimathæa devote large wealth to the honour of his Master's burial? §

And were not all these men following—however remotely—the example of Him who, *though He was rich*, yet for our sakes became poor?

Yes, that absolute surrender of the only perfect wealth has not only set us an example, the spirit of which has been wonderfully followed, but it has altered for us the very notion of wealth. Men have not merely sought to be "rich in good works" and "rich towards God," but they have come to recognize the responsibilities of material wealth. It is impossible now to ask, "May I not do what I will with mine own?" Men have learned—stern facts in modern history have wonderfully quickened the lesson—that *nothing* is our own. We hold every-

---

* 1 Tim. vi. 17–19.   † Acts iv. 37.
‡ Luke xix. 2.   § Mark xv. 46.

thing in trust, to be used for the common good. Not only do we owe duties to our family, but to our town, our nation, to Greater Britain, yea, to the human race. Each and all of them have claims upon us which the world in Christ's time never recognised, but which He has opened our eyes to see; and if we will not learn the lesson peacefully from Christ, it will be forced upon us by the uprising of a down-trodden people.

The words are true enough still, but they are not so bitterly true as when first they were spoken.

A wealthy man then was almost as a matter of course a slave-owner. From his youth he had been trained to crush and keep down his servants, to hold cheap their lives and their honour, to despise the very notion of their rights.

No wonder that "not many rich, not many mighty, not many noble were called."* Still, the apostle did not write "not any." Even in his day the camel, by God's help, had passed the needle's eye. Men had learned (as they may still learn) "not to trust in uncertain riches, but in the living God, who giveth us richly all things to enjoy."†

* 1 Cor. i. 26.   † 1 Tim. vi. 17.

XIII.

THE ORIGIN OF THE LORD'S SUPPER

PROFESSOR GARDNER'S pamphlet on this subject* is very attractive. The tone is modest and conciliatory; the scholarship is of the highest; the difficulties have been carefully considered and the objections anticipated. With much of what he writes, all who have studied the subject will agree—nay, more, they will be grateful for the illustrations which his special knowledge gives; and yet from his main conclusions we feel bound to dissent.

Some persons will retort that all criticism tends in the same direction, and that our only safety lies in the strict conservatism of the late Dean Burgon, who laid down the rule that if a single word in the Bible fall short of being in the fullest sense the Word of God, the whole of our Christianity must be abandoned. Being unwilling to leave any excuses for such counsels of despair, we proceed to examine these new proposals.

Dr. Gardner offers us the choice of two positions. One, to which he apparently inclines, makes the scene of breaking bread, which the synoptists unite in placing at the Last Supper in or about the year

---

* Macmillan and Co., London, 1893.

29, to be antedated by almost a quarter of a century. Our Lord did not say while He was upon earth, "*This is My Body*," but S. Paul in a trance at Corinth in the year 53 heard Him say the words in heaven. More timid or cautious readers are offered an alternative, according to which Christ broke bread and gave it to His disciples upon earth, but nothing further was done. No sacrament of the Lord's Supper was instituted until S. Paul in a vision beheld the scene repeated, and heard a new command, "*This do in remembrance of Me*." He thereupon founded the Eucharist, partly in obedience to the command, partly in imitation of the Eleusinian mysteries, by which he had recently been impressed.

Dr. Gardner, like most of what I may call the more advanced critics, rejects the oral hypothesis respecting the origin of the synoptic Gospels. And no wonder; for this hypothesis is fatal to his speculations. For example, it is essential to his first proposal to hold that S. Paul's Epistle to the Corinthians, which is generally allowed to have been written in the year 58, is far earlier than any of our Gospels. But the advocate of the oral hypothesis replies, "I admit that the synoptic Gospels were not *written* before the eighth decade of the first century, but I insist that a large part of them, including the account of the Last Supper, existed in an oral form a generation earlier. The bulk of S. Peter's Memoirs, which constitute the first cycle of oral Gospel, must have been composed within twelve years of the Ascension, or I cannot account for their wide distribution and their multitudinous variations. And whatever is found in all three Evangelists belongs to the earliest part of S. Peter's work."

Now, there is no question between us that the account of the Last Supper in S. Paul, S. Mark, S. Matthew, and S. Luke comes in great measure from the same source. Dr. Gardner insists upon that fact as strongly as I do. Whether S. Paul or S. Peter is the ultimate authority for it is simply a question of dates. Dr. Gardner, in saying that S. Paul was the author, is ignoring the primitive oral teaching, the existence of which in the first age few people who have examined the subject will venture to deny, however much they may seek to minimise its influence. And I must hold him to that point, as the one essential contention between us.

The truth of the oral hypothesis is established partly by the habits and prejudices of the age, partly by minute study of the resemblances *and divergences* of the same sections in the three Gospels. The very paragraph about the institution of the Lord's Supper furnishes some interesting examples. For S. Luke has some curious reversals of order. He puts the prediction of Judas Iscariot's treachery after the institution of the Lord's Supper, whereas the other two evangelists have put it before the Supper; and, according to the true text, he represents that the cup was given before the bread. Nor is this unparalleled. He presents us with an exactly similar transposition in the early part of his Gospel, where he reverses the order of the second and third temptations. (Luke iv. 5–12; Matthew iv. 5–10.) Such transpositions are easily accounted for, on the supposition that men

ORIGIN OF THE LORD'S SUPPER

learned the Gospel sections by heart, and stored them in a memory which was trustworthy enough when it had mastered the lesson, but was apt to be treacherous during the initial stages. They are almost impossible to account for if the evangelists were copying from a document.

Much of the wording also is strangely altered, not more so than in most passages of the triple tradition; but we should have expected to find this less altered, for it has long been observed that the words of Christ have been more scrupulously preserved in the Gospels than the rest of the narrative. Reverence for the Master's sayings has checked, as I hold, the carelessness or presumption of catechists. Why should it not have done so here? The answer may seem paradoxical, but the very gravity of the occasion would appear to have been the cause for increased changes. At any rate, the same thing has happened in two other utterances of the first importance—the Lord's Prayer and the baptismal formula. S. Luke's recension of the Lord's Prayer, according to the true text (xi. 2 ff.), is much shorter than S. Matthew's (vi. 9 ff.). And S. Matthew's Gospel directs baptism to be administered in the name of the Father, and of the Son, and of the Holy Ghost (xxviii. 19); but S. Luke and S. Paul invariably represent it as administered in the name of the Lord Jesus. (Acts ii. 38, viii. 16, x. 48, xix. 5; Rom. vi. 3; Gal. iii. 27; Col. ii. 12.)

It appears to me that we may account for these changes by the reflex action of the liturgies upon the oral Gospel. Lengthy liturgies certainly did not exist in the first days; but short formularies, at first elastic, but gradually hardened and stereotyped, would connect themselves with the administration of the Sacraments in the several churches. It may be thought strange to believe that in the Church for which S. Luke wrote his Gospel (whether it was Antioch on the Orontes, or any other) the cup should have been regularly given before the bread,* and both the Lord's Prayer and the words used at baptism should have been abbreviated; but on any other supposition I am unable to account for S. Luke's variations. The further you can push the matter back, the easier it is to believe in the existence of diversity of usage; and the less you are encumbered with written documents, the more reasonable will your deductions appear.

My belief in the oral hypothesis is based upon the cumulated results of many years' study; such considerations as these only strengthen it. But a theory which is unwaveringly upheld by the Bishop of Durham must not be lightly set aside out of deference to the opinions of certain critics on the Continent.

It is well known to students of textual criticism that Luke xxii. 19¾-20, have been rejected by Drs. Westcott and Hort as an early interpolation. A copy of S. Luke's Gospel must have reached Corinth, or some other Pauline Church, at an early date. What wonder if the Church authorities, finding in it so strange an inversion of their own custom of administering the Eucharist, should have inserted into the margin from their liturgical formula (which

---

* S. Paul (1 Cor. x. 15-21) supports this custom, but not in 1 Cor. xi. 23-25.

was based on 1 Cor. xi. 25) the words which in the common text distort the whole passage? Their doing so will but illustrate what I have written about the effect of local liturgies upon the local editions of the Gospels.

But if, as I maintain, S. Paul has borrowed from S. Mark (with the usual variations and additions), not S. Mark from S. Paul, how do I account for S. Paul's language: "For I received from the Lord that which I also delivered unto you"?

In the first place, it is to be noticed that the words "receive" and "deliver" ($παραλαβεῖν$, $παραδοῦναι$) are regularly used of tradition ($παράδοσις$), in which a man receives from the Lord, but through a long line of oral teachers. (Mark vii. 4; John i. 11; 1 Cor. xv. 1, 3; Gal. i. 9, 12; Phil. iv. 9, etc.). And it is quite possible that S. Paul merely meant: "I derived from the Lord, through S. Peter and other eye-witnesses." In the passages which Dr. Gardner produces to prove the contrary, this particular word does not occur, and I contend that he has too readily rejected this interpretation.

But even if we allowed that S. Paul alleged in these words a special supernatural revelation, we are not bound to think that he was independent of S. Mark. It is reasonable to suppose that, after his first Communion or his first administration of the Communion to others, being impressed by the solemnity of the occasion and with the words fresh in his mind, he fell into a trance, or had a dream on the following night, in which he saw heaven opened and the Lord Jesus at the Supper-table breaking the bread and delivering it to the apostles. The formulæ, the manual acts, the whole surroundings, would in that case have been projected into the vision from the earthly scene at which he had been so recently assisting. To S. Paul's mind it would bring confirmation of faith; and, unless we deny altogether that God spake in past times in visions unto His saints, we may allow that his belief was warranted. But the historical fact would be the basis of the vision, not the vision the basis of the Eucharistic service.

Dr. Gardner holds that the *agapé*, or love-feast, is older than the Eucharist, and at first was simply a social meal partaken by the whole body of Christians together, without any special religious ceremonies. The Eucharist afterwards was grafted upon it. And that when we read (Luke xxiv. 30; Acts ii. 42) of the breaking bread, nothing more than the *agapé* is intended. To this I object, first that we have no evidence that *agapæ* were ever established in the primitive Church of Jerusalem. The Christians in the first days had no synagogues, nor houses large enough for a joint festival. Nor were such feasts known to the Jewish synagogue, whose practices they largely followed. S. Luke's words, "breaking bread *at home*" (Acts ii. 42), indicate a multitude of small gatherings, not a congregational meal. When S. Jude (12) writes "*your* love feasts," he perhaps points to the fact that love-feasts were unknown to his own Church. Secondly, the phrase "breaking bread" is not, I think, the proper one to describe an ordinary meal. It is an expression never found in the Old Testament, nor, I believe, in any pre-Christian author. The cause for this is obvious. The loaves of the ancients were flat cakes, each of which would generally satisfy one person's appetite. To hand round the loaves, not to break them, would be the office of the master of the house. For to give broken bread was a mark of poverty or slight. (Ezek. xiii. 19.) It was our Lord who introduced a new custom. On two occasions He took some loaves of bread and brake them into pieces to distribute to the multitudes. At the Last Supper He took one loaf, divided it into twelve pieces, and gave one piece to each of the apostles. In imitation of this S. Paul says that *all* the Corinthians at the Eucharist partook of *one* loaf, which symbolized their unity. So completely was this ceremony peculiar to Christ that the disciples at Emmaus recognised Him in the breaking of bread.

Let us turn next to S. John. It is well known that he omits all reference to the institution of the Lord's Supper, but, nevertheless, in the sixth chapter uses Eucharistic language, as though the Communion had already at that early date been established. Dr. Gardner infers from this that he did not accept S. Paul's account, but yet elaborately expanded his phrases. I have for some time suspected that a simpler explanation is the true one. If we had the synoptists alone, we should have gathered that baptism was first instituted after the Resurrection; we learn from S. John iv. 1 that it had been practised by the Twelve throughout our Lord's ministry. May not the same thing be true of the Eucharist? It was solemnly administered on the night of the betrayal, but not for the first time. It had been a covenant of union between Christ and His disciples during their sojourn together. Ready though I am to admit that the discourses in S. John's Gospel have been moulded in the apostle's mind and influenced by the teaching of his life, I cannot allow that they are so altogether an invention as Dr. Gardner teaches. And if not, the language of the sixth chapter receives its simplest solution from the suggestion which I have made, which in itself is highly probable. Hence, too, we understand better how Jesus was recognised in the breaking of bread.

But, setting aside all other considerations, let us boldly meet Dr. Gardner in his own domain of history. At the date when the synoptic Gospels were written (probably 70 to 80 A.D.), the celebration of the Eucharist in Christian congregations was so general, that in each of three Gospels the account of its institution is given, yet in the year 52 Dr. Gardner maintains it was unknown. Soon after that S. Paul first started it at Corinth, then introduced it at Troas (Acts xx. 7), and in other churches of his founding. After that it spread over the East and became universal. The belief also was established that it dated from the Crucifixion. So much was the genius of one man capable of accomplishing!

Is not Dr. Gardner crediting S. Paul with much greater influence than that apostle possessed during his life, or for some time after his death? We are far from admitting, with the Tübingen school of historical criticism, that S. Peter, S. James, and S. John were his enemies. But he was disliked or deserted in many of his own churches. (Gal. iv. 16;

2 Tim. i. 15.) At Jerusalem the prejudice against him was inveterate. (Acts xv. 5; xxi. 21.) The Jews of the dispersion detested him. (1 Thess. ii. 15; Phil. iii. 2.) And no wonder. It is strange that the author of the Epistle to the Galatians was able to mix with Jews at all. If any man was compelled by the activity of enemies to adhere strictly to the truth, it was the great apostle of the Gentiles. He was not able even to force his own form of institution upon his faithful henchman, S. Luke. In spite of his alleged revelations, the other evangelists also adhered to their own formula. By what means was such a man to foist a new ordinance upon the churches and persuade them to believe that it was primitive? What energy and frequency of exhortation must he have used to preserve it when once started? Yet the fact is that in all his extant writings, except the first epistle to the Corinthians, he never so much as alludes to it.

Dr. Gardner thinks that S. Peter and the other apostles, though they knew that Christ had never said, "This is My body," nor solemnly broken bread and given it to them, would have acquiesced in the pious fraud, and given S. Paul that support in his innovation, without which he could not have succeeded. Many Christians will feel a difficulty in accepting this startling supposition, notwithstanding the reasons which are given for it. Nor is it very credible that the Eleusinian mysteries suggested the Last Supper. These mysteries were celebrated annually. The gorgeous pageant owed its attractiveness to its rarity. A weekly or daily fair would pall on the taste of the gayest. But S. Paul contemplated a more frequent repetition. "This do," the command runs, "as often as ye drink." Strictly interpreted, the words mean, "as often as you take a draught of any kind"; and in the Acts of the Apostles, S. Luke apparently describes the Church in the days of its first love as "breaking bread" at every meal, the head of the family acting as priest in his own house, according to the Christian idea. A looser, but intelligible, interpretation is, "As often as ye drink *wine.*" Just when the temptation to self-indulgence is strongest, let appetite be restrained by sacred associations. Let the thought of Him who died hallow your earthly enjoyments.

The resemblance between the Christian ordinance, and both ancestor worship and the Eleusinian mysteries, is no doubt real, but I should account for it by the similarity which exists between all ancient religious rites amongst civilised peoples. Our Lord did not found anything absolutely new in kind. It would be His design, we may believe, to establish a sacrament which would be generally intelligible, because it appealed to old ideas and inherited prepossessions. To eat bread or salt with a person has been, and amongst Arabs still is, to make a sacred bond of friendship with him. Hence in the books of Genesis and Judges so much is made of asking a visitor to eat bread. Hence the Psalmist sees in violated hospitality the climax of ingratitude: "Yea, mine own familiar friend, whom I trusted, who did also eat of my bread, hath laid great wait for me." (xli. 9.) Hence, also, "every sacrifice is salted with

ORIGIN OF THE LORD'S SUPPER

salt." Nor must we forget the ancient custom of sending out portions, whether carried out on a large scale, as with the Spartan kings,* or on quite a small scale in mere dainty bits, the size of which, however, indicated the measure of your esteem. Oceanus says to Prometheus :

Οὐκ ἔστιν ὅτῳ μείζονα μοῖραν νείμαιμ' ἢ σοί.†

Joseph sends messes to his brethren, "and Benjamin's mess was five times so much as any of theirs." (Gen. xliii. 34.) And in the same manner our Lord gave the sop to Judas. "The blood is the life" (Gen. ix. 4), and wine is an ancient surrogate for blood; it is called in Ecclesiasticus the "blood of the grape." ‡ To make blood-brotherhood is a common custom still with African tribes. "Whoso eateth My flesh and drinketh My blood, abideth in Me and I in him" (John vi. 56) is not borrowed from Hellenic thought, but from the common ideas of primitive man. I believe that this covenant of union was made between Christ and the Twelve frequently during His earthly sojourn. I believe that, as in the feeding of the five thousand, it was to some extent offered occasionally to a larger circle. I believe that it was solemnly repeated on the night of the betrayal, and that S. Luke is right in representing it as practised in the earliest days of the Church. For long examination has convinced me that the opening chapters of the Acts of the Apostles are based upon ancient (probably oral) records. And surely if so strange, so

---

* HDT. vi. 57.   † ÆSCHYLUS, P. V., 291.
‡ Prof. W. R. SMITH, *The Religion of the Semites*, p. 213.

simple a ceremony was started from the first and never discontinued, there is no difficulty about it. But if it was neglected for upwards of twenty years, we fail to imagine a power which within the next twenty years could have made it practically universal.

We freely admit, or, rather, have long insisted, that the words, "Do this in remembrance of Me," stand on a lower level in point of historical attestation than the words, "This is My body." They are not guaranteed by S. Peter, but come to us only on the authority of S. Paul. But we are very far indeed from casting suspicion on all our Lord's reputed deeds and words which S. Peter has not recorded. Other persons who were present at the Last Supper had memories besides the *coryphæus* of apostles. In spite of all that Dr. Gardner has urged, we think it simplest to believe that at the Last Supper Christ Himself used both these sentences, although in the churches, which depended for their information on S. Peter, only one of them was preserved.

POSTSCRIPT

In Isaiah lviii. 7, "Deal thy bread to the hungry" may be literally translated, "Break thy bread," etc.; but this would only be the exception to prove the rule. In the case of starving beggars it is proper to give broken meat, but no one might do so in ordinary social life.

XIV.

ON THE DATE OF THE CRUCIFIXION

I.

IT has been noticed from very early times that there are difficulties about the date of the crucifixion of our Lord. Did it take place (1) in the forenoon or the afternoon? (2) On Thursday or Friday? (3) On the fourteenth day of the month Nisan, or the fifteenth? (4) In the year 29 A.D., or any other year between 27 and 35? We propose to consider these four questions in the four chapters of this paper.

Our principal authorities are ultimately, as I believe, S. Peter and S. John. S. Peter's account is found in S. Mark's Gospel, and is followed by S. Matthew and S. Luke. S. John's is peculiar to the fourth Gospel. But there are other authorities to be considered, as we shall see presently.

Let us begin with the difficulty about the hour. S. Peter says: "It was the third hour, and they crucified Him."* "And when the sixth hour had come there was darkness over the whole land until the ninth hour. And at the ninth hour Jesus cried

* Mark xv. 25.

with a loud voice ... and yielded up His life."*
S. John says: "They bring, therefore, Jesus from
Caiaphas to the prætorium, and it was early."†
Again, at the close of the trial, just before sentence
was passed, we read: "And it was the preparation
of the passover; the hour was about the sixth."‡

In the ancient world hours were not a uniform
period of sixty minutes, but one-twelfth of the space
between sunrise and sunset, so that it could always
be said, "Are there not twelve hours in the day?"§
In Palestine the hours in winter might, therefore,
be as short as fifty minutes; in summer, as long
as seventy; but at the passover (March–April),
the time of the year when our Lord was crucified,
the hours would average sixty minutes, and the sun
would rise and set about six o'clock. The last hour
is not called "the twelfth," but "the late hour"
ὀψία.

Ancient sun-dials were necessarily different from
ours. The hours were traced on the section of a
sphere scooped out of a block of stone, and the
gnomon was placed horizontally at the top. The
only fixed hour was noon. If you consult a standard
work on the subject, like Smith's *Dictionary of
Antiquities*, you will find the statement that noon
was the seventh hour. But this is an error. Noon
was the sixth hour; for sunrise was called πρωΐα,
"the early (hour)." The "first hour" was when the
sun had been shining for an hour, just as with us
"one o'clock" is an hour after noon or midnight.

---

* Mark xv. 33, 34 = Matt. xxvii. 45, 46 = Luke xxiii. 44.
† John xviii. 28.   ‡ John xix. 14.   § John xi. 9.

DATE OF THE CRUCIFIXION

Anyone may see this in the parable of the discontented labourers,* in which the master went forth to hire workmen at early morning, at the third hour, the sixth, the ninth, and the eleventh, paying wages at sunset, at which time those who had been hired at the eleventh hour had worked one hour, and not two, as the other hypothesis would require.

According to S. Peter, then, Christ was crucified at 9 a.m., the agony upon the cross lasted six hours, the darkness began at noon and lasted till 3 p.m. At 3 p.m. Christ yielded up His life. But according to S. John, sentence was passed about noon, and as some time would be required for preparation, the crucifixion began in the afternoon. In short, there is a discrepancy of more than three hours.

Here is work for the harmonist. And that ingenious person's versatility does not forsake him. Consult almost any commentary that you please, from the Bishop of Durham's to a Sunday-school treatise, and you will find it stated with more or less of positive assertion that the ancient world had two ways of reckoning the hours: one from sunrise to sunset, which the synoptists have followed; the other, like our own plan, from midnight to midday, which S. John has followed. The latter plan is also called the Roman. It is said to have been in use at Ephesus, where S. John wrote. Martyrologies are quoted to prove this. And so when S. John says "the hour was about the sixth," he means 6 a.m., and all discrepancy vanishes.

* Matt. xx. 1-16.

There are three objections to this attractive explanation. First, it was unknown to the ancient fathers. Irenæus was a native of Asia Minor, so were Polycarp and Papias. Through them so simple a solution of the difficulty would have passed into the Church if there had been any ground for it. But though all kinds of reasons are given, from the symbolical meaning of the number six in Irenæus, to the fulfilment of Daniel in Hippolytus, and the interval which must have lapsed between passing sentence and nailing to the cross in Hesychius,* no one suggests a different reckoning of hours.

Secondly, we should only escape one difficulty by creating another. Christ was brought before Pilate "early." The phrase is an elastic one, as we shall see hereafter. But it is fixed here. Before He was taken to the prætorium our Lord had been brought before the Sanhedrin in their chamber *gazith* on the temple mount "when the early (hour) had come."† True, there had been two examinations the night before—one before Annas, which was merely to pass the time, the other before Caiaphas, in which some energetic committees of the Sanhedrin had, in the formal ἀνάκρισις, procured sufficient material for condemnation; but for all that, the trial before the Sanhedrin proper must be gone through. According to the Talmud, the meeting to try capital cases must be held by daylight. And although Talmudic rules belong to a later date, common sense

---

* Unfortunately S. John gives the time of passing sentence, S. Mark that of nailing to the cross.

† Matt. xxvii. 1.

as well as S. Matthew's language forbid us to think of the assembling of the Sanhedrists much before 6 a.m.

At any rate, Christ could not have reached Pilate before that hour. And if so, the discussion before the procurator began at 6 a.m., or later, and ended about 6 a.m. Yet there is abundant evidence that it was a long one. S. John takes a large part of two chapters to describe it. S. Matthew gives many details which would lengthen it. S. Luke adds that it was interrupted by a visit to Herod, which can hardly have taken less than an hour. From two hours and a half to three hours appears to me to be the *minimum* time required.

But in the third place, this double reckoning of the hours is in itself a very suspicious thing. Certainly it is possible. In Italy twenty-four hours used to be counted on the clock, so that you dined at nineteen and went to bed at twenty-three, and some reformers wish to restore this way of reckoning now. But railways and through trains compelled the Italians to conform to the use of their neighbours, and it is not easy to go back.

In the ancient world, with no telegraphs or railways, and only slow communication by sailing ships, there would be less need for uniformity. Still, the Rev. J. A. Cross[*] has called in question this supposed second method of reckoning the hours, and Professor W. M. Ramsay declares that it is "a mere fiction, constructed as a refuge of despairing harmonisers, and not a jot of evidence for it has ever been

[*] *Classical Review*, June, 1891.

given that would bear scrutiny."* He himself cuts the Gordian knot in heroic fashion by declaring with Professor Godet that the apostles had no watches. "About the sixth hour" with them would signify anywhere between 11 and 1. If the crucifixion really took place at half-past ten, S. Peter might call it the third hour and S. John the sixth without admitting greater inaccuracy than we should feel between 12.5 and 12.10, or than an astronomer would feel about tenths of a second. All is a matter of habit and education.

This is fascinating, and to a great extent true. Divisions of time are rough and few amongst primitive people. Day and night come first, in which the day includes all the twilight; the night is darkness. Then for military purposes the night is divided into three watches.† The officer on duty decides by the position of the stars when the watch is over. On cloudy nights he guesses, for water-clocks and sand-glasses are a later invention. The day is divided into morning, noon, and evening. Then "the heat of the day"‡ (11 a.m. to 2 p.m.), when food is taken and a *siesta*, the "time of the evening meal-offering"§ (3 p.m.), the "verge of the evening"‖ (5 p.m.), when supper is made ready— these with sunrise and sunset complete the divisions. "Steps" in the sun-dial of Ahaz were introduced by that *savant* from Damascus to Jerusalem, but scarcely affected popular language, which was content with the above-mentioned simple indications

* *Expositor*, March, 1893. † Judges vii. 19.
‡ Gen. xviii. 1. § 1 Kings xviii. 29.
‖ Gen. iii. 8.

DATE OF THE CRUCIFIXION

until the heathenish Greeks invaded the Holy Land and polluted it with their abominations. Then for the first time do we read of the "hour,"* which, nevertheless, in the days of Christ had thrown out the old reckoning. The night, also, was now divided into four watches instead of three,† it was, however, occasionally divided into hours.

But even astrology had not broken up the hour into minutes. Astrologers were satisfied with calculating *horo*scopes. S. Augustine has no notion that twins might have a different horoscope.‡ People said: "I will come in the course of an hour," where our forefathers said, "in a minute," we, "in a second," and our children or grandchildren will say, "in the tenth of a second."

Professor Ramsay holds that plain people were perplexed by these minute subdivisions of time, and did not use them. They talked of "the early (hour)," the third, sixth, ninth hours, and "the late (hour)," but neglected the others.

Let us examine the evidence of the New Testament on this interesting question.

There are two adverbs in very common use, "early" and "late" ($\pi\rho\omega\ddot{\iota}$ and $\ddot{o}\psi\epsilon$), and two adjectives, derived from them, "the early (hour)," $\pi\rho\omega\ddot{\iota}a$, 0 o'clock or sunrise, and "the late (hour)," $\dot{o}\psi\prime\iota a$, 12 o'clock or sunset. $\dot{o}\psi\prime\iota a$ entirely supplants the twelfth hour.

Now we must first observe that the adverbs are

---

* Daniel iii. 6; iv. 16 (the time indicated is still vague as in $\ddot{\omega}\rho a$ originally).
† Mark xiii. 35.   ‡ *De civitate*, 2, 6.

used in a double sense, according as they apply to the night or the day. The first watch of the night was called "late" (ὀψέ), and the last watch "early" (πρωΐ), because they contained the period of twilight. But in common use, unless the context decides otherwise, we may be sure that "early" and "late" do not mean the watches of the night, but are said with reference to the day. "Early" means anything between the first streak of dawn (or, indeed, long before that) and seven or eight o'clock in the morning. "Late" means from five or six till midnight or beyond. For as it is now, so was it then. "I sat up very late last night" may mean till 4 a.m. "I got up very early this morning" may mean at 3 a.m., or to an Alpine club man 1 a.m. And so the terms overlap. For, although the day legally ended when darkness was established and three stars were visible, popular language necessarily disregarded legal absurdities. "To-morrow"* in the Bible always means after the night's sleep is over. "Yesterday" is divided from to-day by the night. And S. Matthew writes, quite naturally as we may do, "Late on Saturday night, as it was dawning for Sunday,"† to signify 4.30 a.m., or somewhere thereabouts, on Sunday morning.

But the adjectives, the "early (hour)" and "the late (hour)" are not quite identical in meaning with the adverbs. Being hours, they do not intrude on the night, probably never extending into real darkness. On the other hand, they trespass much further into the day. "The early (hour)" probably lasted, in

* Acts iv. 3.   † Matt. xxviii. 1.

DATE OF THE CRUCIFIXION

popular language, till nearly 9 a.m.; "the late (hour)" certainly was often reckoned from 3 p.m.*

All this proves that the word "hour," in its popular use, retained its original meaning of an indefinite division of time, as distinguished from the strict meaning of one-twelfth of the day, which science was fastening upon it.

But I cannot persuade myself that a serious historian, who gave dates by the hour at all, would follow the carelessness of country people. S. John, as a matter of fact, mentions the seventh† hour and the tenth,‡ S. Matthew the eleventh,§ a Western reading in Acts xix. 10 the fifth and the tenth. So far were the New Testament writers from being tied to the third, sixth, and ninth. S. Luke speaks of an interval of about an hour,|| and about three hours,¶ and S. Mark, "Could ye not watch with Me one hour?"**

These objections are serious; the following, I submit, is fatal. Of all divisions of the day none is so well marked as the dinner-hour. Even in modern life "morning" popularly means the period before dinner, "afternoon" the period after dinner.

In the New Testament we have indications of two substantial meals in the day and one slight refection. Breakfast, as we should call it, is alluded to in Acts xx. 11; dinner in Matt. xxii. 4, Luke xi. 37, 38 xiv. 12, John xxi. 12, Acts x. 10; supper in

* Matt. xiv. 15, 23.　　† John i. 40.
‡ John iv. 52.　　§ Matt. xx. 6, 9.
|| Luke xxii. 59.　　¶ Acts v. 7.
** Mark xiv. 37.

the "Lord's supper," and in many other passages. In Acts x. 10 the dinner-hour is the sixth (=noon), and although the time doubtless fluctuated a little in various grades of society, we can hardly be wrong in saying that for working-men it would not fall later than midday. The apostles had no watches, but men who have lived without watches in the backwoods inform me that they could tell the dinner-hour to within ten minutes, and I feel sure that most of us with a little practice could do the same. The sixth hour, therefore, being either the dinner-hour or falling, in popular phrase, into the afternoon, would never, I maintain, be put loosely for 10.30 a.m., and although Professor Ramsay has done good service, I cannot accept his explanation in this particular.

I incline myself to the old view of a false reading, either in S. Mark or, more probably, in S. John. Eusebius suggests it in the latter, S. Jerome in the former. In manuscripts, except those of the most expensive kind, numerals were expressed for brevity's sake by letters of the alphabet, as we express them by figures. "Third" would be written with a *gamma* (Γ), "sixth" with a *digamma* (F). And these two letters were so very much alike that they were peculiarly liable to be confused. Perhaps S. John really wrote or intended to write "third" (Γ), but a primitive copyist read "sixth" (F).

In the expensive Constantine MSS. and their derivatives numerals are written out at full length, but in the Cambridge *Codex Bezæ* (D) letters of the alphabet are generally used; and that this was the ancient practice, and that it led to confusion

DATE OF THE CRUCIFIXION

from the similarity of the *digamma* to other letters is proved by Acts xxvii. 37, where the true reading is, "We were in all on board the ship *about seventy-six* souls," though the common text has, "We were in all on board the ship *two hundred and seventy-six* souls." Now C stands for two hundred, O for seventy, and F for six. The original text ran, ⲈⲚⲦⲰⲦⲦⲀⲞⲒⲰⲰⲤⲞ̄Ⲋ̄. But the second ω having been accidentally or purposely omitted, the words became ⲈⲚⲦⲰⲦⲦⲀⲞⲒⲰⲤⲞ̄Ⲋ̄. The British Museum manuscript (A) gives another reading, ⲈⲚⲦⲰⲦⲦⲀⲞⲒⲰⲤ̄Ⲟ̄Ⲉ, "two hundred and seventy-five," the *digamma* (F) having been altered into epsilon (E).

At any rate, our general conclusion is that the common explanation of two methods of calculating hours must be abandoned. It is legitimate for anyone to admit that S. Mark differs from S. John, and that, having acknowledged this discrepancy, it is not our province to seek for explanations which cannot now be obtained with any certainty. It is not legitimate, I maintain, to assert any longer that there were two ways of reckoning hours. The controversy has been unnecessarily confused by introducing into it the question of the point in the twenty-four hours at which the day legally begins. But that is an entirely separate matter. The Roman day, like our own, legally began at midnight, the Jewish day at sunset; but the Romans reckoned the hours from sunrise, exactly as did the Jews, the Greeks, and the rest of the civilized world. At the University of Cambridge the year begins on

October 1st, the week on Friday, the day at noon; but these local peculiarities do not affect popular speech. If S. John had known that his Ephesian readers reckoned the hours from midnight he could not have recorded without comment the saying of our Lord, "Are there not twelve hours in the day? If any man walk in the day he stumbleth not," for the longest day would have contained 14 hours 38 minutes, and the shortest day 9 hours 22 minutes.

That S. Mark is right, and that the crucifixion really took place in the forenoon, is rendered probable by two further considerations. First, time was needed to make this lingering torture fatal. It was no uncommon case for criminals to expire at length from mere hunger on the cross.* Besides the breaking of the legs, various other methods were used to accelerate death. They were suffocated by the smoke of fires lighted below, or were torn in pieces by wild beasts. Now Pilate, who was required by the Romans to respect Jewish law, knew that the bodies could not remain suspended beyond sunset on any day,† much less on a Friday. He would, therefore, be anxious to secure as long a time as possible for the law to take vengeance. Secondly, the scene plainly consisted of two parts, the first of which was characterized by gibes, merriment, and triumph, the next by dread, silence, and misgivings. The darkness will account for the change. Three hours of brutal enjoyment were succeeded by three of superstitious terror. For the wicked are super-

---

* TRENCH, *Studies in the Gospels*, p. 313.
† Deut. xxi. 23.

DATE OF THE CRUCIFIXION

stitious beyond the understanding of good men, and nature seemed, with its heavy storm-clouds at midday, to be conspiring against them. We need not believe that they carried lanterns about, as the unimaginative author of the recently-discovered "Gospel according to S. Peter" supposed. But they confessed, "Truly this Man was a Son of God," they smote their breasts, and returned, saddened and solemnised, to their homes.

II.

Was Christ crucified on a Friday or a Thursday?

Let us first look at our authorities. S. Peter's account is, "For it was Preparation, which is the day before a Sabbath."* S. John's, "For it was Preparation"; and again, "It was Preparation of the passover."† With this S. Luke agrees, "And it was a day of Preparation, and a Sabbath was approaching."‡ S. Matthew also describes the next day thus, "On the morrow, which is after the Preparation."§

According to the common and, I believe, unquestionably true view "Preparation" is the Jewish name for Friday, as preparation was on that day made for the coming Sabbath. But the Bishop of Durham (Dr. Westcott) holds that in this particular case it means Thursday,∥ the next day, Friday, being the great festival of the "first day of unleavened bread, on which the paschal lamb was killed." Special preparations would have to be

---

* Mark xv. 42. † John xix. 31, 14.
‡ Luke xxiii. 54. § Matt. xxvii. 62.
∥ *Introduction to the Study of the Gospels*, chap. 6, note.

made for that day by killing the lamb and searching for leaven with a view to the complete destruction of every particle of it, and this preparation on Thursday would take the place of the ordinary preparation on Friday.

Let us see what arguments can be brought to support this view.

It is stated that the term "Sabbath" need not always mean the seventh day of the week. The great day of atonement is called a "Sabbath of rest,"* and the Jews were ordered to rest on some of the greater festivals; notably on the first day of unleavened bread "no manner of work might be done save that which every man must eat."† Now if the first day of unleavened bread was itself a Sabbath, it would necessarily be preceded by a Preparation. S. Luke's language, "It was a day of Preparation, and a Sabbath was approaching," but still more S. John's, which may fairly be translated, "It was Preparation *for* the passover," are held to indicate that the ordinary Preparation is not meant, but the special Preparation for the passover. This indication is strengthened by S. John's further observation, "For the day of that Sabbath was great."‡ Why should he have said this if the weekly Sabbath was intended?

Again, S. Matthew's circumlocution, "On the morrow, which is after the Preparation," is difficult to account for except on the supposition that he was going to write, "Which was the first day of unleavened

* Lev. xxiii. 32.   † Exodus xii. 16.
‡ John xix. 31.

DATE OF THE CRUCIFIXION

bread," but, recollecting that he had already * used that term in a popular † or Galilean sense (it is supposed) to describe the day before, felt precluded from using it in its proper Pentateuchal sense now. Had an ordinary Sabbath followed, he would have written, "On the morrow, which was the Sabbath."

Again, there are numerical calculations which are claimed distinctly to favour Thursday. S. Mark, following S. Peter, writes, "The Son of Man must . . . . rise again *after three days*"; and again, "*After three days* He shall rise again." ‡ But the strongest passage of all is found in S. Matthew, "As Jonah was three days and three nights in the sea monster's belly, so shall the Son of Man be three days and three nights in the heart of the earth." § If other passages are neutral or only slightly favour the longer period, this, it is claimed, demands it. One day and fractions of two nights cannot be extended into three days and three nights. The crucifixion, therefore, must have taken place on a Thursday.

Now I have shown elsewhere,‖ that there are strong reasons for holding that the verse which speaks of the Son of Man being three days and three nights in the heart of the earth, though put into our Lord's mouth, was not really uttered by Him, but is one of those later accretions which

---

* Matt. xxvi. 17.

† According to the law of Moses there were only seven days of unleavened bread; in the New Testament there are eight, one day having been added at the beginning, thus disturbing the reckoning. It is most probable that this had been done by the scribes in their zeal to "'set a hedge about the law." *Cf.* page 170.

‡ Mark viii. 31; ix. 31.   § Matthew xii. 40.

‖ *The Composition of the Four Gospels*, Macmillan.

M

gathered round the primitive Petrine Gospel during its oral stage. I have shown that a group of thirteen or fourteen of these accretions is concerned with the fulfilment of Scripture by Christ as the Messiah; that this group is peculiar to the first Gospel; that it was due to the Aramaic preachers or catechists, for the quotations never follow the Septuagint version as the rest of the Gospel quotations do; and that there was often much straining of evidence to make these fulfilments good. Sometimes the words of the prophet are altered in what we should consider important respects, sometimes S. Peter's Memoirs are altered, to obtain the desired result. All this is undeniable and highly suggestive. It shows that Jewish Christians, educated in Rabbinic methods of exegesis, regarded these distortions as legitimate. Such a trifle as adding a third night to the recognised three days would not appear to them worthy of account.*

Does anyone think this novel and startling? Let him read what the learned Dr. Lightfoot wrote in his *Horæ Hebraicæ*, published A.D. 1644. Briefly it amounts to this: There is in Aramaic a word '*ônāh* of doubtful meaning. The following definitions of it are given in the Talmud: (1) " How much is the space of an '*ônāh?* ' R. Jochanan says, either a day or a night.' ' R. Akiba fixed a day for an '*ônāh* and a night for an '*ônāh*.' But the tradition is that R. Eliezer Ben Azariah said, 'A day and a night

---

* If S. Matthew's Gospel was finally written in Alexandria, where the exact date of the crucifixion might well be obscured, we shall better understand the change.

make an '*ônāh* and a part of an '*ônāh* is as the whole.' It is said of a period of three days, 'R. Ismael saith, Sometimes it contains four '*ônôth*, sometimes five, sometimes six.'"

Now if the Aramaic catechists said, "As Jonah was three '*ônôth* in the sea monster's belly, so shall the Son of Man be three '*ônôth* in the heart of the earth," all inconsistency with the common date of the Resurrection would disappear; and yet the Greek catechists who moulded our "Gospel according to S. Matthew" would, from their knowledge of the Septuagint, naturally translate it in both cases "three days and three nights," though S. Paul uses a word, νυχθήμερον, which might have served their purpose better.

I do not give this as the true explanation. I do not think it is so. But Lightfoot's authority may help to remove some prejudices.*

It is to be noticed that S. Mark's "After three days I shall rise again," is usually altered in the other Gospels, the Acts of the Apostles, and S. Paul into, "On the third day." And in course of time this change reacted on the text of S. Mark. In the Syrian recension, which the English Authorised Version follows, "On the third day" is found in S. Mark also. Now to our ideas a man speaking on Friday of an event which is to happen on Sunday, might describe it as about to happen "on

* S. Mark omits "Jonah" altogether, following S. Peter's Memoirs. S. Luke gives the explanation contained in the *logia*. S. Matthew gives the explanation contained in the *logia*, modified to fulfil Scripture the better. Unquestionably S. Luke's explanation is more original than S. Matthew's.

the third day," but not "after three days." We must not, however, intrude our mathematical prejudices into ancient thought, for there exists a passage which proves decisively that the evangelists saw no distinction between these two phrases. "Sir," writes S. Matthew, "we remember that that Impostor said, while He was yet alive, *After three days* I will rise again. Command therefore that the sepulchre be made sure *until the third day*."*

It is not, I think, impossible that the Jewish carelessness about numbers was partly due to the symbolic meaning which they attached to certain numbers. Three, four, seven, ten, and multiples of these figures, occur in the Bible far oftener than they would do if there were no symbolism to be sought. "Forty" probably signifies one generation of human life, otherwise its frequent occurrence in the Bible is hard to account for. The number *three* is exceptionally suitable here to one who symbolizes. But I certainly do not think that if no symbolic meaning had been sought "two" would have taken its place. The difficulty is deeper.

In fact, we have to deal with the curious custom of inclusive reckoning. It appears to me that inclusive reckoning was the inveterate habit of the vulgar, but that the lawyers in legal documents, where ambiguity would be fatal, avoided it. Hence in the Pentateuch numbers are used as we use them. "Seven days of unleavened bread," for example, are calculated from "the fourteenth day of the month at even until the twenty-first day of the month at

* Matt. xxvii. 63.

DATE OF THE CRUCIFIXION

even."* Assyrian cuneiform inscriptions, I am told by my colleague, the Rev. C. H. W. Johns, exhibit both uses: in legal documents exclusive reckoning prevails, but in ordinary life great confusion and ambiguity exists from the preference for inclusive figures. How inveterate the error was is shown by the Roman method of calculating the days of the month. They reckoned backwards and always inclusively. Thus the last day of April, for example, was called the day before the Kalends of May, and the last day but one *the third day* before the Kalends of May, though it surely ought to be called the second. The same with the nones and the ides. Even older than this was the weekly market. It was held every eighth day, but was called *nundinae*, "the ninth day," instead of "the eighth." Anyone may see by consulting a concordance that the common Biblical expression, "On the third day," signifies, "the day after to-morrow." Our Lord used it thus in the verse, "Behold, I cast out demons, and accomplish healings to-day and to-morrow, and the third day I am perfected." The Hebraist knows that "heretofore" is expressed by two nouns, "yesterday and the day before," literally "yesterday and the third day." In Latin *nudius tertius*, "it is now the third day," means "the day before yesterday."

On the whole, I submit that the argument from arithmetic is decidedly in favour of Friday.

Again, although in deciding between Thursday and Friday S. Luke, especially as his evidence is only given in an "editorial note," cannot be put on a level

* Exodus xii. 18.

with eye-witnesses like S. Peter and S. John, yet at least he may be used to show what was the belief of the Western Church, which on so interesting a question can hardly have been mistaken. After describing our Lord's burial, S. Luke says that the women "rested the Sabbath day according to the commandment, and on the first day of the week"* came the Resurrection. Plainly he regards Friday as the day of burial and therefore of crucifixion, Saturday as the Sabbath, and Sunday as the Resurrection day. It is an intolerable straining of his words to suppose that by "the Sabbath" he meant forty-eight hours, two "Sabbaths" coming consecutively. Such an interpretation is the fruit of sheer desperation.

But I fail to find any authority for the supposition that the Jews in the time of Christ would have applied the name "Sabbath," without some qualification, to any festival except the seventh day, or "Preparation" to any day but Friday. In the Old Testament the Sabbath is not often mentioned, hardly so often as it is in the Gospels and the Acts of the Apostles. But under the Rabbis the sanctity of the day had been made a chief article of faith. The Maccabean patriots had allowed themselves to be cut down to a man sooner than defend themselves on the Sabbath. The Talmudic rules for Sabbath observance form a life study in themselves. There is not a trace in the New Testament of sharing the honour of the day with any other festival however great. Modern Jews draw a distinction between Sabbaths and festivals, much as churchmen do

* Luke xxiii. 56.

DATE OF THE CRUCIFIXION

between Sundays and holy days. The very phrase "twice a week," "first day of the week," where "week" is literally "Sabbath," shows how fixed the language had become.

When S. John wrote, "For the day of that Sabbath was great," I believe he simply meant to remind his Gentile readers how sacred a day the Sabbath was in the eyes of the Jew. For if it be true that S. John, when he wrote in Greek, thought in Aramaic (and I hold that the structure of his sentences proves this) he would not feel any difference between the expressions, "The day of that Sabbath" and "That Sabbath day." Still, I am ready to admit that if (as is practically certain) the Sabbath on this particular year coincided with the festival, such a Sabbath would be superior to ordinary Sabbaths, much as Easter day with churchmen is superior to an ordinary Sunday.*

S. John's expression, "It was Preparation of the passover," will therefore mean, "It was passover Friday," by which phrase I do not mean the seventh day of unleavened bread, for, though that also on this occasion would be a Friday, it was too far removed from the slaying of the paschal lamb to be so designated. "Passover Friday" will be the day on the afternoon of which the paschal lamb was slain, and in the night of which, according to popular language, it was eaten.

The ancient Christians uniformly held that Friday was the day of Christ's death. Modern Greeks still call Friday "Preparation." There seems to be no

* See LIGHTFOOT's *Apostolic Fathers*, i. 1690.

break in the chain of evidence, and I feel very confident that all the arguments to the contrary are unavailing.

III.

Did the crucifixion take place on the fourteenth day of the month Nisan or on the fifteenth?

Nisan (or Abib, as it was called in olden time) was the first month of the Jewish year, and corresponded roughly to our March-April. We cannot fix it more precisely, for in the first place the months were lunar, and were therefore continually varying with respect to the year; in the next place they were settled by observation merely. If some ripe ears of barley could be found as the new moon was expected, the new year was declared to have begun; if not, a month was intercalated. In critical cases therefore a late or early spring might just make the difference. Similarly, if the moon's thin crescent was visible on the expected night, the ensuing day was proclaimed holy as the first day of the month; if not, even though the moon's absence was caused by clouds or rain, a day was intercalated, but of course only one.

By these simple expedients, the calendar was kept fairly accurate without any of those elaborate calculations by which Julius Cæsar put the matter on its present basis. Modern precision, however, was never thought of. The year did not begin on the right day, but on the nearest new moon to the right day, or one month later; the month did not begin at the true new moon, but when the moon was first visible, which would be a day and a half or two days later. The day itself did not begin at sunset, but when

DATE OF THE CRUCIFIXION

from one to three stars were visible. Everything was vague and empirical.

It is impossible, therefore, for us now to recover an ancient Jewish date with any certainty. We cannot be sure to a day, sometimes not to a month. It is however probable that already in the time of Christ contact with Greek civilization had introduced some more systematic methods of calculation.

The Jews were not seriously inconvenienced by the uncertainty of the calendar. Those who lived in the Holy Land received a fortnight's notice of the passover's approach, ten days' notice of the time for selecting the paschal lamb. If therefore they intended to keep the feast in Jerusalem, there was ample time for preparation. The Jews of the dispersion came to pentecost rather than to passover.

On the fourteenth day of Nisan the paschal lamb was slain "between the evenings" (3–5 P.M. according to Josephus), and was eaten the same night. In legal language (as the day legally began at sunset) it was eaten on the fifteenth, but in popular language it was eaten on the night of the fourteenth. To prevent misconception I shall adhere to popular language throughout the rest of this paper, and reckon the days, as we do, from midnight to midnight.

Next day, the fifteenth, was the first day of unleavened bread, one of the greatest festivals in the year, for it commemorated the deliverance from Egypt. Josephus, however, tells us that in the time of Christ the fourteenth was commonly called the first day of unleavened bread, and we find it so styled in the Gospels. We must not suppose that the great festival had been shifted: that was certainly not the case; but the Rabbis in their endeavour "to set a hedge about the law" had required all leaven to be destroyed one day sooner than the law directed, and so there were practically eight days of unleavened bread now. The numbering therefore was altered, the festivals being on the second and the eighth instead of the first and the seventh.

The question is, Did Christ assemble His disciples to eat the passover on the evening of the fourteenth or was He at that time already resting in the grave, the last conflict being over? Strange to say this question has been long debated. Various makeshift answers have been given. But with the increasing sense of honesty which marks our age, some of the best scholars have dared to say, "I do not know."

Let us first read S. Mark's testimony: "Now after two days was the passover and the feast of unleavened bread. . . . And on the first day of unleavened bread when (the Jews) used to sacrifice the passover, the disciples say unto Him, Where wilt Thou that we go and prepare that Thou mayest eat the passover? . . . Say ye to the master of the house, The Teacher saith, Where is My lodging where I must eat the passover with My disciples? . . . And they prepared the passover."

S. Matthew and S. Luke fully confirm this. The latter adds that Jesus said, "I have earnestly desired to eat this passover with you before I suffer."

If we had the synoptists alone, no one would doubt that Jesus ate the passover the night before the crucifixion, and that He was therefore crucified on the fifteenth.

DATE OF THE CRUCIFIXION

But now let us look at S. John.

"*Before*" (not "at") "the feast of the passover Jesus" partook of the last supper. (xiii. 1.) During the meal Judas went out, and the cause of his departure being secret, some supposed, since Judas held the bag, that Jesus said unto him, "Buy what we need for the feast." (xiii. 29.) They were not therefore already concluding the feast, but were looking forward to it. "Judas went out, and it was night." Yet the shops were not shut, as they would have been on the night of the fourteenth, for legally next day's festival would have begun on which no work was allowed. Next morning S. John tells us that the chief priests "themselves entered not into the prætorium, that they might not be defiled; but might eat the passover." (xviii. 28.) They had not, therefore, eaten the passover the night before, but looked forward to doing so that night. "And it was the preparation of the passover" when they crucified Him. (xix. 14.) "The Jews, therefore, since it was preparation, that the bodies might not remain on the cross upon the Sabbath" . . . applied to Pilate that they might be taken down. (xix. 31.) We have seen that the preparation almost certainly means Friday, in which case these verses do not affect the question. They count neither way. Still we have a singularly long list of dates, some of which seem to demand the fourteenth, all permit of it. If we read S. John's Gospel alone, no one would doubt that our Lord was crucified on the fourteenth, and therefore did not partake of the passover.

Exceedingly early tradition favours the fourteenth,

for the Quartodecimans, who kept Good Friday on the fourteenth of Nisan, date from Polycarp, who claimed to follow the practice of S. John.

Let us first glance at some of the solutions which have been offered of this difficult problem at various times.

1. Eusebius suggested and S. Chrysostom developed the idea, which has been very generally held, that the chief priests had been so busily employed in compassing Christ's arrest and conducting His trial, that they had found no time to eat the passover on the proper night, but had put off the duty of doing so till the fifteenth.

But Christ's arrest appears to have taken place after midnight. The passover was eaten when the sun had set. The chief priests were rigid legalists, and would have abundance of time for celebrating the most solemn of their ordinances. Moreover, this supposition leaves two out of S. John's three statements unexplained, *i.e.* it totally fails.

2. The majority, therefore, of modern interpreters have inclined rather to the view that Christ Himself anticipated the passover, eating it one day sooner than usual because He knew that His hour was come, and because He "earnestly desired to eat it with them before He suffered."

But S. Mark distinctly writes that it was the disciples who suggested to Him that the time for eating the passover had come, and that they did so "on the first day of unleavened bread when (the Jews) sacrificed the passover." Nothing can be clearer than this. The usual day, the usual hour, was come. They fancied that He had overlooked it, and they call attention to the necessity of making preparations for the universal religious duty.

Moreover, although the law directed every master of a house to kill the paschal lamb himself, no restriction about place being given, the later centralisation required that the lamb must be slain in the temple. The Jews of the dispersion could not eat the passover except when they went up—perhaps once in their lives—to the Holy City. Now the priests would have refused to sacrifice the lamb a day before the usual time. And the advocates of this view are obliged to maintain that no lamb was obtained. They point out that in the narrative of the last supper neither lamb nor bitter herbs are mentioned. There seems to have been nothing on the table but bread, wine, and one bowl containing fish or salad or other condiment. It was (as S. John describes it) an ordinary supper. This difficulty we shall consider presently. Meanwhile S. Mark's words, "Prepare that Thou mayest eat the passover," and "They made ready the passover," must surely mean the paschal lamb.

3. Rabbinic students have suggested an entirely new explanation which in recent times has gained wide acceptance. They contend that by "eating the passover" S. John meant something quite different from what S. Mark meant by the same expression. S. Mark plainly intended the paschal lamb, but S. John refers to a festal meal which is not mentioned in the Pentateuch but was prescribed by the tradition of the elders. Commonly called the *Chăgĭgāh*, it

could be eaten on any of the seven days of the feast, but was usually taken on the second—the old "first"—day. It was considered of equal or even greater importance than the paschal lamb, and the term, "eating the passover," included it or sometimes alluded to it alone. In S. John, they argue, the expression "eat the passover" must refer to the *Chăgîgāh*, for if the chief priests had defiled themselves by entering the prætorium, such lesser defilement, caused by the presence of Roman eagles and other idolatrous signs, possibly also of leavened bread, would always be removed by washing the body at sunset. There was nothing after such purification to prevent them from eating the passover.

The feeling against idolatry and idolaters was particularly strong in that age, when the Jews were daily brought into contact with it. I can hardly believe that such pollution was so lightly got rid of. Moreover, the Scribes would wish to attend the sacrifice as well as the supper. If the *Chăgîgāh* could be eaten on any of the seven days, why should not the chief priests have postponed it till the third or fourth day, since their presence in Pilate's court was so imperatively demanded. But, indeed, I am rather suspicious about these later Jewish ceremonies. The destruction of Jerusalem, which altered the whole procedure of sacrifice, created a revolution in the observance of the Law. The Talmud, from which our knowledge of the *Chăgîgāh* is derived, was not written until five centuries after the city was destroyed, and is no sure guide to Jewish customs in the time of Christ. No ancient authors imagined

DATE OF THE CRUCIFIXION

that "eating the passover" in S. John meant something quite different from "eating the passover" in S. Mark.

And there is another difficulty. S. John tells us that all our Lord's adherents were excommunicated. (ix. 22; xii. 42.) And if so, it would, I presume, be impossible for them to get a lamb sacrificed except by intrigue, to which they would not stoop.

Professor Hort, a few months before his death, had a correspondence with Professor Sanday on this subject. Only a few extracts from Dr. Hort's letters have been published, but Dr. Sanday, who had advocated the *Chăgĭgāh*, acknowledged himself convinced. He admitted that there is a real discrepancy between the synoptists and S. John, and that none of the explanations which had been offered could be considered satisfactory.*

Meanwhile, my own examination of the synoptic problem had forced upon me another solution on entirely new lines.

When you look at the synoptic Gospels from an historical point of view the first thing that strikes you is the extraordinary fact that they do not bring Christ to Jerusalem until He entered it to be crucified. Now the more you consider this, the more remarkable it becomes.

It cannot represent the whole truth. Even if we rejected the fourth Gospel altogether, we should feel certain, both from antecedent probability and from certain casual expressions in the synoptists (as "O Jerusalem . . . how often would I have gathered thy children together . . ."), that Christ was no stranger

* *The Expositor*, vol. v. p. 183.

in the Holy City. A Judean ministry is quite as necessary as a Galilean.

Whence then came the omission? Did S. Peter entirely pass over the work done in Judæa? I do not think so. The very fact that S. Mark devotes six chapters out of sixteen to events which took place in the precincts of Jerusalem makes me suspicious. Important though the passion was, it seems to be narrated at undue length. The proportions of the history are destroyed.

And when we look closer, there are many things in those six chapters which have no particular affinity to the passion, but would decidedly gain in significance if they were put a year or more before it. They show how public feeling was educated; but that very education could scarcely be completed in a fortnight. Events in real life move much more slowly.

And there is one incident—the cleansing of the temple—which S. John has placed at the beginning, and not at the close, of our Saviour's ministry. It is very much to be noticed that S. John describes the cleansing of the temple as happening at a passover; not at the final passover which is the only one known to S. Mark, but at an earlier passover which Christ passed in Jerusalem, some say three years, some two, those who consider John vi. 4 to be spurious, one year before the crucifixion.

It has been usual to suppose that there were two cleansings of the temple, one at the earlier passover, one at the last. Such a repetition is, to say the least, highly improbable. That Christ should cleanse the temple once, is intelligible; that He should do so when He first came forward as the Messiah, to test the obedience of the Jews and appeal to their religious feelings, I can understand. But to what end would a repetition serve? And if repeated, why should not S. Mark or S. John have told us so?

I know that many persons object to admit so serious a chronological discrepancy in S. Mark, who was S. Peter's interpreter. But let us look at the facts calmly. S. Mark only brings Christ to Jerusalem at the last. Anything which happened at Jerusalem during an earlier visit must therefore either be omitted by S. Mark, transferred into Galilee, or inserted into holy week. The structure of his Gospel permits no other alternative. In short, the Gospel is not arranged on a chronological but on a topical plan.

If you ask how this is, my answer is that S. Peter did not give a complete course of lessons, nor did he arrange them in order. S. Mark, as Papias tells us, did not write in order, because S. Peter's lessons had been adapted to the immediate wants of the pupils, one lesson being given at a time as the occasion demanded. S. Peter left them so, and S. Mark could not supply the defect. He was not an eye-witness, and could not recover the true sequence.

Professor Sanday fully agrees with me on this point. "The simple fact is," he writes, "that the synoptic Gospels are only a series of incidents loosely strung together, with no chronology at all worthy of the name."*

* *Expositor*, vol. v. p. 16.

I earnestly exhort all biblical students to examine into this question of the chronology of the synoptists for themselves. If I am right, the exhausting labours and tortuous explanations of the harmonists, in their endeavour to reconcile what cannot be reconciled, have been wasted.

I wish heartily that any words of mine could save future students of the Gospels from what I am convinced is a useless task. There is so much to be done in more profitable researches, that I grudge the time and energy spent on harmonies. When three evangelists narrate the same events in the same order, we are not entitled to infer that they follow the true chronology, but only that they follow S. Mark, whose order is not chronological.

Now if it be conceded that the cleansing of the temple belonged to the earlier passover, it is clear that the section in which Christ was asked, "By what authority doest Thou these things?" (Mark xi. 27–33) must be transferred to the earlier passover also. And if so, I should transfer several sections which are found in the next chapter, not, perhaps, to the first passover, but rather to one or other of those subsequent visits which our Lord paid to Jerusalem. These are Mark xii. 13–17, "Is it lawful to give tribute to Cæsar?"; 18–27, the seven brethren marrying; 28–36, the great commandment of the law; 38–40, the warning against the Scribes. All these sections have no real connexion with holy week, but will gain in significance if we put them into an earlier period.

And I should then carry these suggestions one

DATE OF THE CRUCIFIXION 179

step further. S. Peter seems to me to have narrated how Christ, who was obedient to the law for our sakes, ate the passover in the Holy City with His disciples on His earlier visit, when He was not yet excommunicate. Then they "made ready the passover," ate the paschal lamb and the bitter herbs, drank the wine, sang the hymn with all the customary ceremonies.

One, two, or more years later, Christ again assembled His disciples for the Last Supper. On this occasion He gave them the sign of the man bearing the pitcher of water. On this occasion He instituted the Eucharist at the close of the meal, and spoke those discourses which S. John has recorded. It was the thirteenth of the month Nisan, and, therefore, not the passover.

S. Mark has fused the two significant suppers into one, by transferring to the latter what really belong to the former. The other evangelists have followed him in this, as in all the rest of his chronological confusions.

Some one may object that S. Luke records this sentence, "I have earnestly desired to eat this *passover* with you before I suffer," thus connecting the two meals together, which I separate by a year or more. This sentence, I reply, is peculiar to S. Luke, and if anyone will read what I have written about S. Luke's "editorial notes,"* and will then examine S. Luke's Gospel to ascertain whether I have not good grounds for what I say, he will not think that verse a serious objection. The thought pressing

* *Composition of the Four Gospels*, pp. 116–127. Macmillan.

hard on our Lord's human mind was, "This is My last meal." The Western catechists have slightly modified the expression of it, or S. Luke himself has inserted the word "passover," as is his wont.

It is possible, however, that there was no such blending of narratives as I have supposed, but that the whole scene should be transferred to the earlier passover, and rehearsed at the Last Supper. Averse though I am to vain repetitions, there is one repetition which I admit would have been full of significance. What if Christ made the personal covenant by the breaking of bread between Himself and His disciples at the first passover in Jerusalem,* renewed it at His second passover (?) in Capernaum (John vi. 4) with a larger company than the Twelve, and in close connexion with the feeding of the five thousand, and finally repeated it a third time on the night on which He was betrayed, with perhaps the additional word that His body, which they were to eat, would soon be broken for them; His blood, which they were to drink, would soon be shed? In this way we shall both make the sacrament more intelligible as a covenant of brotherhood between Himself and His people; we shall explain and justify the mysterious language of S. John vi. 51, which has always been a difficulty with interpreters; we shall justify S. Paul's statement that our Lord Jesus Christ on the same night in which He was betrayed took bread, and we shall reduce S. Mark's chronological error to a *minimum*.

If we understand the Eucharist as originally a

---

* See above, pages 141, 145.

DATE OF THE CRUCIFIXION

covenant of personal allegiance, there is reason to think that it was frequently celebrated during our Lord's ministry. That it was so is indicated by the narrative of the journey to Emmaus, in which our Lord was known by breaking of bread. The two disciples in question had not been present at the Last Supper, yet they understood the act. "Breaking of bread" is quite a new phrase, invented to express a new ceremony.

Our records of Christ's life are fragmentary. If it were not for a single incidental statement in S. John,* we should have concluded confidently that the sacrament of holy baptism was first instituted after the Resurrection. And if we now know that it had been practised by the apostles from the commencement of Christ's ministry, what wonder if the other sacrament had been celebrated too? We might have to modify our conception of it, and regard it as a covenant of union rather than a commemorative sacrifice; in short, as a sacrifice according to the ancient conception of the word rather than the modern, but we should, I think, only understand its real meaning the better for such a change.

The question discussed in this paper is a very serious one. Scholars are beginning to acknowledge freely that there is a contradiction between the synoptists and S. John respecting the day of the month of the crucifixion. The old explanations of the difference are failing or have already failed. The genuineness of the Fourth Gospel is at stake. Under these circumstances I have pointed out that the con-

* John iv. 1, 2.

tradiction does not lie between S. Peter and S. John, both of whom must have known the facts, but between S. Mark and S. John, of whom S. Mark did not know the facts, and may have confused the records, as S. John shows him to have done on other occasions.

IV.

Did the crucifixion take place in the year 29 A.D., or in any other year between 27 and 35?

To argue this question at length would take a volume. Those who wish to see what has been done at it can read Wieseler's *Synopsis*, Salmon's *Introduction to the New Testament*, McClellan's *New Testament*, and an article in the *Church Quarterly Review* for January, 1892. I will try to state the facts briefly, and make some observations upon them.

Christ suffered (1) at the passover, (2) under Pontius Pilate, (3) while Caiaphas was high priest, but (4) while his father-in-law, Annas, who had been high priest several years before, was still living and exercising paramount influence.

We do not know the date of the death or decline in power of Annas, but Pilate resided as Procurator in Judæa ten years (27–37 A.D.). Caiaphas began and ended his term of office sooner. The last passover at which he can have officiated was in A.D. 35. The period, therefore, in which the crucifixion must have taken place is narrowed down to the nine years 27–35 A.D.

Astronomical calculations have been several times

DATE OF THE CRUCIFIXION

made with a view to eliminate some of these years. For as the crucifixion took place on Friday, the 14th (or possibly the 15th) of Nisan, all those years in which the 14th of Nisan cannot have fallen on Friday (or Thursday) may be set aside. By this method the years 28, 29, 31, 32, 34, and 35 have been got rid of, and there remain only 27, 30, and 33, of which 27 is too early and 33 probably too late. Most of the authorities accept the year 30 A.D.

But, as I pointed out in the last chapter, we are never sure to a day which is the first day—or any other day—of the month, and often we cannot be sure to a month when the new year began. Thus an element of uncertainty is introduced which may vitiate all our calculations.

The writer in the *Church Quarterly*, to whom I alluded, takes advantage of this to plead for the year 29. If in that year Nisan fell a month earlier than modern astronomy would allow, Friday, the 14th of Nisan, would coincide with March 18. And it is remarkable that March 18, 29 A.D., was given (Epiphanius tells us*) in some MSS. of the apocryphal *Acts of Pilate* as the true date of the crucifixion.

Dr. Lipsius has written a treatise on the *Acts of Pilate* (*Die Pilatus-Acten*, Kiel, 1886). The text of these acts,† as it exists now, has been tampered with by some scribe who adhered to the chronology of our Lord's ministry, which was compiled by Eusebius. The result is a confused medley. But there is no reason to doubt that Epiphanius gives us the read-

* *C. Hæreses*, li. 1.
† Published in *Studia Biblica*, vol iv.

ing of the Acts which was current in his day, and the very strangeness of the date is considered to be a proof that we have here a genuine tradition.

How far is it supported by the Gospels and by the opinion of the ante-Nicene fathers?

S. Luke and S. John are the only evangelists who give us any further clue to the date. Let us look at S. John's statements first.

(1) ii. 13. "The passover of the Jews [March–April] was nigh and Jesus went up to Jerusalem." *Cf.* ii. 23. [This visit was shortly after His baptism.]

(2) ii. 20. "In forty-six years was this temple built."

(3) iv. 35. "Say ye not, Four months more and harvest comes?"

(4) v. 1. "After these things was a feast [name not given] of the Jews, and Jesus went up to Jerusalem."

(5) vi. 4. "And the passover [March–April], the feast of the Jews, was nigh." [Jesus spent this feast in Galilee.]

(6) vii. 2. "And the feast of the Jews, tabernacles [October], was nigh."

(7) viii. 57. "Thou art not yet fifty years old."

(8) x. 22. "Then came the dedication [December] in Jerusalem; it was winter."

(9) x. 55. "And the passover of the Jews [March–April] was nigh." [At this passover the crucifixion took place.]

Of these nine passages, however, it is probable that the second and third ought to be ruled out as irrelevant. For (1) Dr. E. A. Abbott has shown

(*Classical Review*, viii. 89) that Zerubbabel's temple, and not Herod's, must have been intended by the Jews; and (2) although John iv. 35 might mean "Harvest is four months distant *from the present moment*," in which case our Lord must have been speaking in or near December, for the Jewish harvest began in April, it is almost certain that the verse is a proverb, "Say not ye [when you have planted your barley], 'Four months more and harvest comes'?" for four months was about the *minimum* interval between sowing and reaping in Palestine.

S. Luke's list is shorter.

(1) i. 5. "In the days of Herod" the Great [who died B.C. 4, spring] John's birth was promised.*

(2) ii. 2. "There issued a decree from Augustus Cæsar that all the civilized world should be enrolled. This, a first enrolment, was made when Quirinius was proprætor of Syria."

[Quirinius was proprætor of Syria A.D. 6-10. It is not improbable that he had been proprætor once before, in B.C. 4; not, however, before Herod's death.]

(3) iii. 1. "In the fifteenth year of the reign of Tiberius Cæsar [A.D. 28-29] John the Baptist began to preach."

(4) iii. 23. "And Jesus Himself was beginning to be about thirty years old" at His baptism.

When we look at these dates, the first question that strikes us is, How long did our Lord's ministry last? The earliest answer is that of Irenæus, who

---

* According to S. Luke, therefore, our Lord may have been born during Herod's reign, or shortly after his death. S. Matthew ii. 4 asserts that He was born during Herod's life; S. Luke leaves the question open. This fact is not generally noticed.

puts it at about twenty years, for he began to teach when about thirty years old (Luke iii. 23), and continued till nearly fifty (John viii. 57), and "as he came to save and to sanctify every time of life, it was fitting that he should pass through age as well as youth." Now Irenæus was born in the province of Asia, the very centre of church life in the sub-apostolic age. No one had a better opportunity of getting correct information than he; and he declares that "all the elders who had known John the disciple of the Lord in Asia witness that he gave them this tradition."*

The Bishop of Durham (Dr. Westcott), in his *Commentary on John* (viii. 57), writes: "However strange it may appear, some such view is not inconsistent with the only fixed historical dates which we have with regard to our Lord's life, the date of His birth, His baptism, and the banishment of Pilate."

Suppose the crucifixion to have taken place at the latest possible date, viz., A.D. 35. Fifty years from that would bring us to 16 B.C. Our Lord, if born then, would have been twelve years old at Herod's death, and the flight into Egypt (Matt. ii. 13) must either be rejected as unhistorical or must have lasted several years, and would thus come into conflict with S. Luke ii. 39-41, in which we read that Joseph and Mary, after performing all the requirements of the law respecting Mary's purification, returned to Nazareth and dwelt there, except that they annually visited Jerusalem to keep the passover. Again, Tiberius celebrated his *decennia*, or tenth year

* *Adv. Haer.* xi. 22, 4 ff., v. xxxiii. 3.

DATE OF THE CRUCIFIXION

festivities, in A.D. 24. His fifteenth year, therefore, was 28–29, at which date our Lord would have been forty-four years old, and not, as S. Luke affirms, about thirty. (Luke iii. 23.) In the third place, the census under Quirinius (Luke ii. 2) will be twenty-one years wrong and quite impossible. I wish that the bishop had stated his exact meaning more clearly. It seems to me that ten years is the utmost length to which we can stretch the ministry without throwing overboard S. Luke's chronology altogether. That it really did last about ten years I think not impossible. It would be natural to say "You are not yet fifty" to a man of nearly forty, but, bad though the Jews were as observers, they would hardly say this to a man of thirty-two, especially when "You are not yet forty" would be more suitable for rhetorical reasons, and there does not seem to be any mystical significance in the number fifty that they should choose it on that account.

If the ministry lasted about ten years, the Gospels are seen to be more fragmentary than ever, S. John's feasts are not a complete list, and new significance is given to his rhetorical *hyperbole* in xxi. 25: "There are many other things which Jesus did, and if they be written every one, I suppose that not even the world itself would contain the books which should be written."

On the other hand, the Gnostics, the Clementine homilies, Clement of Alexandria, and other ante-Nicene authorities restrict the ministry to one year, in defence of which opinion they quoted the verse, "To preach the acceptable year of the Lord." (Luke

iv. 12.) These persons have some right to claim the synoptists on their side. The entire absence of dates from S. Mark gives the impression that no great length of time is described in his Gospel, and that impression is heightened by his forty-one "straight-ways." If the events really cover a period of three or more years, my contention of the unchronological character of S. Peter's Memoirs* is fully established. S. Luke seems to me either to have held that the ministry lasted one year only, or to have put the crucifixion about A.D. 33. When he says that the Baptist began to preach in the fifteenth year of Tiberius (A.D. 28–29) he cannot leave more than a year for the ministry, unless the date of the crucifixion be postponed. It is easy, as we have seen, to postpone it, but commentators have not usually taken this course. Assuming that our Lord's ministry lasted three years and a half, and terminated in or about A.D. 30, they have held that S. Luke calculated the reign of Tiberius, not from the death of Augustus in August, A.D. 14, but from a supposed partition of the imperial power two years and a half earlier. For this partition there is no warrant, and we can have little hesitation in setting it aside.

I have shown that all the chronological data in S. Luke are "editorial notes," and stand on a different footing historically from the rest of the Gospel. They are S. Luke's own ideas, the result of his private investigations.

In spite of Professor Ramsay's pleading,† it seems

* *Composition of the Four Gospels*, pp. 21, 22 ; *Synopsis*, p. xi.
† *Expositor*, April-June, 1897.

DATE OF THE CRUCIFIXION

to me to be impossible to get over the historical difficulties which beset S. Luke's account of the census. He alludes to the census again (Acts v. 37), and by his use of the definite article there indicates, to my thinking, that he knew of one census and only one; if that be so, it was certainly the census of A.D. 6, at which the riots took place. But in A.D. 6 Herod the Great had been dead nine years, and his successor, Archelaus, had been deposed. We cannot put the Nativity then. Moreover, the essential part of S. Luke's narrative is that "all went up to be enrolled, each to his own city." The language, strictly interpreted, implies that everyone did this, Jew and Gentile alike, the civilised world over; but let us suppose that S. Luke meant to say that only the Jews did it, nay, only those Jews who dwelt in Palestine, still, is the statement historically conceivable? Professor Ramsay says that the census must have been taken by tribes, and that not in consequence of any order from Augustus, but to suit local feeling. How many Jews in that day knew to what tribe they belonged? Had not tribal distinctions been greatly enfeebled since the return from Babylon? The popular belief is that ten tribes were lost, and although that is clearly contradicted by the New Testament, in which we find S. Paul speaking of his "twelve-tribed nation" (Acts xxvi. 7), and read that he himself belonged to the tribe of Benjamin (Romans xi. 1; Phil. iii. 5), and that Hannah belonged to the tribe of Asher (Luke ii. 36), nevertheless tribal feeling had generally yielded to national unity. Thousands of Jews, however, were ashamed of their nation, and desired to be thought Gentiles. (1 Cor. vii. 18.) Who was to compel them to journey from Galilee to Judæa to be enrolled? But, lastly, S. Luke does not say that the Jews were enrolled by their tribes, but each man by his own city, according to his own family. This would require a general exodus, which, if voluntary, would not satisfy S. Luke's language; if compulsory, I cannot imagine any power which could enforce it. Riots were general and serious as it was; what must they have been if everyone had to discover and remove to the abode of his remote ancestors? No, S. Luke evidently has somewhat misunderstood the situation.

There is a similar historical difficulty about Theudas in Acts v. 36, unless Josephus has made a mistake, which is not unlikely. It is of the utmost importance in apologetics to recognise different degrees of historical attestation in the Gospels. There are occasionally weak links. We must not make the strength of the chain depend on them, but deny that the Gospels are constructed on the chain principle.

But how did those authors who reduced the ministry to one year explain S. John? It was suggested by Mr. H. Browne* that the defining words "the passover" in John vi. 4 are a mistaken gloss, and that the verse originally ran "Now the feast of the Jews was nigh," by which statement a Jew would mean the feast of tabernacles (the same feast which is mentioned in vii. 2), but a Christian would more

* *Ordo sæclorum*, 1844.

DATE OF THE CRUCIFIXION

naturally understand the passover. The words in question are found in every extant manuscript and version of S. John, nor is any doubt of their genuineness asserted by ancient writers. Nevertheless Dr. Hort has obelized them in Westcott and Hort's *Greek Testament*, rather for calling attention to ancient chronologies than to assert that they are really spurious. Unless they were absent from certain manuscripts, which we no longer possess, he does not see how they can have been overlooked.

If they were struck out, S. John's chronology would become beautifully simple. His feasts would run: Passover (March–April; ii. 1 3–23), pentecost (?) (May; v. 1), tabernacles (October; vi. 4, vii. 2), dedication (December; x. 22), passover (March–April; xi. 55), and the whole period would cover one year, together with a few weeks which intervened between the baptism and the first passover.

The one-year ministry would solve many difficulties. It is the only scheme which reconciles S. Luke, S. Matthew, and S. John. Not improbably it is true; the more I consider it, the more attractive it appears. What I wish to emphasize is this consideration, that if we cannot positively decide between one year and ten, we must be prepared to keep our minds open on many biblical controversies.

Eusebius taught that our Lord's ministry lasted four years. He assumed that the unnamed feast in S. John v. 1 was a passover. Many students at a very early date adopted this view, for S. John's curiously indefinite statement, "After these things was *a* feast of the Jews," was altered in the second century into the more natural "*the* feast," which

Christians took for the passover. The first year, therefore (which was probably a short one), ended, according to Eusebius, with the passover of ii. 13–23; the second year with the supposed passover of v. 1; the third with the passover of vi. 4; and the fourth with the passover of xi. 55, at which the crucifixion took place. Eusebius, whose chronological system obtained wide acceptance, argued thus: (1) We read in S. Luke iii. 1 of the high-priesthood of Annas and Caiaphas. Our Lord's ministry must have begun under Annas and ended under Caiaphas. Three high priests came between them. Allowing them one year apiece (John xi. 49–51, xviii. 13) we get four years. (2) Our Lord's ministry began in A.D. 29, the fifteenth year of Tiberius, and a solar eclipse took place during the crucifixion. Phlegon mentions an eclipse of the sun in the year A.D. 33. This also gives four years. (3) Daniel, ix. 27, speaks of three and a half weeks, at the end of which the sacrifice and meat offering should cease. Assume that each week represents a year, and you get three years and a half for the ministry.

The first of these arguments rests on a mistake. S. Luke says that when the Baptist came forth "Annas *or** Caiaphas (as we should express it) was high priest." Caiaphas was the nominee of Rome, Annas exercised the real power. The faithful hesitated to give the sacred title to the puppet who depended for his position on the will of the foreigner.†

* ἀρχιερέως is in the singular according to the true text.

† S. John's language (xi. 49–51, xviii. 13) does not necessarily imply, though it does suggest, that the high priest held office for only one year. Certainly, though the Romans would not tolerate life officers, they allowed the high priest to continue for several years. Annas reigned 6–15 A.D.

The second argument rests on a double mistake. A solar eclipse cannot happen when the moon is at the full, as must be the case during passover, nor can it last longer than eight minutes. True, Eusebius might quote S. Luke, who, according to the true text, attributed the three hours' darkness to an eclipse of the sun; but this he did in one of his "editorial notes," which, as we have seen, express his own opinions, which are not always warranted. Of all the schemes which we have examined this four years (or rather three years and a half) scheme of Eusebius has been the most popular because of the prophecy of Daniel, the meaning of which is at least uncertain. It is supposed also to be supported by S. Luke xiii. 7, "Behold there are three years from the time that I come seeking fruit on this fig tree," though the number "three" in a parable is more likely to have a mystical meaning of completeness, as in S. Luke xi. 5, xiii. 21–32.

Much more may be said for the scheme which makes the ministry last two years and a fraction. This reduces the discrepancy between S. Luke and S. John, and accords with the *Acts of Pilate.*

The unnamed feast of S. John v. 1 is not in the least degree likely to be passover, pentecost, or tabernacles. It is much more probably a minor festival. Wieseler, Meyer, and Godet argue for Purim (March), Dr. Westcott for Trumpets (September).

We have passed in review a great number of subjects of engrossing interest to all biblical students. We have shown that many received opinions need revision. We have pointed out places where further investigation is desirable, and we have submitted some new proposals. Our general conclusion is, that certainty is unattainable, but unless the ministry lasted about ten years, the most probable date for the crucifixion is 9 a.m. to 3 p.m. on Friday, the fourteenth of Nisan, A.D. 29, and that the fourteenth of Nisan probably fell on March 18.

XV.

MR. HALCOMBE'S STRICTURES ON MODERN CRITICISM

I.

MR. HALCOMBE is hard on modern criticism. He never has a good word for modern critics. The Bishop of Durham he has singled out for special attack. The rest, though they are numerous and hold widely divergent opinions, he groups together and condemns without distinction.

Mr. Halcombe forgets that he is a modern critic himself. He has spent years of patient toil on the Gospels, like a critic. He has sedulously marshalled, analysed, and interrogated his facts, like a critic. He has startled us with his conclusions, like a critic. And if a modern critic is not merely one who writes at the close of the nineteenth century, but one who ruthlessly disintegrates books which the Church has always held to be perfect, Mr. Halcombe's treatment of S. Luke's Gospel makes him a very modern critic indeed.

In attempting to state briefly a few of my reasons for not agreeing with him, I have no desire to snatch a victory for the moment. My wish is to help others, if possible, in arriving at truth on this important question. I desire to do full justice to Mr. Halcombe's ability, his industry, and his earnestness, but I am unable to accept his conclusions, and I say so with sincere regret.

Mr. Halcombe's contention is that the Gospels were written in the following order: John, Matthew, Mark, Luke.

Now in putting S. John first Mr. Halcombe does not stand alone. Schleiermacher advocated the same view in the early part of this century. But not even his influence had any appreciable effect on Christian belief. The common sense of the Church refused to give way. But Mr. Halcombe contends that this was the second century order, and appeals to Tertullian to support him. We will not stay to ask why we should prefer the opinion of a third century Montanist to the testimony of the Fathers of the Church. If Mr. Halcombe's supporters had recollected the golden rule, "Verify your references," they would have been met by a more serious difficulty. Tertullian's order, according to all the manuscripts and editions which I have consulted, appears to be: John, Matthew, Luke, Mark.

Here is the Latin text: "Denique nobis fidem ex apostolis Johannes et Matthæus insinuant, ex apostolicis LUCAS ET MARCUS instaurant."

And here is Mr. Halcombe's translation: "This then is our position. From amongst apostles, John and Matthew plant in us the faith; from amongst apostolic men MARK AND LUKE confirm this faith."

And again: "Let the Gospels, *as placed by Ter-*

tullian—John, Matthew, MARK, LUKE—be represented by the letters W O R D."

Their meaning in this order, he argues, is plain to every child; but the common order, O R D W, or the order adopted by modern critics, R O D W, is hopelessly unintelligible.

Mr. Halcombe is fond of rearrangements. He has transposed S. Luke viii. 22–xi. 13 and xi. 14–xiii. 21, but he has written a volume to justify himself in doing so. He has discovered that the Muratorian fragment of the Canon has been tampered with by the seventh century translator, who put S. John's Gospel last, whereas the second century author had put it first; but he has given some, if not probable, reasons for thinking so. I cannot find, however, that he has anywhere told us on what authority he has altered the current text of Tertullian. Until he does this I must suppose the editors of Tertullian to be right. And if so, W O D R will be as unintelligible as any of the other permutations.*

Meanwhile I will give my own account of this question of the order of the Gospels.

Let us transfer ourselves in thought to the year 90 A.D. At that time, according to my belief, the Epistle of S. James had been in existence more than forty years, being the oldest of the New Testament writings; S. Paul's Epistles to the Thessalonians come next, with an age of thirty-eight years; S. Mark's written Gospel was nearly attaining its

---

* A first sketch of this paper appeared in the *Expository Times* (T. and T. Clark), and drew from Mr. Halcombe the admission that he was in error on this point.

majority; S. Matthew's was not much younger; but S. Luke's was only ten years old; and S. John's, if Mr. Halcombe will allow me to say so, was an infant.

All the books of the New Testament, except, perhaps, the Second Epistle of S. Peter, which is of doubtful canonicity, were in existence, but all had a limited circulation. Some Churches probably had none of them, being still content with the old oral teaching. S. Paul's Epistles, however, or at least the longer ones, must have been possessed by many of the Western Churches. Most Churches had one Gospel; few, I imagine, more than one. The Epistle to the Hebrews, the Catholic Epistles, and the Apocalypse, I cannot suppose to have been in use over a wide area at this date.

But the death of S. John, and the rapid removal of the last of the eye-witnesses, must have had a potent effect in creating or stimulating the desire to possess apostolic writings. During the next hundred years the books of the New Testament penetrated everywhere. They were translated into Latin and Syriac. False Gospels, like the recently-discovered Gospel according to S. Peter, or Marcion's edition of S. Luke, or the Ebionite edition of the Gospel according to the Hebrews, competed with them in certain Churches. Tatian's *Dia Tessarôn* was beginning to supplant them in Edessa. But a healthy scepticism arose. Questions were asked. Was a book which claimed admission into the Church written by an apostle? If not, where did it circulate? Who was its sponsor? And so the wheat was separated from the chaff, and the Canon

MR. HALCOMBE'S STRICTURES 199

was gradually closed; though some books, like the Epistles of Barnabas and Clement, the Shepherd of Hermas, the Acts of S. Paul, and the Revelation of S. Peter, were read as Scripture in some Churches for two or three centuries longer.

It is plain that many years must have elapsed before the scattered books of the New Testament were collected into one or (more usually) two volumes. For whenever a Church desired to secure some Gospel or Epistle which it had not used hitherto, the booksellers would make a copy of the work, bind it in a separate volume, and send it in that condition, in which it would remain. For there was precedent for doing so. In the synagogues the books of the Old Testament were kept in a series of rolls. Probably the New Testament was at first kept in rolls also, for the art of binding into a *codex* had been but recently brought into use. And it may be that the sacred books were kept secret amongst the Christians, in which case they would be copied and bound by such of the brethren as could undertake the work.

The small size of the rolls, the cheap paper, the poor binding, accounts for the loss of these primitive books. In less than a century papyrus would be rubbed to pieces. And no books of the New Testament appear to have been written on vellum until the conversion of Constantine. The poor and persecuted Churches could not afford such luxuries, and hence their service books have perished.

Now it is clear that when the twenty-seven books —more or less, for the number was not exactly fixed at first—began to be collected into one or two volumes, some decision must have been made about their relative order.

And it would be contrary to experience for any great pains to be taken at first to fix the order. We cannot suppose a Church Council to have been held for the purpose, or even a local Synod. It is possible that the choice was left to the purchaser or to the scribe. But in the course of years a few principles for arranging the books would become established.

The Gospels almost invariably stand first in existing manuscripts. And this was right; for though written last, they had been composed first, and had circulated in an oral form from very early times. Committing them to writing was indeed for us a matter of the highest moment, but to the primitive Church it had not been so. To the Christians who learned them by heart, and not merely heard them read, it mattered little whether the catechist dictated the lesson from a book or from his memory. Hence the Fathers, in speaking of the Gospels, fail to distinguish between their oral stage and the written stage. They regard them as a product of the first days. And, at least in the case of the synoptic Gospels, they are right in doing so, though many changes and additions were made during the oral period.

There was another reason for putting the Gospels first. In the Old Testament the Law stood first, the Prophets next, the Psalms and writings last. Now the Gospels corresponded to the Law, the Acts of the Apostles to the earlier Prophets (Joshua,

Judges, etc.), the Epistles and Apocalypse to the later Prophets. Psalms and poetical writings the New Testament has none, so fully does the ancient Psalter suffice for devotional needs.

But in what order were the Gospels arranged with respect to one another? Different Churches took, as we should have expected, different views. Most of the Western Churches—by which term Rome and the North African Churches are principally meant—seem to have put the Gospels which were written by apostles first, and then those which were written by the followers of apostles. In nearly all other Churches the order, as far as we can ascertain it, was that which we adopt now.

But which of these two arrangements was the older? I cannot positively say; but let us look at some early authorities. 1. The Muratorian fragment of the Canon (about 170 A.D.) is imperfect; its testimony concerning S. Matthew and S. Mark has been lost, except the last six words, which appear to apply to S. Mark; but it expressly states that S. Luke stood third and S. John fourth. Mr. Halcombe thinks that the seventh century translator has reversed the second century author's order. I wish to do justice to his reasons, but I do not think that the learned will agree with him. 2. Irenæus (about 180 A.D.) says that the true *chronological* order was: (1) the Aramaic edition of S. Matthew; (2) S. Mark; (3) S. Luke; (4) S. John. He does not, however, say that the books were thus placed in his manuscript. Perhaps they were not. Perhaps with him they still formed separate volumes. 3. Clement of Alexandria, "giving the tradition of the primitive fathers," says that "John, last of all, observing that the material facts had been exhibited in the other Gospels, produced at the instigation of his acquaintances, and under the inspiration of the Holy Ghost, a spiritual Gospel."* 4. Tatian's *Dia Tessarôn* opens with S. John i. 1 ff. This creates a slight presumption that Tatian's New Testament put S. John first, but nothing more; the nature of his harmony almost necessitated this commencement. 5. Tertullian (about 200 A.D.) gives the order John, Matthew, Luke, Mark, and argues for it as the necessarily true chronological order. Tertullian was an advocate. I have had occasion to lecture on him several times, and I have formed a poor opinion of his literary honesty. He was a plagiarist, who copied without acknowledgment, sometimes without understanding his authority. If S. John stood first in his New Testament, and that order favoured his argument at the moment, he was not the man to inquire why it stood first. He would flout the fact in the face of his adversary, as if it were irrefutable truth. Now in arguing, as he was, against Marcion, who accepted S. Luke's Gospel only, it was important to maintain the superiority of S. John and S. Matthew. We must therefore discount his language. He argues the question tediously through four long chapters, bringing, after his wont, plenty of positive assertion and plenty of abuse against his opponents, but he never quotes an authority. If he had been able to do so he would not have lost the opportunity.

* EUSEBIUS, *H. E.* vi. 14.

He practically confesses that he has no information. The kind of *a priori* reasons which he presses, though they were the common stock-in-trade of rhetoricians of his stamp, vanish before a single fact, and cannot stand against the statements of Irenæus.

I infer, however, from his testimony that in the Churches of Rome and North Africa, with which he was connected, the order of the Gospels in his time was what he states it to be—John, Matthew, Luke, Mark. Nay, I infer that this order had prevailed at Rome from the day when the Gospels had first been bound into one volume. Otherwise the conviction that this was the true order, could hardly have prevailed so decidedly as Tertullian's arguments prove it to have done.

But I do not believe that the Roman Christians had any good authority for putting the Gospels in that order, even if they had originally intended it to be the chronological order, and not—as on the surface it appears to be—an order according to the dignity of the writers. They knew the date of S. Mark's Gospel, which had probably been written in their city, and they inferred that the other Gospels must be earlier than S. Mark from what they heard of their circulation elsewhere in an oral form.

For notice what follows. Although the pressure of external opinion did not for more than a century alter the rule that apostles should stand first, it did vindicate the priority of S. Matthew to S. John. It had been easy to put S. John first. It must have been very difficult, after he had occupied that post for thirty years or more, to exalt S. Matthew over his head. Nevertheless this was done. All existing manuscripts of the Western Church testify to the order Matthew, John, Luke, Mark. So stand the Gospels in the uncial *Codex Bezæ*, so are they found in the manuscripts of the old Latin version, in the Gothic Version, and in the Apostolical Constitutions.

The instincts of religious people are intensely conservative. S. John could not have been deposed from the post of honour, if the reasons for putting him first could bear examination. Many persons were living who recollected the adoption of the order. If there had been good cause for its retention their voices could not have been silenced. They did succeed in retaining for him the second place, but not the first.

Meanwhile the common arrangement—Matthew, Mark, Luke, John—prevailed throughout the East; but before we discuss it some different orders are worthy of notice. In the *Codex Claromontanus* of S. Paul's Epistles there is bound up a page which contains an exceedingly ancient list of the books of the New Testament (including certain apocryphal authors now rejected), with the number of lines in each. In this list the order of the Gospels is Matthew, John, Mark, Luke.

The Syrian versions, the oldest of which belong to the second century, do not give Mr. Halcombe's order. The fragments of the Curetonian Syriac have at present a peculiar order of their own: Matthew, Mark, John, Luke. But nothing is extant of the version of S. Mark except the last four of those twelve verses with which in the common text S.

MR. HALCOMBE'S STRICTURES 205

Mark is concluded. In the newly-discovered palimpsest, however, of this version, all these twelve verses are omitted, a most significant fact; and S. Luke's Gospel follows S. Mark xvi. 8 immediately on the same page, with no space left between. The four Gospels stand in the common order: Matthew, Mark, Luke, John.

Finally, in the Memphitic and Sahidic versions, the late Bishop Lightfoot detected three stages. In the first the common order—Matthew, Mark, Luke, John—prevailed. Next, S. John was transferred from the last place to the first, Mr. Halcombe's order being thus at last obtained. Soon afterwards the original order was restored.

Meanwhile the practice of putting S. John's Gospel last was becoming general. When S. Jerome revised the old Latin versions, or possibly before this, the Eastern order was introduced at Rome, and from thence gradually spread over Christendom, though two centuries passed before the Vulgate drove out the old Latin versions.

S. Jerome could hardly have succeeded if the arguments had not been on his side. Irenæus was not the only one who knew something about the relative dates of the Gospels. Others whose names have perished must have given their testimony; for Origen was convinced, so were Athanasius, Chrysostom, Augustine, and the other Fathers. The Eastern order is adopted by a canon of the Council of Laodicea (363 A.D.), and in later Councils, in which Western bishops were present to plead for the Western order. I cannot imagine any arguments to have been used against them except those derived from chronology. The Western order appears to me to have been based on the precedence of the authors, the Eastern order on the dates of the writing.

Mr. Halcombe appeals to the Lectionaries of the Greek Church, which, though themselves not earlier than the sixth century, he rightly regards as resting on older usage. It is true that the Eastern Church selected the "Gospels for the day" at Easter and in the weeks immediately following from S. John as a general rule; and it is true that Easter was reckoned the commencemeut of the ecclesiastical year. Hence, in the volume which was prepared for the sole use of the "Gospeller," selections from S. John come first, and except two "Gospels" from S. Mark and two from S. Luke, he is read daily until Whitsunday. But this fact does not prove much. Perhaps the men who arranged the services put S. John first because of his apostolic rank, more probably because the truths which he proclaims are best suited to the most triumphant period of the Church calendar. Certainly, while the *Evangelisterium* held the broken fragments of the Gospels in this order, the Bible on the lectern held them unbroken in the common order. And if this is so, it only confirms my contention that there were two ways of arrangement, one according to dignity, the other according to dates.

Mr. Halcombe will retort that modern critics do not agree with the early Fathers, but strike out for themselves a new and unheard-of order—Mark, Matthew, Luke, John. I reply that I fully accept the order of Irenæus, who was brought up in Asia Minor, where he had often seen and heard Polycarp, the pupil of S. John. But I have shown that our Greek edition of S. Matthew is a slightly later work than the Aramaic edition of S. Matthew to which Irenæus alludes, and thus it becomes a little later than S. Mark.

If, however, we go beyond the date of writing to the time when the oral Gospel was first composed, then the discrepancy becomes greater, and S. Mark is much older than S. Matthew. I rejoice to have Irenæus on my side, and Papias and Origen and others who have a right to be heard. But I do not, any more than Mr. Halcombe, undertake to follow them blindly. Church Councils are not infallible guides in solving literary problems. Take a parallel case. The Catholic Epistles, after some vicissitudes, fell into the order—James, Peter, John, Jude. I should arrange them—James, Jude, Peter, John. S. Paul's Epistles are given in the Muratorian fragment in this order—Corinthians, Ephesians, Philippians, Colossians, Galatians, Thessalonians, Romans, Philemon, Titus, Timothy. Gradually they settled down into their present order. But modern scholars place them—Thessalonians, Corinthians, Galatians,* Romans, Philippians, Colossians, Philemon, Ephesians, 1 Timothy, Titus, 2 Timothy. Would Mr. Halcombe propose to go back to the old order? If he did, would anyone support him?

The ancients did their best. Their proximity to

* I am not yet convinced that the Epistle to the Galatians is the earliest of S. Paul's epistles.

the events gave them certain advantages. Direct testimony, like that of Irenæus, must not lightly be set aside. But we claim the right to review the whole question, and decide it according to the evidence.

II.

The ruler of the feast at Cana, betraying his vulgarity when he thought to parade his wit, made use of the coarse epigram, "Every man at the beginning of a banquet produces his best wines, and when his guests are drunk, then those of an inferior brand: thou hast kept the good wine until now." (S. John ii. 10.)

Mr. Halcombe thinks that the Gospels were produced according to the earthly precedent described by the ruler of the feast, and not according to the divine plan followed by Christ. S. John, he says, came first and culled the choicest fruits of all; S. Matthew followed, selecting the best of what was left; S. Mark and S. Luke, being evangelists, but not apostles, did not presume to record anything, nor even to copy anything, of the highest spiritual value. Indeed, the three synoptists avoided S. John altogether, as towering above their heads. They read, admired, and passed him by. But S. Mark endeavoured to serve the Church by slightly expanding S. Matthew's historical narratives, without presuming to make use of the discourses and the doctrinal portions. S. Luke added a few distinctly "ministerial" details.

Thus the best wine was set forth first, afterwards that which was worse.

To my mind such a plan of composition seems unworthy of God, and incredible in man. To take a single instance, S. Mark on this hypothesis read the words, "Come unto Me all ye that labour and are heavy laden, and I will give you rest." Was it humility which made him deliberately omit them, as too good for so insignificant a creature as himself to record? Or was it a conscious or unconscious feeling that they were unsuited to his readers? A man with such preposterous humility was ill-equipped for the work of an evangelist. Readers so unchristian would not value a Gospel.

But let us see whether Mr. Halcombe's method is followed out in other New Testament writings.

Luther described S. James's Epistle as an epistle of straw. It contains but little Christian doctrine. The spirit is that of the Old Testament, caught from Isaiah and the prophets, and only slightly affected by the Incarnation. If Luther had but known that S. James was the earliest of the Christian writers, his estimate might have been different. He would have seen in the Epistle the pledge of future things and the assurance that the Old Testament is not contrary to the New, but simply earlier and less developed. S. James clings mainly to the Old. His Epistle is Christianity in swaddling clothes.

S. Mark's Gospel might with equal justice be described as a gospel of straw. Give it the first place, and its value is seen. It is the historical basis on which the other synoptic Gospels are built. It is the first-fruits of the Spirit, the glory which led to glory. Put it second or third, and few scholars in this age would admit its right to exist.

Again, we have thirteen Epistles of S. Paul. Read them in their chronological order, as every Bible student ought to do, and you trace step by step the development of the apostle's inner life. They may be arranged into four groups, which to assist the memory may be roughly separated by an interval of five years in each case.

The first group (A.D. 52) contains the Epistles to the Thessalonians, which may almost be described as a youthful effort. The Tübingen critics, with singular lack of appreciation, judged these Epistles to be unworthy of the master-mind, and it is only as a first work that we can defend their genuineness, but as such they are of the highest value. In the second group (A.D. 57) we have the product of manhood. The Epistles to the Corinthians, Galatians, and Romans have no equal, whether we regard them in respect of creative genius, of variety, or of vigour. They have been accepted as undoubtedly Pauline writings by even the most destructive and narrow-minded critics. They are practically unassailable. In the third group (A.D. 62) we have the result of chastened experience. The Epistles to the Philippians, Colossians, Philemon, and Ephesians are the work of the imprisonment. Age, grief, and disappointment have sobered, but given depth to, the apostle's spiritual hopes. To many persons these writings have been the most consolatory of his efforts. Lastly, in the Pastoral

Epistles (A.D. 68) we see the old man retiring from speculation, and devoting himself to organization. The radical has become a moralist. He who boldly trusted to great principles now descends to petty details, for the time of his departure is at hand, and he feels the need of providing successors and endowing them.

Here, then, are all the stages of progress from weakness through strength to maturity and even the beginnings of decay. Everything shows that inspiration quickens, vitalises, energizes, but does not alter the laws of thought nor change the character of the human mind.

Thirdly, let us glance at the earlier period, when writings were, according to the common belief, unknown, and only the outlines of a few great speeches have been preserved. S. Luke has collected in the Acts of the Apostles such information as we possess of the work of this period. Its meagreness and disappointing character are the best proof of its truth. Take S. Stephen's speech, which runs its weary length through fifty-two verses. Except in the last, there is not even an allusion to Christ or to anything Christian. It was in the synagogue that S. Stephen had learned to preach; and if we did not know it, we could hardly have believed that he was an officer of the Church. But S. Paul's sermon at the Pisidian Antioch is not so very much better. S. Peter's speeches attest the fact of the resurrection, and press on the Jewish conscience the guilt of the crucifixion; but except certain allusions to the fulfilment of Scripture, they do nothing more. It is only in the latter part of the book that we find anything like developed doctrine. No doubt the character of the speeches is largely affected by the audience and the surroundings; but, I maintain, it is still more due to the immaturity of the speaker's conceptions. The Christian leaders had not yet attained to the fulness of their later knowledge. Development and progress may be discerned on every side.

For it is a law of the human mind that combating error is the best way to advance knowledge. They who have never joined in controversy have no firm grasp of truth. Hateful and unchristian as theological disputes are apt to become, they have this merit, that they open our eyes. The Arian controversy, though detestable at the time, left the Church richer in the faith. And S. Paul would not have had so sure an apprehension of truth if he had not had to combat heresy in Corinth, Galatia, and Colossæ.

But, Mr. Halcombe may reply, this is true of the doctrinal facts of the New Testament, but the case of the Gospels is different. The evangelists are not theologians or historians interpreting what they narrate, but annalists recording certain words and deeds. Proximity to the event is the one thing needful. The earliest narrator would be the best. For their faces, like that of Moses, shone from their communion with Him who is the Light, and, as years rolled on, the glory would inevitably fade away.

This is precisely the question on which we differ. S. Mark, I maintain, was an annalist. He recorded, almost without comment, what he had learned from S. Peter. But the other evangelists were historians. They interpret for us the facts which they relate. By numerous editorial notes and observations they give us the result of their meditations. By a large number of new sections they increase the store of truth. For thus was Christ's promise fulfilled, that the Holy Spirit should bring back to their remembrance what Christ had spoken to them. In other words, they did not at first understand the full meaning of their trust. They did not see what was most important in Christ's work. Their conceptions of Christianity were crude and one-sided. The deeper truths were brought home to them gradually. The glory, so far from fading away, waxed, as S. Paul says, brighter and brighter in proportion as they severally received the illumination of the Spirit of the Lord.

S. Mark's Gospel, therefore, with its naked history, came first. S. Matthew's and S. Luke's were founded upon it (of course, while they all existed in the oral stage), but they were slowly enriched by the gradual accumulation of facts and teaching collected from a great variety of sources.

All three evangelists, I hold, made it their single aim to give their readers everything trustworthy which they could collect. The common idea, that they picked and selected what was specially adapted to their readers, I most confidently reject. The simple fact that S. Matthew's Gospel—the Gospel of the Eastern Church—has always been more popular amongst Gentile Christians than S. Luke's

—the Gospel of the West—upsets this most erroneous notion. I cannot doubt that S. Matthew would have given much to include in his Gospel the parable of the Prodigal Son, or that S. Luke would have given still more for the history of the Syrophœnician woman's daughter, for that is the only recorded case of mercy granted by Christ to a Gentile,* and is therefore the one fact by which his readers would be most powerfully affected. He did not give it, because he had never heard of it. It belongs to the second edition of S. Peter's memoirs, which never reached the West till the Gospels were written.

But though there was no conscious selection of what was proper, the inevitable pressure of circumstances and locality must unconsciously have moulded the development. S. Matthew's Gospel, being built up in the East, deals with the inferiority of the Law to the Gospel, the fulfilment of Scripture in Christ, the guilt of the Jewish nation in crucifying Him. It thus justifies and explains the destruction of Jerusalem, which was the one event of Providence which demanded explanation with the Jews.

If I wanted to describe the special features of this Gospel, I should call it the proclamation of Christianity amid the ruins of the Holy City. The catechists, who gradually shaped it, had the coming destruction before their eyes, and it was not finally written until that destruction was an accomplished fact.

S. Luke, on the other hand, felt very slightly the

* The centurion's servant (Matt. viii. 5-13; Luke vii. 1-10) was probably a Jew, and the centurion himself was certainly a proselyte.

pressure of this terrible tragedy. A Gentile himself, whose work lay amongst Gentiles, he could view with comparative equanimity the events which were so overwhelming to his neighbours. For him the universality of the Gospel, and its applicability to all ages and nations, to the poor, the sick, the lost, the dying, was the essential thing. Brought up under S. Paul, he teems with the Pauline spirit. And though he delights to colour his page with details of Jewish ritual and Semitic thought, he does so with the feelings of an artist, and not because he cares for such trivialities in themselves. His Gospel is the Gospel of humanity.

But if S. Matthew's Gospel and S. Luke's show traces of progress in spiritual and intellectual understanding, S. John's does so sevenfold. His opening verses reveal a depth of knowledge to which S. James never attained. Not that S. James would have contradicted them, or doubted their truth. But it is one thing to see truth when it is set before you; it is another to set it forth yourself. There is such a thing as latent knowledge. The grander the truth, the more simple and obvious it is when once enunciated; but for all that it is long in coming. "The Spirit divideth to every man severally as He wills."

I suppose no one now would hold that the Gospels were written in a state of ecstasy; that the evangelists, scarcely conscious of what they were doing, held the pen while the Holy Spirit directed it. Such crude conceptions of inspiration are not favoured by Mr. Halcombe nor by any other competent observer of the facts. We agree that the inspired writers give what they had learned. I hold that they had learned it after a long search. I believe that S. John's ideas are clear, because they are the product of a life of thought. Christ's speeches, as he records them, must not be regarded as *verbatim* reports, made as it were by the help of a shorthand writer. What Christ really said was, I maintain, often simpler and briefer. The thought is Christ's, the clothing of it is S. John's. The cast of the sentence, the choice of words, are not seldom the evangelist's contribution. This is proved by a strongly-marked style and a peculiar vocabulary, not to be found in the synoptic writers. The speeches and the narratives had been turned over in his mind and reproduced in his oral teaching for a generation. Every year they acquired some new polish, some fresh illustration. He had repeated them, till he did not sharply distinguish between the original saying and the inspired commentary. Indeed, these are perpetually mixed up. Sometimes we can see the distinction, but oftener it eludes us; so completely is the interpretation blended with the text.

This process demands time. Mr. Halcombe holds that S. John's Gospel was completed, published, and received as canonical a few weeks after the author had been blindly asking, "Lord, dost Thou at this time restore the kingdom to Israel?" I, on the contrary, require at least several decades of experience, meditation, and prayer for the education of the greatest of the evangelists.

I do not believe that it was easier to write a

Gospel than to write an Epistle. I deny that the one was a mere effort of memory, the other the product of thought. And, therefore, I cannot admit that S. John when he followed S. Peter about as a dumb companion,* never to our knowledge opening his mouth, was engaged in composing or had already completed and was known as the author of those weighty chapters which have in many respects given us a nobler conception of Christ than we can gain from any other source, and have done more to solace the sufferer than the other evangelists put together.

If Christ Himself during His period of humiliation grew in wisdom as perceptibly as He grew in stature, and needed thirty years' meditation, study of Scripture, and prayer before He broke silence, much more did His youthful servant need experience and training before he commenced to write. Pontius Pilate or Caiaphas might have given us a life of Christ, which in many respects would have been fuller and more correct, historically and legally, than what the evangelists have given. We should value such a document highly for critical purposes, but it would not have been a Gospel. And why? The consecrated thought would not have been there; the sympathetic insight, which we define as inspiration, would not have discerned the treasure which should bless ages unborn.

It is impossible to separate S. John's Gospel from his first Epistle. To say that the Epistle was written as a preface to the Gospel is perhaps going too far,

---

* So he invariably appears in Acts iii.–viii.

but the two works teem with the same ideas, and can hardly have been written at very different epochs. Now the tone of the Epistle is sad. It speaks of antagonism. The struggle against opposing forces is constant and severe. But in the first years of Christianity the apostles were triumphant. The people magnified them. The attempts of the rulers and the Sadducees to crush them failed because they were the heroes of the hour. Their converts were numbered by thousands. They carried everything before them. The Master's triumphant return was their daily expectation.

In a few years this state of things began to change. S. Stephen was martyred by a mob acting under lynch law. A general persecution followed, and the brethren were scattered. A little later Herod Agrippa I. slew S. James the son of Zebedee. This brutal murder brought him so much popularity that he resolved to strike a blow at the ringleader, S. Peter. It was long before the Roman authorities were aroused, but they were aroused at last, and then the outlook was black indeed.

Now if S. John wrote, as Mr. Halcombe says, in the earliest days of Christianity, he would have been more or less than human, if his writings had not reflected the triumph of the moment. They must have been inspired with hope and the sense of coming victory. But, on the contrary, they are permeated with gloom, and with the feeling that though not crushed, or capable of being crushed, yet the revelation of Christ in many quarters was not making way. And this is true of the Gospel as much as of the Epistle. Look, for example, at the use which S. John makes of that word, "the world," in both of them. It is not a new word. S. Mark uses it twice; S. Luke three times in his Gospel, and once in the Acts of the Apostles. SS. Peter, Paul, Matthew, James, and the author of the Epistle to the Hebrews employ it still more frequently. But with S. John it is a keyword. He repeats it twenty-one times in the Epistle, seventy-eight times in the Gospel. And its meaning has been deepened. S. Luke spoke of all the kingdoms of the world. S. Paul teaches that the world by nature knew not God. But with S. John the kingdom of the world is the antithesis of the kingdom of God. Ignorance has been succeeded by active hatred. No compromise is possible. "We are of God, and the whole world lieth in the evil one." This is the result of ripe experience. This is a sign that the power of Rome was stirring itself. Tertullian thought it impossible for the Roman emperors ever to become Christian. His opinion was the natural, if too literal, deduction from the teaching of S. John.

Again, the fulfilment of Scripture by Christ was an engrossing study in the first ages. It was the subject of endless discussion with the Jews. But it was not merely a weapon to confute or persuade them; it was one of the strongest means of establishing the Christians themselves, both Jews and Gentiles, in the faith. S. Peter began the investigation on the day of Pentecost, and it was continued not only in the East, as S. Matthew's

Gospel testifies, but by S. Paul in his Epistles, by S. Luke in the Acts of the Apostles, in S. Peter's First Epistle, and in the Epistle to the Hebrews. S. John draws attention to four fulfilments, which are not expressly noticed elsewhere. They all relate to the passion, and all occur in the nineteenth chapter. (1) They parted My garments among them, and upon My vesture did they cast lots. (2) When I was thirsty, they gave Me vinegar to drink. (3) A bone thereof shall not be broken. (4) They shall look on Him whom they pierced. S. Mark knows nothing of these fulfilments. Some of them, especially the third, are so recondite that they are not likely to have been discovered in the primitive times.

S. John not only gives the incident of the drawing of a sword and cutting off the high priest's domestic servant's ear on the night of the arrest, but says that S. Peter committed the outrage and Malchus suffered it. If both men were dead, there could be no harm in publishing their names. Otherwise some trouble might be apprehended, or why did the synoptists suppress the information?

S. John, after completing his Gospel, added another chapter by way of supplement. The object was to correct a false opinion which was current, that his own exemption from death had been predicted by Christ. If he felt death to be drawing near, we can understand his anxiety to remove a stumbling-block from the faith of his friends. But if he wrote immediately after the Ascension, what time had there been for the rumour to spread, and what probability that it was not correct? It was an inference, an extension, of Christ's words, but at least a very reasonable extension. Lapse of time alone was showing it to be false, and lapse of time alone justified S. John in interpreting so positively our Lord's obscure words respecting S. Peter. For the prophecy, "When thou wast young, thou girdedst thyself, and walkedst whither thou wouldest; but when thou shalt be old, another shall gird thee, and carry thee whither thou wouldest not," does not on the face of it point to martyrdom. Only after S. Peter's death could S. John have unreservedly explained it so. Again, look for a moment at the form of the sentence: "This spake He, signifying by what death he should glorify God." How unnatural to write thus of the departure of your dearest friend, if he was still by your side. How natural if the severance had taken place five years or upwards. There is joy for the comrade who has entered upon his rest, thankfulness that the fiery trial has ended in triumph, regret that such honour should be denied to himself. Here is a typical specimen of S. John's style. The simplest words teem with the deepest meaning.

It appears from v. 2, vii. 2, xi. 18, xviii. 40, and other passages, that the Gospel was written for foreigners and persons unacquainted with Jewish customs and Jewish topography. It cannot, therefore, have been written in the first days when S. John himself lived in Jerusalem, and almost the whole of the Church was resident in that city. Indeed, if written then, it would most certainly have been written in Aramaic.

It is objected that if S. John wrote after the destruction of Jerusalem he ought not to have said, "There *is* in Jerusalem at the sheep (gate) a pool ... with five porches." "There *was*" would have been the necessary word. No doubt the five porches were destroyed, and the pool filled up with the rubbish. But S. John had never visited the city since its destruction. He may not have known the full extent of the demolition. It was natural for the old man to picture the scene as he remembered it in happier days. It is characteristic of great age to live in the distant past. I cannot regard this as an insuperable difficulty.

The theory of inspiration which underlies the views advocated in this paper may seem to some people subversive of belief. I have not found it so. It may make belief more difficult, but it seems to be more in accord with the facts, and therefore in the long-run preserves faith by preventing a conflict with reason.

God's way of revealing Himself is never exactly what we should have expected. He chooses to employ human agents with all their weakness and liability to make mistakes. Inspiration quickens their spiritual perception, but does not altogether preserve them from errors of fact.* Christ might have written down His own message for us on some sheets of vellum which could have been legible to this day. Nay, the phonograph might have been invented before the fulness of time came,

---

* See, for example, Matt. i. 9, 11; Mark ii. 26; Luke ii. 2; John xii. 3; Acts v. 36, vii. 16.

that we might still hear for ourselves the Sermon on the Mount in the very tones with which it was delivered. But by granting none of these things, God seems to warn us against putting our trust in the flesh. After all, we are not saved by the Gospels, but by Christ.

III.

Mr. Halcombe claims to have settled the Gospel difficulties by putting S. John first, retaining the other Gospels in the common order, but dissecting and reconstructing S. Luke. He is satisfied that he has succeeded, and points out in proof that any-one, after mastering his "constructive principles," could tell at sight from which Gospel any particular section came, without any previous knowledge of the Gospels.

So of old the Ptolemaic astronomers insisted that they must be right in making the earth the centre of the universe, and the sun a satellite revolving round the earth, because they could account on this supposition for all the motions of the heavenly bodies. Their system of cycles and epicycles, processions and recessions, was beautifully complete. Were they not able to predict an eclipse? Moreover, the circle was a perfect figure, worthy of the divine perfection of the Creator, incomparably superior to the battered and distorted ellipse.

It is easy to construct a system. If you carefully analyse and arrange the facts, leaving nothing out of consideration and exaggerating nothing, it will be impossible to refute you. The question is, whether your system is natural, self-evident, and capable of asserting its own truth, or a mass of improbabilities, strung together in defiance of law and habit and ascertained fact.

Copernicus maintained that the sun was the centre of the solar system. Galileo supported him. Kepler discovered the laws of the motions in an ellipse. Newton hit upon the idea of gravity. Gradually an easy and natural explanation of the movements of the heavenly bodies was produced, and the result is that no one now believes in the Ptolemaic system, or if anyone occasionally advocates a return to it, he gets no hearing from scientific men.

Mr. Halcombe himself seems to be astonished at the "constructive principles" on which the evangelists, according to his theory, worked. He admits that no other books were ever composed on such literary rules. To my mind it is a sufficient refutation of his scheme that it would be just as easy and far more natural to adopt Tertullian's order in reality, and put S. Mark last instead of third. Then, at least, we should secure symmetry. We should say that S. John came first and gathered the choicest fruit, S. Matthew reaped the second crop, and S. Luke the third; but S. Mark was too late for the harvest, and was compelled to be content with the gleanings.

My advice to the student is, Try a simpler plan. Give up the idea that inspiration sets aside the laws of human thought. Look at a parallel case. Inspiration was promised by Christ Himself to the apostles for their speeches. "Do not premeditate

... it shall be given you at the moment what ye shall speak. It is not you that speak, but the Holy Spirit." That I fully accept and believe. Nevertheless, on examining those speeches of the apostles which have been preserved, and which may therefore be assumed to be in a special manner inspired, I do not find them faultless. Take S. Paul's speech before Ananias and the Sanhedrin. (Acts xxiii.) The commencement, "Brethren, I have lived with a perfectly good conscience before God until this day," appears to me to be singularly deficient in the meekness and gentleness of Christ. The abusive epithet, "You whitewashed wall," seems too insulting for a Christian to use towards any man; it gave the bystanders an opportunity of retort, of which they made full and effective use. The appeal to party rancour, "I am a Pharisee, the pupil of a Pharisee; I am on my trial for the hope of the resurrection of the dead," was—I allude to the last clause—untrue in fact and unjustifiable in intent. The apostle himself admitted this when the excitement was over. (xxiv. 21.) "Compassed with infirmity" is our verdict on him in his speeches. Human nature is there with its faults as well as its virtues.

The same human nature may be perceived when he took his pen in hand. That it was a noble nature, towering high above ordinary men, I strongly maintain. But it was not perfect. Inspiration quickened S. Paul's perception of truth, but it did not protect him from faults of temper, nor from using bad grammar, broken sentences, questionable logic, and inexact quotations.

And if this cannot be gainsaid, why should we think with Mr. Halcombe that "the Gospels, as first given to men, exhibited a perfect unity of design and execution"? Why should we believe that "their parts may be as nicely adjusted to each other as the machinery of the Nasmyth hammer"? Was not human agency employed in their production? And where men are employed, will there not always be an element of imperfection? Or what did S. Paul mean when he wrote, "We have this treasure in earthen vessels, that the exceeding greatness of its power may be of God"?

If Mr. Halcombe's "constructive principles" require S. Luke to have written certain parts of his Gospel in a way in which no man ever wrote before or since, the conclusion which I should draw is that the constructive principles are wrong.

Put the sun into the centre of the solar system. Put S. Mark first among the evangelists. All will then become plain. S. Mark will be restored to his real post of honour. Instead of being a miserable epitomizer of S. Matthew, afraid to copy anything which possessed high spiritual value, he is S. Peter's faithful interpreter, the pioneer in producing the noblest works with which God has been pleased to enrich the Church. S. Matthew and S. Luke are beholden to him for the historical framework of their Gospels. It was their task to collect new matter, and incorporate it with the old.

The first principle which I lay down is this, that the original telling of a story will be the fullest and most picturesque. Later repetitions will give

MR. HALCOMBE'S STRICTURES

the essential points of the story in less rugged diction, but will curtail and confuse the circumstantial details.

That this principle is true in ordinary life needs no proof. But in the Gospels the case is not quite the same. The story was not merely told, but learned by heart and frequently repeated. The habits of the time made this compulsory. We shall never understand the growth of the Gospels unless we realise the pains taken to give every Christian child (and every adult, as far as he was capable of receiving it) an education in the faith, according to the ordinary methods of the day, by making him commit long passages to memory.

Still, though the process of reducing the bulk of material would be carried on at a slower rate under these safeguards, it would be in constant operation. The catechist would unconsciously yield to the pressure of circumstances. Why should he burden his pupil's memory with details, to the exclusion of important matters? Why give names of persons and places in which the learner could take no interest, rather than great principles which would guide him through life? In the course of forty years the shrinkage in narrative would be great; all the greater because newly-added parables and discourses were always swelling the lessons, and compelling the catechist to find space for them by abbreviating the original records.

Now the process of Gospel formation was carried on simultaneously in two districts, which were jealous of each other, and seldom held intercommunications.

The Eastern catechists, centred round Jerusalem, produced, as I hold, in oral form, S. Matthew's Gospel, under his guidance and with his contributions; the Western catechists, under S. Paul, produced the third Gospel, of which one of them, S. Luke, became ultimately the writer. Both sets of catechists started with S. Mark's version of S. Peter's Memoirs (except that S. Luke received about two-thirds of it only), and grafted into it such additional records as they from time to time obtained from S. Matthew or other sources.

Both of them unconsciously and gradually altered S. Mark's teaching, not only by reducing its bulk, but by modifying its statements. But they did this differently, according to their national proclivities. The Jews were strict in adhering to the facts, but contemptuous of picturesque ornament. The Gentiles loved the picturesque, but were not so careful of the facts.

If, then, we strike out of S. Matthew and S. Luke all the verses which have no parallel in S. Mark, and then compare what is left of them with S. Mark and with each other, we shall find, if I am right, that S. Mark is always the fullest, and that of the others S. Matthew's is shortest, but seldom contradicts S. Mark; S. Luke's is of medium length, but more frequently contradicts S. Mark. Above all, whenever S. Matthew and S. Luke support one another, S. Mark must agree with them; when they contradict one another, S. Mark will usually agree with one of them against the other, or give something from which both the divergent statements have been derived.

MR. HALCOMBE'S STRICTURES

This would be true absolutely if S. Mark had written his Gospel at the first, and if the East and West held no communications with each other. Instead of that, S. Mark did not write for about forty years. During that time the records were dwelling in his mind, and were continually produced in his catechetical teaching. They were therefore reduced in bulk and altered in form like the rest, only this process was very much slower than with the other Gospels, because one man's memory does not make so many changes as are made if a story passes through the minds and memories of from six to twelve.

It is not denied that all this has been done; only Mr. Halcombe gives a different and (as I think) impossible account of how it was done. Instead of following the natural and self-evident plan which I have sketched, he proposes another. He holds that S. Matthew wrote first of the three; that S. Mark took his Gospel, struck out of it all those passages which he thought too good for himself to touch or for his readers to know, and then proceeded to amplify the residuum. Where S. Matthew had used six words he expanded them to ten or twelve. Such a process in ordinary literature produces prosy and insipid narratives. But here the effect was the opposite. Not a word is unnecessary or out of place. The dry bones of S. Matthew's jejune chronicles have been clothed with flesh.

In the next place, S. Luke, Mr. Halcombe teaches, took both the Gospels, but, having a less humble estimate of himself than S. Mark had shown, retained a number of the more valuable sections. For the rest, he picked one word from S. Matthew, the next from S. Mark, the third was his own. Yet, instead of producing a patchwork, the result was homogeneous. The world has decided that his Greek is more classical than that of the others. Not a sentence is out of place, not a word is superfluous. "Dovetailing" does not usually turn out so well. If anyone doubts this, let him read Tatian's *Dia Tessarôn*. But then Tatian had some respect for his authorities, and could not bring himself to alter or omit a sentence from any one of them. S. Luke, according to the documentary hypothesis, had no such scruples. Though he was not an eyewitness, but derived his information second-hand, he capriciously altered it without misgiving. Witness his account (in the Revised Version) of the new cloth and the old garment. (Luke v. 36 = Mark ii. 21 = Matt. ix. 16.) Such wanton levity I cannot attribute to S. Luke, and therefore I cling to the oral hypothesis, which preserves the evangelists' character, by denying that any of them had had the advantage of seeing the Gospel of his fellows.

S. Luke's chief object in writing was, Mr. Halcombe teaches, to correct S. Matthew's chronology, which is confessedly wrong, and is supposed to have been causing doubt in the Church. Now S. Luke corrects it by following almost invariably S. Mark. If he had told his pupils that in matters of chronology S. Mark, when he differs from S. Matthew, is always right, would not that have sufficed? It would seem so, for observe the final issue of his labours. No sooner

MR. HALCOMBE'S STRICTURES

was his perfect adjustment of chronology published, than some enemy, according to Mr. Halcombe, spoilt it all. A malicious, or well-meaning but ill-informed, person secured S. Luke's manuscript, and transposed about a couple of chapters, with the result that Gospel difficulties have troubled the Church ever since, until Mr. Halcombe discovered the fraud.

Papias tells us that S. Mark's chronology is wrong. If so, S. Matthew and S. Luke, who, I maintain, follow it as almost their only guide, must be wrong also.* This is, I believe, the true account of the matter. The question is fundamental. If I am right, Mr. Halcombe and the harmonists have spent years of exhausting labour to very little purpose. The Gospels, I say, were put together originally for convenience of Church lessons, with only slight regard for chronological sequence. S. Mark arranged the sections in their present order, and not S. Peter. S. Mark had not the knowledge, even if he had the desire, to secure the correct sequence.

Whether S. Luke, when he promised in his preface to "write in order," meant chronological order or not we cannot decide. The words in themselves are ambiguous. A hundred beads lying on a table at random are not arranged in order. Put them on a string and they become so. If you arrange them carefully with regard to colour, you have a better claim to have put them in order. But if you prefer to arrange them according to size, who will deny that you have kept your promise? So if S. Luke strung together the sections of the

* See *Composition of the Four Gospels*, pp. 21-24, 146.

Gospels with suitable prefaces and conclusions, as he has done, he wrote "in order." The Greek word which he uses ($καθεξῆς$) merely means "strung in a row." If he put them into chronological order, he did better still. But if he put them in the most convenient order for Church services, he has surely done well enough. Even if he intended to write in chronological order (which is very far from certain), we have no reason to suppose that inspiration would prove an infallible guide in such a matter, or that it was possible at that date for a man in his position to arrive at the real sequence of events. If true chronology was necessary for the Church, would not God's providence have prevented such a perversion of it as Mr. Halcombe supposes? It is a poor thing to say that the Gospels once were perfect, if we can only do so by maintaining that they were corrupted immediately.

IV.

But, to turn to another point of the inquiry, when a man writes in a foreign language he is apt to use the idioms of his mother tongue.

A Frenchman seldom writes idiomatic English. When he attempts to do so, an Englishman who knows French can generally detect a multitude of French idioms underlying the English words. Much more in days of old, when a Jew undertook to write Greek, was he likely to introduce Semitic idioms into his work, especially if that work was a translation from Aramaic. Semitic languages co-ordinate rather than subordinate their sentences. The conjunction "and" occurs with monotonous frequency. S. John's Gospel is a good example of this. "And," "therefore," "because," have almost driven out the rich array of Hellenic connecting particles; and this because the apostle thinks in Aramaic, though he writes in Greek. Now S. Mark was S. Peter's interpreter, to translate (as I have shown) his Aramaic lessons for the Greek catechumens, not (as is commonly supposed) to translate S. Peter's Greek into Latin. "And" is his favourite conjunction. One of the strongest internal arguments against the genuineness of the last twelve verses is the sudden reduction in the frequency of this word.

But S. Mark has another peculiarity. To connect narratives he writes "straightway." Forty-one times does this word occur. It is apparently a mannerism, arising from want of literary skill in securing variety.

S. Matthew makes short work with this "straightway." S. Luke in nearly every instance gets rid of it. And so their style is improved; there is less monotony and tediousness.

It is an axiom in such cases that the crude and uncouth shall come first. S. Mark's translation was used by the other Greek catechists, but every one of them would contribute something to improve it, until it reaches its most polished form in S. Luke's edition. The oldest form of the Gospel is that which is fullest in matter, but rudest in expression.

So far we have dealt with broad principles. Now I will give two petty details, to confirm what has been said.

All the evangelists use a certain number of Latin words, connected for the most part with Roman money, law, or military rule. Such words were necessarily current in countries which were under Roman government, but to introduce them into a Greek treatise was a disfigurement. It was false in art and offensive to correct taste. Now S. Mark uses the Latin *centurio* for a centurion. He so writes it three times in the fifteenth chapter. But S. Matthew and S. Luke substitute for it the Greek equivalent, ἑκατοντάρχης. According to Mr. Halcombe's view, S. Mark found the correct Greek word in S. Matthew's Gospel, and deliberately altered it into the incorrect. This, I submit, is incredible.

Again, the word "man" is frequently expressed in Aramaic by the phrase "son of man." Thus in John i. 6 the Peshito Syriac gives, "There was a son of man sent from God, whose name was John." This expression was unknown to Greek authors, and would mislead the Greek reader. Now in Mark iii. 28 it is written, "Verily I say unto you that all things shall be forgiven to *the sons of men*, their sins and the blasphemies wherewith soever they shall blaspheme." This in S. Matthew's parallel (xii. 31) becomes, "Wherefore I say unto you, every sin and blasphemy shall be forgiven to *men*" (for which the Peshito, of course, gives "to *the sons of men*"). Here S. Mark, translating S. Peter's Aramaic, has evidently reproduced the Aramaic idiom instead of substituting the proper Greek equivalent, but some Greek catechist has seen the mistake and corrected it. According to Mr. Halcombe, however, S. Mark found the correct

MR. HALCOMBE'S STRICTURES 235

idiom in S. Matthew, and deliberately, without reason, substituted for it the unintelligible Aramaic idiom. This also I consider to be incredible.

I could bring forward some cogent proofs to show that S. Luke had never read S. Matthew's Gospel; but I prefer to ask my readers to study the question for themselves. Let them take the first two chapters of S. Matthew, and endeavour to fit them into the first two chapters of S. Luke, so as to secure a continuous history of what really happened. Let them do this honestly, without consulting a commentary or a harmony, and if they have a strong sense of historical truth, they will see that neither of these writers was acquainted with what his fellow had written.

Harmonists appear to me to have no hesitation in putting a strain upon our sense of truth, in order to secure the "inerrancy" of Holy Scripture.

Thus in the case of S. Peter's denials, according to Mr. Halcombe's view, S. John was the first to write an account of what happened. He did so within a few weeks of the events, when everything was fresh in his memory. He knew that our Lord had twice predicted S. Peter's fall, that S. Peter had been guilty of *six* denials, and that the cock crew twice. Instead, however, of giving us the truth, the whole truth, and nothing but the truth, he has recorded the first prediction, the first, third, and fourth denials, and the first cock-crowing. What reason can be given for his suppressing one-half of the incidents? We know of none that will bear examination.

Shortly afterwards S. Matthew, knowing the

whole truth, and having S. John's Gospel before him, deliberately suppressed one-half of the truth, and gave us only what his brother apostle had omitted. Again we ask, Why should he have done this? and we are referred to the principles on which he is held to have constructed his Gospel, which principles we do not admit.

Soon afterwards S. Mark, with the two Gospels before him, wrote an account in which he followed S. Matthew in selecting the prediction and the denials, but recorded both the cock-crowings (there are great textual difficulties here, of which Mr. Halcombe takes no account), and altered S. Matthew's simple expression "wept bitterly" into a word the meaning of which has never been cleared up. Some translate, "He buried his face in his mantle and wept"; others, "He wept profusely"; others, "He began to weep"; others, "When he thought thereon, he wept." Is it not more probable that S. Matthew altered S. Mark's obscure word into a simple one than that S. Mark altered S. Matthew's lucid phrase into an incomprehensible one? I should say that the priority of S. Mark is much supported by this one case.

And whence did S. Mark learn about the "twice"? Did our Lord really speak the word, S. Peter recollect it, and S. Mark record it, though other catechists let it drop, as I hold? Or did S. Mark infer from the context that He must have spoken it? And if S. Mark was indeed so anxious to put the narrative right on the smaller matter, why did he not correct "thrice" into "six times," and give us the six denials? Or did he not perceive that there were six?

S. Luke comes next, and having the three Gospels will surely at last give us the whole truth. Not so. He picks and chooses in a bewildering way, following S. John in recording the first prediction and the third denial, but in other particulars preferring S. Matthew.

And why is this improbable doubling of incidents, which not even Tatian allows, forced upon us? Because "standing and sitting are not the same thing"; because one narrative has, "Woman, I know Him not"; another, "Man, I am not." For the sake of these, and a few other minute differences, the fourfold "thrice" is disregarded, the fourfold narratives are declared to be half the truth. Historical probability yields to verbal precision. Yet such a protest against the worship of verbal accuracy do inspired writers make, that the *Shemá*, which every pious Jew in our Lord's time is believed to have repeated daily, is given in four different forms by three evangelists, but not once correctly. (Mark xii. 30, 33; Matthew xxii. 37; Luke x. 27.) It may be expected that every Jew would know the names of the twelve tribes, yet a list of them is given in the Apocalypse in which Joseph and Manasseh are put instead of Ephraim and Manasseh, Levi is inserted though he had no lot with his brethren, Dan is excluded. (Rev. vii. 5-8.) Facts like these meet us everywhere when we undertake a careful study of the New Testament, and they warn us against believing in verbal inspiration. If we do, our faith will receive a shock every time it encounters a difficulty, a shock from which I would fain rescue the devout reader. Verbal inspiration has been generally surrendered, not because it is impossible, for of that we do not profess to judge, but because it is not supported by the evidence.

Again, one of the most strongly-marked narratives in the Gospels is, I should say, the healing of blind Bartimæus. It is narrated by all the synoptists in almost identical words. Yet because S. Matthew speaks of two men, while S. Mark and S. Luke only mention one, and because S. Luke puts the encounter at the entrance into Jericho, though S. Mark, in a singularly tautological sentence, which would naturally lead to confusion, puts it on the departure from that city, Mr. Halcombe is compelled by his principles to maintain that four blind men were healed on three separate occasions. All four cried out, " Thou son of David," an unusual phrase, not found in S. Mark or S. Luke in any other miracle. In every case the multitudes bade them to be silent. In every case they cried the more or the louder. In every case Jesus put the question, " What wilt thou that I should do?" In every case, after receiving sight, they followed Jesus on the way.

Mr. Halcombe has some misgivings. In his second volume he speaks doubtfully of the multiplication of this miracle. I have not seen the second edition of his first volume, and cannot tell whether he there completes the retractation. If he does not, why does he not insist that S. Matthew's narrative of the Gerasene demoniacs is distinct from S. Mark's and

S. Luke's? For not only did the one take place at Gadara, the other at Gerasa, but in S. Matthew two men were healed, in S. Mark and S. Luke only one. The chronology also is different. Dr. Stanley Leathes is more courageous. He holds that the Gadarene and Gerasene miracles were quite distinct, and that on two separate occasions a herd of swine rushed down the steep and were choked in the lake,* a necessary conclusion if "inerrancy" is to be maintained.

But Mr. Halcombe insists that the Gospels are not fragmentary but complete records. He has divided them into 364 sections, and is confident that our Lord's ministry lasted four years, neither more nor less. Now 31 of the sections apply to the period before our Lord's ministry began, or to the ministry of the Baptist; so only 333 remain for Christ, of which S. John records 102. In four years there are 1461 days, and Christ did or said some ministerial thing on 333 out of 1461 days. He was therefore silent on three days out of four, and did not lead the life of incessant toil which Christians have fondly imagined. The work of the second year consists of fifteen incidents only. Is not the mere statement of this fact a sufficient refutation? (John xxi. 25.) I have considered already† the very difficult question of the duration of our Lord's ministry, and my conclusions do not agree with Mr. Halcombe's.

The critical study of the Gospels demands more attention from English Biblical students than it has

---

* See *The Churchman*, December, 1892, p. 121.
† See p. 185.

hitherto received. It is a fascinating pursuit in itself, and one that leads to most important consequences. It makes the Gospels easier to understand, and protects us from treating them arbitrarily. In the infancy of the new science alarmingly destructive results were obtained, which appeared to threaten the foundations of the faith. There are still writers who advocate what I consider false views. They can only be met by diligent and honest examination of the facts. The truth has nothing to fear. The higher criticism, when applied without partiality or distortion of the evidence, strongly supports the general trustworthiness of the Gospels. It proves that the essential points are those best attested; but it also proves, what most scholars have already learned from other facts, that what is called verbal inspiration must be given up.

The Gospels do not preserve the exact utterances of Christ. One example may suffice to prove this. S. Mark writes that our Lord said to the Syrophœnician woman, "For this saying go thy way, the demon is gone out of thy daughter." But S. Matthew writes, "O woman, great is thy faith; be it unto thee even as thou wilt." Shall we, after the manner of Tatian, piece these sentences together and maintain that Christ said, "O woman, great is thy faith; for this saying, go thy way; be it unto thee even as thou wilt; the demon is gone out of thy daughter." This on the Nasmyth hammer hypothesis is, of course, possible. But does any serious historian suppose that Christ was guilty of such verbosity? My solution of the difficulty is this: We do not know the exact words which Christ used. S. Mark gives us what S. Peter recollected of them. But the catechists of Jerusalem, aware that S. Peter's words in this case were capable of a false interpretation—as though the girl had been cured by her mother's merit and not by her mother's faith—took upon themselves to alter the phrase in the interests of truth. Their doing so, presumptuous as it must appear to the traditional exegete, proves that the primitive Christians, under the guidance of the apostles, were not such slaves of the letter as modern commentators would make them.

The same observation I hold to be true of nearly every saying of Christ. Even where three evangelists agree *verbatim*, as they very seldom do for more than six or seven words together, the only safe conclusion is that they have reproduced S. Peter's recollections with greater accuracy than usual. And if the substance rather than the letter of Christ's words is given us, why should we suppose that less important matters—as dates—are to be trusted? S. John says that the anointing at Bethany took place six days before the passover, S. Mark two days. S. Matthew says that while Christ was speaking the parable of the new wine in the old bottles Jairus came to announce that his daughter was dead. S. Mark and S. Luke say that Jairus came several months after this, according to Mr. Halcombe's own chronology, and announced that his daughter was living, but *in extremis*. Are these discrepancies "superficial appearances," or clear indications that the adjustments of the Nasmyth hammer are not to be expected?

God, I repeat, has been pleased to employ human agents for making known the truth. "We know in part" might have been said by the evangelists as much as by S. Paul. The diversities in their narratives prove that they did not possess, and therefore could not bequeath to us, a perfect record of Christ's words and deeds. We have what God in His providence has been pleased to give us. We have records which exhibit the belief of whole Churches in the primitive days. They have sufficed for Christians in all days. They will suffice for us, in the power of the same Spirit who inspired the men that wrote them, and is ready to inspire us to understand them, to the saving of our souls.

XVI.

THEORIES OF MESSRS. BADHAM AND JOLLEY*

THESE books have little in common, except a belief that the oral hypothesis does not account for the origin of the synoptic Gospels. Mr. Badham does not concern himself about the oral hypothesis. He is satisfied with documents and redactors. Mr. Jolley is more reasonable. He admits that for forty years (oral) tradition, together with personal reminiscences, supplied the wants of the Churches. He admits that the (oral) tradition grew larger as the personal reminiscences grew less, until, on the death of the last eye-witness, our written Gospels superseded both. But Mr. Badham does not take account of those forty years. Until the first document appeared—close upon 70 A.D.—he leaves the whole question to silence.

Yet surely forty years, in which the number of Christians amounted to myriads, and Churches, each with its cycle of oral teaching, were established in most parts of the inhabited world, would

* *The Formation of the Gospels.* By F. P. BADHAM, M.A. 2nd Edition. London: 1892.
The Synoptic Problem for English Readers. By ALFRED J. JOLLEY. London: 1892.

exercise a preponderating influence upon the formation of the Gospels. Tradition, I believe, was neither so vague nor so fluctuating as some persons have imagined. It had a distinct source in S. Peter's teaching—not his "preaching," as Mr. Badham says. On that point turns the whole controversy. Preaching varies. New subjects drive out the old, or if sometimes the same story is told, it is told in different words. Our Gospels could not have been formed in that way. The very existence of the catechists proves that a compact body of lessons was drawn up, which they taught to the catechumens. Those who had mastered these lessons became catechists themselves, and carried the same teaching into every corner of the Roman world.

Thus S. Peter's Memoirs formed a framework into which, from time to time, the personal reminiscences of other witnesses were worked. In every Church the oral Gospel must have had peculiarities of its own, but at the end of forty years a broad distinction lay between the tradition of the East and that of the West.

Our three Gospels are the final result. S. Mark's is neutral, giving little besides S. Peter's teaching. S. Matthew's gives the same teaching, enriched by the accumulations of the East. S. Luke has gathered materials from every available source. Having no knowledge of the subject himself, he has been a diligent collector. Aramaic documents, fragments of the *Logia*, and new contributions are worked up into one remarkable whole.

The oral hypothesis has the supreme advantage of making each evangelist give us all that he knew. He did not pick and choose from an enormous mass of floating amorphous matter; nor did he, by a free use of scissors and paste, patch together cuttings from a number of lengthy documents; but, as a faithful historian, he recorded all that he could collect. And his work was not originally intended for the use of the Church Catholic, but (as S. Luke plainly says in his preface) for the local congregation, whose oral Gospel he had committed to writing.

After these preliminary remarks, let us proceed to our task. Professor Stanton wrote for the *Expositor* of March, 1893, respecting Dr. B. Weiss's theory of the Gospels, "Weiss does not appear to have made any converts. There is an arbitrariness about the explanations offered by this theory which renders it very unattractive." Before the number was published a convert was forthcoming. Mr. Jolley has accepted Dr. Weiss's views, and made them the basis of this book.

According to his theory (1) S. Mark's Gospel was used by the other two evangelists. Mr. Badham denies this. So, of course, do those who hold the oral hypothesis. I think that it is refuted by an examination of the proper names in S. Mark. Under oral teaching I should expect a large proportion of those proper names to be gradually riddled out and lost, especially in the Gentile Churches; for what wise teacher would burden the memory of his pupils with foreign names in which they could take no interest? But if an historian like S. Luke had S. Mark's written Gospel before him, I should expect that, whatever else he neglected, he would preserve the whole of the proper names, for names and dates are the backbone of history. Well, how does the matter stand? I find that out of eighty-six proper names in S. Mark, twenty-five, and these the rarest and most interesting to an historian, have disappeared from S. Luke's parallel passages.

(2) S. Matthew and S. Luke wrote independently, and were not acquainted with each other's Gospels. Mr. Jolley has no difficulty in showing this by comparing Matt. i., ii. with Luke i., ii.; but Mr. Badham is forced by his theory to hold that S. Luke had Matt. i., ii. (or rather the source from which it was taken) before him when he wrote. In proof of this he submits, amongst other considerations, that "the star in the east" (ὁ ἀστὴρ ἐν τῇ ἀνατολῇ) "is surely alluded to in the Day-spring" (ἀνατολή) "from on high . . . to guide our feet into the way of peace"!

(3) All three evangelists drew largely upon an earlier document which has perished. This document, commonly called the *Logia*, is styled by Mr. Jolley the Primitive Gospel, or for brevity P.G. He restores it on the lines of Dr. Weiss, and prints an English version of it at full length. It constitutes the main feature of his book, and he demands for it the patient examination which it is sure to get at the hand of scholars.

I reserve my remarks on P.G. for the present, and pass on to describe how Mr. Jolley holds our three Gospels to have originated. (1) S. Mark wrote down what he recollected of S. Peter's teachings, combining with it certain portions of P.G. Out of his 666 verses, I reckon that, according to Mr. Jolley, 427 are Petrine, and 239 come from P.G. (2) S. Matthew's Gospel—I call it so for convenience; it is really a composite work, as Messrs. Badham and Jolley agree in thinking—is built, Mr. Jolley holds, upon S. Mark, with much more copious extracts from P.G., some personal reminiscences and traditions, "the latter of which are not always trustworthy." (3) S. Luke not only used S. Mark and P.G., but also a document unknown to the other evangelists, and of Ebionite tendency. Out of S. Luke's 1151 verses it certainly supplies 212, probably 218, possibly 313. But this is not all; in the history of the Passion and Resurrection it is largely used in combination with S. Mark. It may give some idea of this document to state that, according to Mr. Jolley, S. Luke's two introductory chapters come from it; so do the stories of the Rich Man and Lazarus, the Good Samaritan, the Prodigal Son, the Widow's Son of Nain, and some other, but by no means all, nor even the most striking, of the narratives which deal with poverty and wealth.

Mr. Badham's account of the origin of the Gospels is altogether different. Whereas Mr. Jolley writes, "The Petrine character of the second Gospel is universally admitted," Mr. Badham denies it. Papias, he says, has been misunderstood from the first. S. Mark, so far from being the author of the second Gospel, is the author of all that is peculiar in S.

Luke's Gospel, of much that is common to S. Matthew and S. Luke, of more than half of the Acts of the Apostles, and of the whole of the Epistle to the Hebrews. Of the second Gospel he only wrote the last twelve verses, which textual critics declare to be not genuine.

Historical criticism has done much to restore honour to S. Mark, but Mr. Badham in this respect surpasses everyone. Those portions of S. Luke which we call Pauline are really Petrine; it is S. Mark's Gospel that was written by an unknown Pauline Christian. These views Mr. Badham published as a Bachelor of Arts in 1891 in a pamphlet of ninety-nine pages. As a Master of Arts he published in 1892 a volume at least six times as large, greatly improved in tone, with new and various pleadings, concluding with the three Gospels in English, according to the Authorised Version, printed in red type, black type, or italics, to indicate the sources in detail. Earnest work like this demands attention. We cannot afford to treat it as Mr. Jolley does.

Mr. Badham holds (1) that the earliest document (A) was written before the destruction of Jerusalem, the next (B) after the flight to Pella. A and B were speedily combined into AB. (2) Somewhat later a Pauline Christian, with A, B, and AB in his hands, but with little original knowledge, produced our second Gospel. This was "an improved harmony," intended to supersede AB, but not A and B. The writer omits very large portions, especially of B. (3) S. Mark in Rome (*circ.* A.D. 72) writes down what he remembers of "the Preaching of S. Peter." His work soon perished, but not before the greatest part of it—in fact, all but forty verses—had been incorporated into other writings. (4) S. Luke composed our third Gospel by combining "the Preaching of S. Peter" with S. Mark's Gospel. He omits some passages, especially of the latter work. He had A, B, and AB before him, but seldom used them. (5) Our first Gospel was made up of AB and a few sections from "the Preaching of S. Peter." Contrary to most critics, Mr. Badham makes this the last of the synoptic Gospels.

It is not surprising that increased examination has caused Mr. Badham to somewhat shift his ground. In his second edition he includes in "the Preaching of S. Peter" Luke i. 5–iii. 3; iii. 7–14, 18–20; iv. 5–8, and many other sections, verses, or even half verses, which he treated differently in his first edition. I think he has rather weakened his case by these changes. Strange to say, in both editions he includes in the "Preaching" S. Luke's genealogy, which would form a curious sermon. Mr. Badham's theories are based upon doublets and inconsistencies. Let us look at the doublets in S. Matthew. Mr. Badham denies that the same document could have held the following doublets. (1) "This is Elijah which is to come," "Elijah is come already." (2) "The sign of Jonah" (twice). (3) "More tolerable for Sodom" (twice). (4) "Trees known by their fruit" (twice). (5) "Unfruitful trees hewn down and burnt" (twice). (6) "Greatest be your servant" (twice). (7) "Every idle word that men shall speak they shall give account thereof in the day of judgment," "Whosoever shall say to his brother, Raca, shall be in danger of the judgment." It is unnecessary to continue the list. S. Matthew uses the phrase, "There shall be wailing and gnashing of teeth," six times; "The end of the world," five times; "Eternal life," seven times. The conclusion which Mr. Badham, it seems, would have us draw is, that when a phrase occurs twice diversity of documents is proved, when it occurs more than twice identity. But will anyone admit that? That there is one doublet in S. Matthew (ix. 27-34 = xii. 22-24) is made probable by S. Luke's parallel. That there is another (xii. 41 = xvi. 4), and several in S. Luke, will scarcely be denied by those who have studied the question; but Mr. Badham's four lists, with an aggregate of one hundred doublets, can only excite our amazement.

Mr. Badham, however, rightly follows Dr. Weiss and others in maintaining that the central third of S. Luke (ix. 51-xviii. 14) is not, as it appears to claim to be, an account of events which happened during the last journey to Jerusalem, but "the mainstock of a record, covering," not "the whole period of our Lord's life," but a considerable part of His ministry. His arguments on this point are mostly convincing. Chapter viii., also, is interesting in its suggestion that "S. Peter's Preaching" is arranged according to subject-matter. In many cases there is good reason to think so. In chapter x. a less successful attempt is made to show that Tatian used "the Preaching of S. Peter," as well as our four

Gospels, in drawing up his *Dia Tessarôn*. Chapter xi. maintains that certain sections of the Acts of the Apostles are a continuation of the "Preaching of S. Peter." He goes further than I should go in extending these sections over the whole book. Chapter xii. deals with the authorship of the Epistle to the Hebrews. Those who think the Epistle to have been written by S. Luke will, if they accept Mr. Badham's views, have no objection to transfer the authorship to S. Mark. To others Mr. Badham's reasons are not likely to be convincing. Chapter xv. deals with the inconsistencies. They are weaker than the doublets. The first I consider the only good one. "How strange it is to hear Christ enjoining secrecy on the leper when great multitudes are present." (Matt. viii. 1, 4.) True, but Matt. viii. 1, I maintain, is an "editorial note." It is absent from S. Mark and S. Luke. It is only one of those connecting links which bind narratives together, but are not based on the original authority, and are sometimes demonstrably wrong.

Mr. Badham assumes that Matt. xvii. 21 is genuine. A critic should take care to use a good text. How strange it is, he continues, "to hear Christ bidding certain women, *All* hail, when the context (Matt. xxviii. 1) only assures us of the presence of two." When Shakespeare wrote, "Cæsar, all hail," he did not imply that several persons were present. The Greek is simply Χαίρετε. A critic should work upon the Greek text and not upon the "authorised" English version. In pages 77 and 78 Mr. Badham gives lists of words peculiar to A and B. He derives the imperative ἐξετάσατε from ἐκτάζειν. When a writer, who is capable of such errors, speaks about Greek style, the reader will learn to discount his confident assertions.

The list on page 77 contains twenty-one words peculiar to A, and the list on page 78 nineteen words peculiar to B. What reason can be given why we should not add the lists together and say that they give us forty words peculiar to S. Matthew? They are mostly such. κατ' ὄναρ occurs five times in Matt. i., ii., once in Matt. xxvii. 19, and nowhere else. Would it not be fair to argue, on Mr. Badham's principles, that the author, who has shown such a predilection for the phrase in chapters i., ii., cannot have written the next twenty-four chapters? In this case the argument, I believe, would be in accordance with the facts, but it would wreck Mr. Badham's theory. But there are further inaccuracies to be noticed. ἀθῷος occurs in Matt. xxvii. 24 only, for it is a false reading in Matt. xxvii. 4. The same may be said of ἀπέναντι, which is a true reading once, but false twice. The accents οἰκίακος, ἡλιός, ἀλαλός, στείρα, ἑώς, ἀνάστασίς, ἐκ νέκρων are wrong. πυρετω, ὡρα (dative), and ἀθῶος require ι subscript. Many of these "peculiar words" are found in S. John, S. Paul, S. James, and other writers; several occur in the Acts of the Apostles, which was not written by the author of A or B.

Mr. Badham has a greater show of reason when he argues, from the discrepancies in the order of narration between S. Matthew and S. Mark, that two documents, A and B, were used and pieced together differently. But even so, he cannot account for S. Matthew's order; he only reduces the number of variations. The explanation that the Eastern catechists omitted numerous sections of S. Peter's Memoirs in order to put the Sermon on the Mount near the beginning of the ministry, and then turned back and gathered up the fragments that remained, preserving in both cases the relative order, seems to me to be far more probable.

The strange difficulty which those critics who support the documentary hypothesis feel about the preservation of the same order of narration in oral tradition, extending, as it does, even to minute particulars, is surely unwarranted. Systems of mnemonics were largely used by the ancients, and they were necessarily based on order and association. There are clergy now who can repeat the litany from beginning to end without book; if they changed the order of a single petition their memory would break down.

It will be seen that both these authors deny the unity of S. Mark, or of the "Triple Tradition," and expand the volume of the *Logia*. Mr. Badham's B corresponds in the main to the *Logia*. Mr. Jolley's P.G. professes to restore it. They both hold that the second Gospel (S. Mark) made free use of the *Logia*. Herein I cannot agree with them. If S. Mark had the *Logia*, why did not he make more use of it? An evangelist who deliberately omitted the Sermon on the Mount, the Lord's Prayer, the longer parables and discourses, when he had them before him in writing, is an incomprehensible enigma.

But the other evangelists are hardly better. What should have induced S. Matthew to omit the parables of the Prodigal Son, the Rich Fool, the Rich Man and Lazarus, or the journey to Emmaus? Why should S. Luke have omitted the healing of the Syrophœnician woman's daughter? The critic who accepts the oral hypothesis has an intelligible answer. They omitted what they had never heard.

No critic who works on the documentary hypothesis has ever accounted for the multitudinous diversities in the identical sections of the triple or double tradition. Those who attempt the task say that the evangelists, although they had documents, and used them as guides to the order, and in a few other respects, trusted rather for their language to local oral tradition, because the congregation for which they wrote would tolerate nothing else. If that is the state of the case, apostolic authority had sunk rather low. Cannot we dispense with these imaginary documents if they were of so little use?

But when once you leave the triple tradition, the question of order appears to be fatal to the documentary hypothesis. Look at Mr. Jolley's order. He divides P.G. into seventeen chapters of about twenty-two verses each. S. Matthew copies them in the following order (to save space the first verse only is given): i. 1, 3, 6, 8, 9; ii. 1, 5; xv. 18; v., 14; ii. 7; xiii. 6; ii. 11; v. 19; ii. 12, 15; ix. 5; xii. 18; v. 15; viii. 25; xii. 11; ii. 18; ix. 10; . 17; xiv. 9; ii. 21, 23; xiv. ii.; ii. 24. I need not continue the catalogue, though I have only come to the end of Matt. vii. S. Mark's order is no better; S.

Luke's is even worse. Did three men, working independently on the same document, ever copy it so erratically? Does anyone believe after this that Mr. Jolley's "hypothesis explains all the facts"?

Mr. Badham's chief argument for identifying S. Luke's original matter with "the Preaching of S. Peter" is the statement of Papias, that S. Mark wrote, "but not in order." Our second Gospel, Mr. Badham insists, is a conspicuously orderly document, because nearly every event follows "immediately" after the preceding; but the central third of S. Luke's is as famous for disorder. Without denying the latter assertion, I protest against the former. S. Mark's Gospel is not orderly. Papias explains why it is not so in the next sentence. It consists of lessons loosely strung together, because S. Peter did not assay to write a continuous history, but adapted his teaching to the needs of his pupils at the moment. A better description of S. Mark's Gospel could not be given. His fifty-six "immediately's" are merely "editorial" connecting links, and cannot be pressed.

We are asked to believe that all the supposed documents, and combinations of documents, came into existence by a mushroom growth at Jerusalem, Pella, Rome, or other places between the years 68–72 A.D., and published, as a rule, before 80. Yet they were so widely circulated that three evangelists, living at widely-severed places, had a copy of all of them, except the heretical Ebionite work.

We cannot suppose that the evangelists got copies sooner or more surely than other men. Therefore, at least a hundred copies must have been made and circulated with extraordinary rapidity. Yet they all perished. Not even at Ephesus, at Alexandria, or at Rome did a copy remain. Nay, such was the ignorance of the earliest fathers of the Church that they confused S. Mark's work with S. Luke's, and the mistake has been continued till Mr. Badham has at last exposed it.

I think it is time that men began to consider once more the claims of the oral hypothesis.

Five years later Mr. Badham produces another book,* in which he comes forward as a pupil of Hilgenfeld, and adopts for a motto a quotation from S. Augustine.

Are we to understand that he has adopted all the opinions of Hilgenfeld to the exclusion of his own? He does not, like Stesichorus, begin with the palinode—

οὐκ ἔστ' ἔτυμος λόγος οὗτος,

or, like an Act of Parliament, state precisely how much of previous acts is rescinded. It is clear from his sixteenth chapter that he has not renounced the whole of his scheme, but there are considerable modifications of it. For in the "Formation" S. Mark is a dull copyist, with little original matter; in the "Indebtedness" he is an artist, who develops a picture from S. Matthew's sketch. We should like to know whether he adheres to his opinions about the author and the contents of the "Preaching of Peter." Must we continue to believe in that, or may we conclude, as he now does, with a thankful

* *S. Mark's Indebtedness to S. Matthew.* London: 1897.

Requiescat, applied, however, to each and all of A, B, AB, and P?

There is nothing absurd in the contention that S. Matthew wrote first and S. Mark abbreviated him. Such has been the belief of the great majority of Christians from S. Augustine to Keim. It was not the opinion of the Early Church from Papias onwards, nor is it generally accepted now; but Mr. Badham wishes to bring us back to S. Augustine's opinion, and it is well for us to consider what he has to say.

He possesses, I think, the advantages and disadvantages of what I may call—without meaning anything offensive—microscopic eyesight. He sees ambiguities, glosses, inflations, and inaccuracies which, to a man with normal vision, are often nothing of the kind. His argument rests upon them, and he fails to take a wider view.

For example, certain sections of S. Matthew—notably chapters viii., ix., xiv. 1-12—present a very much shorter recension of the narrative than is found in the other Gospels. But many parts of S. Matthew are only slightly shorter than S. Mark, while not a few are even longer, and contain the very glosses and inflations which are held to be proofs of S. Mark's posteriority. There is no attempt made to explain this difference.

Again, it has been generally allowed that S. Mark wrote for Gentile readers, S. Matthew for Jews. It would be more consonant with modern ideas to say that S. Matthew's Gospel had gradually grown up in a Jewish community, where it had gathered to itself a large number of Judaic elements, such as allusions to the Law and fulfilments of prophecy. S. Mark, though he was originally taught the Gospel in Jerusalem, had lived for many years in Pauline Churches, and had learned to provide for Gentile congregations. He may, therefore, have allowed a few things to drop out of his teaching which had only attraction for Jews, and he inserted certain explanations of Semitic customs. Concede this, and you have replied to Mr. Badham's chapter on "The un-Judaic character of S. Mark."

Ancient historians claimed the privilege—which is now only conceded to novelists—of knowing the secret motives and private conversations of their heroes. Probably some of the speeches in the Gospels give rather what the occasion demanded than what was actually said. These were literary usages which imposed upon no one. Hence there is no call for the remarks on page thirty-nine about Herodias and her daughter.

Mr. Badham's evangelists are the slaves of a very few documents, but he now allows them the pleasure of an occasional gossip with their contemporaries, which assisted their imagination, but could not add to their knowledge. Has he never heard of the large and energetic Church of Jerusalem, which still "compassed sea and land to make one proselyte"? Did not its emissaries penetrate to Antioch, Rome, Alexandria, and other centres of thought? Did not its preachers and teachers follow in the footsteps of S. Paul, and supply the wants of his newly-founded Churches, sometimes leavening his teaching? And were there not scores of Christians in Jerusalem who had seen our Lord, heard Him converse, and had been witnesses of the crucifixion? Could not they confirm or add to S. Peter's recollections? Could not they fill in his outline sketches, explaining many an ambiguity, and often supplying a motive? The Tübingen leaders placed the birth of our Gospels in the second century. It seems unreasonable to admit that S. Matthew and S. Mark wrote soon after 70 A.D., and yet to surround them with the same atmosphere of ignorance. "These things were not done in a corner."

Mr. Badham never takes into consideration the question whether the oral hypothesis may not be the true key to the synoptic problem. And this is to be regretted, because under that hypothesis most of the difficulties which trouble him disappear. For example, the cumbrous array of primitive documents —supposed to have been scattered broadcast over the Churches, and yet to have perished in spite of their priceless value, and left not a trace behind— vanish into thin air. Again, Mr. Badham's chief purpose is to crush out of their phantom existence, by argument and ridicule, those pets of the critics, Ur-Marcus and Ur-Matthäus. In oral tradition we seldom use these terms; but, in spite of what Mr. Badham has put forth, I fear that most of those who have studied the question will agree with me that they are indispensable under any theory of documents.

If S. Mark in any passage is opposed to both the other Gospels, it is perfectly open to me, as a supporter of the oral hypothesis, to assume that he has consciously or unconsciously departed from his original wording. If he has four sections which they have not, I infer that these were the latest additions to his Gospel. That they should, in taking their places there, thrust out a few verses which once were there, is highly probable; and so Mr. Badham's fifth chapter becomes unnecessary. If many of S. Mark's picturesque descriptions are curtailed in both the other Gospels, the reason may be that whatever is not requisite to make sense, is liable to be riddled out in oral teaching. At the same time, I am free to admit that some of them are later accretions, and so I deal with chapter iv.

If St. Luke omits thirty-six of S. Mark's sections, I can point out that S. Mark's oral teaching was carried westwards about 47 A.D., before the said sections were incorporated into it. If he gives us sixteen scraps out of the omitted sections, I reply that the scraps were sent to him by his correspondents. Thus we secure all the advantages of an oral Ur-Marcus, which is a very elastic thing, without the inextricable perplexities of a documentary one, which is a rigid thing.

If S. Mark contains few of the narratives which appear to come to us from non-Petrine sources, it is because he buried himself in Cyprus, out of reach of progressive activities. If S. Matthew is rich in such new matter, it is because his oral Gospel continued to move, perhaps, ten years longer in Jerusalem, before it was taken to its final *habitat* (Alexandria?). During those ten years it must have been so amplified, corrected, and polished, that the chapter on S. Mark's abruptness is not required.

S. Luke, besides keeping up communications with Jerusalem by letter and visitors, resided in Palestine for two years during S. Paul's imprisonment, and doubtless used his opportunity to collect new materials. Under the oral hypothesis we can explain his order, his additions, and—most difficult of all—his omissions. We can do so without the slightest demand on the reader's credulity, and without making any of the evangelists a literary monster.

In contrast to all this, Mr. Badham accounts for the omissions as excisions! And the only reason for them offered is that a Gospel must be kept within certain limits. Perhaps so, as we have seen above (p. 13), yet the omitted sections contain things which are far too valuable to have been struck out. The difficulty about S. Luke's order Mr. Badham does not seem to have felt. But he does not often consider the points which make against him. For example, he dwells on the abruptness produced by the omission from Mark xiv. 65 of the question, "Who is he that smote Thee?" but he does not tell us how these words, on his own principle, found their way into S. Luke.

It is desirable that a critic of the Gospels should work upon the Greek text, and in a good edition. Mr. Badham appears to work on the English Revised Version, and, when he refers to the Greek, to use the *textus receptus*, not even in Scrivener's edition. How else can we account for κράββατος instead of κράβαττος? The latter form is accepted by all modern editors, and is rendered necessary by the line in the *Moretum*—

"Membra levat sensim vili demissa grabato."

How else account for εὐθέως instead of εὐθύς? How else does he accuse S. Mark of the redundancy, "Them that trust in riches"? Even the Revisers in their margin condemn this reading. Ταλιθά κοῦμι is not correct in Mark v. 41, but ταλειθά κούμ. For κούμει is the Hebrew form; in Syriac the final consonant is written but not vocalised, because it was not usually pronounced. Ἐφφαθά, by the way, is not Aramaic.

Attention to Greek syntax is still more desirable in those who would lead others. And what shall we say of the assertion that εἰς τὸ πέραν πρὸς Βηθσαϊδα(ν) *might* mean, "To the opposite side *from* Bethsaida"? To which is appended the note, "Βηθσαϊδαν may just as well be a genitive as an accusative. *Cf.* οὐαί σοι Βηθσαϊδαν, Matt. xi. 21; similarly ℵ, E, Luke x. 13. Although it is more natural to take Βηθσαϊδαν in Mark vi. 45 as an accusative, it must be remembered that S. Luke may have been influenced by the fact above noticed, that this interpretation is difficult to reconcile with verse fifty-three." In the Greek Testament πρός with the genitive occurs once, and then not in a local sense; πρός with the accusative occurs about seven hundred times. I do not believe that any Greek author in any age could have used πρός with the proper name of a place in the genitive to mean simply "from." Liddell and Scott quote Sophocles, *Antigone*, 1037, but that is a false reading. Granted, therefore, that Βηθσαιδάν is not necessarily an accusative, but a curious collateral indeclinable form of Βηθσαιδά—Dr. Hort compared it with Γολγοθάν—I confidently assert that no native Greek could have understood by it "from Bethsaida." What would be the use of language if "to London" could occasionally mean "from London"?

Again, in Mark iii. 21 the various reading ἐξίσταται αὐτούς cannot be primitive, because no writer in the first century would have put it for ἐξίστησιν αὐτούς. The LXX. are never guilty of such a mistake. As a matter of fact, however, Cod. D. does not read ἐξίσταται, but ἐξέσταται, a mere blunder, which points, however, to ἐξέστη. The Greek of Cod. D. in this passage, as in many others, has been altered to correspond to the Latin, and the double error in syntax and in accidence detects the change. Mr. Badham's alternative suggestion that if ἐξέστη be read, perhaps ὄχλος is the subject to it, makes one ask with surprise, Do you think so?

I have not the space here to work through the whole of Mr. Badham's objections. Many of them are very well known of old. Many of them appear to me forced, exaggerated, inapplicable, or capable of being used to prove the opposite. The cumulative effect is not what he would wish it to be.

The strongest reason for upholding the priority of S. Mark is the difficulty of believing that any Christian in writing a Gospel would deliberately strike out of it what has always been dearest to the hearts of his brethren. Put S. Mark first, and he is invaluable; put him anywhere else, and he is inexplicable. What sort of Christians would desire to purchase brevity by the excision of the story of our Lord's birth, the Sermon on the Mount, the account of the Son of Man in glory (Matt. xxv.), with the longer parables and much discourse matter? The very fact of S. Mark's comparative unpopularity is a decisive answer.

To come to details, I find it hard to believe that if S. Mark had had S. Matthew's ἑκατόνταρχος before him he would have changed it into the Latin κεντυρίων; harder to believe that he altered S. Matthew's τοῖς ἀνθρώποις into the Aramaic τοῖς υἱοῖς τῶν ἀνθρώπων, which misleads some of his readers to this day (Mark iii. 28 = Matt. xii. 31); impossible to believe that he habitually altered S. Matthew's smoother and more polished sentences into the rugged, uncouth, Semitic co-ordinations, with hardly any other conjunction than "and." In fact, that monotonous monosyllable does more than outweigh what Mr. Badham has put into the opposite scale.

If S. Mark started with a small nucleus of oral teaching, and slowly expanded it as his master supplied new class-lessons, we should inevitably find some of those connexions which Mr. Badham thinks awkward, abrupt, and inconsequent. But is not this exactly what Papias says about S. Mark? What right has anyone to transfer the words of Papias to some other document, and then to condemn S. Mark as secondary, for the very reasons which most surely establish his priority?

XVII.

PAPIAS ON S. MATTHEW*

THE writer of this book undertakes to examine the exact meaning of Papias in the sentence, Ματθαῖος μὲν οὖν Ἑβραΐδι διαλέκτῳ τὰ λόγια †συνεγράψατο, ἡρμήνευσε δ' αὐτὰ ὡς ἦν δυνατὸς ἕκαστος, which I should render, "Matthew procured the compilation of the Utterances (of our Lord, in Aramaic), and each man translated them (into Greek), according to his ability," but he would offer something like the following: "Matthew collected and explained the Old Testament prophecies concerning the Messiah; and his treatise was the storehouse from which early Christians drew their Messianic discussions."

There was room in English theological literature for a new work on Papias, for above twenty years have passed since Bishop Lightfoot penned his famous Essays for the *Contemporary Review;* and the progress which has been made during the intervening period in the historical criticism of the Gospels has inevitably caused much of what he wrote to need reconsideration. We cannot think, however, that this treatise has supplied the want.

* London: Longmans. 1894. † v. l. συνετάξατο, p. 16.

The author does not seem to us to possess the necessary qualifications. For example, he tells us, "The word ἡρμήνευσε (= interpreted) may be taken to mean either 'explained' or 'translated,'" and he finally decides in favour of "explained." Now I put it to anyone, whether "John wrote a treatise in French and William interpreted it," can mean anything but that William translated it, or paraphrased it, or in some way made it intelligible to the English reader. In Greek, where antithesis is the backbone of composition, the necessity for so understanding the sentence is much greater, and we cannot think highly of the critical insight of an author who does not feel this instinctively. But this simple fact is fatal to our author's contention, for even if λόγια might mean "(Messianic) prophecies," S. Matthew cannot have filled five books by merely copying them out and writing them down, but we know from Eusebius that such was the length of the treatise in question.

Again, it is clear from these pages that the writer has no knowledge of Aramaic or even of Hebrew. This is surely a serious defect in treating of Papias, and many a weary page does it needlessly inflict upon us. A man cannot satisfactorily deal with the Septuagint without some knowledge of Hebrew. Look also at the following extract: "Aramaic was not a learned language. The Christians of Palestine, whose mother-tongue it was, understood it perfectly. The Greek Christians did not understand it at all. Where, then, is the meaning that 'everyone interpreted it as he was able'?" (p. 4.) Now I admit that Pales-

PAPIAS ON S. MATTHEW

tinian Aramaic was in a very formless and fluctuating state, but Papias does not assert that "everyone" translated it. The verb is in the singular, and the distributive ἕκαστος is used. If three or four persons attempted the task, the language will be sufficiently accounted for. If Papias himself was one of them— and he talks elsewhere of his translations of the Utterances—those who have ever tried to render Aramaic into Greek will feel the force of the self-depreciatory, apologetic way in which he speaks of his efforts.

But if our author is seriously handicapped by his ignorance of Semitic languages, what must we think of his Greek scholarship? Examine the following examples:—

(1) οὐχ ὥσπερ σύνταξιν τῶν κυριακῶν ποιούμενος λογίων, "not as making a systematic disquisition *upon* the Dominical oracles." (p. 2.)

(2) Ματθαῖος τὰ λόγια συνεγράψατο, " Matthew wrote *on* the (Messianic) prophecies." (p. 83.)

(3) καὶ ὃς ἂν μεθοδεύῃ τὰ λόγια τοῦ Κυρίου, " and whosoever shall pervert the oracles *of (concerning)* the Lord." (p. 67.)

(4) διαβεβαιούμενος ὑπὲρ αὐτῶν ἀλήθειαν, "*having* thoroughly established the truth concerning them." (p. 9.) Apparently he regards this word as a reduplicated perfect.

(5) "The word *exotericus* has a recognised meaning which appears very apt for the interpretation of this passage. It means that which is contained in writing as opposed to mere oral instruction." (p. 18.)

These translations are either careless or perverse,

and yet they are thrust on us when much depends upon them. We shall presently maintain that our author's main argument rests on a false rendering of a Greek sentence, and that in another place he takes up a most important position in defiance of the fundamental rules of Greek syntax.

After stating the problem which he proposes to solve by an entirely new method, the writer proceeds to discuss the date at which Papias published his "Exposition of the Utterances of our Lord," or, as he calls it, "Exposition of Messianic prophecies." This he places at "not earlier than A.D. 80, or later than A.D. 98. About A.D. 90 would seem to be the most probable date." (p. 31.) Bishop Lightfoot had given "A.D. 130–140, or even later," and other authorities, who differ widely from each other, have accepted this. But our author argues from the tenses of the Greek verbs which are used that Papias must have written during the lives of Aristion and John the Elder, who had been disciples of the Lord, and therefore cannot have lived much later than A.D. 100. The tenses of the verbs, however, merely show that these two men were living at the time when Papias was pursuing his inquiries.*

* The rule in English Reported Speech is that the leading verb affects all the verbs in the speech following. Thus, "I *am* glad to see you It *was* a fine day yesterday. You *will* be glad to hear that I *shall* commence harvest to-morrow," becomes, "He told me that he *was* glad to see me; it *had been* a fine day yesterday. I *should* be glad to hear that he *would* commence harvest to-morrow," "should" and "would" being not subjunctives but past tenses of the indicative. But in Greek, when the leading verb is in a past tense, although the mood of the verbs following may be changed into the optative or not at the option of the writer, the tenses *must* remain the same as they

The context shows that he did this in the early days of his episcopate, or even before his consecration, a whole generation before he began to write. Why else should he speak of it as a chapter in his history which had long been closed? Why else should he insist on the pains with which he had learned the traditions by heart, and on the excellence of the memory by means of which he had retained them? Here, then, we perceive a mistake so fatal to the whole argument, that were it not for the extreme importance of the Papias question, we might well decline to pursue the subject any further.

The Emperor Caius is said to have expressed a wish that the whole Roman people had but one neck, that he might have had the pleasure of severing it. And a certain class of critics trace everything back to Papias, in the hope that if they can discredit him, they may shake the foundations of early Church history. In this chapter the real question is the date of the apostle John's death, which our author tries to put thirty years earlier than ancient authorities place it. It was John the Presbyter—not John the Apostle —who (we are assured) lived till nearly the close of the first century, and most people ignorantly or wilfully confused him with the son of Zebedee. In

---

were in the direct speech. Therefore the only correct way to translate the quotation from Papias is, "And if at times I was visited by one of the pupils of the Fathers, I would examine him upon the discourses of the Fathers, as to what Andrew, Peter, Philip, Thomas, James, John, Matthew, or any other of our Lord's disciples (once) *had said*, or what Aristion, or the Presbyter John, our Lord's disciples (still) *said*." And upon this way of translating this crucial passage we must insist, though it is not found in the usual text books.

particular, Irenæus, the pupil of Polycarp, had been led in his youth to believe that Polycarp had conversed with the beloved apostle. In later life, he discovered the deception. What was he to do? If he confessed the truth, he would sink in the popular estimation; if he told a lie, he would imperil his soul. He resolved at last to act a lie. Throughout his writings he calls John the "disciple" of Jesus, never the "apostle." Those who were in the secret knew that John the Presbyter is sometimes intended, but the mass of readers are deceived into supposing that it was always the Apostle.

We should have thought that Irenæus (like Papias, the author of the Muratorian fragment on the Canon, and other writers) borrowed the title "disciple" from the Gospels, especially from the fourth Gospel. But in any case we cannot allow the existence of the Christian Church to be ignored. In 180 A.D. there must have been hundreds of Christians in Asia Minor and elsewhere who had derived from tradition a tolerably correct idea of the date of the apostle's decease, and who would thus have had a guide to the meaning of Papias which we no longer possess. It is impossible to suppose that Polycarp, Papias, and Irenæus, even if they had wished to do so, could have misled the whole Church.

The next point of discussion is the meaning of the word λόγια. Our author complains that the early Latin Fathers perversely translate it by *verba*, *eloquia*, or *sermones*, connecting it with the idea of words, oratory, or discourses; not till we come to

Rufinus is the proper rendering *oracula* given, which connects it with oracles, prophecies, and Scripture.

Now the early writers include S. Jerome, who was a practised translator, and possessed a competent knowledge of Hebrew, Greek, and Latin. It seems to me that his rendering is perfectly right. For λόγια is properly an adjective, the neuter plural of λόγιος, which means " an eloquent man." And although in profane authors λόγιον is sometimes applied to an oracle, it is rather as the utterance of the god than as the χρησμός. Our author confesses that he can see no difference between λόγια and λόγοι in the Septuagint. We should as soon look for a difference between "he spake" and "he said."

If we turn to the Hebrew, we shall find this reasoning corroborated. λόγιον commonly represents אִמְרָה, a poetical and rather rare word, derived, however, from the commonest verb in the language, אָמַר, "to say." In the LXX., therefore, λόγιον simply recalls τάδε λέγει ὁ Κύριος, "*thus saith the Lord,*" and this is the meaning which underlies the word, not only in the LXX., but in Philo, Josephus, and the early Christian Fathers. It is never used of ordinary human utterances, but both in sacred and profane writers is confined to the divine. The context alone can decide whether the "Utterances of the Lord" are the Utterances of Jehovah or the Utterances of the Lord Jesus. I deem it therefore superfluous to examine the twenty-six passages which our author has laboriously collected. As well might we collect examples to prove that *text* always means a verse of Scripture.

In a certain class of writers it invariably does so, but if you look beyond them, you will find the wider meaning asserting itself.

Papias uses the word λόγιον three times in the few fragments of his work which have reached us. I agree with our author that there is a presumption that he uses it always in the same sense, but I insist that in the fragment about S. Mark we *must* translate (s.v.l.) "not as though he were making a catena of *our Lord's Utterances*," and therefore I should claim this rendering for the two other passages also. "S. Matthew," therefore, "procured the compilation of the Utterances of our Lord," and the title of the lost work of Papias was, "An Exposition of the Utterances of our Lord," nor do I know of any reason why this rendering should be called in question. Much has been said about the silliness of Papias, but if he, on writing a treatise upon the Messianic prophecies taken from the Old Testament, instead of calling it ἐξήγησις τῶν περὶ τοῦ Χριστοῦ προφητειῶν, deliberately preferred the title ἐξήγησις λογίων Κυριακῶν, so far from sneering at the mental calibre of Irenæus for understanding him to mean "An exposition of the words of our Lord," I should say that no Greek could have taken the sense to be otherwise. Dr. Resch, in his *Agrapha*, has gone so far as to use λόγιον in the singular for every Utterance which he can discover of extra-canonical sayings of Jesus, and I think that he is perfectly justified in doing so.

But our author, following the early Tübingen school, has very much to say about the heterodoxy of this primitive bishop. Papias was not only a credulous fool, but he warned his readers against expecting to find any spiritual food in S. Paul's Epistles. He wrote things which Eusebius dared not, or would not, quote. His book perished because it was shocking to post-Nicene orthodoxy.

Now the quotations which have reached us from Papias are not always very pleasant or satisfactory reading, but we have no right to suppose that they are fair samples of the bulk of the five books. Take a similar case. The fragments of the "Gospel according to the Hebrews" are far from satisfactory, but they owe their preservation to their very strangeness. The work as a whole was so orthodox that S. Jerome, after transcribing it, and translating it into both Greek and Latin, pronounced it to be the original of S. Matthew, and similarly the orthodox divines of the post-Nicene period gave Papias the title of the Great. Should his work ever be discovered—and who can say that it will not be?— we feel sure that it will not shock the Christian conscience. Destructive criticism, we are confident, will profit as little by it as by the discovery of Tatian's *Dia Tessarôn*.

Bishop Lightfoot, following the old commentators, argued that Papias, in his allusions to S. Matthew and S. Mark, was describing the genesis of our first and second Gospels. As far as S. Mark goes, he may well have been right. Of course, our author says that this cannot be so, for Papias complains of lack of order, whereas S. Mark's Gospel is as orderly as any. The answer is easy. As long as men fancy that Papias—or his authority—preferred S. John's order or S. Matthew's to S. Mark's, the observation made by John the Presbyter will be perplexing. But if they will look at the reasons which the Presbyter himself produces, they will see that the criticism is a far-reaching one. The lack of chronology was inherent in the methods of compilation. The Gospel of S. Mark consists of a number of detached lessons, issued originally by S. Peter without any regard to chronology, and subsequently strung together by S. Mark with only the rudest attempt to recover the true sequence. Long consideration of the subject has convinced me that this is the true account of the matter. S. Mark's arrangement is altogether wrong, and therefore the other synoptists, who follow his arrangement, are wrong also. John the Presbyter may well have pointed out this from personal knowledge and conversation with eye-witnesses.

In the case of S. Matthew's Gospel, it is not so easy to believe that Dr. Lightfoot was right. Historical criticism has convinced us of the priority of S. Mark to S. Matthew. It follows from this that S. Matthew's Gospel is a composite work, of which the Apostle can only have written some parts, and the Presbyter is probably speaking of those parts only. But what parts did he write? The *Logia*, we reply, by which we understand those " Utterances of the Lord " which go to make up the Sermon on the Mount and other discourses and parables which are absent from S. Mark, but are found in the first Gospel, and large portions of them in the third. Our author holds that S. Matthew wrote only those eleven quotations from the Old Testament which are peculiar to the first Gospel, and are mostly introduced by the editorial phrase, "That it might be fulfilled which was spoken by the Lord through the prophets, saying."

Of course, our author holds that S. Matthew's supposed collection of prophecies was larger than this. Papias can hardly have written five books to explain eleven texts. And other Gospels, which have perished, may have incorporated the whole, or nearly the whole, of S. Matthew's treatise. In particular, the Gospel which Justin Martyr is assumed to have used, is supposed to have been much richer in this department.

If such a collection did exist—whoever was the author—it seems to me more probable that Justin quoted from it direct than from any supposed Gospel containing it. But what I wish to point out is, that these eleven quotations in our first Gospel are no part of the original work. They are comparatively late accretions, never essential to the narrative or really blended with it. The narrative is older and independent. If, therefore, S. Matthew died, as our author insists, about A.D. 63, having already compiled this book, how much older may the other parts of the Gospel be?

It is clear that the study of Messianic prophecy was an absorbing topic of the time. Every preacher would contribute something to it, and no subject was more popular in sermons. I hold that the collection of Messianic texts was a gradual growth, and that the oldest narratives embedded in our Gospels may sometimes be detected by their lack of this element. Justin Martyr's Gospel quotations present a large number of very interesting problems, but I see nothing in the partial examination of a few of them, with which our author is content, to set aside the account of Dr. Abbott in his article on the Gospels in the *Encyclopædia Britannica.* I go even beyond the Rev. J. A. Cross, in holding that during the oral stage every considerable Church must have had a Gospel of its own, identical with those of other Churches in many points, but differing from them, sometimes considerably, both in contents and in wording. With S. Luke i. 1-4 before us, we can hardly deny that some of these Gospels had been partially committed to writing, enough perhaps to account for the language of 1 Tim. v. 18; but we see insuperable objections to the idea that Justin, in the middle of the second century, when, as he informs us, the Gospels were already read in Churches, used any other Gospel than the four which we possess.

XVIII.

THE GIFT OF TONGUES

I.

TWO rival interpretations, which I may call the ancient and the modern, are usually set before the student in this difficult subject. But the leading commentators in recent years have so decidedly inclined to the modern view that Dr. Schaff, in his *History of the Church* (I. 232), pronounces the ancient to be generally abandoned.

This, perhaps, is saying too much. Generally abandoned it may be amongst those who have seriously studied the question, but as long as the "Authorised" Version continues to be read in churches, the ancient interpretation is likely to commend itself to the mass of Christians.

I propose in this paper to examine the whole matter; and I may state at the outset that, though the arguments against the ancient explanation are in my opinion decisive, the modern is beset by difficulties even more formidable. There remains a third interpretation, which has never made much way, because it seems to possess the difficulties of both the others with the advantages of neither. But I shall endeavour to show that, when strengthened by some new explanations, it is at least worthy of careful consideration.

I take Dr. Wordsworth, the late Bishop of Lincoln, as the most uncompromising advocate of the ancient view. In his Commentary on Acts ii. 4 he maintains that the apostles on the day of Pentecost were gifted with the tongues of all nations, and retained this gift in full force throughout the rest of their ministry, because Christ sent them to preach to all nations; and they being unlettered men, not trained to public speaking (Acts iv. 13), could not, he argues, have done their work without this supernatural aid. S. Peter himself, with his Galilean accent (Matt. xxvi. 73), could never have been an acceptable speaker even to an audience of Jews.

To confirm this view the Bishop quotes S. Cyril in Cramer's *Catena*, "They spake with languages which they had never learnt, and thus was fulfilled the prophecy: 'There is neither speech nor language, but their voices are heard among them.'" And he insists with S. Chrysostom and S. Augustine that "the miracle of Pentecost is the antithesis of the confusion of tongues at Babel. There the one language had been divided into many; here the many languages are united in one man."

Now in the first place, we have no scriptural warrant for the contrast between the gift of Pentecost and the confusion of Babel. Nor is the rendering of Psalm xix. 3, which S. Cyril follows, admitted to be true. The psalmist is speaking of the stars and other heavenly bodies, which have no speech or language, and yet with clearest voice proclaim the

THE GIFT OF TONGUES

glory of God. But Professor Cheyne gives reasons for regarding the whole verse as a gloss.*

In the second place, the ancient Fathers did not distinguish between what is contrary to nature, and what is simply beyond nature's unaided powers. The more startling and stupendous a miracle was, the more worthy it appeared to them to be of God's working. The question, "Is anything too hard for the Lord?" put an end for them to controversy. They had not realised, as we have, the supremacy of law or the uniformity of the divine operation. They would not have understood, while they would have rejected as blasphemous, the assertion of Meyer, "The sudden communication of a faculty of speaking foreign languages is neither logically possible nor psychologically and morally conceivable."†

Far be it from me to endorse Meyer's dogmatism. Till "man is the measure of all things," it is not for us to say what is impossible when the human mind is supernaturally acted upon by the Divine Spirit. A thing may be difficult to imagine and hard to believe, but our duty is to weigh the evidence for it, and not to reject it for *à priori* reasons. But it is when we consider the question in the light of contemporary history that we find Bishop Wordsworth's contention least supported.

S. Paul, who "spake with tongues more than all" the Corinthians (1 Cor. xiv. 18), was once preaching at Lystra when the natives "cried out in the speech of Lycaonia, 'The gods have come down to us

* Commentary on the Psalms.
† Commentary on Acts ii. 4.

in the likeness of men.' And they called Barnabas Zeus, and Paul Hermês, because Paul was the leader in speaking." And they proceeded to offer sacrifice to them. (Acts xiv. 11.) It is reasonably clear that S. Luke, in this passage, intends to convey the impression that it was the use of the Lycaonian dialect which made the apostles so slow in perceiving the intention of the barbarians.

S. Luke carefully records that S. Paul spoke in "Hebrew" at Jerusalem: he does not tell us that he spoke in Latin at Rome. The fact that he wrote his Epistle to the Romans in Greek is an indication that he used Greek in his addresses. And when S. Luke records his sermons at other places in Greek, without any hint that he is giving us only a translation of what was said, there is a presumption that these also were originally delivered in the Greek language.

Again, in the *locus classicus* on the question (1 Cor. xiv. 1 ff.) much special pleading is required to uphold Bishop Wordsworth in his contention that the persons of whom S. Paul is there writing always understood what they said when they spake with a tongue. To an unprejudiced mind it seems abundantly plain that they did not. "If I pray in a tongue," S. Paul writes of himself, "my spirit prayeth, but my understanding reaps no harvest." (*v.* 14.)

Once more, if this view be correct, why should speaking with tongues have been granted at the conversion of Cornelius (Acts x. 46), or at that of the twelve men at Ephesus (Acts xix. 6)? Were they also to become evangelists and devote themselves to foreign work?

THE GIFT OF TONGUES

And why should the gift have been so freely bestowed at Corinth, that S. Paul was constrained to lay down the rule that not more than three persons must exercise it at any one assembly? There was no missionary purpose there. "No one hearkens" (ver. 2) or listens to what is said. For when the novelty was gone, the manifestation was not interesting.

I have shown elsewhere* that we have good evidence that S. Peter employed S. Mark to translate his " Memoirs of the Lord" into Greek for the use of the Hellenists at Jerusalem, and that Silvanus performed a like service for S. Peter's first Epistle (p. 24; 1 Peter v. 12). Yet if S. Peter possessed the gift of languages to the degree which Bishop Wordsworth supposed, no such need of extraneous help could have arisen. Nay, instead of the Hebraic style and strong provincialisms which mark some of the apostolic writings, we should have expected the purest Greek of the age, or even a polyglot edition.

S. Paul bids those who had the gift of speaking with a tongue to "pray that they might interpret." This can only mean that ordinarily they could not interpret. It would be meaningless, if not blasphemous, to pray for this power if they had always a full, conscious grasp of what they were uttering.

Lastly, it has been held to be one of the most marvellous providential orderings which attended the "fulness of the times" that the widespread use of the Greek language made the acquisition of foreign tongues less necessary to a missionary of the first

* *Composition of the Four Gospels*, pp. 15, 32.

century than it has been at any other age. Yet this "preparation of the way of the Lord" would have been wasted if the apostles had been supernaturally endued with the gift of languages.

Contemporary history, therefore, gives little support and many contradictions to the ancient interpretation; and, in the face of these, we do not feel justified in throwing the burden of belief in this unparalleled marvel on the faith of the brethren.

But before we come to the modern view, let us glance at some other less important attempts to solve the problem.

S. Luke's language in Acts ii. 4 ff. readily *admits* of the explanation that the miracle did not lie in the tongue of the speaker, but in the ears of the listener. The speaker *may* have used his own mother tongue, and the several hearers heard the words in the language of their birth.

One speech on the day of Pentecost would thus have sufficed for the fifteen dialects which S. Luke enumerates. And Dr. Schaff actually maintains this view. He holds that the Holy Spirit directly intervened and interpreted the words during their passage through the air, so as to present them to the ears of the numerous listeners, to each in his native tongue.*

But in this way the whole of S. Peter's speech in Acts ii. 14 ff. might have been heard in divers languages, whereas it evidently was not. For S. Peter alludes to those who had been "speaking with a tongue" in the third person. "*These* are not

* *Hist. Church*, i. 231.

drunken, as ye suppose." (*v.* 15.) Which fact, if it does not prove that S. Peter had not exercised the gift himself, at least shows that the manifestations had ceased before he began his address. The very name, "speaking with a tongue," shows that the miracle lay in the tongue of the speaker, and not in the ear of the listener, and this extravagant view may be set aside.

Others have pointed out that the simpler emotions are expressed by sounds which are readily comprehended. Laughter, crying, sobs, sighs, huzzas, the shrieks of frenzy and the groans of despair, are either identical in all languages, or at least require no interpretation. There are songs without words. Music is a kind of language. Rhapsody does not need definite expression. The primitive language of Paradise may have been intelligible to all.

But this explanation, while it comes very far short of satisfying S. Luke's words, " They began to speak with *other* tongues," is finally set aside by S. Paul's testimony that interpretation was the custom. Not only was a man to "pray that he might interpret," but he was to keep silence if none of those who were present could do so. "Interpretation of tongues" is classed as a spiritual gift by the side of speaking with tongues (1 Cor. xii. 10), but a universal language would not need interpretation.

Some, therefore, have pleaded that instead of reverting back to the simple language of Paradise, we have here a foretaste of the complex language of heaven, where all will understand, because all languages will be united into one comprehensive whole.

These, however, are speculations with which it is impossible to deal. Language itself may be unnecessary in the future state. We do not know and it is vain to argue on such a subject. At any rate, we cannot imagine anything of the kind being anticipated on earth.

We turn, therefore, at last to what I have called the modern view.

If the ancient view was founded on S. Luke, and scarcely took account of S. Paul, modern teachers plead with much force that, if we wish to understand what the gift really was, we must concentrate our attention on S. Paul's words, as those of one who himself possessed it, and had frequently witnessed its manifestations in others, whereas it is not *certain* that S. Luke enjoyed either of these advantages.

The late Dean Stanley discussed the whole question in his Commentary on the First Epistle to the Corinthians, and concluded that speaking with a tongue was a trance or ecstasy, which in moments of great religious fervour, especially at the moment of conversion, seized the early believers; and this fervour vented itself in expressions of thanksgiving, in fragments of psalmody, or hymnody, or prayer, which to the speaker himself conveyed an irresistible sense of communion with God, and to the bystander an impression of some extraordinary manifestation of power; but not necessarily any instruction or teaching, and sometimes even having the appearance of wild excitement, like that of madness or intoxication.

He compares with it the ecstatic states amongst

the Montanists in the second century, and amongst the Irvingites of the nineteenth, giving some valuable illustrations.

The Dean of Canterbury, Dr. Farrar,* is more explicit. The *glòssolalia*, or 'speaking with a tongue,' is connected with 'prophesying,' that is, exalted preaching and magnifying God. The sole passage by which we can hope to understand it is the section of the first Epistle to the Corinthians. (xii.—xiv. 33.) It is impossible for anyone to examine that section carefully without being forced to the conclusion that at Corinth, at any rate, the gift of tongues had not the least connexion with foreign languages. . . . They did not speak as men ordinarily speak. The voice they uttered was awful in its range, in its tone, in its modulations, in its startling, penetrating, almost appalling power."

For myself, I must confess that I have done what Dr. Farrar pronounces to be impossible; for I have read through the section in question with all the care that I could command, and have been forced to the conclusion that, though some of S. Paul's illustrations undoubtedly favour the theory of incoherent noises, yet his application of them does not do so, and, on the whole, foreign languages are certainly implied.

Again, I see nothing to indicate the awe-inspiring tones which Dr. Farrar imagines. S. Paul's disparaging words, "Sounding brass or clanging cymbal," "A trumpet giving an uncertain sound," seem to me to be directed against the folly of using foreign languages when no foreigners were present. Concrete

* *Life of S. Paul*, i. 95.

languages are certainly implied in the eulogistic rhetorical description, "The tongues of men and of angels." But "no one hearkens" (*v.* 2) does not imply an overwhelming, irresistible, spirit-stirring appeal, but the contempt of familiarity. It is because "I do not understand the speech" that "the speaker is a foreigner to me, and I am a foreigner to him." It is "the private man," and not the expert, who will be at a loss how to say "Amen" to your prayer, and will think you must be mad. All difficulty will vanish if a version be supplied. And the apostle's sole advice is, keep silence, or "pray that ye may interpret."

If the word "new" were not in all probability a false reading in Mark xvi. 17, we should have the testimony, not of S. Mark, for the passage is not genuine, but of a first century record, that the apostles were to "speak with new tongues." Irenæus* understood foreign languages to have been used, for he writes, "They spake with all kinds of tongues" (παντοδαπαῖς γλώσσαις), and adds that the gift was possessed by many in his day, though he does not claim to have heard any of them. S. Paul's illustrative quotation from Isaiah, "By men of strange tongues" (ἑτερογλώσσοις) "and by the lips of strangers will I speak unto this people," naturally implies diversity of language.

But all these objections, important though they are, become as nothing to my mind compared with the rejection of S. Luke's testimony in the Acts of the Apostles.

* *Adv. Har.*, v. 6, 1.

S. Luke writes that men of fifteen nations or tribes expressed their astonishment in the words, "Are not all these which speak Galileans? And how hear we them every one in our own language, wherein we were born?" Dr. Farrar replies, "We have been taking too literally S. Luke's dramatic reproduction of the vague murmurs of a throng who mistook the *nature* of the gift of which they witnessed the reality." But S. Luke himself endorses their view, for he writes in calm history, "They began to speak with *other* tongues, as the Spirit gave them utterance." We have here something different from "dramatic reproduction." Either we must admit that diversity of language was employed, or we are forced to accept the contention of Meyer, that S. Luke's account is "not historical." And if we once admit that S. Luke's account is not historical, I do not see how we are to hold that the Acts of the Apostles was written by S. Luke or by anyone of the first century. For this is a different case from that of an "editorial note" in the Gospels. Inaccuracies in those were caused by the imperfect knowledge in the editor;* but S. Luke was a companion of S. Paul, who possessed the gift in a high degree. S. Luke also regarded the gift as one of the greatest wonders of those wondrous days. Even if he had never heard it exercised, he must, at least, have conversed about it with S. Paul, or with some other person who possessed it. For, though it had probably become rare at the time when he wrote, it had been in full force during the first days of his discipleship. The

* *Composition of the Four Gospels*, p. 116 ff.

historian of the Church, collecting materials, can never have been so entirely mistaken on a point of the greatest interest and importance.

But further, if it be true, as I have maintained,[*] that the early sections of the Acts of the Apostles are based on oral teaching, the case is still more difficult; for the oral sections must have been drawn up at a very early date, when hundreds of Christians were living who had been present at the Pentecostal manifestation. There is no reason to doubt that the oral sections were taught at Corinth, and even stirred up the Corinthians to covet earnestly the gift. The Corinthians themselves would have corrected the accounts if they differed so widely from their own experience of the truth.

In short, if the narrative in the Acts of the Apostles be not historical but "dramatic," it will be difficult to maintain that the whole book as we now have it was not put forth early in the second century, the former part of it being based on oral teaching altered and adapted to suit the false and exaggerated notions respecting the nature of the gift of tongues current in that age, the latter part on a journal kept by some companion of S. Paul, which journal the editor somewhat carelessly embedded in his work. According to such a supposition, S. Luke cannot have been the author of the book. This view I am not prepared to admit, least of all in support of a theory which S. Paul's words are so far from demanding that they appear to me absolutely to exclude it.

[*] *Composition of the Four Gospels*, p. 91.

THE GIFT OF TONGUES

Must we, then, hold that the gift of tongues at Pentecost was different in kind from "speaking with a tongue" at Corinth? Were the apostles at first endowed with the power of using language which they had never learned, but, as love grew cold or men neglected to put the gift to a proper use, did it degenerate into rhapsody? Had the Corinthians heard of the miracle of the first days, and were they, in their ambition, falsely emulating it? Is there something more in S. Paul's disparaging words than appears on the surface? Can it be that he is repressing the indignation of his heart?

It may be so. Some view of this kind appears to be accepted by the Bishop of Gloucester and Bristol, Mr. Lias, and other recent English commentators. To those who cannot accept the solution which I shall presently propound (and there must be many such), I would commend this as the best escape from the difficulty. The question *how* such power could have been bestowed will then remain unanswered. It was simply the gift of God. But in any case the evidence shows that the gift was granted on rare occasions for a few moments to a select number of persons by the unknown operation of the Holy Spirit. Those who used it, at least at Corinth and in the case of S. Paul himself, neither understood what they were saying nor had any power of controlling the flow of words, save perhaps that of ceasing to speak. And it was simply a sign to unbelievers. It arrested the attention of those who could not otherwise be induced to listen. When it had done that its utility departed.

II.

Having now settled preliminaries, let us turn to the opinion of the late Dean Alford, which is different from both the ancient and the modern view. S. Luke's "speaking with other tongues" he held to be identical with S. Paul's "speaking with a tongue," and in both cases there was, he maintained, "a sudden and powerful inspiration of the Holy Spirit, by which the disciples uttered, not of their own mind, but as mouthpieces of the Spirit, the praises of God in various languages, hitherto, and possibly at the time itself, unknown to them." *

Change "possibly" into "certainly," and this view will meet the facts of the case. The utterances were spoken, as Dean Stanley said, "in ecstasy," the speaker being as unconscious of what he was saying, and as incapable of recollecting what he had said and done when the ecstasy was over, as one who talks in his sleep or in the hypnotic state.

If the reader asks how this could be done, I would first refer him to the mysterious phenomenon of demoniacal possession. If this was something more than brain or nerve disorder, and was the effect of an external power so completely taking hold of a man as to control his thoughts and his words, how much more may have been accomplished by the Holy Spirit? The very term "speaking with a tongue" may have signified that the tongue was the human member used, the thoughts and words were supplied from elsewhere.

* Commentary on Acts ii. 4.

But as the real nature of demoniacal possession is unknown, I would point out that another and simpler explanation is at least possible. The phenomenon of "speaking with tongues" may have been the result of an abnormally excited memory.

That people should under certain conditions speak passages of considerable length in a language which they do not understand, by recalling and repeating what they have heard others say, it may be years before, is a well-tested fact.

In certain abnormal states—as madness, febrile delirium, somnambulism, catalepsy, etc.—"a multitude of facts," writes Mr. E. H. Lecky, "which are so completely forgotten that no effort of the will can revive them, and that the statement of them calls up no reminiscences . . . . may be reproduced with intense vividness."

Persons during delirium have been heard to speak in a language which they had known in their childhood, but which for many years had passed from their memory. And it cannot be shown that any impression once made on the tablet of the mind is ever fully forgotten, for sensations long dormant may be awakened by some startling crisis.

Sir Francis Beaufort, in describing his experience when rescued from drowning, said that "every incident of his former life seemed to glance across his recollection in a retrograde succession, not in mere outline, but the picture being filled with every minute and collateral feature," forming "a kind of panoramic view of his entire existence, each act of it being

accompanied by a sense of right and wrong." *
This fact is confirmed by numerous other examples.

But to return to the question of unknown languages. A case is narrated by S. T. Coleridge of a young woman of four or five and twenty, who could neither read nor write, and who was seized with a nervous fever, during which she continuously talked Latin, Greek, and Hebrew in very pompous tones and with a most distinct enunciation. Sheets of her ravings were taken down from her mouth, and at last it was found that she had been for some years servant to a Protestant pastor, who was in the habit of walking up and down a passage of his house adjoining the kitchen and reading aloud to himself portions of his favourite authors.

In the *Contemporary Review* for January, 1886, Mr. Richard Heath has collected a number of instances of abnormal memory, quite apart from fever, in an article on "The Little Prophets of the Cevennes."

A girl of seven years, who, when awake, was dull, awkward, and without any taste for music, warbled in her sleep in a manner exactly resembling the sweetest tones of a small violin. She performed, in a clear and accurate manner, elaborate pieces of music. A year or two passed away, and she began to discourse on a variety of topics in a way which excited the astonishment of those who knew her limited means of information. She was known to conjugate correctly Latin verbs, and to speak several sentences in French.

* KAY, *Memory*, p. 237.

THE GIFT OF TONGUES

The case of the Little Prophets is still more to the point, because we have not isolated instances, but as many as six hundred affected in the same way at once. The manifestation lasted over thirteen years, bursting out *at intervals* from the year 1688 to 1701 A.D. It did not take place during sleep, but in broad daylight. Children of three years old and upwards preached sermons in correct French, which they could not ordinarily use, with appropriate emphasis and gestures impossible to a child. Some of the sermons were three-quarters of an hour long. The Prophets "first swooned and appeared without any feeling, then broke out into exhortations — fervent, eloquent, correct, well-chosen, appropriate, mostly in good French." There was nothing hysterical or wildly excited about their manner, only they were insensible to pain and could not be induced to stop. "The boldness of the young boy astonished me," writes an eye-witness. "It was, indeed, a marvel to see an ignorant and timid child undertake to teach the people, to preach in a language he was incapable of speaking at another time, expressing himself magnificently, and presiding like a bishop in an assembly of Christians."

All these phenomena, which a few of the priests at the time attributed to demoniacal possession, are confidently put down by Mr. Heath to a memory unduly excited by the most appalling persecutions. The children were one and all repeating the sermons which had been preached by their pastors long before. If this can be done, it is enough for my purpose. We need not follow Mr. Heath into his further contention, that some at least of the children were reproducing what their parents or ancestors had heard long before the children were born. Or, if we do so, it shall be to show that science also demands faith, and that the supposable possibilities of the memory are greater than is commonly thought. Individuals die, but their offspring carry on the memory of all the impressions which their ancestors acquired or received. What we call instinct in animals—for example, the faculty by which a bird not only always builds the same kind of nest, but without any teaching knows how to set about it—is probably to a great extent inherited memory, which is strongest in those who are intellectually weakest. "We are one person with our ancestors." And "if we are unable to conceive memory working at such a pitch," as it did in the Little Prophets, "it is because our imagination, not being adequately sustained by knowledge, is unequal to conceive the degree to which this sacred lore had been burnt into the soul of a long-suffering people."

But I leave this question to the men of science. It is enough for my purpose that they maintain that "it is impossible to put any limits to the power of memory." For if only the more ordinary manifestations of an abnormally excited memory be conceded me, the gift of tongues will cease to be, as Meyer said, impossible and inconceivable. Exercised within the limits which the evidence shows it to have been confined, it becomes so simple and natural, that some persons, who do not greatly value the removal of a stumbling-block from the way of the Faith, will

THE GIFT OF TONGUES

accuse me of rationalistically explaining away what the Church has always held to be a stupendous miracle.

Such a charge would surely be more fairly brought against those who advocate what I have called the "modern view," according to which there was neither miracle nor mystery in the matter, but all the phenomena were due to excitement or hysteria (real at Pentecost, sometimes simulated at Corinth), which the ignorance of the age attributed to supernatural causes.

According to my view, though the means used may have been in large measure natural, yet the providential ordering which brought the event about at that particular crisis was miraculous. It was a miracle, not of power, but of providence. As in the draught of fishes or the stilling of the storm, there may have been little or nothing supernatural in the occurrence itself; the miracle lay in its occurring at the precise moment when it did. The choice of time, the preparation of the speakers beforehand, the selection of suitable words, the restriction of the gift to particular persons betoken the work of Him who 'moves in a mysterious way His wonders to perform.' But the exciting cause may finally have been, not mere mental tension, but the direct impulse of the Holy Spirit working in that way. We do not necessarily destroy the miracle when we point out the means by which it may have been wrought.

If it be objected, that according to my showing there was some degree of deception about it, for the ignorance of the age magnified its mystery, and even

S. Paul cannot have known its real cause: that, I reply, is true of God's working in every age. Our ignorance necessarily increases or diminishes its mystery. If God is to communicate with men at all, we cannot see how He can do so without making use of the state of human knowledge at the time. He who made the bow in the cloud a sign to the patriarchs could not have done so in an age which familiarly calls it the rainbow and explains its origin by the laws of optics.

At no time or place were there better opportunities for men to overhear religious addresses in foreign languages than in Jerusalem at the time of Christ. Pilgrims from all parts of the world filled the city with foreign speech. Many earnest preachers must have seized on the opportunity to make what to many was their only visit to the Holy City a turning point in their religious lives. Such a discourse, overheard but not comprehended, while some foreigner in the market-place or street corner addressed a small knot of his compatriots in his native tongue, would suffice. The words, the intonations, the impassioned appeals of the orator could be reproduced by this marvellous power which we have been describing, as accurately as by the latest discoveries in modern electricity.

In support of this hypothesis, it is to be noticed that they "who spake with tongues" are never said to have given utterance to distinctly Christian teaching. They did but record "the mighty works of God" as any Rabbi would have done. It is plain that the words spoken in the ecstatic state, even when interpreted or understood, were of no special utility to Christians. Accustomed to the higher tone of S. Paul and his evangelists, the Corinthians found little profit in these Rabbinic exhortations. Even the apostle's utterances "in a tongue" were deficient in spirituality. "As it is, brethren, if I come to you speaking with tongues, what shall I profit you, unless I speak to you by revelation or by knowledge or by prophecy or by teaching?" The words spoken "in a tongue" must be derived from some better source than they ever yet had been, if they were, when interpreted, to appeal successfully to the conscience of Christians. S. Peter's speech, delivered in his native Aramaic on the day of Pentecost, has been preserved to us at least in outline, but all the utterances of the tongues, both there and elsewhere, have perished. They contained no new revelation to keep them alive.

Some mockers, we read, attributed the utterances to intoxication. These, as Dean Alford pointed out, might be the native Jews, to whom the strange languages would be unintelligible, while the words spoken in their own language would contain no sign.

We are told that some of the hundred and twenty spoke more than others, "in proportion as the Spirit enabled them to speak." Some, perhaps, used several languages in succession, some only one. They appear to have burst out all at once, mixing with the crowd, and speaking simultaneously. So they did afterwards at Corinth. But what had been effective amongst a multitude in the open air ill-suited the four walls of a church. The assembly became such a Babel that a stranger coming in and not understanding the languages would be likely, S. Paul feared, to account them all as mad.

The rapt ecstatic state, the unconscious utterances, the blank of memory when the speaker regained his faculties will account for S. Paul's classing this as the lowest of spiritual gifts. The recipient was entirely passive. Some assurance he obtained: "He established himself"; but if all our gifts are multiplied for us when we share them with others, speaking with tongues brought no such blessing. When the novelty was worn off, it became a weariness to the Church, an occasion for discontent and jealousy. There was danger that it would cease to be a spiritual power and degenerate into nothing but ecstasy. "In the church I had rather speak five words with my understanding, that I may teach others also, than ten thousand words in a tongue."

We read that the gift of tongues was granted on the day of Pentecost, at the conversion of Cornelius, and of the twelve men at Ephesus, in the Church of Corinth, and in the case of S. Paul. We have no indication of its presence in other churches, nor are we entitled to regard it as anything but rare and exceptional. When, however, it was granted, it was, as is usual with God's gifts, granted with profusion. At Corinth "every one had .... a tongue." But S. Paul's prediction, "As for tongues they shall cease," was probably very soon fulfilled. If, as Irenæus affirms, isolated cases occurred even in the second century, they were few and final. For the incoherent cries of the Montanists, the Irvingites, and others, I take to be different in kind, as it has been usual to regard them.

One difficulty remains. What must we understand by the "gift of interpretation"?

There were no interpreters on the day of Pentecost. The several nations heard their own language spoken, and needed not the assistance of a translator. But S. Paul in the first Epistle to the Corinthians alludes six times to the class of interpreters. First, in xii. 10 he reckons "interpretation of tongues" as one of the spiritual gifts. Secondly, in xii. 30 he asks, "Do all interpret?" Thirdly, in xiv. 5 he writes, "Greater is he that prophesieth, than he that speaketh with tongues, except he interpret." Fourthly, in verse 13 he directs, "Let him that speaketh with a tongue pray that he may interpret." Fifthly, in verse 26 he says, "Every one hath .... an interpretation"; and lastly, in verse 27, "If any man speak with a tongue, let it be by two at a time, or at the most three, and in turn, and let one interpret."

We have seen that if, according to the ancient view, the speaker understood what he was saying, the office of the interpreter was unnecessary; and if, according to the modern view, speaking with tongues consisted of incoherent cries, interpretation was impossible.

According to our view, interpretation would be both possible and necessary; but, as it is contrary to God's usual working to supply supernaturally what can be readily produced by human effort, we should expect it to be assigned to one who understood the language. And when S. Paul writes, "Let one interpret," he perhaps means no more than this. For at a port like Corinth, all languages would be spoken and few languages would not be understood by some member of the Church, which was largely composed of slaves, the very class of persons who in ancient days undertook this kind of work. The "gift of interpreting" may thus have depended on a knowledge of the language, supplemented by the power to speak boldly and acceptably in public.

If anyone thinks that a "spiritual gift" must necessarily convey to him who was endued with it some more distinctly miraculous power than this, let him remember that S. Paul in the same list classes among spiritual gifts "faith," "the word of wisdom," and "the word of power."

But S. Paul contemplates the case of a man acting as his own interpreter, for he writes, "Greater is he that prophesieth, than he that speaketh with tongues, except he interpret," and again, "Let him pray that he may interpret."

We need not suppose that the apostle expected that, though the "speaking with a tongue" was done in ecstasy, the interpretation was to be made consciously when the ecstatic state was over. S. Paul "spake with tongues" himself, and knew the limitations under which the gift was exercised. If my theory is right, the speaker on recovering consciousness had no recollection of what he had said. And it is not probable that S. Paul, knowing this, bids him seek and pray for a new power: a power which appears, at least to us, to be different in kind. Much though S. Paul wished to rebuke the spiritual pride of the Corinthians, he would hardly take this means of doing so.

Did he, then, intend that both the speech and the interpretation should be spoken in ecstasy? This is possible, and *may* have been brought about by the providential ordering of the Holy Spirit, though it is difficult for us to see the necessity of it. As, however, we do not know the extent to which the "interpretations" were exact translations of what had been said, an utterance in a foreign tongue, followed immediately by an utterance in the vernacular, might be popularly mistaken for a speech and its interpretation, provided no one was present who understood both languages; for the general tenor of these utterances must usually have been much the same. Moreover, S. Paul is not describing anything which (as far as we know) ever had been done, or was done, but something which he (perhaps from imperfect knowledge) supposes to be attainable.

But I incline myself to a simpler explanation. The term "interpretation" may not only have been applied to *bonâ fide* translations of utterances in a tongue, but to any utterance made in the vernacular during the state of ecstasy, so that when S. Paul writes "Pray that ye may interpret," he merely means "Pray that your utterance may be granted in the vernacular," that thus it may be directly profitable to the hearers. That utterances in the vernacular were made in ecstasy, we know from the account of the day of Pentecost, where natives of Judæa are enumerated amongst those who heard the disciples speak in their own language. And even the Little Prophets sometimes preached in their native *patois*, reproducing, as I suppose, the words which had been used by the peasants in family worship.

I have written this paper chiefly from a sense of the very serious danger of calling in question the historical truth of the Acts of the Apostles, but also in the hope of helping those who find the common views on this difficult subject a trial to their faith. My prayer is that the truth in this, as in all other matters, may ultimately prevail, whether it be found to accord with my own ideas or not.

XIX.

THE BEAUTIFUL GATE OF THE TEMPLE

Acts iii. 1–10.

THE translation "beautiful" gate or door (ὡραία πύλη, θύρα) is not correct according to derivation or classical usage. ὡραῖος coming from ὥρα should mean "timely," and is applied to fruits in their season or human beings in their prime. The idea of beauty is foreign to it, except as an inference; that must be expressed by καλός. However, already in the Septuagint the meaning "beautiful" is established, and S. Luke, over whom the Septuagint exercised a paramount influence, naturally used the word in this sense. We may therefore set aside the conjecture favoured by Lightfoot, the learned author of *Horæ Hebraicæ*, that ὡραία is a translation of חולדה. Nothing is known of such a name, and the Vulgate rendering *speciosa* points to the sense in which S. Luke's word was understood traditionally.

No other author is known to mention any gate or door of the Temple bearing the name of "beautiful." We are therefore left to inference and conjecture in determining its locality. Opinion has fluctuated, and still fluctuates, between four gates—

two external and two internal. (1) The gate leading to the city over the Tyropœon Bridge, at the south-west corner of the outer court; (2) the gate "Shushan" or "the Lily," leading from the centre of Solomon's Porch on the east side of the Temple to the brook Kidron, Gethsemane, and the Mount of Olives; (3) Nicanor's Gate, leading from the Court of the Women, through the Court of Israel, into the Court of the Priests; (4) the eastern gate of the Court of the Women. That this last is the true position it will be my endeavour to show.

It is well known that there are two words in the Greek Testament which are indifferently translated "Temple" in the Authorised English Version, viz., ὁ ναός, which is the house proper; the sanctuary, the church as opposed to the churchyard; and τὸ ἱερόν, "the holy ground," which includes the whole of the sacred precincts. And as the church could only be entered by officiating priests, the churchyard alone was trodden by our Lord and by the people in general. Herod, however, had surrounded it with highly decorated porticoes, in which people were sheltered from sun and rain in those latter days.

Now when we examine S. Luke's narrative closely, we see that the beggar was lying *outside* "the holy ground"; he asked alms of those who were entering "into the holy ground." After the miracle was performed he entered with S. Peter and S. John "into the holy ground," and when the service was over the people retired into Solomon's Porch, where S. Peter addressed them.

Hence Captain Conder and others have argued

that the "Beautiful Gate" was that which led into the Court of the Gentiles from the city by way of the Tyropœon Bridge, while yet others have fastened on the gate "Shushan"; and for many years I considered that one or other of these gates must be intended. Captain Conder's position seemed much the better of the two, because S. Peter and the great mass of the worshippers would enter from the city by the Tyropœon Bridge, whereas only a few villagers from outside would be likely to approach by Shushan. And the lame man would be sure to select a frequented spot, if he could find an unoccupied corner.

"Nulla crepido vacat?"—*Juvenal* v. 8.

It is, however, much to be noticed that S. Luke fluctuates between "gate" ($\pi\acute{u}\lambda\eta$) and "door" ($\theta\acute{u}\rho a$). (Acts iii. 2, 10.) If "gate" in the ancient world belonged to a wall, and "door" to a house, we may be sure that "beautiful door" would not be applied to any of the outer gates of the Temple, which were highly fortified. Indeed, the Temple was the strongest fortress in the city, and its approaches were defended with all the means known to ancient warfare. A "door" points to some internal entrance leading from room to room. A variation so slight and incidental is surely full of significance.

There is good *à priori* reason to think that the expression "holy ground" would be used sometimes in an exoteric sense to include all of the thirty-five acres which constituted the "mountain of the house," sometimes in an esoteric sense to designate those portions only of the Temple which were really holy, because no Gentile foot might tread them on penalty of death. To these alone, I maintain, could the grander word ἅγιος be applied.

There are seven degrees in holiness according to Jewish reckoning: (1) All the world is holy, for "the earth is the Lord's and the fulness thereof"; (2) Jerusalem is the holy city; (3) the Temple precincts are holy ground; (4) the sacred enclosure within them is in a special sense holy; (5) the Court of the Priests is holier still; (6) the ναός, or sanctuary, surpasses all these; but (7) yields to the part beyond the veil—the holy of holies, the very dwelling-place of Jehovah.

Now when a Jew boasted of his greatness, Palestine is the holy land, Jerusalem the holy city, the Temple the holy place—he magnifies and expands everything in the exuberance of his heart. But the narrower exclusive feeling is always close in the background. "This people which knoweth not the Law is accursed." "All are not Israel which are of Israel." "Israel after the flesh" is distinct from "the Israel of God"; and assuredly the Court of the Gentiles was profane and not holy.

Indeed, there was much to make him think so. Apart from the occasional presence of Gentiles this court was a mart for the sale of oxen, sheep, and doves, and for the purchase of the half-shekel for the Temple tax: sacred transactions indeed; but anyone who knows how barter is conducted in the East will appreciate the feelings of scruple. The loud chaffering of purchasers, the lowing of oxen, the stench and dung, made this part of the Temple profane indeed.

Now there is no question that the Court of the Gentiles is regularly called "holy." Indeed τὸ ἱερόν in most cases undoubtedly points to it or its porticoes. But we have a good deal more than *à priori* reasons for holding that sometimes the stricter sense prevails. Thus in Acts xxi. 28 the charge is brought against S. Paul that he had brought Gentiles "into the holy ground," εἰς τὸ ἱερόν. This cannot mean the whole Temple area, for Gentiles might freely roam over the greater part of this at all times of the day, even during the most solemn festivals. The sense must be restricted to the inner enclosure, viz., the Court of the Women or the Court of the Priests, from which Gentiles were rigorously excluded. In the next verse the same restricted meaning is plainly required. It is probable also in xxi. 30; xxii. 17; xxiv. 6, 12, 18; xxv. 8; xxvi. 21. And if these passages, or any of them, be granted there can be no difficulty in extending it to the third chapter and the Beautiful Gate.

If, then, it be granted that some inner door, leading from the Court of the Gentiles to the more holy parts, is intended, how shall we determine which door? Nicanor's Gate, made of Corinthian bronze, is especially extolled for beauty by Josephus, and hence has been selected by the late Professor Lumby and others. But there seem to be insuperable objections to this view. Nicanor's Gate did not lead from profane into holy ground, but from the Court of the Women into the Court of the Priests*; nor is it probable that a beggar would be placed where few people passed. Moreover, as S. Peter was "going up to catch the hour of prayer" he was not going into the Court of the Priests to offer sacrifice, but into the Court of the Women for worship. Now worshippers entered by the eastern gate, and thus we are brought to that position.

For the Court of the Women was the regular place of assembly for the services. Women sat in a gallery above, the men stood on the ground-floor below. There was, I estimate, standing ground for about 15,000 people, which, except at the great festivals, would be ample accommodation.

Many authorities, *e.g.* Dr. Edersheim, agree with me about the position of the Gate, but not for the reason which I have given, nor with the degree of assurance of which the case admits. The fact that τὸ ἱερόν is used in the New Testament in two senses, has, I believe, hitherto escaped notice, although it is intrinsically probable, and on examination certain.

---

* The so-called "Court of Israel," or "Court of the Men," was not a court at all, but the narrow space between the walls, which were double everywhere.

XX.

APOLLOS

A STUDY IN PRE-PAULINE CHRISTIANITY

WHEN S. Paul in his third missionary journey settled down at Ephesus, he found that a Christian Church had long been established there. Possibly it dated from the great day of Pentecost, when "Jews from Asia," of which province Ephesus was the capital, had been present at the Feast. (Acts ii. 9.) His old acquaintances, Aquila and Priscilla, were amongst the members. His future helper, Apollos, had but recently departed. There were twelve other brethren, of whom we shall have something to say presently, and doubtless there were a few more of whom nothing is known. That it was a small and struggling community is indicated by the fact that it had never separated from Judaism. Whatever of special love-feasts, eucharists, and other Christian ordinances were kept, must have been celebrated, as they usually were in those earliest days (Acts ii. 46), in the private houses of the brethren. Public services were supplied by the synagogue. S. Paul, on his first visit, joined himself to that synagogue and preached on the Sabbath. (Acts xviii. 19.) On his second visit he did so again. It was his rule "to become a Jew to the Jews, that he might gain the Jews." And either experience had taught him how to avoid giving offence, or the Jews of that synagogue were unusually docile. Perhaps, having welcomed the Christians from the first, they had incurred the enmity of other synagogues, and did not like to recede. For in a city like Ephesus there must have been several synagogues. Anyhow, three months elapsed before the apostle found it advisable to separate the brethren.

The first thing which struck S. Paul, on his second visit, and has perplexed the interpreters of the Acts of the Apostles ever since, was the existence of the twelve brethren, who "had been baptized into John's baptism." (Acts xix. 1.)

These men were in the same condition in which Apollos had recently been. The two cases are placed together by the historian, and will throw light upon one another.

What, then, was exactly the position of Apollos, when Aquila and Priscilla "took him unto them, and expounded to him the way of God more accurately"? (Acts xviii. 26.)

He was, we read, "an eloquent man and mighty in the Scriptures." So much might be predicated of many a Jewish Rabbi. But he "had been instructed in the way of the Lord, and spake and taught accurately the facts concerning Jesus." He was therefore a Christian, and, indeed, in some sort, a Christian minister. He was "fervent in spirit," but he had this defect that "he knew only the baptism of John."

APOLLOS

Now when we combine this statement with S. Paul's question to the Twelve, "Unto what then were ye baptized?" and their answer, "Unto John's baptism," it becomes evident that the words are not to be taken in any transcendental sense, but as a plain allegation of fact. Apollos and the others had received, not Christian, but pre-Christian baptism.

It is usually assumed that they had all been baptized by one of John's disciples, and not a few have inferred that the twelve had been baptized by Apollos himself. To me it seems almost certain that the rite had in all cases been administered by John the Baptist in person.

For these men were Jews, and every true Israelite recognised the moral obligation of going on pilgrimage to the city of David at least once in his life. A place like Ephesus sent many scores of Jews every Pentecost to keep the Feast. Jews of Jerusalem also migrated to the city of Artemis, and settled down there for the purpose of trade. It is practically certain that there would be at least twelve men then living at Ephesus, who in their youth had shared in the general enthusiasm, when "all Jerusalem and all Judæa and all the region round about Jordan" had gone forth to John's baptism.

For a short season John had in very truth been "a burning and a shining light." But I see no indication that his work was continued by his disciples after his death. Already in his lifetime he had begun to "decrease." Jesus "made and baptized more disciples than John." And when once

John had pointed out the Lamb of God, his work was accomplished. It was impossible that he should appoint any other successor than our Lord.

Moreover, if these twelve men had been baptized by Apollos, why did he not impart to them his more perfect knowledge before leaving Ephesus? He was in no hurry to go. According to the Western text of the Acts, certain Corinthians, who were sojourning in Ephesus, invited him to return with them to their country. To leave his converts, without so much as introducing them to Aquila, is a more heartless thing than we like to suppose him guilty of. No one can have had such claims upon him as these firstfruits of his ministry.

Aquila, if I read his character aright, was no orator. He could not stand up in the synagogue, like Apollos, and address the congregation. But he had worked side by side with S. Paul at their common trade. And he invited to his house and held private conversations with such as were willing to hear a plain man talk on religious questions. He had initiated Apollos into certain mysteries of the faith, and he would gladly have initiated the others, if they had consulted him.

But we have yet to grapple with the central difficulty of this remarkable narrative. How comes it that Apollos, a Christian minister, "knew only the baptism of John"?

Dr. F. Blass, Professor of Classical Philology in the University of Halle, put forward in his *Commentary on the Acts of the Apostles* the idea that Apollos had learned what he knew of Christianity from some written book, and not from the mouth of a Christian teacher.

If such a book existed at that early date (about 50 A.D.), we should all agree with Dr. Blass that it must have been S. Mark's Gospel, or some first edition thereof.

It is much to be noticed that of late years independent investigators, working on different lines and from different standpoints, have been forced to the conclusion that our Gospels, or their component parts, were in existence at a very early date. We who remember the time when the most strenuous efforts of our apologists were needed to prevent the Gospels from being relegated to the second century, cannot but rejoice at the change which has come over critical opinion. Far be it from me to quarrel with anyone who, being a competent scholar, puts forth opinions so exceedingly welcome.

But still it is our bounden duty dispassionately to examine the grounds for this opinion, and to reject it, or at least postpone its acceptance, if we are not satisfied.

Hence the editor of the *Expository Times** pertinently pointed out that the word "instructed" in the sentence: "Apollos was instructed in the way of the Lord (Jesus)," is the rare and significant κατηχεῖσθαι, "to be catechized," which is expressly assigned to oral teaching.

If this objection could not be removed, Dr. Blass's theory must fall to the ground. And therefore he soon replied to it, and argued that κατηχεῖσθαι has

* *Expository Times* (T. and T. Clark), vol. vii. p. 241.

not a very strict meaning as to where the instruction comes from, whether from a book directly or from a person. He continues that in Rom. ii. 18, κατηχεῖσθαι, and in John xii. 34, ἀκούω, "to hear," are used of book knowledge, even as Plato (*Phædrus*, 268 c.) writes ἐκ βιβλίου ποθὲν ἀκούσας, "having caught up from some book." Thus, he concludes, even ἀκούω itself does not necessarily imply oral instruction.

I find myself unable to agree with these expositions. To begin with the last, Plato is describing a quack doctor, a mere ignoramus, who sets up for a physician because he has happened upon a few pills and "has heard [some prescriptions] from a pamphlet." It seems to me that there is a sting in the condensed phrase: "*Heard* from a pamphlet." Plato wishes to insinuate that the impostor can neither read nor write, but has employed some one to decipher the MS. for him.

Again, the accomplished Jew of Rom. ii. 18, who poses as a guide to the blind, an instructor of fools, a teacher of infants, "cannot be one of the vulgar crowd of Jews, but must be able to study the law for himself, like the Jews of Berœa." True, but even such a Rabbi was once an unconscious babe, and began, like Timothy, "to know the Holy Writings," with other boys at the feet of the *Chazzan*, who "catechized them out of the law." Learning by heart, as I have shown above,* was almost the only conception of education in the East. And the catechumens were certainly not allowed to

* See page 94.

finger the sacred rolls. Their teacher read a passage to them; they (probably) copied it down upon their tablets, and then recited it, like modern Chinese boys, at the top of their voices, until by noise and repetition it "was dinned into them," as the word implies, and so became a life possession.

Learning the law by heart is so contrary to modern habits that a Western reader does not readily grasp the idea. Yet when the Pharisees said, "This multitude which knoweth not the law is accursed" (John vii. 49), they were speaking of men who, from their tender years, had habitually heard the Pentateuch read in the synagogue, and were far better acquainted with it than most devout Englishmen are with the New Testament. Only as they could not repeat it *verbatim*, they fell short of the standard which the Pharisees expected.

To come to the next passage (John xii. 34), "We have *heard* out of our Bible that the Messiah abideth for ever." The Pharisees, who speak thus, may either be recalling the catechetical lessons of their youthful days, or they may be proudly boasting of their regularity in attendance at the synagogue. Or, as our Gospels are not built upon the reports of shorthand writers, but on the free recollections of "illiterate men," the exact words which the Pharisees used may have been altered into what a layman would say. There are plenty of ways of escape for those who question whether "heard" can ever mean "read."

But, indeed, as ἀναγνῶναι, "to read," means strictly "to read aloud," the familiar phrase, "Did ye never read?" points, I think, to the public reading of Scriptures in the synagogue rather than to private study. Copies of the Septuagint may have been fairly common amongst Greek-speaking Jews, but the Hebrew Bible was not so accessible. In the face of "Ye search the Scriptures" (John v. 39), we can hardly doubt that some Rabbis possessed the sacred rolls, but at a later date touching them "defiled the hands," and must have been discouraged both at that time and long before, or such a notion would never have arisen.

I freely admit that the sentence "I *heard* from Mr. Smith this morning that he had been ill" conveys to the educated Englishman the idea that you had received a letter from him in which the fact was stated. But the transference is due to the penny post, which has superseded the verbal message of the courier. My contention is that oral teaching in the time of the apostles was so familiar an institution that the word which denotes it must be supposed to have its proper meaning, unless the context demands some other rendering. Now κατηχεῖσθαι occurs only eight times in the New Testament. And in six of these (Luke i. 4, Acts xviii. 25, Rom. ii. 18, 1 Cor. xiv. 19, Gal. vi. 6 *bis*) it seems to me to have its full meaning. Twice (Acts xxi. 21, 24) it is used in its primitive sense respecting the Church at Jerusalem, which "has had dinned into its ears" the falsehood that S. Paul induced the Jews of the Dispersion to give up circumcising their children and offering sacrifices in the temple when they became followers of Christ.

It may be that clearer examples of ἀκοῦσαι, in the wider sense of μαθεῖν, can be produced from classical authors. These would require to be examined on their own merits. I only ask for delay and consideration before we accept the laxity of use for which Dr. Blass contends. I find nothing to correspond to it in the Septuagint, which has very great weight in determining the meaning of New Testament words.

Dr. Blass admits that S. Mark's Gospel already at that early date must have reached Apollos in its present mutilated form, the concluding verses being lost, which I think probably corresponded to Matt. xxviii. 8-10, 16-20, in the latter of which the disciples are ordered to baptize into the name of the Father and of the Son and of the Holy Ghost. But this admission throws immense difficulties in the way. For if the Gospel circulated so many years during S. Mark's lifetime, why did he not replace these lost verses? He was alive when 2 Tim. iv. 11 was written (A.D. 66), and even when 1 Peter v. 13 was written—probably a much later date.

Again, if S. Mark's Gospel had been widely circulated in primitive times, how came S. Matthew and S. Luke to present so many variations from it? Much longer time is needed for the oral stage to produce the state of text which we actually find in the synoptists.

For these reasons, although I strongly hold that St. Mark's Gospel—or about two-thirds of it—existed in oral form some years before A.D. 50, I do not see my way to concede that the written

Gospel was in existence at that date. I shall offer some further reasons for this reluctance below.

But to return to Apollos. He had been baptized by John. He had been taught to expect the Messiah at once. Possibly Jesus had been pointed out to him as such. He then, according to the Western text of Acts xviii. 25, returns to Alexandria, where rumours would reach him from time to time of what was happening in Palestine. He would hear of our Lord's ministry, of His mighty works, His rejection, crucifixion, and resurrection. For a long time report would give him only the broad outlines of the facts, but in the course of twelve or fifteen years one of those catechists, whom the Church of Jerusalem sent out in large numbers, visited the metropolis of Egypt. This itinerant was neither apostle, evangelist, nor preacher. He had learned by heart, and was anxious to teach others, "the facts concerning Jesus," and he formed a class for that purpose. Apollos became one of the pupils, and, like Theophilus, was "orally instructed" in the way of the Lord, until he became perfect and was able to teach others also. For when he came to Ephesus, "being fervent in spirit," he could not keep silence, but "*repeated by rote*, and taught accurately the facts concerning Jesus."

I once more adopt the Western reading, ἀπελάλει, but I have ventured to assign to it *meo periculo* a new interpretation. The word is so rare that it is only known to occur again in Lucian, *Nigrinus*, sec. xxii., where the authorities explain it "to chatter much." But this rendering does scant justice to Lucian, and is plainly unsuited to S. Luke. It seems to me that as the ordinary sense, "to forbid," found in ἀπαγορεύω and in ἀπεῖπον, is out of the question, it is not impossible that in the silver age ἀπολαλῶ may have been used for ἀπὸ στόματος λαλῶ or ἀπὸ γλώσσης λαλῶ, both of which phrases signify "to repeat by rote." If "to speak off the mouth" and "to speak off the tongue" were English phrases to denote *ex tempore* discourse, "to speak off" would be likely soon to acquire the same meaning.

My interpretation, if true, will give new point to the quotation from Lucian, who is describing the miseries of parasites at their patron's dinner table, and complains, amongst other things, that they are called upon for *recitations* of passages unfit for publication, to amuse the company. At the same time, it is so admirably adapted to what S. Luke, according to my view of the situation, wanted to say, that I feel bound, for that very reason, not to press it too strongly. It is something, however, to have found a meaning which gives point to both passages, and if only the rendering, "glibly recite," be conceded, I shall be content.

Apollos had been baptized by John: ought he to seek rebaptism? His master had told him, "I baptize with water . . . but the Messiah will baptize with the gifts of the Holy Spirit." But the Messiah's ministry was over. He had ascended into the heavens. Apollos could not approach Him. Was it necessary, or desirable, or indeed of any use, to apply to one of His disciples? The question, like many questions which agitated the Church in the first age, was a difficult one. Christ Himself had been baptized by John, and in this had "fulfilled all righteousness." What was enough for our Lord may well have been thought enough for His servants. The catechist, who had taught Apollos, had not been sent to baptize. Like S. Paul, he preferred to keep to his own department. I can well believe that even evangelists were wont to keep the question of baptism in the background, lest in their haste they should introduce false brethren and informers into the fold. Rebaptism is never popular. The Anabaptists were particularly hated. Roman Catholics now on receiving a man insist only on conditional rebaptism, or they would find great difficulties in imposing it. For it is a slur on your original baptism, a confession that your first teacher was incapable. I can well believe that Apollos, knowing the efficacy of John's baptism, and not yet having experienced the superiority of Christian baptism, deliberately decided to abide as he was. And if he felt thus, what wonder if the other twelve men, who were only laymen, should follow his example? Neither Alexandria nor Ephesus had been visited by an apostle, by the laying on of whose hands the gifts of the Spirit were bestowed. And, until he met Aquila, Apollos had seen no one who had received those gifts.

Much difficulty has been introduced into the situation by the assumption that the case of these men was exceptional. The truth I suspect to be that S. Paul was exceedingly familiar with such cases.

APOLLOS

John's disciples were scattered everywhere over the Roman Empire, and S. Paul, in the course of his journeys, must have encountered them repeatedly. Nor were the converts of the great day of Pentecost less numerous or much more grounded in the faith. They had received Christian baptism, and had witnessed some of the gifts of the Spirit; but they had been imperfectly instructed, and their Christianity was defective in doctrine.

When S. Paul met Christians in Churches which no apostle had visited, his desire was to " impart to them some spiritual gift." (Rom. i. 11, etc.) To this end he asked, " Did you receive any spiritual gift when you were made Christians?" This means, " Have you ever come in contact with an apostle? Did he ever lay his hands upon you?" The twelve replied, " We did not even hear that gifts of the Spirit were granted." By this they admit the possibility of such gifts, for the saying of the Baptist had taught them so much; but they were not aware that the gifts were already obtainable. They probably expected to have to wait for them until they reached the other world. S. Paul—no doubt after a good deal of instruction—baptized them into the name of the Lord Jesus, and then laid his hands upon them, and their faith was confirmed by the possession at last of these gifts.

There is something attractive in the picture of the unity of early times, when the ordinary Jew, the disciple of the Baptist, and the full-grown Christian could worship in the same synagogue, and felt no call to excommunicate and curse one another. Let us remember that this was only possible because Christianity was at a very low ebb. These Christians believed that Jesus was the Christ, but in nothing else did they, as a rule, differ from the Jews. They insisted on the necessity of circumcision. They upheld sacrifices as the only atonement. They regarded the crucifixion as a stumbling-block. They ignored it as far as possible, holding that it was only a necessary prelude to the resurrection. They did not preach Christ crucified. The sermons of Apollos differed very little from the sermons of an ordinary Rabbi. The catechetical teaching of Apollos was accurate, but his doctrine was grievously defective. Aquila, who had been trained under S. Paul, felt its hollowness. S. Paul's activity inevitably led to disruption.

We, in these days, may pray for unity and strive for unity, but let us remember that unity may be bought too dear. If we got it by renouncing all that is valuable in our creed, we should have reason to regret that the old days of cursing have passed away.

XXI.

THAT PROPHECY IS CONDITIONAL

WHEN the storm was at its height, S. Paul had stood up as a prophet amongst the shivering passengers, and inspired them with new hope by proclaiming in the name of the Lord, "There shall be no loss of life amongst you . . . . for there stood by me this night an angel of God, whose I am, and whom also I serve, saying, Fear not, Paul; thou must stand before Cæsar: and, lo, God hath granted thee all them that sail with thee. Wherefore, sirs, be of good cheer: for I believe God, that it shall be even as it was spoken unto me. Howbeit we must be cast upon a certain island." (Acts xxvii. 22–26.)

But now the wished-for island, whose name and locality, be it observed, had not been revealed to the apostle, is at hand. They have cast anchor upon its shores, and are only waiting for daybreak to thrust the ship aground and make their final venture. Meanwhile the selfish and cowardly Phœnician sailors, taking advantage of the ignorance of the passengers about naval tactics, proceed to lower into the sea the solitary boat which the ship possesses, and which at the beginning of the storm they had secured with so much difficulty, pretending that they were going to make the ship safer and steadier by extending some anchors from the prow.

A more dastardly deed was never heard of. We may thank God that in these days the British sailor makes it a point of honour to be the last to leave the sinking ship, not the first to make off with the boat and secure his own safety.

S. Paul, however, had been shipwrecked before. He had acquired by experience some knowledge of practical navigation. He saw that when you have four anchors at the stern it was folly or madness to stretch other anchors from the prow. He looked through the lying pretext to the infamous design which underlay it, and appealed to the arms of the soldiers to stop the rascality of the sailors. "Except these abide in the ship, ye cannot be saved."

A period of intense anxiety and peril is a test of character, and the apostle, during this fortnight of storm, had been steadily rising in the estimation of his fellows. The centurion accepts his advice; the soldiers cut the ropes, and let the boat fall into the sea. At that stage it was probably impossible to do anything to save it. And so the men who possessed the requisite knowledge to handle the ship were forcibly kept on board, and by their advice and assistance the seventy-six[*] souls escaped safe to land.

But now what are we to say of S. Paul's consistency? Had he forgotten the promise of God? Had he lost faith in his own prophecy? Did he

[*] See above, page 156.

believe that the reckless wickedness of a dozen men would change the divine purpose towards the remaining threescore?

S. Paul, it may be, held a different theory of prophecy from that which prevailed in heathen lands, and is too often accepted in modern Christian circles.

Let us look at a similar case in his own history.

He was journeying towards Jerusalem on that very visit which led to his present imprisonment, and very nearly terminated in his death.

At Cæsarea, in the house of Philip the Evangelist, he was met by a certain prophet of the name of Agabus. This man took S. Paul's girdle, bound with it his own hands and feet, in imitation of the symbolism of the ancient prophets, and said, "Thus saith the Holy Ghost, So shall the Jews at Jerusalem bind the man that owneth this girdle, and shall deliver him into the hands of the Gentiles."*

The Christians who heard these words had the fullest belief in prophecy and in the power of God, but they did not therefore say, "This prediction must be fulfilled, and will be fulfilled, whatever steps we take to hinder it."

Such a view of prophecy is to be found in Herodotus and the Greek tragedians, who learned it from Persia and the oriental fatalists.

The Christians, having been trained on the Old Testament, were better instructed, and looked upon this prophecy as a kindly warning whereby the disaster might be set aside. "Both we," writes S.

---

* Acts xxi. 11.

Luke, "and they of that place besought him not to go up to Jerusalem."

So then the biblical view of prophecy is that a prediction is not necessarily a statement concerning the future which must at all hazards be fulfilled. On the contrary, a prediction of disaster is a hint, that you may take the proper steps to avert the disaster, a prediction of blessing is an encouragement, that you may persevere in the right steps to secure it. Repentance may turn aside the punishment; wickedness may forfeit the reward.

This is no unwarranted inference. Jeremiah writes, "At what instant I shall speak concerning a nation .... to pluck it up, and to break it down, and to destroy it; if that nation ... turn from their evil, I will repent of the evil that I thought to do unto them. And at what instant I shall speak concerning a nation .... to build it and to plant it; if it do evil in my sight .... I will repent of the good, wherewith I said I would benefit them."*

And in accordance with this principle, although the prophets for more than a century had been unanimous in predicting captivity for Judah, at the very last hour before the siege began Jeremiah went down to the house of the king with the promise that if he would execute judgement and do righteousness the city should be spared.

Look again at the prophecy of Jonah. He made the proclamation, "Yet forty days, and Nineveh shall be destroyed."† There was as definite a prediction as could be desired, and upon it the whole book of

---

* Jeremiah xviii. 7–10.   † Jonah iii. 6.

PROPHECY IS CONDITIONAL

Jonah turns. But the forty days passed, and Nineveh was not destroyed. The prophecy was not fulfilled. Jonah was very angry, but not surprised. On the contrary, it was what he had all along expected. He was certain that he would never have been sent if Jehovah had not a gracious purpose towards the hated foreigner. "I knew that Thou art a gracious God, and full of compassion, slow to anger, and plenteous in mercy, and repentest Thee of the evil."*

Hence, very needless difficulty has been felt about our Lord's parable of the unmerciful servant, in which the master of the house, after forgiving his slave the debt of ten thousand talents, *changed his mind* when that slave showed no pity towards his fellow-slave, and cast him into prison until he should repay the whole of the money.†

To one who remembers the biblical idea of prophecy and divine promises this is perfectly normal. The promise was conditional, and the conditions not being fulfilled, the promise was withdrawn.

The doctrine of God's repentance has been almost forgotten in popular theology. Our notions of God's sovereignty have driven it out of view. It seems so much easier to regard God as absolutely unchangeable, irresistible in might, working out His own purposes in spite of the puny efforts of man, that we end in making Him a tyrant, implacable, unmerciful, as far removed as possible from that Heavenly Father which our Lord came to reveal.

* Jonah iv. 2. † Matthew xviii. 34.

S. Augustine was the first to emphasize this side of the truth, which at one time became so exaggerated that everything upon earth, every incident in our lives, our deeds, yea, even our thoughts were held to have been predestined from all eternity. Yea, a certain definite number of privileged persons had been elected to salvation. And no effort of the individuals themselves, or of their friends or fellow-Christians, could alter the numbers either way in a single case.* Missionary zeal was therefore folly, and a dreary fatalism ate out the heart of evangelistic endeavour.

This was but a one-sided exaggeration of the truth. There is a sense in which God's electing love is true. It is taught by S. Paul, and is recognised in our Thirty-nine Articles. But we must not let it destroy the other side of the question.

Granted that the conflicting truths are irreconcilable by the human understanding. That was to be expected, for God is beyond us, and above us. He is infinite, eternal, past finding out, and not to be measured by our puny thought.

It is therefore necessary when we think of Him to acquiesce in much which we cannot understand. It is easy to believe in the absolute freedom of the human will; it is easy to insist that everything is fixed by fate and unalterable. It is difficult to combine what is true in both systems, and be content to wait for the solution of the mystery until we know even as we are known.

* This perversion of truth culminated in the Lambeth Articles, which are truly blasphemous, A.D. 1595. They never possessed full authority.

Meanwhile, let us hold fast to this doctrine of God's repentance. The language in which it is expressed may be only an adaptation to our human intelligence, but it contains a great truth. It makes prayer a reality, it opens a door of hope to the returning penitent, it encourages us to work for the good of mankind, it restores to us a loving Father, to whom we can turn with confidence in our perplexities and our sorrows, it opens the way for the Incarnation. "God sent not His Son into the world to condemn the world; but that the world through Him might be saved."*

When our Saviour stood before the High Priest on His last trial the Levitical police blindfolded Him and struck Him on the face, saying, "Prophesy unto us, thou Christ, Who is he that smote Thee?"† That is a good example of the vulgar idea of a prophet. But, setting aside the question of our Lord's unique nature, and not pretending to decide what He could say and what He could not during the period of His voluntary earthly humiliation, we must insist that the prophets, as prophets, had no such power as these police attributed to Him, and as the uneducated mind is apt to attribute to every prophet. Prediction was but rarely conceded them. They were preachers of righteousness, not guides as to the future. And when prediction was granted them it was not concerned with trivial matters of no consequence, but with the welfare of nations or of individual souls. The prophets did not speak as soothsayers, but as they were moved by the Holy Ghost; and their

* John iii. 17.   † Matthew xxvi. 68.

utterances were conditional, and not the declaration of an unalterable fate.

Nothing is so destructive of faith as a false or one-sided view of God. The Christian teacher must always be anxious to vindicate God's character. And while we insist most that the problem is insoluble, we most earnestly protest against those easy methods of solving it which end in degrading the idea of God, and exaggerating or denying the liberty of man.

God is supreme, and God has created man in His own image. He seems to have willingly and mysteriously given up some part of His own omnipotence in acting thus, for He created a being who could disobey Him and thwart His gracious purposes. It rests with ourselves whether we will do this. We may become like God by setting Him always before us, by letting the thought of Him rule our hearts, our affections, and our thoughts; by seeking in Christ for the true glorification of human nature, by working in the power of the Spirit till every thought is hallowed, every act sanctified.

XXII.

THE AUTHORSHIP OF THE EPISTLE TO THE HEBREWS

IT has been pointed out by one of our greatest theologians, who has recently been taken to his rest (Dr. Hort), that if we would understand the difficulties which S. Paul had to encounter and the helps which he received in his work, if we would penetrate to the meaning of his Epistles and realise the errors against which he is contending, we must find out something about the religious condition of those Jews in the Dispersion who in God's good providence had prepared the way for his teaching, but in most cases did all that they could to prevent the Gentiles from going further upon it than their prejudices and slowness of heart permitted them to go themselves.

For example, it has now been held for a generation that the heresy which meets us in the Epistle to the Colossians originated from the Essenes. And a flood of light has seemed to be thrown upon the extreme obscurity of that Epistle by this assumption. So teaches Bishop Lightfoot in his work on Colossians.

There is, however, one objection which appears to be fatal. The monastic communities which the

Essenes founded were most of them round the shores of the Dead Sea. A few were scattered over Judæa, and perhaps in Galilee, but certainly not in Asia Minor, much less in Europe. The Essenes did not send missionaries abroad, and were too exclusive and bigoted to influence perceptibly the thought of distant countries. The Colossian heresy is probably to be found in the ordinary beliefs of the Jews of the Dispersion, who, as we know from the case of Philo in Egypt, had often departed very far from the teaching of the Pharisees in which S. Paul had been trained.

Now it seems to me that in the Epistle to the Hebrews we may find something of what is wanted. That Epistle for a long time was but hesitatingly admitted into the Canon, because it is anonymous, and not even a tradition existed respecting its authorship.

We may put the matter thus: Of all the New Testament authors S. Luke alone was capable of writing it. S. Paul, who was rude in speech, *could* not have produced its smoothly-written, rhetorical periods. Of extra-canonical writers who have come down to us S. Clement of Rome is the most probable. But, as Origen says, who wrote the Epistle in very truth God knoweth.

A less discerning age began to advocate the Pauline authorship, which in the Western Church, where the Epistle was generally read in a version, has been extensively held. By this means its admission into the Canon was made easier. We may be thankful for the result, although we cannot admit the cause. Luther pleaded for Apollos, a suggestion which it is impossible to deal with, for Apollos to us is little more than a name.

Internally the treatise contains very few and slight indications of persons, or time, or place. We cannot suppose that the superscription, "To Hebrews,"* is original, and it would be quite easy to maintain that the Epistle was written by a Gentile, and was addressed exclusively to Gentiles.† We should only have one more proof of what S. Paul and S. Luke abundantly indicate, that the Gentile Christians of the first days accepted the Old Testament, and studied it and valued it as highly as they have done ever since.

On the whole, however, it is perhaps more probable that we have here the exhortation of a Jew to his fellow-countrymen. And as he not only wrote in Greek, but gives the clearest proof that Greek was his mother tongue and the Septuagint his Bible, we may be certain that he was a Jew of the Dispersion. What I wish to point out is that there is reason to believe that he had never paid a visit to Palestine or seen the Temple and its services.

For, in the first place, how comes it that not even once in the whole treatise is the Temple mentioned or alluded to? The argument turns on the high priesthood of Christ, a most valuable and stimulating idea,

---

* By "Hebrews" Aramaic-speaking Jews are intended. This Epistle is in Greek, and is certainly addressed to Hellenists. The idea that the Epistle was originally written in Hebrew cannot be upheld.

† The persons addressed are not so much warned against lapsing back into Judaism as of giving up religion altogether, "forsaking the assembling of themselves together" and "falling away."

which is not merely novel in itself, but is not even hinted at in any of the other books of the New Testament, although in subsequent days it was made much of, and has been used to explain the work of Christ far more than the common conception that He is the Messianic King or even the True Prophet.

The writer, therefore, deals with the holy place and the holy of holies, with the altars, the high priest, the priests; none of them, however, does he connect with the Temple, but always with the "Tent of Meeting," the Tabernacle in the wilderness.

It has been suggested that he deliberately ignored the Temple, regarding the building of it as a retrograde movement, a mistake due to the decline in spirituality which marked the period of David and Solomon.

But this is not convincing. I cannot think that the building of the Temple was a mistake, or that the regal period was inferior to that of the judges. Surely it was very far superior, and the Temple was a real necessity. The nation could not have done without it.

Now it would not have been easy for a resident in Jerusalem, who was familiar with the imposing structure of the Temple and with the solemnity of its services, to have shut his eyes to it altogether when he was writing on such a topic. But suppose that our author had never seen it; suppose that his acquaintance with Judaism was derived from hearing the law read, as it was read at every service of the synagogue; and it becomes natural for him to think in the language of the Pentateuch. He cannot

AUTHORSHIP OF THE HEBREWS 335

indeed have been wholly ignorant of the existence of the Temple. Every Jew was proud of it, every pious Jew paid taxes to support it, and every Christian had heard how Christ visited it; but as he derives his facts from the Pentateuch, his thoughts turn more readily to that humbler edifice of which the Pentateuch makes mention.

There are several other things which seem to me to indicate a literary rather than a practical acquaintance with the Jewish ordinances.

First comes the extraordinary assertion that the innermost sanctuary of the Tabernacle, the holy of holies, contained the golden altar of incense. (Heb. ix. 4.) *

We know that the holy of holies in Herod's Temple contained nothing at all, for the sacred vessels which used to be stored there had been lost or melted down in Babylon, and no attempt was made to replace them. But anyone who had attended the Temple services, and seen the priest enter twice every day to burn incense on the golden altar, could never have forgotten that most impressive sight, as S. Luke describes it in the first chapter of his Gospel.

This writer knew perfectly well—for he insists

* That θυμιατήριον means "a censer" here is rightly rejected by Bishop Westcott in his commentary on the passage. The texts which he produces (Exodus xxx. 6, xl. 5; Leviticus iv. 7, xvi. 12-18; and especially 1 Kings vi. 22, "The altar which belonged to the sanctuary," *i.e.* the holy of holies), explain how the author of the Epistle may have been misled if he derived his knowledge from books; but to my mind it is clear that he believed the "holy of holies" to "hold" the altar of incense in exactly the same sense in which it "held" the Ark of the Covenant.

upon it—that the holy of holies could only be entered once a year, and by the high priest alone. He seems to have supposed that incense also was burnt once a year only, instead of being the most conspicuous feature of the daily ritual.

Again, he tells us, "And every priest indeed standeth day by day ministering and offering oftentimes the same sacrifices." (x. 11.) A man who only read the Pentateuch might well believe that every priest was on duty every day; but we know that the priests in the time of Christ were divided into twenty-four courses, which served a week at a time, only therefore twice in the year. We know that the great mass of priests never offered sacrifice at all, and that to all of them doing so was a comparatively rare occurrence.

The writer makes no mention of the Levites, of the musical services, or the chanting of the psalms. These things, which impressed the visitor more than anything, are not mentioned in the law.

And though it would be most unfair to conclude from his silence that our author was not aware of their existence, a Jew of the Dispersion, who only read his Bible, would not be likely to think of them.

In xiii. 10, which is confessedly difficult, I think we have another example of want of personal acquaintance with contemporary Jewish ritual.

The thesis of the Epistle is that Christ is the true High Priest, the only Priest who satisfies our aspirations.

In order to prove this, the writer deals with the

ceremonial of the great day of atonement, which fell once a year.

Why did he fasten on that day? Because it is the only day on which the high priest was especially ordered to officiate.

As a matter of fact, the high priest, if he valued his sacerdotal office, took part in the services (we are told) every Sabbath and festival. But in the evil days of Sadduceeism, when the high priest was a prince first, a prelate afterwards, the religious duties were often disliked and ignored. And in any case, one who only read the law would never gather that it was usual for him to officiate oftener.

Now the law briefly directs that on the day of atonement "the bullock of the sin-offering, and the goat of the sin-offering, whose blood was brought in to make atonement in the holy place, shall be carried forth without the camp; and they shall burn in the fire their skins, and their flesh, and their dung." (Leviticus xvi. 27.)

These were burnt—not as sacrifices; the Hebrew word is different*—not on an altar, there was but one altar for burnt sacrifice in our Lord's time, but as refuse outside the camp. In the time of the Temple, we are told, the place selected for the purpose was that where the ashes of the altar were thrown.

But in earlier times the notion of one altar was unknown. Elijah, Elisha, Samuel, and other leaders of religion built or rebuilt altars on every hill and under every green tree. It is, therefore, natural

* שָׂרף בָּאֵשׁ, to consume with fire. הִקְטִיר, to burn incense, fat, etc., sacrificially.

that our author should—perhaps truly—suppose, as he certainly seems to me to do, that in primitive times an altar of earth was built outside the camp for burning these victims.

That altar, he says, was very different from the altar inside the camp. The latter was connected with mirth and jollity. The worshipper came before it to feast with Jehovah, to eat flesh and drink wine. His family and friends came with him, portions were sent to favoured persons, and the priests got their share.

But the altar outside the camp had none of those symbols of joy. No flesh was eaten, no cakes were baked, no wine or oil was poured forth. All was sadness and fasting and mourning, symbolical of God's wrath against sin.

On this interpretation the whole passage becomes coherent. "It is good," the context says, "that the heart be established by grace, not by meats, wherein they that occupied themselves were not profited." The oldest form of sacrifice, that in which the worshipper came to feast, and to invite Jehovah to partake with him, was not satisfying. The human heart which has once awoke to its need demands something of a more serious nature. Our altar—the Christian altar—is one at which neither worshipper nor priest nor Levite was ever permitted to eat or to make merry. The victims offered upon it were entirely consumed. Not even their skins became the perquisite of the priest.

The carcases were carried, as if under a curse, outside the holy precincts. No room was found for them in the assembly of God's people. They were taken outside to be wholly consumed by fire.

"Wherefore Jesus also, that He might sanctify the people through His own blood, suffered without the gate." The cross — the true altar — was not erected upon holy ground. Calvary was, as we now know it to have been — though no other ancient author gives us any clue to its locality — outside the walls of Jerusalem. And He, "who became a curse for us," endured thereon mysteriously the wrath of God, Himself the Victim and Himself the Priest.

"Let us therefore," the writer continues, "go forth unto Him without the camp, bearing His reproach."

In the early days of Christianity thousands of Jews had enrolled themselves under the banner of the cross, because they could be Jews first, Christians afterwards.

But now a different state of things existed. The Jewish authorities had decisively pronounced against Christianity. The Christian Jew had to consider whether he valued Christ enough to endure excommunication for His sake. Was he willing to go forth with Him outside the city, bearing His reproach?

Many baptized Christians found that they could not do so. They had not the burning faith, the true insight of this most highly inspired man. They looked at things temporal, and were attracted by them. Their heart-strings were tied to the Temple and its services. They had loved the altar from their childhood, had felt its consolation, and were satisfied with it. They could not believe that God would break His covenant, destroy the city, burn the Temple, and overthrow the altar. They were proud of the walls of Zion. They were ready to die in defence of Jerusalem. And so they had their desire, and perished in the breaking of their idol.

It was not every Jew that had so deep a sense of sin, so strong a desire for holiness, as to be dissatisfied with his religious opportunities. To S. Peter the law was a "yoke which neither we nor our fathers were able to bear." To S. Paul it was "the schoolmaster to bring us to Christ," but of itself it made him cry, "O wretched man that I am, who shall deliver me from the body of this death?" To this writer it was weak and unprofitable, incapable of satisfying the longing of the soul. But to less exalted natures it was perfectly sufficient. You committed a sin, you offered the duly-appointed sacrifice, Jehovah was appeased, and everything was well for time and for eternity.

This writer goes far beyond even S. Paul in spiritual discernment on this point. The law is "old and decaying, ready to vanish away." "It is impossible that the blood of bulls and goats should ever have taken away sin." They were but a symbol, an earthly counterpart of the true heavenly sacrifice. Christ, the eternal High Priest, has come, and by the one offering of Himself, once for all, has made the true, the only possible atonement.

INDEX

Abbott, Dr. E. A., 276.
Abnormal Memory, 291 f.
Acts of the Apostles, oral sections in, 288.
— date of composition of, 287 f.
— of Pilate, 183.
Aeschylus quoted, 145.
Agabus, 325.
Agape, 140, 309.
Alexandria, 21, 99, 162, 260.
Alford, Dean, 290.
Allegorizing, 113.
Altar of burnt offering, 337.
— incense, 335.
Ammonian sections, 38, 51.
Anabaptists, 320.
Ananias, S. Paul's rebuke of, 225.
Annas, date of his influence, 182.
Anointing of our Lord's feet, 51.
Anonymous sections of the Gospels, 105, 146.
Apollos, 42, 52, 68, 309-322, 333.
Apophthegms, disconnected, 54.
Aquila and Priscilla, 309 ff., 320 ff.
Aramaic, the language spoken by our Lord, 34.
— the language of the earliest oral teaching, 18.
— idioms in Greek translations, 234.
— writing legible, 60.
Assimilation of doublets, ix, 48, 111.

Assyrian inscriptions, 165.
Astronomical calculations, 182, 223.
Athanasius, S., 205.
Atonement, Day of, 337.
Augustine, S., 153, 205, 257, 278, 328.

Badham, Mr., *Formation of the Gospels*, 243-256.
— *Indebtedness of S. Mark*, 256-264.
Baptismal formula, variations in the, 137, 321.
Barnabas, Epistle of, 199.
Barns, Rev. T., 99.
Bartimæus, healing of, 238.
Beaufort, Sir F., on drowning, 291.
Beautiful Gate of the Temple, 303-308.
Bethany, the Anointing at, 51, 241.
— the unnamed village in Luke x. 38., 26.
— same village as Bethphage? 71.
Bethsaidas, were there two? 71.
Bezæ Codex, 263.
Blass, Prof. F., 312.
Breaking of bread, 140, 142, 144, 181.
Browne, H., 190.

Burgon, Dean, 134.
Burton, Prof., 27.

Cæsarea, S. Luke's residence at, 100.
Caiaphas, 217.
— date of his power, 182.
Calendar, the Jewish, 168, 183.
Call of SS. Peter, Andrew, James, and John, 50.
Camel and needle's eye, 125-133.
Catechists, defence of their existence, 67, 96.
— Eastern and Western, 228.
— modify the tradition, 2, 58.
— wrote our Gospels, 11, 98.
Catholic Epistles, order of, 207.
Census under Quirinius, 183 ff.
Centurio, Latin word in S. Mark, 234, 264.
Cevennes, Little prophets of the, 292 ff.
Chăgîgāh, 173.
Charge to the Seventy, 51, 108.
— Twelve, 21, 23, 51, 107.
Chazzan, 314.
Cheyne, Prof., 279.
Christ our High Priest, 333 f.
Chronology, defective, 15, 21, 33, 38, 105, 273 f.
Chrysostom, S., 172, 205, 278.
Church lessons fix the length of the Gospels, 12 ff.
Churches, Gospels attest the belief of, 117.
Claromontanus Codex, 204.
Cleansing of the Temple, 176.
Clement of Alexandria, 187, 201.
— of Rome, 199, 332.
Clementine Homilies, 67, 187.
Cloak used as blanket, 112.

Coleridge, S. T., 292.
Conder, Captain, 76, 305.
Conditional prophecy, 323-330.
Conflations, 40-55.
— list of, in S. Luke, 50-55.
Confusion of tongues, 278.
Contentment, a false translation, 43.
Converts ill instructed, 321 f.
Copernicus, 224.
Corinth, speaking with tongues at, 281.
Cornelius, conversion of, 77, 280.
Court of the Gentiles, 306.
— men, 308.
— priests, 307.
— women, 307 f.
Cramer's Catena, 278.
Cross, Rev. J. A., 151, 276.
Crucifixion, date of, 147-194.
Cyril, S., 278.

Dalmanutha, 71.
Daniel, prophecy of weeks, 150, 193.
Dates in S. Luke's writings, 75.
— from internal evidence, 106.
— of the Crucifixion, 147-194.
Demons, on casting out, 45.
Denials, S. Peter's, 235.
Dinner hour, 155 f.
Divergences a proof of originality, 123.
Divisions of time, 152.
Documentary hypothesis, 1, 59, 64, 91, 101, 102, 136, 230.
Doublets assimilated, ix, 48, 111.
— meaning of the term, x.

"Early," "Early hour," 153.
Eclipse of the sun, 192 f.

INDEX

Edersheim, Dr. A., 308.
Editions of S. Mark, three, 1–10, 42, 105, 117.
Editorial Notes, 43, 58, 72, 179.
Eleusinian mysteries, 135, 143.
Ellicott, Bishop, 24, 289.
Ephesus, Church at, 309.
— S. Paul at, 309.
— the twelve disciples at, 42, 310 ff.
Ephphatha, 262.
Epiphanius, 183.
Eschatological discourses, 21, 28, 54, 55.
Essenes, 331 f.
Ethiopian Eunuch, 77.
Eucharist, when first instituted, 141, 180.
— in private houses, 309.
— at Troas, 142.
— resemblance to Eleusinian mysteries, 144.
Eucharistic language in John vi., 141, 180.
Eusebian canons, 38.
Eusebius, 172, 183, 191, 273.
Excommunication, 117, 339.
Exultation of our Lord, 52.

Farrar, Dean, 285.
Fatalism, 325 ff.
Feeding of the five thousand, locality of, 71.
Fulfilments of Scripture, 219.

Gadarene miracle of the swine, 239.
Gardner, Prof. P., on the origin of the Lord's Supper, 134–146.
Gates of the Temple, 304 ff.
Gaulanitis, 72.

"Generation, this is an evil," 52.
God, reluctance to use His name, 103.
Gnostics, 187.
Godet, Prof., 152.
Gospels for every Sunday, 13.
— limited in length, 14.
— read in Church, 13, 17, 55, 231.
— Greek oral version of, 62.
— bound in a codex, 199 f.
— order of, in a codex, 200 ff.
Greek syntax, 27, 262, 268.

Halcombe, Rev. J. J., strictures on modern criticism, 195–242.
— dissects and reconstructs S. Luke, 195, 223.
— in error about Tertullian, 196 f.
— puts S. John's Gospel first, 208, 223.
— multiplies S. Peter's denials, 235.
Harmonists' duplicate speeches, 32, 33.
— tortuous explanations of, 24, 38, 149, 178, 235.
Heath, Mr. R., 292.
Hebrews, Gospel according to the, 273.
— Epistle to the, 331–340.
— meaning of, 333.
Hellenists, 61.
Hermas, Shepherd of, 199.
Herod the Great, 185.
— Agrippa I., 218.
Hesychius, 150.
High Priesthood of Christ, 333.
Hilgenfeld, Prof., 256.

Hippolytus, 150.
Holiness, degrees of, 306.
Holy of holies, 334 ff.
Horace quoted, 89.
Hort, Prof., 175, 331.
Hour, meaning of the word, 148.
— of the crucifixion, 147-159.
Hours, two ways of reckoning? 149.
Hyperbole, 125, 129, 187.

Identical passages, 30-39.
Inclusive reckoning, 164.
Intercalated months, 13, 168.
Inspiration, 34, 78, 215, 222, 238, 242.
Interpretation, the gift of, 281, 299 ff.
Irenæus, 150, 185 f., 201, 207.

Jairus, 241.
James the Apostle martyred, 117, 218.
James, S., the earliest Christian writer, 209.
Jeremiah, 326.
Jerome, S., 205.
Jerusalem, 54.
— church of, 258.
John the Baptist, 310 ff.
— preaching of, 40 ff.
— disciples of, 41, 42, 52, 311.
— the Presbyter, 269, 274.
John, S., oral teaching of, 67.
— writes for foreigners, 221.
— corrects S. Mark's dates, 171 f, 182.
— speeches not *verbatim* reports, 216.
— fulfilments of Scripture, 220.
— Jewish feasts in, 184, 191.

John, S., the sheep (gate), 222.
— on S. Peter's martyrdom, 220.
— first epistle of, 217 f.
Johns, Rev. C. H. W., 165.
Jolley, Mr., *The Synoptic problem;* 243-256.
Jonah, 161, 163, 326.
Joppa, 117.
Justin Martyr, 275 f.
Juvenal quoted, 305.

Keim, Prof., 257.
Kennett, Rev. R. H., 100.
Kenosis, doctrine of, 33, 114, 130, 329.
Kepler, 224.

Lambeth Articles, 328.
Laodicea, Council of, 205.
"Late," "Late hour," 153.
Law, the, a burden or a comfort? 340.
Learning by heart, 94, 137.
Leathes, Prof., 239.
Lecky, Mr. E. H., 291.
Lectionaries, 13, 206.
Lias, Rev. J. J., 289.
Lightfoot, *Horæ Hebraicæ*, 162, 303.
— Bishop, 205, 265, 273, 331.
Lipsius, Dr., 183.
Liturgies, 137, 139.
Logia, meaning of, 16, 270 ff.
— contents of, 274.
— Aramaic, 17, 19, 61.
— borrow Marcan scraps, 18.
— how they reached S. Luke, 7, 19, 105.
— undated, 16, 18, 28, 49.
— differently arranged by SS. Matthew and Luke, 19, 28, 35.

INDEX 345

Lord's Supper, Origin of, 134-146.
— when first instituted, 141, 180.
Lucian quoted, 318 f.
Luke, S., artist and historian, 25, 49, 63, 74, 80.
— knowledge of geography, 83.
— a Catechist, 63.
— used S. Mark's oral Gospel, 2, 27, 105.
— sometimes discards S. Mark, 42, 65.
— used the *logia*, 19, 28, 35, 49, 65, 105.
— how he got the *logia*, 7, 28, 41, 64.
— travel narrative, 20, 23-29, 77, 93, 250.
— literary methods of, 20, 27, 46.
— analysis of his Gospel, 23.
— proper names, 74-90.
— omissions, 3, 64, 245, 261.
— dates, 75, 185.
— editorial notes, 179.
— meaning of preface, 68, 78, 92, 231, 245, 274.
— first two chapters, 235.
— characteristics of his gospel, 214 f.
— limited information, 49, 78, 104 f.
Lumby, Prof., 307.
Luther, M., 209, 333.
Lycaonia, language of, 279.

Mark, S., connexion with SS. Peter and Paul, 5, 6, 281.
— lived at Cyprus, 260.
— an annalist, 74, 212.
— a Catechist, 98.
— picturesqueness of, 9.
— priority of, 1, 41, 59, 209, 213, 226, 236, 264.

Mark, S., oral gospel a gradual growth, 1, 317.
— various editions of, 1, 42, 105, 117, 214.
— list of second edition sections, 4.
— contents of third edition, 8, 9, 260.
— not acquainted with the *logia*, 60, 253.
— wrote for Gentiles, 258.
— date of his Gospel, 313, 317.
— unchronological, 15, 39, 176, 188, 273.
— misplaces cleansing of the Temple, 176.
— groundwork of SS. Matthew and Luke, 23, 27, 77.
— SS. Matthew and Luke agree against him, 3, 41 f., 46, 59.
— agreements with S. John, 10.
— describes Jesus as Son of God, 119.
— testimony to the Resurrection, 115-124.
— proper names in, 56-73.
— xvi. 9-20 not genuine, 62, 115 f., 233, 286, 317.
— — whence to be supplied, 122, 317.
Marcion, 202.
Marshall, Prof., 59, 64, 103.
Matthew, S., a theologian, 74.
— peculiarities of, 214.
— some parts abbreviated, 257.
— reluctance to use God's name, 103.
— Gospel a composite work, 38, 99, 247, 274.
— — written at Alexandria? 21, 99, 162, 260.

346 NEW TESTAMENT PROBLEMS

Matthew, S., written for Hellenistic Jews, 257.
— — popular among Gentiles, 213.
— *logia*, how arranged, 21, 35.
— first two chapters, 235.
— contains second edition of S. Mark, 3.
Meals, hour of, 155.
Memory, abnormal, 291 f.
Memphitic version, 205.
Meyer, Prof., 279, 287, 294.
Ministry, length of our Lord's, 89, 185, 239.
Miseries of the lost, 54.
Mixture, 41, 48.
Mnemonics, 66, 253.
Moretum quoted, 262.
Moule, Ven. Archdeacon, 96.
Muratorian fragment, 197, 201.
Mystical interpretation, 113.

Nain, widow's son of, 247.
Nasmyth hammer, 226, 241.
Nazareth, 50.
Needle's eye, 127 ff.
New cloth and old garment, 230.
Newton, Sir I., 224.
Nicanor's gate, 307.
Nisan or Abib, 168.
Nugent, Lord, quoted, 127.
Numerals expressed in MSS. by letters, 156.

Oral teaching during forty years, 243.
— modern instances of, 94.
— learning by heart, 137.
Oral hypothesis, arguments for:
(1) Gives freedom, 1, 20, 56, 138, 259 f.

(2) Accounts for variations and resemblances, 91, 107, 135.
(3) Accounts for omissions, 64, 245.
(4) Preserves the Evangelist's good character, 230.
(5) Does not postulate lost documents, 1, 59, 102, 259.
(6) Proper names in S. Mark, 56 ff.
(7) — S. Luke, 74, 87 ff.
(8) Assimilation of doublets, ix, 48, 111.
(9) Patristic quotations, 101.
— objections considered, 91.
— value in apologetics, 103, 135.
Order, variations in, 17, 22, 35, 254.
— according to subject matter, 65.
— — locality, 67.
— essential in mnemonics, 66.
Origen, 205, 332.

Papias, Bishop of Hierapolis, a native of Asia Minor, 150.
— says that S. Mark was S. Peter's translator, 5, 247, 257.
— — did not write in order, 11, 77, 177, 231, 255.
— that S. Matthew wrote the *logia* in Hebrew, 16, 265-276.
— his "expositions," 17.
Papyrus used for MSS., 199.
Parables, the seven, in Matt. xiii., 21, 28.
Paschal Lamb, 169, 173.
Passion, history of the, 2, 106.
Passover, 179.
Patristic quotations, 101.

INDEX

Paul, S., order of his epistles, 207, 210.
— speech before the Sanhedrin, 225.
— shipwreck, 323 f.
— Acts of, 199.
— unpopularity of, 143.
Pella, 248, 255.
Pentecost, speaking with tongues at, 283.
Peræan Ministry, 24.
Peter, S., his denials, 235.
— resides at Joppa, 117.
— speeches in the Acts, 211.
— Herod tries to murder, 218.
— connexion with S. Mark, 5. 6, 93, 177, 244.
— his "Memoirs" in Aramaic, 61, 98, 105.
— — defective in dates and proper names, 68.
— Gospel according to, 159, 198.
— Revelation of, 199.
Pharisees accuse our Lord of being in league with Satan, 46.
— our Lord eats with, 53.
— discourse at breakfast table of, 53.
— — dinner table, 54.
— woes against, 21, 28.
Philip the evangelist, 325.
Philippi, S. Luke's home, 99, 105.
Philo, 332.
Phœnician sailors, 323 f.
Pilate, 217.
— date of, 182.
— Acts of, 183.
Plato quoted, 130.
Plummer, Dr., 27.
Polycarp, 150, 172, 207.
Popularity of the early Christians, 117, 218.

Prayer, 52.
"Preparation," meaning of, 159.
Pre-Pauline Christianity, 309-322.
— beliefs, 322, 339 f.
Priests seldom officiated, 336.
"Primitive Gospel," 246 ff.
Prodigal Son, 29, 247.
Progressive revelation, 217.
Proper names in S. Mark, 56-74.
— S. Luke, 74-90.
Prophecy conditional, 323-330.
"Prophesy, thou Christ," 329.
Ptolemaic astronomy, 223.
Purse, 111.

Quartodecimans, 12, 172.
Quirinius, census of, 187.

Ramsay, Prof., 77, 84, 151, 188 ff.
Rebaptism, 320.
Repentance, God's, 327.
Repetition of utterances improbable, 32, 33, 37, 49, 176.
Resch, Dr. A., 272.
Resurrection, an historical fact, 123.
— five accounts of, 123.
— S. Mark's testimony to, 115-124.
Revelations, S. Paul's, 139.
Rich man and Lazarus, 29, 131, 247.
Robinson, Prof. J. A., 100.

Sabbath, 160.
— synonym for festival? 166.
Sacrifices, ancient idea of, 145, 181, 338.
— favour the rich, 131.
Sahidic version, 205.
Salmon, Rev. Provost, 96.
Salt, ceremony of eating, 144.

Samaritan, the Good, 52, 247.
Sanday, Prof., 59, 68, 97, 175.
Satan, our Lord's miracles attributed to, 46.
Schaff, Dr., 277.
Schleiermacher, 196.
Scraps of S. Mark, 7.
"Sell your cloak and buy a sword," 104-114.
Semitic co-ordination of sentences, 264.
Sermon on the Mount, 21, 28, 50.
Shakespeare quoted, 126.
Shipwreck, S. Paul's, 323.
Shoes and staff forbidden? 108 ff.
Shushan, 305.
Sign from heaven demanded, 48.
Silvanus, 62, 281.
Silver coins, 107 f.
Smith, Mr., of Jordanhill, 84.
— Prof. W. Robertson, 145.
Son of Man, 234, 264.
Southey quoted, 129.
Spiritual gifts, 321.
Stanley, Dean, 284.
Stanton, Prof., 62, 66, 103, 245.
Stesichorus quoted, 256.
Sunday services, 13.
Synagogues used by Christians, 309.
Synoptists differ from S. John about the day of the crucifixion, 170 ff.
— misplace cleansing of the Temple, 176.
— are not chronological, 177.
Syria, 99.
Syrian versions, 204 f.
Syrophœnician woman, 240.

Talitha cumi, 262.

Tatian's Dia Tessarôn, 38, 51, 108, 198, 202, 230, 250, 273.
Temple, Beautiful Gate of, 303-308.
— not mentioned in the Epistle to the Hebrews, 333.
— not a retrogression, 333.
— Zerubbabel's, 185.
Tertullian, 196 f., 202, 224.
Theodoret, 109.
Theophilus, 68, 97.
Theudas, 190.
Thursday, day of crucifixion? 159 ff.
Tiberius, 186.
Tongues, the gift of, 277-302.
— confusion of, 278.
Tradition, oral, 139.
Translation never exact, 18.
Travel-narrative, S. Luke's, 20, 23-29, 77, 93.
Trilogy of parables, 29.
Troas, the Eucharist at, 142.
Tübingen critics, 259, 272.
Twelve, an address to the, 53.
Twelve tribes, names of the, 237.
Twidale, Rev. T., 95.

Unconscious cerebration, 107.
Unchronological arrangement, 22, 50.
Unity may be bought too dear, 322.
Unjust Steward, 29.
Unleavened bread, eight days of, 161.
Unmerciful servant, the, 327.
Ur-Marcus, 1, 259 f.
Ur-Matthäus, 259.

Weiss, Prof. B., 245, 250.

INDEX

Westcott, Bishop, supporter of oral tradition, 138.
— on reckoning of hours, 149.
— crucifixion on Thursday, 159.
— length of our Lord's ministry, 186.
— abused by Halcombe, 195.
Western order of Gospels, 204.
— readings, 312, 318.
Woods, Rev. F. H., 66.
World, teaching respecting the, 219.
Wordsworth, Ch., Bishop, 278.

Year of the crucifixion, 182-194.

ἀγάπη, 140.
ἅγιος, 306.
ἀθῷος, 252.
ἀκούω, 314, 317.
ἀμφιάζει, 31.
ἀμφιέννυσιν, 31.
ἀναγνῶναι, 315.
ἀνάκρισις, 150.
ἀνατολή, 246.
ἀπαγορεύω, 319.
ἀπελάλει, 318.
ἀπεῖπον, 319.
ἀπέναντι, 252.
ἀπὸ γλώσσης λαλεῖν, 319.
ἀπὸ στόματος λαλεῖν, 319.
αὐτάρκης, 43.
διαβεβαιούμενος, 267.
ἑκατοντάρχης, 234, 264.
ἐν τῷ λαλῆσαι, 27.
ἐξετάσατε, 252.
ἐξήγησις, 272.
ἐξίσταται, 263.
ἑτερογλώσσοις, 286.
ἐφοβοῦντο γάρ, 1.
ἡρμήνευσε, 266.
θυμιατήριον, 335.
θύρα, 305.
ἱερόν, 304, 307.
καθεξῆς, 232.
καλός, 303.
κάμιλος, 127.
κατηχεῖσθαι, 313, 316.
κατ' ὄναρ, 252.
κράβαττος, 261.
κυριακῶν λογίων σύνταξις, 267.
λόγιον, 266, 270, 272.
μήπω, 120.
μοῖραν νέμειν, 145.
ναός, 304, 306.
νυχθήμερον, 163.
ὄψε, ὀψία, 153.
παράδοσις, 139.
παραδοῦναι, 139.
παραλαβεῖν, 139.
πρὸς Βηθσαϊδάν, 262.
πρωΐ πρωΐα, 148, 153.
πύλη, 305.
ῥάβδος, 109.
σοε, 157.
συνεγράψατο, 16, 264.
συνετάξατο, 16, 264.
τοῖς υἱοῖς τῶν ἀνθρώπων, 264.
χαίρετε, 251.
ὡραῖος, 303.

PLYMOUTH
WILLIAM BRENDON AND SON
PRINTERS

A CATALOGUE OF BOOKS AND ANNOUNCEMENTS OF METHUEN AND COMPANY PUBLISHERS : LONDON 36 ESSEX STREET W.C.

CONTENTS

	PAGE
FORTHCOMING BOOKS,	2
POETRY,	12
BELLES LETTRES, ANTHOLOGIES, ETC.	12
ILLUSTRATED AND GIFT BOOKS,	16
HISTORY,	17
BIOGRAPHY,	19
TRAVEL, ADVENTURE AND TOPOGRAPHY,	21
NAVAL AND MILITARY,	23
GENERAL LITERATURE,	24
PHILOSOPHY,	26
SCIENCE,	27
THEOLOGY,	27
FICTION,	32
BOOKS FOR BOYS AND GIRLS,	42
THE PEACOCK LIBRARY,	42
UNIVERSITY EXTENSION SERIES,	42
SOCIAL QUESTIONS OF TO-DAY	43
CLASSICAL TRANSLATIONS,	44
EDUCATIONAL BOOKS,	44

JULY 1901

JULY 1901.

MESSRS. METHUEN'S ANNOUNCEMENTS

Belles Lettres

STUDIES IN DANTE. By PAGET TOYNBEE. *Crown 8vo. 6s.*
Among the subjects dealt with are 'Dante's Latin Dictionary,' 'Dante and the Lancelot Romance,' Dante's references to Pythagoras, Dante's obligations to Alfraganus, to Orosius, to Albertus Magnus; Dante's theories as to the spots on the moon, the seven examples of munificence in the Convivio, the Commentary of Benvenuto da Imola on the *Divina Commedia*, etc., etc.

Methuen's Standard Library

THE FRENCH REVOLUTION. By THOMAS CARLYLE. Edited by C. R. L. FLETCHER, Fellow of Magdalen College, Oxford. *Three Volumes. Crown 8vo. 6s. each.*
This edition is magnificently equipped with notes by a scholar who has given three years to its preparation.

THE LIFE AND LETTERS OF OLIVER CROMWELL. By THOMAS CARLYLE. With an Introduction by C. H. FIRTH, M.A., and Notes and Appendices by Mrs. LOMAS. *Three Volumes. 6s. each.*
This edition is brought up to the standard of modern scholarship by the addition of numerous new letters of Cromwell, and by the correction of many errors which recent research has discovered.

CRITICAL AND HISTORICAL ESSAYS. By LORD MACAULAY. Edited by F. C. MONTAGUE, M.A. *Three Volumes. Crown 8vo. 6s. each.*
The only edition of this book completely annotated.

Little Biographies

Fcap. 8vo. Each Volume, cloth, 3s. 6d.; leather, 4s. net.

Messrs. METHUEN are publishing a new series bearing the above title. Each book contains the biography of a character famous in war, art, literature or science, and is written by an acknowledged expert. The books are charmingly produced and well illustrated. They form delightful gift books.

THE LIFE OF JOHN HOWARD. By E. C. S. GIBSON, D.D., Vicar of Leeds. With 12 Illustrations.

The Works of Shakespeare

General Editor, EDWARD DOWDEN, Litt. D.

Messrs. METHUEN are publishing an Edition of Shakespeare in single Plays. Each play is edited with a full Introduction, Textual Notes, and a Commentary at the foot of the page.

KING LEAR. Edited by W. J. CRAIG. *Demy 8vo.* 3s. 6d.

The Little Library

'The volumes are compact in size, printed on thin but good paper in clear type, prettily and at the same time strongly bound, and altogether good to look upon and handle.'—*Outlook.*

Pott 8vo. Each Volume, cloth, 1s. 6d. *net; leather,* 2s. 6d. *net.*

Messrs. METHUEN are producing a series of small books under the above title, containing some of the famous books in English and other literatures, in the domains of fiction, poetry, and belles lettres. The series contains several volumes of selections in prose and verse.

The books are edited with the most sympathetic and scholarly care. Each one contains an Introduction which gives (1) a short biography of the author, (2) a critical estimate of the book. Where they are necessary, short notes are added at the foot of the page.

Each book has a portrait or frontispiece in photogravure, and the volumes are produced with great care in a style uniform with that of 'The Library of Devotion.'

CHRISTMAS BOOKS. By W. M. THACKERAY. Edited by S. GWYNN.

ESMOND. By W. M. THACKERAY. Edited by S. GWYNN.

CHRISTMAS BOOKS. By CHARLES DICKENS. Edited by GEORGE GISSING.

THE EARLY POEMS OF ROBERT BROWNING. Edited by W. H. GRIFFIN.

OUR VILLAGE. By Miss MITFORD. (First Series.) Edited by E. V. LUCAS.

THE COMPLEAT ANGLER. By ISAAC WALTON. Edited by J. BUCHAN.

THE ESSAYS OF ELIA; First and Second Series. By CHARLES LAMB. Edited by E. V. LUCAS.

STEPS TO THE TEMPLE, AND OTHER POEMS. By ROBERT CRASHAW. Edited by EDWARD HUTTON.

A SENTIMENTAL JOURNEY. By LAURENCE STERNE. Edited by H. W. PAUL.

Illustrated Books and Books for Children

THE ESSAYS OF ELIA. By CHARLES LAMB. With 70 Illustrations by A. GARTH JONES, and an Introduction by E. V. LUCAS. *Demy 8vo.* 10s. 6d.

This is probably the most beautiful edition of Lamb's Essays that has ever been published. The illustrations display the most remarkable sympathy, insight, and skill, and the introduction is by a critic whose knowledge of Lamb is unrivalled.

THE VISIT TO LONDON. Described in verse by E. V. LUCAS, and in coloured pictures by F. D. BEDFORD. *Small 4to.* 6s.

This charming book describes the introduction of a country child to the delights and sights of London. It is the result of a well-known partnership between author and artist.

A GALLANT QUAKER. By Mrs. MARGARET H. ROBERTSON. Illustrated by F. BUCKLAND. *Crown 8vo.* 6s.

The Little Blue Books for Children.
Edited by E. V. LUCAS.

Illustrated. Square Fcap, 8vo. 2s. 6d.

Messrs. METHUEN have in preparation a series of children's books under the above general title. The aim of the editor is to get entertaining or exciting stories about normal children, the moral of which is implied rather than expressed. The books will be reproduced in a somewhat unusual form, which will have a certain charm of its own. The first three volumes arranged are:

1. THE CASTAWAYS OF MEADOW BANK. By T. COBB.

2. THE BEECHNUT BOOK. By JACOB ABBOTT. Edited by E. V. LUCAS.

3. THE AIR GUN: or, How the Mastermans and Dobson Major nearly lost their Holidays. By T. HILBERT.

History

CROMWELL'S ARMY: A History of the English Soldier during the Civil Wars, the Commonwealth, and the Protectorate. By C. H. FIRTH, M.A. *Crown 8vo.* 7s. 6d.

An elaborate study and description of Cromwell's army by which the victory of the Parliament was secured. The 'New Model' is described in minute detail, and the author, who is one of the most distinguished historians of the day, has made great use of unpublished MSS.

MESSRS. METHUEN'S ANNOUNCEMENTS 5

A HISTORY OF RUSSIA FROM PETER THE GREAT TO ALEXANDER II. By W. R. MORFILL, Jesus College, Oxford. *Crown 8vo.* 7s. 6d.
This history, by the most distinguished authority in England, is founded on a study of original documents, and though necessarily brief, is the most comprehensive narrative in existence. Considerable attention has been paid to the social and literary development of the country, and the recent expansion of Russia in Asia.

A HISTORY OF THE POLICE IN ENGLAND. By Captain MELVILLE LEE. *Crown 8vo.* 7s. 6d.
This highly interesting book is the first history of the police force from its first beginning to its present development. Written as it is by an author of competent historical and legal qualifications, it will be indispensable to every magistrate and to all who are indirectly interested in the police force.

ECTHESIS CHRONICA. Edited by Professor LAMBROS. *Demy 8vo.* *net.* [*Byzantine Texts.*

A HISTORY OF ENGLISH LITERATURE: From its Beginning to Tennyson. By L. ENGEL. Translated from the German by J. H. FREESE. *Demy 8vo.* 7s. 6d.
This is a very complete and convenient sketch of the evolution of our literature from early days. The treatment is biographical as well as critical, and is rendered more interesting by the quotation of characteristic passages from the chief authors.

A HISTORY OF THE BRITISH IN INDIA. By A. D. INNES, M.A. With Maps and Plans. *Crown 8vo.* 7s. 6d.

Biography

THE LIFE OF ROBERT LOUIS STEVENSON. By GRAHAM BALFOUR. *Two Volumes. Demy 8vo.* 25s. *net.*
This highly interesting biography has been entrusted by Mr. Stevenson's family to his cousin, Mr. Balfour, and all available materials have been placed at his disposal. The book is rich in unpublished MSS. and letters, diaries of travel, reminiscences of friends, and a valuable fragment of autobiography. It also contains a complete bibliography of all Stevenson's work. This biography of one of the most attractive and sympathetic personalities in English literature should possess a most fascinating interest. The book will be uniform with The Edinburgh Edition.

THE LIFE OF FRANÇOIS DE FENELON. By VISCOUNT ST. CYRES. *Demy 8vo.* 10s. 6d.
This biography has engaged the author for many years, and the book is not only the study of an interesting personality, but an important contribution to the history of the period

THE CONVERSATIONS OF JAMES NORTHCOTE, R.A. AND JAMES WARD. Edited by ERNEST FLETCHER. With many Portraits. *Demy 8vo.* 10s. 6d.
This highly interesting, racy, and stimulating book, contains hitherto unpublished utterances of Northcote during a period of twenty-one years. There are many reminiscences of Sir Joshua Reynolds, much advice to young painters, and many references to the great artists and great figures of the day.

Travel, Adventure and Topography

HEAD-HUNTERS, BLACK, WHITE, AND BROWN. By A. C. HADDON, Sc.D., F.R.S. With many Illustrations and a Map. *Demy 8vo.* 15s.

A narrative of adventure and exploration in Northern Borneo. It contains much matter of the highest scientific interest.

A BOOK OF BRITTANY. By S. BARING GOULD. With numerous Illustrations. *Crown 8vo.* 6s.

Uniform in scope and size with Mr. Baring Gould's well-known books on Devon, Cornwall, and Dartmoor.

General Literature

WOMEN AND THEIR WORK. By the Hon. Mrs. LYTTELTON. *Crown 8vo.* 2s. 6d.

A discussion of the present position of women in view of the various occupations and interests which are or may be open to them. There will be an introduction dealing with the general question, followed by chapters on the family, the household, philanthropic work, professions, recreation, and friendship.

ENGLISH VILLAGES. By P. H. DITCHFIELD, M.A., F.S.A. Illustrated. *Crown 8vo.* 6s.

A popular and interesting account of the history of a typical village, and of village life in general in England.

SPORTING MEMORIES. By J. OTHO PAGET. *Demy 8vo.* 12s. 6d.

This volume of reminiscences by a well-known sportsman and Master of Hounds deals chiefly with fox-hunting experiences.

Science

DRAGONS OF THE AIR. By H. G. SEELEY, F.R.S., With many Illustrations. *Crown 8vo.* 6s.

A popular history of the most remarkable flying animals which ever lived. Their relations to mammals, birds, and reptiles, living and extinct, are shown by an original series of illustrations. The scattered remains preserved in Europe and the United States have been put together accurately to show the varied forms of the animals. The book is a natural history of these extinct animals, which flew by means of a single finger.

Messrs. Methuen's Announcements

Theology

REGNUM DEI. THE BAMPTON LECTURES OF 1901. By A. ROBERTSON, D.D., Principal of King's College, London. *Demy 8vo. 12s. 6d. net.*

This book is an endeavour to ascertain the meaning of the 'Kingdom of God' in its original prominence in the teaching of Christ. It reviews historically the main interpretations of this central idea in the successive phases of Christian tradition and life. Special attention is given to the sense in which St. Augustine identified the Church with the Kingdom of God. The later lectures follow out the alternative ideas of the Church, and of its relation to civil society which the Middle Ages and more recent types of Christian thought have founded upon alternative conceptions of the Kingdom of God.

A HISTORY OF THE OLD TESTAMENT. By G. W. WADE. With Maps. *Crown 8vo. 6s.*

This book presents a connected account of the Hebrew people during the period covered by the Old Testament; and has been drawn up from the Scripture records in accordance with the methods of historical criticism. The text of the Bible has been studied in the light thrown upon it by the best modern commentators; but the reasons for the conclusions stated are not left to be sought for in the commentaries, but are discussed in the course of the narrative. Much attention has been devoted to tracing the progress of religion amongst the Hebrews, and the book, which is furnished with maps, is further adapted to the needs of theological students by the addition of geographical notes, tables, and a full index.

THE AGAPE AND THE EUCHARIST. By J. F. KEATING, D.D. *Crown 8vo. 3s. 6d.*

THE IMITATION OF CHRIST. A Revised Translation, with an Introduction, by C. BIGG, D.D., Canon of Christ Church. *Crown 8vo. 3s. 6d.*

A new edition, carefully revised and set in large type, of Dr. Bigg's well-known version.

Oxford Commentaries

General Editor, WALTER LOCK, D.D., Warden of Keble College, Dean Ireland's Professor of Exegesis in the University of Oxford.

THE ACTS OF THE APOSTLES: With Introduction and Notes by R. B. RACKHAM, M.A. *Demy 8vo. 10s. 6d.*

The Churchman's Library

General Editor, J. H. BURN, B.D., Examining Chaplain to the Bishop of Aberdeen.

THE OLD TESTAMENT AND THE NEW SCHOLARSHIP. By J. W. PETERS, D.D. *Crown 8vo. 6s.*

COMPARATIVE RELIGION. By J. A. MACCULLOCH. *Crown 8vo.*

THE CHURCH OF CHRIST. By E. T. GREEN. *Crown 8vo.*

A POPULAR INTRODUCTION TO THE OLD TESTAMENT. Edited by A. M. MACKAY. *Crown 8vo.*

The Churchman's Bible

General Editor, J. H. BURN, B.D.

Messrs. METHUEN are issuing a series of expositions upon most of the books of the Bible. The volumes will be practical and devotional, and the text of the authorised version is explained in sections, which will correspond as far as possible with the Church Lectionary.

ISAIAH. Edited by W. E. BARNES, D.D., Fellow of Queen's College, Cambridge. *Two Volumes.* 2s. *net each.*

THE EPISTLE OF ST. PAUL THE APOSTLE TO THE EPHESIANS. Edited by G. H. WHITAKER. 1s. 6d. *net.*

The Library of Devotion

Pott 8vo, cloth, 2s.; *leather,* 2s. 6d. *net.*

'This series is excellent.'—THE BISHOP OF LONDON.
'Very delightful.'—THE BISHOP OF BATH AND WELLS.
'Well worth the attention of the Clergy.'—THE BISHOP OF LICHFIELD.
'The new "Library of Devotion" is excellent.'—THE BISHOP OF PETERBOROUGH.
'Charming.'—*Record.* 'Delightful.'—*Church Bells.*

THE THOUGHTS OF PASCAL. Edited with an Introduction and Notes by C. S. JERRAM, M.A.

ON THE LOVE OF GOD. By ST. FRANCIS DE SALES. Edited by W. J. KNOX-LITTLE, M.A.

A MANUAL OF CONSOLATION FROM THE SAINTS AND FATHERS. Edited by J. H. BURN, B.D.

THE SONG OF SONGS. Being Selections from ST. BERNARD. Edited by B. BLAXLAND, M.A.

Leaders of Religion

Edited by H. C. BEECHING, M.A. *With Portraits, Crown 8vo.* 3s 6d.

A series of short biographies of the most prominent leaders of religious life and thought of all ages and countries.

BISHOP BUTLER. By W. A. SPOONER, M.A., Fellow of New College, Oxford.

Educational Books

COMMERCIAL EDUCATION IN THEORY AND PRACTICE. By E. E. WHITFIELD, M.A. *Crown 8vo.* 5s.

An introduction to Methuen's Commercial Series treating the question of Commercial Education fully from both the point of view of the teacher and of the parent.

EASY GREEK EXERCISES. By C. G. BOTTING, M.A. *Crown 8vo.* 2s.

DEMOSTHENES: The Olynthiacs and Philippics. Translated upon a new principle by OTHO HOLLAND. *Crown 8vo.* 2s. 6d.

MESSRS. METHUEN'S ANNOUNCEMENTS

A SOUTH AFRICAN ARITHMETIC. By HENRY HILL, B.A., Assistant Master at Worcester School, Cape Colony. *Crown 8vo. 3s. 6d.*

This book has been specially written for use in South African schools.

JUNIOR EXAMINATION SERIES. Edited by A. M. M. STEDMAN, M.A. *Fcap. 8vo. 1s.*

FRENCH EXAMINATION PAPERS. By F. JACOB, B.A.

LATIN EXAMINATION PAPERS. By C. G. BOTTING, M.A.

ALGEBRA EXAMINATION PAPERS. By AUSTEN S. LESTER, M.A.

ENGLISH GRAMMAR EXAMINATION PAPERS. By W. WILLIAMSON, B.A.

Fiction

THE HISTORY OF SIR RICHARD CALMADY: A Romance. By LUCAS MALET, Author of 'The Wages of Sin.' *Crown 8vo. 6s.*

This is the first long and elaborate book by Lucas Malet since 'The Wages of Sin.' It is a romance on realistic lines, and will certainly be one of the most important novels of the last ten years.

This novel, the scene of which is laid in the moorland country of the northern part of Hampshire, in London, and in Naples, opens in the year of grace 1842. The action covers a period of about three and thirty years; and deals with the experiences and adventures of an English country gentleman of an essentially normal type of character, subjected—owing to somewhat distressing antecedent circumstances—to very abnormal conditions of life. The book is frankly a romance; but it is also frankly a realistic and modern one.

THE SERIOUS WOOING: A Heart's History. By Mrs. CRAIGIE (JOHN OLIVER HOBBES), Author of 'Robert Orange.' *Crown 8vo. 6s.*

LIGHT FREIGHTS. By W. W. JACOBS, Author of 'Many Cargoes.' Illustrated. *Crown 8vo. 3s. 6d.*

A volume of stories by Mr. Jacobs uniform in character and appearance with 'Many Cargoes.'

CLEMENTINA. By A. E. W. MASON, Author of 'The Courtship of Morrice Buckler,' 'Miranda of the Balcony,' etc. Illustrated. *Crown 8vo 6s.*

A spirited romance of the Jacobites somewhat after the manner of 'Morrice Buckler.' The Old Pretender is introduced as one of the chief characters.

A WOMAN ALONE. By Mrs. W. K. CLIFFORD, Author of 'Aunt Anne.' *Crown 8vo. 3s. 6d.*

A volume of stories.

THE STRIKING HOURS. By EDEN PHILLPOTTS, Author of 'Children of the Mist,' 'Sons of the Morning,' etc. *Crown 8vo. 6s.*

The annals of a Devon village, containing much matter of humorous and pathetic interest.

Messrs. Methuen's Announcements

FANCY FREE. By EDEN PHILLPOTTS, Author of 'Children of the Mist.' Illustrated. *Crown 8vo.* 6s.

A humorous book. Uniform with 'The Human Boy.'

TALES OF DUNSTABLE WEIR. By GWENDOLINE KEATS (ZACK). Author of 'Life is Life.' *Crown 8vo.* 6s.

A volume of stories after the style of 'Zack's' well-known first book 'Life is Life.'

WITH ESSEX IN IRELAND. By the Hon. EMILY LAWLESS. Cheaper Edition. *Crown 8vo.* 6s.

A cheaper edition of a book which won considerable popularity in a more expensive form some years ago.

A NEW NOVEL. By Mrs. B. M. CROKER. *Crown 8vo.* 6s.

THE PROPHET OF BERKELEY SQUARE. By ROBERT HICHENS, Author of 'Flames,' 'Tongues of Conscience,' etc. *Crown 8vo.* 6s.

A new long novel.

THE ALIEN. By F. F. MONTRESOR, Author of 'Into the Highways and Hedges.' *Crown 8vo.* 6s.

THE EMBARRASSING ORPHAN. By W. E. NORRIS. *Crown 8vo.* 6s.

ROYAL GEORGIE. By S. BARING GOULD, Author of 'Mehalah.' With eight Illustrations by D. MURRAY SMITH. *Crown 8vo.* 6s.

FORTUNE'S DARLING. By WALTER RAYMOND, Author of 'Love and Quiet Life.' *Crown 8vo.* 6s.

THE MILLION. By DOROTHEA GERARD, Author of 'Lady Baby.' *Crown 8vo.* 6s.

FROM THE LAND OF THE SHAMROCK. By JANE BARLOW, Author of 'Irish Idylls.' *Crown 8vo.* 6s.

THE WOOING OF SHEILA. By GRACE RHYS. *Crown 8vo.* 6s.

RICKERBY'S FOLLY. By TOM GALLON, Author of 'Kiddy.' *Crown 8vo.* 6s.

A GREAT LADY. By ADELINE SERGEANT, Author of 'The Story of a Penitent Soul.' *Crown 8vo.* 6s.

MARY HAMILTON. By LORD ERNEST HAMILTON. *Crown 8vo.* 6s.

MASTER OF MEN. By E. PHILLIPS OPPENHEIM. *Crown 8vo.* 6s.

BOTH SIDES OF THE VEIL. By RICHARD MARSH, Author of 'The Seen and the Unseen.' *Crown 8vo.* 6s.

THE THIRTEEN EVENINGS. By GEORGE BARTRAM, Author of 'The People of Clopton.' *Crown 8vo.* 6s.

THE SKIRTS OF HAPPY CHANCE. By H. B. MARRIOTT WATSON. Illustrated. *Crown 8vo.* 6s.

A NEW NOVEL. By E. H. COOPER, Author of 'Mr. Blake of Newmarket.' *Crown 8vo.* 6s.
This book, like most of Mr. Cooper's novels, is chiefly concerned with sport and racing.

THE YEAR ONE: A Page of the French Revolution. By J. BLOUNDELLE BURTON, Author of 'The Clash of Arms.' *Crown 8vo.* 6s.
A vivid story of the Reign of Terror in France in 1792, when the year 1 of the Republic calendar commenced.

THE DEVASTATORS. By ADA CAMBRIDGE, Author of 'Path and Goal.' *Crown 8vo.* 6s.

JOHN TOPP: Pirate. By WEATHERBY CHESNEY. *Crown 8vo.* 6s.
A book of breathless adventure.

The Novelist

Messrs. METHUEN are issuing under the above general title a Monthly Series of Novels by popular authors at the price of Sixpence. Each Number is as long as the average Six Shilling Novel.

XXIII. THE HUMAN BOY. EDEN PHILLPOTTS.
[*July.*

XXIV. THE CHRONICLES OF COUNT ANTONIO. ANTHONY HOPE.
[*August.*

XXV. BY STROKE OF SWORD. ANDREW BALFOUR.
[*September.*

Methuen's Sixpenny Library

A New Series of Copyright Books.
NEW VOLUMES

THE CONQUEST OF LONDON. DOROTHEA GERARD. [*July.*

THE MUTABLE MANY. ROBERT BARR. [*August.*

A VOYAGE OF CONSOLATION. SARA J. DUNCAN.
[*September.*

THE WAR WITH THE BOERS: A Sketch of the Boer War of 1899-1901. With Maps and Plans. By H. SIDEBOTHAM. (Double number. 1s.) [*October.*

A CATALOGUE OF

MESSRS. METHUEN'S
PUBLICATIONS

Poetry

Rudyard Kipling. BARRACK-ROOM BALLADS. By RUDYARD KIPLING. 68*th Thousand.* *Crown 8vo.* 6s. *Leather,* 6s. *net.*
'Mr. Kipling's verse is strong, vivid, full of character. . . . Unmistakeable genius rings in every line.'—*Times.*
'The ballads teem with imagination, they palpitate with emotion. We read them with laughter and tears; the metres throb in our pulses, the cunningly ordered words tingle with life; and if this be not poetry, what is?'—*Pall Mall Gazette.*

Rudyard Kipling. THE SEVEN SEAS. By RUDYARD KIPLING. 57*th Thousand.* *Cr. 8vo. Buckram, gilt top.* 6s. *Leather,* 6s. *net.*
'The Empire has found a singer; it is no depreciation of the songs to say that statesmen may have, one way or other, to take account of them.'—*Manchester Guardian.*
'Animated through and through with indubitable genius.'—*Daily Telegraph.*

"Q." POEMS AND BALLADS. By "Q." *Crown 8vo.* 3s. 6d.

"Q." GREEN BAYS: Verses and Parodies. By "Q." *Second Edition.* *Crown 8vo.* 3s. 6d.

H. Ibsen. BRAND. A Drama by HENRIK IBSEN. Translated by WILLIAM WILSON. *Third Edition.* *Crown 8vo.* 3s. 6d.

A. D. Godley. LYRA FRIVOLA. By A. D. GODLEY, M.A., Fellow of Magdalen College, Oxford. *Third Edition.* *Pott 8vo.* 2s. 6d.
'Combines a pretty wit with remarkably neat versification. . . . Every one will wish there was more of it.'—*Times.*

A. D. Godley. VERSES TO ORDER. By A. D. GODLEY. *Crown 8vo.* 2s. 6d. *net.*

J. G. Cordery. THE ODYSSEY OF HOMER. A Translation by J. G. CORDERY. *Crown 8vo.* 7s. 6d.

Herbert Trench. DEIRDRE WED: and Other Poems. By HERBERT TRENCH. *Crown 8vo.* 5s.

Edgar Wallace. WRIT IN BARRACKS. By EDGAR WALLACE. *Crown 8vo.* 3s. 6d.

Belles Lettres, Anthologies, etc.

R. L. Stevenson. VAILIMA LETTERS. By ROBERT LOUIS STEVENSON. With an Etched Portrait by WILLIAM STRANG. *Third Edition.* *Crown 8vo. Buckram.* 6s.
'A fascinating book.'—*Standard.*
'Unique in Literature.'—*Daily Chronicle.*

G. Wyndham. THE POEMS OF WILLIAM SHAKESPEARE. Edited with an Introduction and Notes by GEORGE WYNDHAM, M.P. *Demy 8vo. Buckram, gilt top.* 10s. 6d.
This edition contains the 'Venus,' 'Lucrece,' and Sonnets, and is prefaced with an elaborate introduction of over 140 pp.
'We have no hesitation in describing Mr. George Wyndham's introduction as a masterly piece of criticism, and all who love our Elizabethan literature will find a very garden of delight in it.'—*Spectator.*

Edward FitzGerald. THE RUBAIYAT OF OMAR KHAYYAM. Translated by EDWARD FITZGERALD. With a Commentary by H. M. BATSON, and a Biography of Omar by E. D. ROSS. 6s. Also an Edition on large paper limited to 50 copies.
'One of the most desirable of the many reprints of Omar.'—*Glasgow Herald.*

W. E. Henley. ENGLISH LYRICS. Selected and Edited by W. E. HENLEY. *Crown 8vo. Gilt top.* 3s. 6d.
'It is a body of choice and lovely poetry.'—*Birmingham Gazette.*

Henley and Whibley. A BOOK OF ENGLISH PROSE. Collected by W. E. HENLEY and CHARLES WHIBLEY. *Crown 8vo. Buckram, gilt top.* 6s.

H. C. Beeching. LYRA SACRA: An Anthology of Sacred Verse. Edited by H. C. BEECHING, M.A. *Crown 8vo. Buckram.* 6s.
'A charming selection, which maintains a lofty standard of excellence.'—*Times.*

"Q." THE GOLDEN POMP. A Procession of English Lyrics. Arranged by A. T. QUILLER COUCH. *Crown 8vo. Buckram.* 6s.

W. B. Yeats. AN ANTHOLOGY OF IRISH VERSE. Edited by W. B. YEATS. Revised and Enlarged Edition. *Crown 8vo.* 3s. 6d.

W. M. Dixon. A PRIMER OF TENNYSON. By W. M. DIXON, M.A. *Cr. 8vo.* 2s. 6d.
'Much sound and well-expressed criticism. The bibliography is a boon.'—*Speaker.*

W. A. Craigie. A PRIMER OF BURNS. By W. A. CRAIGIE. *Crown 8vo.* 2s. 6d.
'A valuable addition to the literature of the poet.'—*Times.*

G. W. Steevens. MONOLOGUES OF THE DEAD. By G. W. STEEVENS. *Foolscap 8vo.* 3s. 6d.

L. Magnus. A PRIMER OF WORDSWORTH. By LAURIE MAGNUS. *Crown 8vo.* 2s. 6d.
'A valuable contribution to Wordsworthian literature.'—*Literature.*

Sterne. THE LIFE AND OPINIONS OF TRISTRAM SHANDY. By LAWRENCE STERNE. With an Introduction by CHARLES WHIBLEY, and a Portrait. 2 *vols.* 7s.

Congreve. THE COMEDIES OF WILLIAM CONGREVE. With an Introduction by G. S. STREET, and a Portrait. 2 *vols.* 7s.

Morier. THE ADVENTURES OF HAJJI BABA OF ISPAHAN. By JAMES MORIER. With an Introduction by E. G. BROWNE, M.A. and a Portrait. 2 *vols.* 7s.

Walton. THE LIVES OF DONNE, WOTTON, HOOKER, HERBERT AND SANDERSON. By IZAAK WALTON. With an Introduction by VERNON BLACKBURN, and a Portrait. 3s. 6d.

Johnson. THE LIVES OF THE ENGLISH POETS. By SAMUEL JOHNSON, LL.D. With an Introduction by J. H. MILLAR, and a Portrait. 3 *vols.* 10s. 6d.

Burns. THE POEMS OF ROBERT BURNS. Edited by ANDREW LANG and W. A. CRAIGIE. With Portrait. *Second Edition. Demy 8vo, gilt top.* 6s.

F. Langbridge. BALLADS OF THE BRAVE; Poems of Chivalry, Enterprise, Courage, and Constancy. Edited by Rev. F. LANGBRIDGE. *Second Edition. Cr. 8vo.* 3s. 6d. *School Edition.* 2s. 6d.
'The book is full of splendid things.'—*World.*

Methuen's Standard Library

Gibbon. MEMOIRS OF MY LIFE AND WRITINGS. By EDWARD GIBBON. Edited, with an Introduction and Notes, by G. BIRKBECK HILL, LL.D. *Crown 8vo.* 6s.
'An admirable edition of one of the most interesting personal records of a literary life. Its notes and its numerous appendices are a repertory of almost all that can be known about Gibbon.'—*Manchester Guardian.*

Gibbon. THE DECLINE AND FALL OF THE ROMAN EMPIRE. By EDWARD GIBBON. A New Edition, Edited with Notes, Appendices, and Maps, by J. B. BURY, LL.D., Fellow of Trinity College, Dublin. *In Seven Volumes. Demy 8vo. Gilt top. 8s. 6d. each. Also Cr. 8vo. 6s. each.*

'At last there is an adequate modern edition of Gibbon. . . . The best edition the nineteenth century could produce.'—*Manchester Guardian.*

'A great piece of editing.'—*Academy.*

Gilbert White. THE NATURAL HISTORY OF SELBORNE. By GILBERT WHITE. Edited by L. C. MIALL, F.R.S., assisted by W. WARDE FOWLER, M.A. *Crown 8vo. 6s.*

C. G. Crump. THE HISTORY OF THE LIFE OF THOMAS ELLWOOD. Edited by C. G. CRUMP, M.A. *Crown 8vo. 6s.*

This edition is the only one which contains the complete book as originally published. It contains a long Introduction and many Footnotes.

Dante. LA COMMEDIA DI DANTE ALIGHIERI. The Italian Text edited by PAGET TOYNBEE, M.A. *Demy 8vo. Gilt top. 8s. 6d. Also Crown 8vo. 6s.*

Tennyson. THE EARLY POEMS OF ALFRED, LORD TENNYSON. Edited, with Notes and an Introduction by J. CHURTON COLLINS, M.A. *Crown 8vo. 6s.*

An elaborate edition of the celebrated volume which was published in its final and definitive form in 1853. This edition contains a long Introduction and copious Notes, textual and explanatory. It also contains in an Appendix all the Poems which Tennyson afterwards omitted.

Jonathan Swift. THE JOURNAL TO STELLA. By JONATHAN SWIFT. Edited by G. A. AITKEN. *Crown 8vo. 6s.*

Chesterfield. THE LETTERS OF LORD CHESTERFIELD TO HIS SON. Edited, with an Introduction by C. STRACHEY, and Notes by A. CALTHROP. *Two Volumes. Crown 8vo. 6s. each.*

The Works of Shakespeare

General Editor, EDWARD DOWDEN, Litt.D.

Messrs. METHUEN have in preparation an Edition of Shakespeare in single Plays. Each play will be edited with a full Introduction, Textual Notes, and a Commentary at the foot of the page.

The first volumes are:

HAMLET. Edited by EDWARD DOWDEN. *Demy 8vo. 3s. 6d.*

'Fully up to the level of recent scholarship, both English and German.'—*Academy.*

ROMEO AND JULIET. Edited by EDWARD DOWDEN, Litt.D. *Demy 8vo. 3s. 6d.*

'No edition of Shakespeare is likely to prove more attractive and satisfactory than this one. It is beautifully printed and paged and handsomely and simply bound.'—*St. James's Gazette.*

The Novels of Charles Dickens

Crown 8vo. Each Volume, cloth 3s. net; leather 4s. 6d. net.

With Introductions by Mr. GEORGE GISSING, Notes by Mr. F. G. KITTON, and Topographical Illustrations.

THE PICKWICK PAPERS. With Illustrations by E. H. NEW. *Two Volumes.*

'As pleasant a copy as any one could desire. The notes add much to the value of the edition, and Mr. New's illustrations are also historical. The volumes promise well for the success of the edition.'—*Scotsman.*

NICHOLAS NICKLEBY. With Illustrations by R. J. WILLIAMS. *Two Volumes.*

BLEAK HOUSE. With Illustrations by BEATRICE ALCOCK. *Two Volumes.*

OLIVER TWIST. With Illustrations by G. H. NEW.

THE OLD CURIOSITY SHOP. With Illustrations by G. M. BRIMELOW. *Two Volumes.*

BARNABY RUDGE. With Illustrations by BEATRICE ALCOCK. *Two Volumes.*

Little Biographies

Fcap. 8vo. Each volume, cloth, 3s. 6d.

THE LIFE OF DANTE ALIGHIERI. By PAGET TOYNBEE. With 12 Illustrations.

'This excellent little volume is a clear, compact, and convenient summary of the whole subject.'—*Academy.*

THE LIFE OF SAVONAROLA. By E. L. S. HORSBURGH, M.A. With Portraits and Illustrations.

The Little Library

With Introductions, Notes, and Photogravure Frontispieces.

Pott 8vo. Each Volume, cloth 1s. 6d. net, leather 2s. 6d. net.

'Altogether good to look upon, and to handle.'—*Outlook.*
'In printing, binding, lightness, etc., this is a perfect series.'—*Pilot.*
'It is difficult to conceive more attractive volumes.'—*St. James's Gazette.*
'Very delicious little books.'—*Literature.*
'Delightful editions.'—*Record.*
'Exceedingly tastefully produced.'—*Morning Leader.*

VANITY FAIR. By W. M. THACKERAY. With an Introduction by S. GWYNN. *Three Volumes.*

THE PRINCESS. By ALFRED, LORD TENNYSON. Edited by ELIZABETH WORDSWORTH.

IN MEMORIAM. By ALFRED, LORD TENNYSON. Edited, with an Introduction and Notes, by H. C. BEECHING, M.A.

THE EARLY POEMS OF ALFRED, LORD TENNYSON. Edited by J. C. COLLINS, M.A.

MAUD. By ALFRED, LORD TENNYSON. Edited by ELIZABETH WORDSWORTH.

A LITTLE BOOK OF ENGLISH LYRICS. With Notes.

EOTHEN. By A. W. KINGLAKE. With an Introduction and Notes.

CRANFORD. By Mrs. GASKELL. Edited by E. V. LUCAS.

THE INFERNO OF DANTE. Translated by H. F. CARY. Edited by PAGET TOYNBEE.

THE PURGATORIO OF DANTE. Translated by H. F. CARY. Edited by PAGET TOYNBEE, M.A.

JOHN HALIFAX, GENTLEMAN. By Mrs. CRAIK. Edited by ANNIE MATHESON. *Two Volumes.*

A LITTLE BOOK OF SCOTTISH VERSE. Arranged and edited by T. F. HENDERSON.

A LITTLE BOOK OF ENGLISH PROSE. Arranged and edited by Mrs. P. A. BARNETT.

SELECTIONS FROM WORDSWORTH. Edited by NOWELL C. SMITH, Fellow of New College, Oxford.

SELECTIONS FROM WILLIAM BLAKE. Edited by M. PERUGINI.

PRIDE AND PREJUDICE. By JANE AUSTEN. Edited by E. V. LUCAS. *Two Volumes.*

PENDENNIS. By W. M. THACKERAY, Edited by S. GWYNN. *Three Volumes.*

LAVENGRO. By GEORGE BORROW. Edited by F. HINDES GROOME. *Two Volumes.*

The Little Guides

Pott 8vo, cloth 3s. ; leather, 3s. 6d. net.

OXFORD AND ITS COLLEGES. By J. WELLS, M.A., Fellow and Tutor of Wadham College. Illustrated by E. H. NEW. *Fourth Edition.*

'An admirable and accurate little treatise, attractively illustrated.'—*World.*

CAMBRIDGE AND ITS COLLEGES. By A. HAMILTON THOMPSON. Illustrated by E. H. NEW.

'It is brightly written and learned, and is just such a book as a cultured visitor needs.'—*Scotsman.*

THE MALVERN COUNTRY. By B. C. A. WINDLE, D.Sc., F.R.S. Illustrated by E. H. NEW.

SHAKESPEARE'S COUNTRY. By B.C.A. WINDLE, F.R.S., M.A. Illustrated by E. H. NEW. *Second Edition.*

'One of the most charming guide books. Both for the library and as a travelling companion the book is equally choice and serviceable.'—*Academy.*

SUSSEX. By F. G. BRABANT, M.A. Illustrated by E. H. NEW.

'A charming little book; as full of sound information as it is practical in conception.'—*Athenæum.*

'Accurate, complete, and agreeably written.'—*Literature.*

WESTMINSTER ABBEY. By G. E. TROUTBECK. Illustrated by F. D. BEDFORD.

'A delightful miniature hand-book.'—*Glasgow Herald.*

'In comeliness, and perhaps in completeness, this work must take the first place.'—*Academy.*

'A really first-rate guide-book.'—*Literature.*

Illustrated and Gift Books

Tennyson. THE EARLY POEMS OF ALFRED, LORD TENNYSON. Edited, with Notes and an Introduction by J. CHURTON COLLINS, M.A. With 10 Illustrations in Photogravure by W. E. F. BRITTEN. *Demy 8vo. 10s. 6d.*

Gelett Burgess. GOOPS AND HOW TO BE THEM. By GELETT BURGESS. With numerous Illustrations. *Small 4to. 6s.*

Gelett Burgess. THE LIVELY CITY OF LIGG. By GELETT BURGESS. With 53 Illustrations, 8 of which are coloured. *Small 4to. 6s.*

Phil May. THE PHIL MAY ALBUM. *4to. 6s.*

'There is a laugh in each drawing.'—*Standard.*

A. H. Milne. ULYSSES; OR, DE ROUGEMONT OF TROY. Described and depicted by A. H. MILNE. *Small quarto. 3s. 6d.*

'Clever, droll, smart.'—*Guardian.*

Edmund Selous. TOMMY SMITH'S ANIMALS. By EDMUND SELOUS. Illustrated by G. W. ORD. *Fcap. 8vo. 2s. 6d.*

A little book designed to teach children respect and reverence for animals.

'A quaint, fascinating little book: a nursery classic.'—*Athenæum.*

S. Baring Gould. THE CROCK OF GOLD. Fairy Stories told by S. BARING GOULD. *Crown 8vo. 6s.*

'Twelve delightful fairy tales.'—*Punch.*

M. L. Gwynn. A BIRTHDAY BOOK. Arranged and Edited by M. L. GWYNN. *Demy 8vo. 12s. 6d.*

This is a birthday-book of exceptional dignity, and the extracts have been chosen with particular care.

John Bunyan. THE PILGRIM'S PROGRESS. By JOHN BUNYAN. Edited, with an Introduction, by C. H. FIRTH, M.A. With 39 Illustrations by R. ANNING BELL. *Crown 8vo. 6s.*

'The best "Pilgrim's Progress."'—*Educational Times.*

F. D. Bedford. NURSERY RHYMES. With many Coloured Pictures by F. D. BEDFORD. *Super Royal 8vo.* 2s. 6d.

S. Baring Gould. A BOOK OF FAIRY TALES retold by S. BARING GOULD. With numerous Illustrations and Initial Letters by ARTHUR J. GASKIN. *Second Edition. Cr. 8vo. Buckram.* 6s.

S. Baring Gould. OLD ENGLISH FAIRY TALES. Collected and edited by S. BARING GOULD. With Numerous Illustrations by F. D. BEDFORD. *Second Edition. Cr. 8vo. Buckram.* 6s.
'A charming volume.'—*Guardian.*

S. Baring Gould. A BOOK OF NURSERY SONGS AND RHYMES. Edited by S. BARING GOULD, and Illustrated by the Birmingham Art School. *Buckram, gilt top. Crown 8vo.* 6s.

H. C. Beeching. A BOOK OF CHRISTMAS VERSE. Edited by H. C. BEECHING, M.A., and Illustrated by WALTER CRANE. *Cr. 8vo, gilt top.* 3s. 6d.

History

Flinders Petrie. A HISTORY OF EGYPT, FROM THE EARLIEST TIMES TO THE PRESENT DAY. Edited by W. M. FLINDERS PETRIE, D.C.L., LL.D., Professor of Egyptology at University College. *Fully Illustrated. In Six Volumes. Cr. 8vo.* 6s. each.

VOL. I. PREHISTORIC TIMES TO XVITH DYNASTY. W. M. F. Petrie. *Fourth Edition.*

VOL. II. THE XVIITH AND XVIIITH DYNASTIES. W. M. F. Petrie. *Third Edition.*

VOL. IV. THE EGYPT OF THE PTOLEMIES. J. P. Mahaffy.

VOL. V. ROMAN EGYPT. J. G. Milne.

VOL. VI. EGYPT IN THE MIDDLE AGES. STANLEY LANE-POOLE.

'A history written in the spirit of scientific precision so worthily represented by Dr. Petrie and his school cannot but promote sound and accurate study, and supply a vacant place in the English literature of Egyptology.'—*Times.*

Flinders Petrie. RELIGION AND CONSCIENCE IN ANCIENT EGYPT. By W. M. FLINDERS PETRIE, D.C.L., LL.D. Fully Illustrated. *Crown 8vo.* 2s. 6d.
'The lectures will afford a fund of valuable information for students of ancient ethics.'—*Manchester Guardian.*

Flinders Petrie. SYRIA AND EGYPT, FROM THE TELL EL AMARNA TABLETS. By W. M. FLINDERS PETRIE, D.C.L., LL.D. *Crown 8vo.* 2s. 6d.
'A marvellous record. The addition made to our knowledge is nothing short of amazing.'—*Times.*

Flinders Petrie. EGYPTIAN TALES. Edited by W. M. FLINDERS PETRIE. Illustrated by TRISTRAM ELLIS. *In Two Volumes. Cr. 8vo.* 3s. 6d. each.
'Invaluable as a picture of life in Palestine and Egypt.'—*Daily News.*

Flinders Petrie. EGYPTIAN DECORATIVE ART. By W. M. FLINDERS PETRIE. With 120 Illustrations. *Cr. 8vo.* 3s. 6d.
'In these lectures he displays rare skill in elucidating the development of decorative art in Egypt.'—*Times.*

C. W. Oman. A HISTORY OF THE ART OF WAR. Vol. II.: The Middle Ages, from the Fourth to the Fourteenth Century. By C. W. OMAN, M.A., Fellow of All Souls', Oxford. Illustrated. *Demy 8vo.* 21s.
'The whole art of war in its historic evolution has never been treated on such an ample and comprehensive scale, and we question if any recent contribution to the exact history of the world has possessed more enduring value.'—*Daily Chronicle.*

S. Baring Gould. THE TRAGEDY OF THE CÆSARS. With numerous Illustrations from Busts, Gems, Cameos, etc. By S. BARING GOULD. *Fifth Edition. Royal 8vo.* 15s.

'A most splendid and fascinating book on a subject of undying interest. The great feature of the book is the use the author has made of the existing portraits of the Caesars and the admirable critical subtlety he has exhibited in dealing with this line of research. It is brilliantly written, and the illustrations are supplied on a scale of profuse magnificence.' —*Daily Chronicle.*

F. W. Maitland. CANON LAW IN ENGLAND. By F. W. MAITLAND, LL.D., Downing Professor of the Laws of England in the University of Cambridge. *Royal 8vo.* 7s. 6d.

'Professor Maitland has put students of English law under a fresh debt. These essays are landmarks in the study of the history of Canon Law.'—*Times.*

John Hackett. A HISTORY OF THE CHURCH OF CYPRUS. By JOHN HACKETT, M.A. With Maps and Illustrations. *Demy 8vo.* 15s. net.

A work which brings together all that is known on the subject from the introduction of Christianity to the commencement of the British occupation. A separate division deals with the local Latin Church during the period of the Western Supremacy.

E. L. Taunton. A HISTORY OF THE JESUITS IN ENGLAND. By E. L. TAUNTON. With Illustrations. *Demy 8vo.* 21s. net.

'A history of permanent value, which covers ground never properly investigated before, and is replete with the results of original research. A most interesting and careful book.'—*Literature.*

'A volume which will attract considerable attention.'—*Athenæum.*

H. de B. Gibbins. INDUSTRY IN ENGLAND: HISTORICAL OUTLINES. By H. DE B. GIBBINS, Litt.D., M.A. With 5 Maps. *Second Edition. Demy 8vo.* 10s. 6d.

H. E. Egerton. A HISTORY OF BRITISH COLONIAL POLICY. By H. E. EGERTON, M.A. *Demy 8vo.* 12s. 6d.

'It is a good book, distinguished by accuracy in detail, clear arrangement of facts, and a broad grasp of principles.'—*Manchester Guardian.*

Albert Sorel. THE EASTERN QUESTION IN THE EIGHTEENTH CENTURY. By ALBERT SOREL. Translated by F. C. BRAMWELL, M.A. *Cr. 8vo.* 3s. 6d.

C. H. Grinling. A HISTORY OF THE GREAT NORTHERN RAILWAY, 1845-95. By C. H. GRINLING. With Illustrations. *Demy 8vo.* 10s. 6d.

'Mr. Grinling has done for a Railway what Macaulay did for English History.'—*The Engineer.*

Clement Stretton. A HISTORY OF THE MIDLAND RAILWAY. By CLEMENT STRETTON. With numerous Illustrations. *Demy 8vo.* 12s. 6d.

'A fine record of railway development.'—*Outlook.*

'The volume is as exhaustive as it is comprehensive, and is made especially attractive by its pictures.'—*Globe.*

W. Sterry. ANNALS OF ETON COLLEGE. By W. STERRY, M.A. With numerous Illustrations. *Demy 8vo.* 7s. 6d.

'A treasury of quaint and interesting reading. Mr. Sterry has by his skill and vivacity given these records new life.'—*Academy.*

G. W. Fisher. ANNALS OF SHREWSBURY SCHOOL. By G. W. FISHER, M.A. With numerous Illustrations. *Demy 8vo.* 10s. 6d.

'This careful, erudite book.'—*Daily Chronicle.*

'A book of which Old Salopians are sure to be proud.'—*Globe.*

J. Sargeaunt. ANNALS OF WESTMINSTER SCHOOL. By J. SARGEAUNT, M.A. With numerous Illustrations. *Demy 8vo.* 7s. 6d.

A. Clark. THE COLLEGES OF OXFORD: Their History and their Traditions. Edited by A. CLARK, M.A., Fellow of Lincoln College. *8vo.* 12s. 6d.

'A work which will be appealed to for many years as the standard book.'—*Athenæum.*

MESSRS. METHUEN'S CATALOGUE 19

T. M. Taylor. A CONSTITUTIONAL AND POLITICAL HISTORY OF ROME. By T. M. TAYLOR, M.A., Fellow of Gonville and Caius College, Cambridge. *Crown 8vo. 7s. 6d.*
'We fully recognise the value of this carefully written work, and admire especially the fairness and sobriety of his judgment and the human interest with which he has inspired a subject which in some hands becomes a mere series of cold abstractions. It is a work that will be stimulating to the student of Roman history.'—*Athenæum.*

J. Wells. A SHORT HISTORY OF ROME. By J. WELLS, M.A., Fellow and Tutor of Wadham Coll., Oxford. *Third Edition.* With 3 Maps. *Crown 8vo. 3s. 6d.*
This book is intended for the Middle and Upper Forms of Public Schools and for Pass Students at the Universities. It contains copious Tables, etc.
'An original work written on an original plan, and with uncommon freshness and vigour.'—*Speaker.*

O. Browning. A SHORT HISTORY OF MEDIÆVAL ITALY, A.D. 1250-1530. By OSCAR BROWNING, Fellow and Tutor of King's College, Cambridge. *In Two Volumes. Cr. 8vo. 5s. each.*
VOL. I. 1250-1409.—Guelphs and Ghibellines.
VOL. II. 1409-1530.—The Age of the Condottieri.

O'Grady. THE STORY OF IRELAND. By STANDISH O'GRADY, Author of 'Finn and his Companions.' *Crown 8vo. 2s. 6d.*

Byzantine Texts
Edited by J. B. BURY, M.A., Litt.D.

ZACHARIAH OF MITYLENE. Translated into English by F. J. HAMILTON, D.D., and E. W. BROOKS. *Demy 8vo. 12s. 6d. net.*

EVAGRIUS. Edited by Professor LÉON PARMENTIER and M. BIDEZ. *Demy 8vo. 10s. 6d. net.*

THE HISTORY OF PSELLUS By C. SATHAS. *Demy 8vo. 15s. net.*

Biography

R. L. Stevenson. THE LETTERS OF ROBERT LOUIS STEVENSON TO HIS FAMILY AND FRIENDS. Selected and Edited, with Notes and Introductions, by SIDNEY COLVIN. *Fourth and Cheaper Edition. Crown 8vo. 12s.*
LIBRARY EDITION. *Demy 8vo. 2 vols. 25s. net.*
'Irresistible in their raciness, their variety, their animation ... of extraordinary fascination. A delightful inheritance, the truest record of a "richly compounded spirit" that the literature of our time has preserved.'—*Times.*

J. G. Millais. THE LIFE AND LETTERS OF SIR JOHN EVERETT MILLAIS, President of the Royal Academy. By his Son, J. G. MILLAIS. With 319 Illustrations, of which 9 are in Photogravure. *Second Edition. 2 vols. Royal 8vo. 32s. net.*
'This splendid work.'—*World.*
'Of such absorbing interest is it, of such completeness in scope and beauty. Special tribute must be paid to the extraordinary completeness of the illustrations.'—*Graphic.*

S. Baring Gould. THE LIFE OF NAPOLEON BONAPARTE. By S. BARING GOULD. With over 450 Illustrations in the Text and 12 Photogravure Plates. *Large quarto. Gilt top. 36s.*
'The main feature of this gorgeous volume is its great wealth of beautiful photogravures and finely-executed wood engravings, constituting a complete pictorial chronicle of Napoleon I.'s personal history from the days of his early childhood at Ajaccio to the date of his second interment.'—*Daily Telegraph.*

W. A. Bettesworth. THE WALKERS OF SOUTHGATE : Being the Chronicles of a Cricketing Family. By W. A. BETTESWORTH. Illustrated. *Demy 8vo. 7s. 6d.*
'A most engaging contribution to cricket literature ... a lasting joy.'—*Vanity Fair.*

G. S. Layard. THE LIFE OF MRS. LYNN LINTON. By G. S. LAYARD. With Portraits. *Demy 8vo. 12s. 6d.*
'Mrs. Lynn Linton is here presented to us in all her moods. She lives in the book; she is presented to us so that we really know her.'—*Literature.*
'A thoroughly good book, very interesting, and at the same time in very good taste.'—*Daily Graphic.*
'Mr. Layard may be congratulated on having produced an honest and interesting record of a notable woman.'—*Athenæum.*

Stanley Lane-Poole. THE LIFE OF SIR HARRY PARKES. By STANLEY LANE-POOLE. *A New and Cheaper Edition. Crown 8vo. 6s.*

Helen C. Wetmore. THE LAST OF THE GREAT SCOUTS ('Buffalo Bill'). By his Sister, HELEN C. WETMORE. With Illustrations. *Demy 8vo. 6s.*
'The stirring adventures of Buffalo Bill's career are described vigorously and picturesquely, and with a directness that inspires the fullest confidence.'—*Glasgow Herald.*
'A narrative of one of the most attractive figures in the public eye.'—*Daily Chronicle.*

Constance Bache. BROTHER MUSICIANS. Reminiscences of Edward and Walter Bache. By CONSTANCE BACHE. With Sixteen Illustrations. *Crown 8vo. 6s. net.*

P. H. Colomb. MEMOIRS OF ADMIRAL SIR A. COOPER KEY. By Admiral P. H. COLOMB. With a Portrait. *Demy 8vo. 16s.*

C. Cooper King. THE STORY OF THE BRITISH ARMY. By Colonel COOPER KING. Illustrated. *Demy 8vo. 7s. 6d.*
'An authoritative and accurate story of England's military progress.'—*Daily Mail.*

R. Southey. ENGLISH SEAMEN (Howard, Clifford, Hawkins, Drake, Cavendish). By ROBERT SOUTHEY. Edited, with an Introduction, by DAVID HANNAY. *Second Edition. Crown 8vo. 6s.*
'A brave, inspiriting book.'—*Black and White.*

W. Clark Russell. THE LIFE OF ADMIRAL LORD COLLINGWOOD. By W. CLARK RUSSELL. With Illustrations by F. BRANGWYN. *Fourth Edition. Crown 8vo. 6s.*
'A book which we should like to see in the hands of every boy in the country.'—*St. James's Gazette.*

Morris Fuller. THE LIFE AND WRITINGS OF JOHN DAVENANT, D.D. (1571-1641), Bishop of Salisbury. By MORRIS FULLER, B.D. *Demy 8vo. 10s. 6d.*

J. M. Rigg. ST. ANSELM OF CANTERBURY: A CHAPTER IN THE HISTORY OF RELIGION. By J. M. RIGG. *Demy 8vo. 7s. 6d.*

F. W. Joyce. THE LIFE OF SIR FREDERICK GORE OUSELEY. By F. W. JOYCE, M.A. *7s. 6d.*

W. G. Collingwood. THE LIFE OF JOHN RUSKIN. By W. G. COLLINGWOOD, M.A. With Portraits, and 13 Drawings by Mr. Ruskin. *Second Edition. 2 vols. 8vo. 32s. Cheap Edition. Crown 8vo. 6s.*

C. Waldstein. JOHN RUSKIN. By CHARLES WALDSTEIN, M.A. With a Photogravure Portrait. *Post 8vo. 5s.*

A. M. F. Darmesteter. THE LIFE OF ERNEST RENAN. By MADAME DARMESTETER. With Portrait. *Second Edition. Cr. 8vo. 6s.*

W. H. Hutton. THE LIFE OF SIR THOMAS MORE. By W. H. HUTTON, M.A. With Portraits. *Second Edition. Cr. 8vo. 5s.*
'The book lays good claim to high rank among our biographies. It is excellently, even lovingly, written.'—*Scotsman.*

S. Baring Gould. THE VICAR OF MORWENSTOW: A Biography. By S. BARING GOULD, M.A. A new and Revised Edition. With Portrait. *Crown 8vo. 3s. 6d.*
A completely new edition of the well known biography of R. S. Hawker.

Travel, Adventure and Topography

Sven Hedin. THROUGH ASIA. By SVEN HEDIN, Gold Medallist of the Royal Geographical Society. With 300 Illustrations from Sketches and Photographs by the Author, and Maps. 2 vols. *Royal 8vo.* 20s. *net.*

'One of the greatest books of the kind issued during the century. It is impossible to give an adequate idea of the richness of the contents of this book, nor of its abounding attractions as a story of travel unsurpassed in geographical and human interest. Much of it is a revelation. Altogether the work is one which in solidity, novelty, and interest must take a first rank among publications of its class.'—*Times.*

F. H. Skrine and E. D. Ross. THE HEART OF ASIA. By F. H. SKRINE and E. D. ROSS. With Maps and many Illustrations by VERESTCHAGIN. *Large Crown 8vo.* 10s. 6d. *net.*

'This volume will form a landmark in our knowledge of Central Asia. . . . Illuminating and convincing.'—*Times.*

R. E. Peary. NORTHWARD OVER THE GREAT ICE. By R. E. PEARY, Gold Medallist of the Royal Geographical Society. With over 800 Illustrations. 2 vols. *Royal 8vo.* 32s. *net.*

'His book will take its place among the permanent literature of Arctic exploration.'—*Times.*

T. H. Holdich. THE INDIAN BORDERLAND: being a Personal Record of Twenty Years. By Sir T. H. Holdich, K.C.I.E. Illustrated. *Demy 8vo.* 15s. *net.*

'Probably the most important work on frontier topography that has lately been presented to the general public.'—*Literature.*

'Interesting and inspiring from cover to cover, it will assuredly take its place as the classical on the history of the Indian frontier.'—*Pilot.*

'A work that should long remain the standard authority.'—*Daily Chronicle.*

A. B. Wylde. MODERN ABYSSINIA. By A. B. WYLDE. With a Map and a Portrait. *Demy 8vo.* 15s. *net.*

'The most valuable contribution that has yet been made to our knowledge of Abyssinia.'—*Manchester Guardian.*

'A book which will rank among the very best of African works.'—*Daily Chronicle.*

'A repertory of information on every branch of the subject.'—*Literature.*

Alex. Hosie. MANCHURIA. By ALEXANDER HOSIE. With Illustrations and a Map. *Demy 8vo.* 10s. 6d. *net.*

A complete account of this important province by the highest living authority on the subject.

'This book is especially useful at the present moment when the future of the country appears uncertain.'—*Times.*

E. A. FitzGerald. THE HIGHEST ANDES. By E. A. FITZGERALD. With 2 Maps, 51 Illustrations, 13 of which are in Photogravure, and a Panorama. *Royal 8vo,* 30s. *net.* Also a Small Edition on Hand-made Paper, limited to 50 Copies, 4to, £5, 5s.

'The record of the first ascent of the highest mountain yet conquered by mortal man. A volume which will continue to be the classic book of travel on this region of the Andes.'—*Daily Chronicle.*

F. W. Christian. THE CAROLINE ISLANDS. By F. W. CHRISTIAN. With many Illustrations and Maps. *Demy 8vo.* 12s. 6d. *net.*

'A real contribution to our knowledge of the peoples and islands of Micronesia, as well as fascinating as a narrative of travels and adventure.'—*Scotsman.*

H. H. Johnston. BRITISH CENTRAL AFRICA. By Sir H. H. JOHNSTON, K.C.B. With nearly Two Hundred Illustrations, and Six Maps. *Second Edition. Crown 4to.* 18s. *net.*

'A fascinating book, written with equal skill and charm—the work at once of a literary artist and of a man of action who is singularly wise, brave, and experienced. It abounds in admirable sketches.'—*Westminster Gazette.*

L. Decle. THREE YEARS IN SAVAGE AFRICA. By LIONEL DECLE. With 100 Illustrations and 5 Maps. *Second Edition. Demy 8vo.* 10s. 6d. *net.*

A. Hulme Beaman. TWENTY YEARS IN THE NEAR EAST. By A. HULME BEAMAN. *Demy 8vo.* With Portrait. 10s. 6d.

Henri of Orleans. FROM TONKIN TO INDIA. By PRINCE HENRI OF ORLEANS. Translated by HAMLEY BENT, M.A. With 100 Illustrations and a Map. *Cr. 4to, gilt top.* 25s.

Chester Holcombe. THE REAL CHINESE QUESTION. By CHESTER HOLCOMBE. *Crown 8vo.* 6s.

'It is an important addition to the materials before the public for forming an opinion on a most difficult and pressing problem.'—*Times.*

'It is this practical "note" in the book, coupled with the fairness, moderation, and sincerity of the author, that gives it, in our opinion, the highest place among books published in recent years on the Chinese question.'—*Manchester Guardian.*

J. W. Robertson-Scott. THE PEOPLE OF CHINA. By J. W. ROBERTSON-SCOTT. With a Map. *Crown 8vo.* 3s. 6d.

'A vivid impression ... This excellent, brightly written epitome.'—*Daily News.*
'Excellently well done. ... Enthralling.' —*Weekly Dispatch.*

S. L. Hinde. THE FALL OF THE CONGO ARABS. By S. L. HINDE. With Plans, etc. *Demy 8vo.* 12s. 6d.

A. St. H. Gibbons. EXPLORATION AND HUNTING IN CENTRAL AFRICA. By Major A. ST. H. GIBBONS. With full-page Illustrations by C. WHYMPER, and Maps. *Demy 8vo.* 15s.

A. H. Norway. NAPLES: PAST AND PRESENT. By A. H. NORWAY, Author of 'Highways and Byways in Devon and Cornwall.' With 40 Illustrations by A. G. FERARD. *Crown 8vo.* 6s.

In this book Mr. Norway gives not only a highly interesting description of modern Naples, but a historical account of its antiquities and traditions.

S. Baring Gould. DARTMOOR: A Descriptive and Historical Sketch. By S. BARING GOULD. With Plans and Numerous Illustrations. *Crown 8vo.* 6s.

'A most delightful guide, companion, and instructor.'—*Scotsman.*
'Informed with close personal knowledge.' —*Saturday Review.*

S. Baring Gould. THE BOOK OF THE WEST. By S. BARING GOULD. With numerous Illustrations. *Two volumes.* Vol. I. Devon. *Second Edition.* Vol. II. Cornwall. *Crown 8vo.* 6s. each.

'Bracing as the air of Dartmoor, the legend weird as twilight over Dozmare Pool, they give us a very good idea of this enchanting and beautiful district.'— *Guardian.*

S. Baring Gould. A BOOK OF BRITTANY. By S. BARING GOULD. With numerous Illustrations. *Crown 8vo.* 6s.

Uniform in scope and size with Mr. Baring Gould's well-known books on Devon, Cornwall, and Dartmoor.

S. Baring Gould. THE DESERTS OF SOUTHERN FRANCE. By S. BARING GOULD. 2 vols. *Demy 8vo.* 32s.

J. F. Fraser. ROUND THE WORLD ON A WHEEL. By JOHN FOSTER FRASER. With 100 Illustrations. *Crown 8vo.* 6s.

'A classic of cycling, graphic and witty.'— *Yorkshire Post.*

R. L. Jefferson. A NEW RIDE TO KHIVA. By R. L. JEFFERSON. Illustrated. *Crown 8vo.* 6s.

J. K. Trotter. THE NIGER SOURCES. By Colonel J. K. TROTTER, R.A. With a Map and Illustrations. *Crown 8vo.* 5s.

W. Crooke. THE NORTH-WESTERN PROVINCES OF INDIA: THEIR ETHNOLOGY AND ADMINISTRATION. By W. CROOKE. With Maps and Illustrations. *Demy 8vo.* 10s. 6d.

A. Boisragon. THE BENIN MASSACRE. By CAPTAIN BOISRAGON. *Second Edition.* Cr. 8vo. 3s. 6d.

H. S. Cowper. THE HILL OF THE GRACES: OR, THE GREAT STONE TEMPLES OF TRIPOLI. By H. S. COWPER, F.S.A. With Maps, Plans, and 75 Illustrations. *Demy 8vo.* 10s. 6d.

W. B. Worsfold. SOUTH AFRICA. By W. B. WORSFOLD, M.A. With a Map. *Second Edition. Cr. 8vo. 6s.*

'A monumental work compressed into a very moderate compass.'—*World.*

Katherine and Gilbert Macquoid. IN PARIS. By KATHERINE and GILBERT MACQUOID. Illustrated by THOMAS R. MACQUOID, R.I. With 2 maps. *Crown 8vo. 1s.*

'A useful little guide, judiciously supplied with information.'—*Athenæum.*

A. H. Keane. THE BOER STATES: A History and Description of the Transvaal and the Orange Free State. By A. H. KEANE, M.A. With Map. *Crown 8vo. 6s.*

Naval and Military

F. H. E. Cunliffe. THE HISTORY OF THE BOER WAR. By F. H. E. CUNLIFFE, Fellow of All Souls' College, Oxford. With many Illustrations, Plans, and Portraits. *In 2 vols. Vol. I., 15s.*

'The excellence of the work is double; for the narrative is vivid and temperate, and the illustrations form a picture gallery of the war which is not likely to be rivalled.... An ideal gift book.'—*Academy.*

G. S. Robertson. CHITRAL: The Story of a Minor Siege. By Sir G. S. ROBERTSON, K.C.S.I. With numerous Illustrations, Map and Plans. *Second Edition. Demy 8vo. 10s. 6d.*

'A book which the Elizabethans would have thought wonderful. More thrilling, more piquant, and more human than any novel.'—*Newcastle Chronicle.*

'As fascinating as Sir Walter Scott's best fiction.'—*Daily Telegraph.*

R. S. S. Baden-Powell. THE DOWNFALL OF PREMPEH. A Diary of Life in Ashanti, 1895. By Maj.-Gen. BADEN-POWELL. With 21 Illustrations and a Map. *Third Edition. Large Crown 8vo. 6s.*

R. S. S. Baden-Powell. THE MATABELE CAMPAIGN, 1896. By Maj.-Gen. BADEN-POWELL. With nearly 100 Illustrations. *Fourth and Cheaper Edition. Large Crown 8vo. 6s.*

J. B. Atkins. THE RELIEF OF LADYSMITH. By JOHN BLACK ATKINS. With 16 Plans and Illustrations. *Third Edition. Crown 8vo. 6s.*

H. W. Nevinson. LADYSMITH: The Diary of a Siege. By H. W. NEVINSON. With 16 Illustrations and a Plan. *Second Edition. Crown 8vo. 6s.*

Barclay Lloyd. A THOUSAND MILES WITH THE C.I.V. By Captain BARCLAY LLOYD. With an Introduction by Colonel MACKINNON, and a Portrait and Map. *Crown 8vo. 6s.*

Filson Young. THE RELIEF OF MAFEKING. By FILSON YOUNG. With Maps and Illustrations. *Crown 8vo. 6s.*

J. Angus Hamilton. THE SIEGE OF MAFEKING. By J. ANGUS HAMILTON. With many Illustrations. *Crown 8vo. 6s.*

'A thrilling story.'—*Observer.*

H. F. Prevost Battersby IN THE WEB OF A WAR. By H. F. PREVOST BATTERSBY. With Plans, and Portrait of the Author. *Crown 8vo. 6s.*

'The pathos, the comedy, the majesty of war are all in these pages.'—*Daily Mail.*

Howard C. Hillegas. WITH THE BOER FORCES. By HOWARD C. HILLEGAS. With 24 Illustrations. *Second Edition. Crown 8vo. 6s.*

'A most interesting book. It has many and great merits.'—*Athenæum.*

'Has extreme interest and scarcely less value.'—*Pall Mall Gazette.*

H. C. J. Biss. THE RELIEF OF KUMASI. By Captain H. C. J. BISS. With Maps and Illustrations. *Second Edition. Crown 8vo. 6s.*

'Pleasantly written and highly interesting. The illustrations are admirable.'—*Queen.*

'We should say it will remain the standard work on its very interesting subject.'—*Globe.*

E. H. Alderson. WITH THE MOUNTED INFANTRY AND THE MASHONALAND FIELD FORCE, 1896. By Lieut.-Colonel ALDERSON. With numerous Illustrations and Plans. *Demy 8vo.* 10s. 6d.

Seymour Vandeleur. CAMPAIGNING ON THE UPPER NILE AND NIGER. By Lieut. SEYMOUR VANDELEUR. With an Introduction by Sir G. GOLDIE, K.C.M.G. With 4 Maps, Illustrations, and Plans. *Large Crown 8vo.* 10s. 6d.

Lord Fincastle. A FRONTIER CAMPAIGN. By Viscount FINCASTLE, V.C., and Lieut. P. C. ELLIOTT-LOCKHART. With a Map and 16 Illustrations. *Second Edition. Crown 8vo.* 6s.

E. N. Bennett. THE DOWNFALL OF THE DERVISHES: A Sketch of the Sudan Campaign of 1898. By E. N. BENNETT, Fellow of Hertford College. With a Photogravure Portrait of Lord Kitchener. *Third Edition. Crown 8vo.* 3s. 6d.

W. Kinnaird Rose. WITH THE GREEKS IN THESSALY. By W. KINNAIRD ROSE. With Illustrations. *Crown 8vo.* 6s.

G. W. Steevens. NAVAL POLICY: By G. W. STEEVENS. *Demy 8vo.* 6s.

D. Hannay. A SHORT HISTORY OF THE ROYAL NAVY, FROM EARLY TIMES TO THE PRESENT DAY. By DAVID HANNAY. Illustrated. 2 *Vols. Demy 8vo.* 7s. 6d. *each.* Vol. I., 1200-1688.
'We read it from cover to cover at a sitting, and those who go to it for a lively and brisk picture of the past, with all its faults and its grandeur, will not be disappointed. The historian is endowed with literary skill and style.'—*Standard.*

E. L. S. Horsburgh. WATERLOO: A Narrative and Criticism. By E. L. S. HORSBURGH, M.A. With Plans. *Second Edition. Crown 8vo.* 5s.
'A brilliant essay—simple, sound, and thorough.'—*Daily Chronicle.*

H. B. George. BATTLES OF ENGLISH HISTORY. By H. B. GEORGE, M.A., Fellow of New College, Oxford. With numerous Plans. *Third Edition. Cr. 8vo.* 6s.
'Mr. George has undertaken a very useful task—that of making military affairs intelligible and instructive to non-military readers—and has executed it with a large measure of success.'—*Times.*

General Literature

S. Baring Gould. OLD COUNTRY LIFE. By S. BARING GOULD. With Sixty-seven Illustrations. *Large Cr. 8vo. Fifth Edition.* 6s.
'"Old Country Life," as healthy wholesome reading, full of breezy life and movement, full of quaint stories vigorously told, will not be excelled by any book to be published throughout the year. Sound, hearty, and English to the core.'—*World.*

S. Baring Gould. AN OLD ENGLISH HOME. By S. BARING GOULD. With numerous Plans and Illustrations. *Crown 8vo.* 6s.
'The chapters are delightfully fresh, very informing, and lightened by many a good story. A delightful fireside companion.'—*St. James's Gazette.*

S. Baring Gould. HISTORIC ODDITIES AND STRANGE EVENTS. By S. BARING GOULD. *Fifth Edition. Crown 8vo.* 6s.

S. Baring Gould. FREAKS OF FANATICISM. By S. BARING GOULD. *Third Edition. Cr. 8vo.* 6s.

S. Baring Gould. A GARLAND OF COUNTRY SONG: English Folk Songs with their Traditional Melodies. Collected and arranged by S. BARING GOULD and H. F. SHEPPARD. *Demy 4to.* 6s.

S. Baring Gould. SONGS OF THE WEST: Traditional Ballads and Songs of the West of England, with their Melodies. Collected by S.

Baring Gould, M.A., and H. F. Sheppard, M.A. In 4 Parts. *Parts I., II., III.,* 3s. each. *Part IV.,* 5s. *In one Vol., French morocco,* 15s.

'A rich collection of humour, pathos, grace, and poetic fancy.'—*Saturday Review.*

S. Baring Gould. YORKSHIRE ODDITIES AND STRANGE EVENTS. By S. BARING GOULD. *Fifth Edition. Crown 8vo.* 6s.

S. Baring Gould. STRANGE SURVIVALS AND SUPERSTITIONS. By S. BARING GOULD. *Cr. 8vo. Second Edition.* 6s.

Marie Corelli. THE PASSING OF THE GREAT QUEEN: A Tribute to the Noble Life of Victoria Regina. By MARIE CORELLI. *Small 4to.* 1s.

Cotton Minchin. OLD HARROW DAYS. By J. G. COTTON MINCHIN. *Cr. 8vo. Second Edition.* 5s.

W. E. Gladstone. THE SPEECHES OF THE RT. HON. W. E. GLADSTONE, M.P. Edited by A. W. HUTTON, M.A., and H. J. COHEN, M.A. With Portraits. *Demy 8vo. Vols. IX. and X.,* 12s. 6d. each.

M. N. Oxford. A HANDBOOK OF NURSING. By M. N. OXFORD, of Guy's Hospital. *Crown 8vo.* 3s. 6d.

'The most useful work of the kind that we have seen. A most valuable and practical manual.'—*Manchester Guardian.*

E. V. Zenker. ANARCHISM. By E. V. ZENKER. *Demy 8vo.* 7s. 6d.

Emily Lawless. A GARDEN DIARY. By the Hon. EMILY LAWLESS. *Demy 8vo.* 7s. 6d. net.

S. J. Duncan. ON THE OTHER SIDE OF THE LATCH. By SARA JEANNETTE DUNCAN (Mrs. COTES), Author of 'A Voyage of Consolation.' *Crown 8vo.* 6s.

W. Williamson. THE BRITISH GARDENER. By W. WILLIAMSON. Illustrated. *Demy 8vo.* 10s. 6d.

Arnold White. EFFICIENCY AND EMPIRE. By ARNOLD WHITE. *Crown 8vo.* 6s.

'Stimulating and entertaining throughout, it deserves the attention of every patriotic Englishman.'—*Daily Mail.*
'A notable book.'—*Literature.*
'A book of sound work, deep thought, and a sincere endeavour to rouse the British to a knowledge of the value of their Empire.'—*Bookman.*
'A more vigorous work has not been written for many years.'—*Review of the Week.*

A. Silva White. THE EXPANSION OF EGYPT: A Political and Historical Survey. By A. SILVA WHITE. With four Special Maps. *Demy 8vo.* 15s. net.

'This is emphatically the best account of Egypt as it is under English control that has been published for many years.'—*Spectator.*

Chas. Richardson. THE ENGLISH TURF. By CHARLES RICHARDSON. With numerous Illustrations and Plans, *Demy 8vo.* 15s.

'As a record of horses and courses, this work is a valuable addition to the literature of the Turf. It is crammed with sound information, and with reflections and suggestions that are born of a thorough knowledge of the subject.'—*Scotsman.*
'A book which is sure to find many readers; written with consummate knowledge and in an easy, agreeable style.'—*Daily Chronicle.*
'From its sensible introduction to its very complex index, this is about the best book that we are likely for some time to see upon the subject with which it deals.'—*Athenæum.*

Philip Trevor. THE LIGHTER SIDE OF CRICKET By Captain PHILIP TREVOR (DUX). *Crown 8vo.* 6s.

A highly interesting volume, dealing with such subjects as county cricket, village cricket, cricket for boys and girls, literary cricket, and various other subjects which do not require a severe and technical treatment.

'A wholly entertaining book.'—*Glasgow Herald.*
'The most welcome book on our national game published for years.'—*County Gentleman.*

Peter Beckford. THOUGHTS ON HUNTING. By PETER BECKFORD. Edited by J. OTHO PAGET, and Illustrated by G. H. JALLAND. *Demy 8vo.* 10s. 6d.

'Beckford's "Thoughts on Hunting" has

long been a classic with sportsmen, and the present edition will go far to make it a favourite with lovers of literature.'—*Speaker.*

E. B. Michell. THE ART AND PRACTICE OF HAWKING. By E. B. MICHELL. With 3 Photogravures by G. E. LODGE, and other Illustrations. *Demy 8vo.* 10s. 6d.
'No book is more full and authoritative than this handsome treatise.'
—*Morning Leader.*

H. G. Hutchinson. THE GOLFING PILGRIM. By HORACE G. HUTCHINSON. *Crown 8vo.* 6s.
'Without this book the golfer's library will be incomplete.'—*Pall Mall Gazette.*

J. Wells. OXFORD AND OXFORD LIFE. By Members of the University. Edited by J. WELLS, M.A., Fellow and Tutor of Wadham College. *Third Edition. Cr. 8vo.* 3s. 6d.

C. G. Robertson. VOCES ACADEMICÆ. By C. GRANT ROBERTSON, M.A., Fellow of All Souls', Oxford. With a Frontispiece. *Pott 8vo.* 3s. 6d.
'Decidedly clever and amusing.'—*Athenæum.*

Rosemary Cotes. DANTE'S GARDEN. By ROSEMARY COTES. With a Frontispiece. *Second Edition. Fcp. 8vo.* 2s. 6d. *Leather,* 3s. 6d. *net.*
'A charming collection of legends of the flowers mentioned by Dante.'—*Academy.*

Clifford Harrison. READING AND READERS. By CLIFFORD HARRISON. *Fcp. 8vo.* 2s. 6d.
'An extremely sensible little book.'—*Manchester Guardian.*

L. Whibley. GREEK OLIGARCHIES: THEIR ORGANISATION AND CHARACTER. By L. WHIBLEY, M.A., Fellow of Pembroke College, Cambridge. *Crown 8vo.* 6s.

L. L. Price. ECONOMIC SCIENCE AND PRACTICE. By L. L. PRICE, M.A., Fellow of Oriel College, Oxford. *Crown 8vo.* 6s.

J. S. Shedlock. THE PIANOFORTE SONATA: Its Origin and Development. By J. S. SHEDLOCK. *Crown 8vo.* 5s.
'This work should be in the possession of every musician and amateur. A concise and lucid history and a very valuable work for reference.'—*Athenæum.*

A. Hulme Beaman. PONS ASINORUM; OR, A GUIDE TO BRIDGE. By A. HULME BEAMAN. *Fcap 8vo.* 2s.
A practical guide, with many specimen games, to the new game of Bridge.

E. M. Bowden. THE EXAMPLE OF BUDDHA: Being Quotations from Buddhist Literature for each Day in the Year. Compiled by E. M. BOWDEN. *Third Edition.* 16mo. 2s. 6d.

F. Ware. EDUCATIONAL REFORM. By FABIAN WARE, M.A. *Crown 8vo.* 2s. 6d.

Sidney Peel. PRACTICAL LICENSING REFORM. By the Hon SIDNEY PEEL, late Fellow of Trinity College, Oxford, and Secretary to the Royal Commission on the Licensing Laws. *Crown 8vo.* 1s. 6d.

Philosophy

L. T. Hobhouse. THE THEORY OF KNOWLEDGE. By L. T. HOBHOUSE, Fellow of C.C.C., Oxford. *Demy 8vo.* 21s.
'The most important contribution to English philosophy since the publication of Mr. Bradley's "Appearance and Reality."'—*Glasgow Herald.*

W. H. Fairbrother. THE PHILOSOPHY OF T. H. GREEN. By W. H. FAIRBROTHER, M.A. *Second Edition. Cr. 8vo.* 3s. 6d.

'In every way an admirable book.'—*Glasgow Herald.*

F. W. Bussell. THE SCHOOL OF PLATO. By F. W. BUSSELL, D.D., Fellow of Brasenose College, Oxford. *Demy 8vo.* 10s. 6d.

F. S. Granger. THE WORSHIP OF THE ROMANS. By F. S. GRANGER, M.A., Litt.D. *Crown 8vo.* 6s.

Science

E. H. Colbeck. DISEASES OF THE HEART. By E. H. COLBECK, M.D. With numerous Illustrations. *Demy 8vo.* 12s.

W. C. C. Pakes. THE SCIENCE OF HYGIENE. By W. C. C. PAKES. With numerous Illustrations. *Demy 8vo.* 15s.
'A thoroughgoing working text-book of its subject, practical and well-stocked.' —*Scotsman.*

A. T. Hare. THE CONSTRUCTION OF LARGE INDUCTION COILS. By A. T. HARE, M.A. With numerous Diagrams. *Demy 8vo.* 6s.

J. E. Marr. THE SCIENTIFIC STUDY OF SCENERY. By J. E. MARR, F.R.S., Fellow of St. John's College, Cambridge. Illustrated. *Crown 8vo.* 6s.
A volume, moderate in size and readable in style, which will be acceptable alike to the student of geology and geography, and to the tourist.'—*Athenæum.*

J. Ritzema Bos. AGRICULTURAL ZOOLOGY. By Dr. J. RITZEMA BOS. Translated by J. R. AINSWORTH DAVIS, M.A. With an Introduction by ELEANOR A. ORMEROD, F.E.S. With 155 Illustrations. *Crown 8vo.* 3s. 6d.
'The illustrations are exceedingly good, whilst the information conveyed is invaluable.'—*Country Gentleman.*

Ed. von Freudenreich. DAIRY BACTERIOLOGY. A Short Manual for the Use of Students. By Dr. ED. VON FREUDENREICH, Translated by J. R. AINSWORTH DAVIS, M.A. *Second Edition, Revised. Crown 8vo.* 2s. 6d.

Chalmers Mitchell. OUTLINES OF BIOLOGY. By P. CHALMERS MITCHELL, M.A. *Illustrated. Cr. 8vo.* 6s.
A text-book designed to cover the new Schedule issued by the Royal College of Physicians and Surgeons.

George Massee. A MONOGRAPH OF THE MYXOGASTRES. By GEORGE MASSEE. With 12 Coloured Plates. *Royal 8vo.* 18s. net.
'A work much in advance of any book in the language treating of this group of organisms. Indispensable to every student of the Myxogastres.'—*Nature.*

C. Stephenson and F. Suddards. ORNAMENTAL DESIGN FOR WOVEN FABRICS. By C. STEPHENSON, of the Technical College, Bradford, and F. SUDDARDS, of the Yorkshire College, Leeds. With 65 full-page plates. *Demy 8vo. Second Edition.* 7s. 6d.
'The book is very ably done, displaying an intimate knowledge of principles, good taste, and the faculty of clear exposition.'—*Yorkshire Post.*

C. C. Channer and M. E. Roberts. LACE-MAKING IN THE MIDLANDS, PAST AND PRESENT. By C. C. CHANNER and M. E. ROBERTS. With 16 full-page Illustrations. *Crown 8vo.* 2s. 6d.
An interesting book, illustrated by fascinating photographs.'—*Speaker.*

Theology

W. R. Inge. CHRISTIAN MYSTICISM. The Bampton Lectures for 1899. By W. R. INGE, M.A., Fellow and Tutor of Hertford College, Oxford. *Demy 8vo.* 12s. 6d. net.
'It is fully worthy of the best traditions connected with the Bampton Lectureship.'—*Record.*

Lady Julian of Norwich. REVELATIONS OF DIVINE LOVE. By the LADY JULIAN of Norwich. Edited by GRACE WARRACK. *Crown 8vo.* 6s.
A partially modernised version, from the MS. in the British Museum of a book which Dr. Dalgairns terms 'One of the most remarkable books of the Middle Ages.' Mr. Inge in his Bampton Lectures on Christian Mysticism calls it 'The beautiful but little known *Revelations.*'

R. M. Benson. THE WAY OF HOLINESS: a Devotional Commentary on the 119th Psalm. By R. M. BENSON, M.A., of the Cowley Mission, Oxford. *Crown 8vo.* 5s.
'His facility is delightful, and his very sound and accurate theological sense saves him from many of the obvious dangers of such a gift. Give him a word or a number and at once there springs forth a fertile stream of thought, never commonplace, usually both deep and fresh. For devotional purposes we think this book most valuable. Readers will find a great wealth of thought if they use the book simply as a help to meditation.'—*Guardian.*

Jacob Behmen. THE SUPERSENSUAL LIFE. By JACOB BEHMEN. Edited by BERNARD HOLLAND. *Fcap 8vo.* 3s. 6d.

S. R. Driver. SERMONS ON SUBJECTS CONNECTED WITH THE OLD TESTAMENT. By S. R. DRIVER, D.D., Canon of Christ Church, Regius Professor of Hebrew in the University of Oxford. *Cr. 8vo.* 6s.
'A welcome companion to the author's famous "Introduction."'—*Guardian.*

T. K. Cheyne. FOUNDERS OF OLD TESTAMENT CRITICISM. By T. K. CHEYNE, D.D., Oriel Professor at Oxford. *Large Crown 8vo.* 7s. 6d.
A historical sketch of O. T. Criticism.

Walter Lock. ST. PAUL, THE MASTER-BUILDER. By WALTER LOCK, D.D., Warden of Keble College. *Crown 8vo.* 3s. 6d.
'The essence of the Pauline teaching is condensed into little more than a hundred pages, yet no point of importance is overlooked.'—*Guardian.*

F. S. Granger. THE SOUL OF A CHRISTIAN. By F. S. GRANGER, M.A., Litt.D. *Crown 8vo.* 6s.
A book dealing with the evolution of the religious life and experiences.
'A remarkable book.'—*Glasgow Herald.*
'Both a scholarly and thoughtful book.'—*Scotsman.*

H. Rashdall. DOCTRINE AND DEVELOPMENT. By HASTINGS RASHDALL, M.A., Fellow and Tutor of New College, Oxford. *Cr. 8vo.* 6s.

H. H. Henson. APOSTOLIC CHRISTIANITY: As Illustrated by the Epistles of St. Paul to the Corinthians. By H. H. HENSON, M.A., Fellow of All Souls', Oxford, Canon of Westminster. *Cr. 8vo.* 6s.

H. H. Henson. DISCIPLINE AND LAW. By H. HENSLEY HENSON, M.A., Fellow of All Souls', Oxford. *Fcap. 8vo.* 2s. 6d.

H. H. Henson. LIGHT AND LEAVEN: HISTORICAL AND SOCIAL SERMONS. By H. H. HENSON, M.A. *Crown 8vo.* 6s.

J. Houghton Kennedy. ST. PAUL'S SECOND AND THIRD EPISTLES TO THE CORINTHIANS. With Introduction, Dissertations, and Notes, by JAMES HOUGHTON KENNEDY, D.D., Assistant Lecturer in Divinity in the University of Dublin. *Crown 8vo.* 6s.

Bennett and Adeney. A BIBLICAL INTRODUCTION. By W. H. BENNETT, M.A., and W. F. ADENEY, M.A. *Crown 8vo.* 7s. 6d.
'It makes available to the ordinary reader the best scholarship of the day in the field of Biblical introduction. We know of no book which comes into competition with it.'—*Manchester Guardian.*

W. H. Bennett. A PRIMER OF THE BIBLE. By W. H. BENNETT. *Second Edition.* Cr. 8vo. 2s. 6d.
'The work of an honest, fearless, and sound critic, and an excellent guide in a small compass to the books of the Bible.'—*Manchester Guardian.*

C. F. G. Masterman. TENNYSON AS A RELIGIOUS TEACHER. By C. F. G. MASTERMAN. *Crown 8vo.* 6s.
'A thoughtful and penetrating appreciation, full of interest and suggestion.'—*World.*

William Harrison. CLOVELLY SERMONS. By WILLIAM HARRISON, M.A., late Rector of Clovelly. With a Preface by 'LUCAS MALET.' *Cr. 8vo. 3s. 6d.*

Cecilia Robinson. THE MINISTRY OF DEACONESSES. By Deaconness CECILIA ROBINSON. With an Introduction by the Lord Bishop of Winchester. *Cr. 8vo. 3s. 6d.*

'A learned and interesting book.'—*Scotsman.*

E. B. Layard. RELIGION IN BOYHOOD. Notes on the Religious Training of Boys. By E. B. LAYARD, M.A. *18mo. 1s.*

T. Herbert Bindley. THE OECUMENICAL DOCUMENTS OF THE FAITH. Edited with Introductions and Notes by T. HERBERT BINDLEY, B.D., Merton College, Oxford. *Crown 8vo. 6s.*

A historical account of the Creeds.

H. M. Barron. TEXTS FOR SERMONS ON VARIOUS OCCASIONS AND SUBJECTS. Compiled and Arranged by H. M. BARRON, B.A., of Wadham College, Oxford, with a Preface by Canon SCOTT HOLLAND. *Crown 8vo. 3s. 6d.*

W. Yorke Fausset. THE *DE CATECHIZANDIS RUDIBUS* OF ST. AUGUSTINE. Edited, with Introduction, Notes, etc., by W. YORKE FAUSSET, M.A. *Cr. 8vo. 3s. 6d.*

J. H. Burn. THE SOUL'S PILGRIMAGE: Devotional Readings from the published and unpublished writings of GEORGE BODY, D.D. Selected and arranged by J. H. BURN, B.D. *Pott 8vo. 2s. 6d.*

F. Weston. THE HOLY SACRIFICE. By F. WESTON, M.A., Curate of St. Matthew's, Westminster. *Pott 8vo. 6d. net.*

À Kempis. THE IMITATION OF CHRIST. By THOMAS À KEMPIS. With an Introduction by DEAN FARRAR. Illustrated by C. M. GERE. *Second Edition. Fcap. 8vo. 3s. 6d. Padded morocco, 5s.*

'Amongst all the innumerable English editions of the "Imitation," there can have been few which were prettier than this one, printed in strong and handsome type, with all the glory of red initials.'—*Glasgow Herald.*

J. Keble. THE CHRISTIAN YEAR. By JOHN KEBLE. With an Introduction and Notes by W. LOCK, D.D., Warden of Keble College. Illustrated by R. ANNING BELL. *Second Edition. Fcap. 8vo. 3s. 6d. Padded morocco. 5s.*

'The present edition is annotated with all the care and insight to be expected from Mr. Lock.'—*Guardian.*

Oxford Commentaries

General Editor, WALTER LOCK, D.D., Warden of Keble College, Dean Ireland's Professor of Exegesis in the University of Oxford.

THE BOOK OF JOB. Edited, with Introduction and Notes, by E. C. S. GIBSON, D.D., Vicar of Leeds. *Demy 8vo. 6s.*

'The publishers are to be congratulated on the start the series has made.'—*Times.*

'Dr. Gibson's work is worthy of a high degree of appreciation. To the busy worker and the intelligent student the commentary will be a real boon; and it will, if we are not mistaken, be much in demand. The Introduction is almost a model of concise, straightforward, prefatory remarks on the subject treated.'—*Athenæum.*

Handbooks of Theology

General Editor, A. ROBERTSON, D.D., Principal of King's College, London.

THE XXXIX. ARTICLES OF THE CHURCH OF ENGLAND. Edited with an Introduction by E. C. S. GIBSON, D.D., Vicar of Leeds, late Principal of Wells Theological College. *Second and Cheaper Edition in One Volume. Demy 8vo. 12s. 6d.*

'We welcome with the utmost satisfaction

a new, cheaper, and more convenient edition of Dr. Gibson's book. It was greatly wanted. Dr. Gibson has given theological students just what they want, and we should like to think that it was in the hands of every candidate for orders.'—*Guardian.*

AN INTRODUCTION TO THE HISTORY OF RELIGION. By F. B. JEVONS, M.A., Litt.D., Principal of Bishop Hatfield's Hall. *Demy 8vo.* 10s. 6d.

'The merit of this book lies in the penetration, the singular acuteness and force of the author's judgment. He is at once critical and luminous, at once just and suggestive. A comprehensive and thorough book.'—*Birmingham Post.*

THE DOCTRINE OF THE INCARNATION. By R. L. OTTLEY, M.A., late fellow of Magdalen College, Oxon., and Principal of Pusey House. *In Two Volumes. Demy 8vo.* 15s.

'A clear and remarkably full account of the main currents of speculation. Scholarly precision . . . genuine tolerance . . . intense interest in his subject—are Mr. Ottley's merits.'—*Guardian.*

AN INTRODUCTION TO THE HISTORY OF THE CREEDS. By A. E. BURN, B.D., Examining Chaplain to the Bishop of Lichfield. *Demy 8vo.* 10s. 6d.

'This book may be expected to hold its place as an authority on its subject.'—*Spectator.*

THE PHILOSOPHY OF RELIGION IN ENGLAND AND AMERICA. By ALFRED CALDECOTT, D.D., *Demy 8vo.* 10s. 6d.

'Singularly well-informed, comprehensive, and fair.'—*Glasgow Herald.*
'A lucid and informative account, which certainly deserves a place in every philosophical library.'—*Scotsman.*

The Churchman's Library

General Editor, J. H. BURN, B.D., Examining Chaplain to the Bishop of Aberdeen.

THE BEGINNINGS OF ENGLISH CHRISTIANITY. By W. E. COLLINS, M.A. With Map. *Cr. 8vo.* 3s. 6d.

'An excellent example of thorough and fresh historical work.'—*Guardian.*

SOME NEW TESTAMENT PROBLEMS. By ARTHUR WRIGHT, M.A., Fellow of Queen's College, Cambridge. *Crown 8vo.* 6s.

'Real students will revel in these reverent, acute, and pregnant essays in Biblical scholarship.'—*Great Thoughts.*

THE KINGDOM OF HEAVEN HERE AND HEREAFTER. By CANON WINTERBOTHAM, M.A., B.Sc., LL.B. *Cr. 8vo.* 3s. 6d.

'A most able book at once exceedingly thoughtful and richly suggestive.'—*Glasgow Herald.*

THE WORKMANSHIP OF THE PRAYER BOOK: Its Literary and Liturgical Aspects. By J. DOWDEN, D.D., Lord Bishop of Edinburgh. *Crown 8vo.* 3s. 6d.

'Scholarly and interesting.'—*Manchester Guardian.*

EVOLUTION. By F. B. JEVONS, M.A., Litt.D., Principal of Hatfield Hall, Durham. *Crown 8vo.* 3s. 6d.

'A well-written book, full of sound thinking happily expressed.'—*Manchester Guardian.*

The Churchman's Bible

General Editor, J. H. BURN, B.D.

Messrs. METHUEN are issuing a series of expositions upon most of the books of the Bible. The volumes will be practical and devotional, and the text of the authorised version is explained in sections, which will correspond as far as possible with the Church Lectionary.

THE EPISTLE OF ST. PAUL TO THE GALATIANS. Explained by A. W. ROBINSON, Vicar of All Hallows, Barking. *Fcap. 8vo.* 1s. 6d. net.

'The most attractive, sensible, and instructive manual for people at large, which we have ever seen.'—*Church Gazette.*

ECCLESIASTES. Explained by A. W. STREANE, D.D. *Fcap. 8vo.* 1s. 6d. net.

'Scholarly suggestive, and particularly interesting.'—*Bookman.*

MESSRS. METHUEN'S CATALOGUE   31

THE EPISTLE OF PAUL THE APOSTLE TO THE PHILIPPIANS. Explained by C. R. D. BIGGS, B.D. *Fcap. 8vo.* 1s. 6d. *net.*

Mr. Biggs' work is very thorough, and he has managed to compress a good deal of information into a limited space.'
—*Guardian.*

THE EPISTLE OF ST. JAMES. Edited by H. W. FULFORD, M.A. *Fcap. 8vo.* 1s. 6d. *net.*

The Library of Devotion

Pott 8vo, cloth, 2s.; *leather,* 2s. 6d. *net.*

'This series is excellent.'—THE BISHOP OF LONDON.
'Very delightful.'—THE BISHOP OF BATH AND WELLS.
'Well worth the attention of the Clergy.'—THE BISHOP OF LICHFIELD.
'The new " Library of Devotion " is excellent.'—THE BISHOP OF PETERBOROUGH.
'Charming.'—*Record.* 'Delightful.'—*Church Bells.*

THE CONFESSIONS OF ST. AUGUSTINE. Newly Translated, with an Introduction and Notes, by C. BIGG, D.D., late Student of Christ Church. *Third Edition.*
'The translation is an excellent piece of English, and the introduction is a masterly exposition. We augur well of a series which begins so satisfactorily.'—*Times.*

THE CHRISTIAN YEAR. By JOHN KEBLE. With Introduction and Notes by WALTER LOCK, D.D., Warden of Keble College, Ireland Professor at Oxford.

THE IMITATION OF CHRIST. A Revised Translation, with an Introduction, by C. BIGG, D.D., late Student of Christ Church. *Second Edition.*
A practically new translation of this book, which the reader has, almost for the first time, exactly in the shape in which it left the hands of the author.

A BOOK OF DEVOTIONS. By J. W. STANBRIDGE, B.D., Rector of Bainton, Canon of York, and sometime Fellow of St. John's College, Oxford.
'It is probably the best book of its kind. It deserves high commendation.'—*Church Gazette.*

LYRA INNOCENTIUM. By JOHN KEBLE. Edited, with Introduction and Notes, by WALTER LOCK, D.D., Warden of Keble College, Oxford.
'This sweet and fragrant book has never been published more attractively.'—*Academy.*

A SERIOUS CALL TO A DEVOUT AND HOLY LIFE. By WILLIAM LAW. Edited, with an Introduction, by C. BIGG, D.D., late Student of Christ Church.
This is a reprint, word for word and line for line, of the *Editio Princeps.*

THE TEMPLE. By GEORGE HERBERT. Edited, with an Introduction and Notes, by E. C. S. GIBSON, D.D., Vicar of Leeds.
This edition contains Walton's Life of Herbert, and the text is that of the first edition.

A GUIDE TO ETERNITY. By Cardinal BONA. Edited, with an Introduction and Notes, by J. W. STANBRIDGE, B.D., late Fellow of St. John's College, Oxford.

THE PSALMS OF DAVID. With an Introduction and Notes by B. W. RANDOLPH, D.D., Principal of the Theological College, Ely.
A devotional and practical edition of the Prayer Book version of the Psalms.

LYRA APOSTOLICA. With an Introduction by Canon SCOTT HOLLAND, and Notes by H. C. BEECHING, M.A.

THE INNER WAY. Being Thirty-six Sermons for Festivals by JOHN TAULER. Edited, with an Introduction, by A. W. HUTTON, M.A.

Leaders of Religion
Edited by H. C. BEECHING, M.A. With Portraits, *Crown 8vo.* 3s. 6d.

A series of short biographies of the most prominent leaders of religious life and thought of all ages and countries.

The following are ready—

CARDINAL NEWMAN. By R. H. HUTTON.

JOHN WESLEY. By J. H. OVERTON, M.A.

BISHOP WILBERFORCE. By G. W. DANIELL, M.A.

CARDINAL MANNING. By A. W. HUTTON, M.A.

CHARLES SIMEON. By H. C. G. MOULE, D.D.

JOHN KEBLE. By WALTER LOCK, D.D.

THOMAS CHALMERS. By Mrs. OLIPHANT.

LANCELOT ANDREWES. By R. L. OTTLEY, M.A.

AUGUSTINE OF CANTERBURY. By E. L. CUTTS, D.D.

WILLIAM LAUD. By W. H. HUTTON, M.A.

JOHN KNOX. By F. MACCUNN.

JOHN HOWE. By R. F. HORTON, D.D.

BISHOP KEN. By F. A. CLARKE, M.A.

GEORGE FOX, THE QUAKER. By T. HODGKIN, D.C.L.

JOHN DONNE. By AUGUSTUS JESSOPP, D.D.

THOMAS CRANMER. By. A. J. MASON.

BISHOP LATIMER. By R. M. CARLYLE and A. J. CARLYLE, M.A.

Other volumes will be announced in due course.

Fiction

Marie Corelli's Novels
Crown 8vo. 6s. each.

A ROMANCE OF TWO WORLDS. *Twenty-Second Edition.*

VENDETTA. *Sixteenth Edition.*

THELMA. *Twenty-Fifth Edition.*

ARDATH: THE STORY OF A DEAD SELF. *Thirteenth Edition.*

THE SOUL OF LILITH. *Tenth Edition.*

WORMWOOD. *Eleventh Edition.*

BARABBAS: A DREAM OF THE WORLD'S TRAGEDY. *Thirty-sixth Edition.*

'The tender reverence of the treatment and the imaginative beauty of the writing have reconciled us to the daring of the conception, and the conviction is forced on us that even so exalted a subject cannot be made too familiar to us, provided it be presented in the true spirit of Christian faith. The amplifications of the Scripture narrative are often conceived with high poetic insight, and this "Dream of the World's Tragedy" is a lofty and not inadequate paraphrase of the supreme climax of the inspired narrative.'—*Dublin Review.*

THE SORROWS OF SATAN. *Forty-Fourth Edition.*

'A very powerful piece of work.... The conception is magnificent, and is likely to win an abiding place within the memory of man.... The author has immense command of language, and a limitless audacity.... This interesting and remarkable romance will live long after much of the ephemeral literature of the day is forgotten.... A literary phenomenon... novel, and even sublime.'—W. T. STEAD in the *Review of Reviews.*

THE MASTER CHRISTIAN.

[160th Thousand.

'It cannot be denied that "The Master Christian" is a powerful book; that it is one likely to raise uncomfortable questions in all but the most self-satisfied readers, and that it strikes at the root of the failure of the Churches—the decay of faith—in a manner which shows the inevitable disaster heaping up.... The good Cardinal Bonpré is a beautiful figure, fit to stand beside the good Bishop in "Les Misérables"... The chapter in which the Cardinal appears with Manuel before Leo XIII. is characterised by extraordinary realism and dramatic intensity... It is a book with a serious purpose expressed with absolute unconventionality and passion... And this is to say it is a book worth reading.'—*Examiner.*

Anthony Hope's Novels

Crown 8vo. 6s. each.

THE GOD IN THE CAR. *Ninth Edition.*
'A very remarkable book, deserving of critical analysis impossible within our limit; brilliant, but not superficial; well considered, but not elaborated; constructed with the proverbial art that conceals, but yet allows itself to be enjoyed by readers to whom fine literary method is a keen pleasure.'—*The World.*

A CHANGE OF AIR. *Sixth Edition.*
'A graceful, vivacious comedy, true to human nature. The characters are traced with a masterly hand.'—*Times.*

A MAN OF MARK. *Fifth Edition.*
'Of all Mr. Hope's books, "A Man of Mark" is the one which best compares with "The Prisoner of Zenda."'—*National Observer.*

THE CHRONICLES OF COUNT ANTONIO. *Fourth Edition.*
'It is a perfectly enchanting story of love and chivalry, and pure romance. The Count is the most constant, desperate, and modest and tender of lovers, a peerless gentleman, an intrepid fighter, a faithful friend, and a magnanimous foe.'—*Guardian.*

PHROSO. Illustrated by H. R. MILLAR. *Fifth Edition.*
'The tale is thoroughly fresh, quick with vitality, stirring the blood.'—*St. James's Gazette.*

SIMON DALE. Illustrated. *Fifth Edition.*
'There is searching analysis of human nature, with a most ingeniously constructed plot. Mr. Hope has drawn the contrasts of his women with marvellous subtlety and delicacy.'—*Times.*

THE KING'S MIRROR. *Third Edition.*
'In elegance, delicacy, and tact it ranks with the best of his novels, while in the wide range of its portraiture and the subtilty of its analysis it surpasses all his earlier ventures.'—*Spectator.*

QUISANTE. *Third Edition.*
'The book is notable for a very high literary quality, and an impress of power and mastery on every page.'—*Daily Chronicle.*

Gilbert Parker's Novels

Crown 8vo. 6s. each.

PIERRE AND HIS PEOPLE. *Fifth Edition.*
'Stories happily conceived and finely executed. There is strength and genius in Mr. Parker's style.'—*Daily Telegraph.*

MRS. FALCHION. *Fourth Edition.*
'A splendid study of character.'—*Athenæum.*

THE TRANSLATION OF A SAVAGE.
'The plot is original and one difficult to work out; but Mr. Parker has done it with great skill and delicacy.'—*Daily Chronicle.*

THE TRAIL OF THE SWORD. Illustrated. *Seventh Edition.*
'A rousing and dramatic tale. A book like this, in which swords flash, great surprises are undertaken, and daring deeds done, in which men and women live and love in the old passionate way, is a joy inexpressible.'—*Daily Chronicle.*

WHEN VALMOND CAME TO PONTIAC: The Story of a Lost Napoleon. *Fifth Edition.*
'Here we find romance—real, breathing, living romance. The character of Valmond is drawn unerringly.'—*Pall Mall Gazette.*

AN ADVENTURER OF THE NORTH: The Last Adventures of 'Pretty Pierre.' *Second Edition.*
'The present book is full of fine and moving stories of the great North, and it will add to Mr. Parker's already high reputation.'—*Glasgow Herald.*

THE SEATS OF THE MIGHTY. Illustrated. *Eleventh Edition.*
Mr. Parker has produced a really fine historical novel.'—*Athenæum.*
'A great book.'—*Black and White.*

THE BATTLE OF THE STRONG: a Romance of Two Kingdoms. Illustrated. *Fourth Edition.*
'Nothing more vigorous or more human has come from Mr. Gilbert Parker than this novel. It has all the graphic power of his last book, with truer feeling for the romance, both of human life and wild nature.'—*Literature.*

THE POMP OF THE LAVILETTES. *Second Edition.* 3s. 6d.
'Unforced pathos, and a deeper knowledge of human nature than Mr. Parker has ever displayed before.'—*Pall Mall Gazette.*

MESSRS. METHUEN'S CATALOGUE

S. Baring Gould's Novels

Crown 8vo. 6s. each.

ARMINELL. *Fifth Edition.*
URITH. *Fifth Edition.*
IN THE ROAR OF THE SEA. *Seventh Edition.*
MRS. CURGENVEN OF CURGENVEN. *Fourth Edition.*
CHEAP JACK ZITA. *Fourth Edition.*
THE QUEEN OF LOVE. *Fifth Edition.*
MARGERY OF QUETHER. *Third Edition.*
JACQUETTA. *Third Edition.*
KITTY ALONE. *Fifth Edition.*
NOÉMI. Illustrated. *Fourth Edition.*
THE BROOM-SQUIRE. Illustrated. *Fourth Edition.*
THE PENNYCOMEQUICKS. *Third Edition.*
DARTMOOR IDYLLS.
GUAVAS THE TINNER. Illustrated. *Second Edition.*
BLADYS. Illustrated. *Second Edition.*
DOMITIA. Illustrated. *Second Edition.*
PABO THE PRIEST.
WINEFRED. Illustrated. *Second Edition.*
THE FROBISHERS.

Conan Doyle. ROUND THE RED LAMP. By A. CONAN DOYLE. *Seventh Edition. Crown 8vo. 6s.*
'The book is far and away the best view that has been vouchsafed us behind the scenes of the consulting-room.'—*Illustrated London News.*

Stanley Weyman. UNDER THE RED ROBE. By STANLEY WEYMAN, Author of 'A Gentleman of France.' With Illustrations by R. C. WOODVILLE. *Sixteenth Edition. Crown 8vo. 6s.*
'Every one who reads books at all must read this thrilling romance, from the first page of which to the last the breathless reader is haled along. An inspiration of manliness and courage.'—*Daily Chronicle.*

Lucas Malet. THE WAGES OF SIN. By LUCAS MALET. *Thirteenth Edition. Crown 8vo. 6s.*

Lucas Malet. THE CARISSIMA. By LUCAS MALET, Author of 'The Wages of Sin,' etc. *Fourth Edition. Crown 8vo. 6s.*

Lucas Malet. THE GATELESS BARRIER. By LUCAS MALET, Author of 'The Wages of Sin.' *Third Edition. Crown 8vo. 6s.*
'The story is told with a sense of style and a dramatic vigour that makes it a pleasure to read. The workmanship arouses enthusiasm.'—*Times.*

W. W. Jacobs. A MASTER OF CRAFT. By W. W. JACOBS, Author of 'Many Cargoes.' Illustrated. *Fourth Edition. Crown 8vo. 3s. 6d.*
'Can be unreservedly recommended to all who have not lost their appetite for wholesome laughter.'—*Spectator.*
'The best humorous book published for many a day.'—*Black and White.*

W. W. Jacobs. MANY CARGOES. By W. W. JACOBS. *Twenty-fifth Edition. Crown 8vo. 3s. 6d.*

W. W. Jacobs. SEA URCHINS. By W. W. JACOBS. *Crown 8vo. 3s. 6d.*

Edna Lyall. DERRICK VAUGHAN, NOVELIST. *42nd thousand.* By EDNA LYALL. *Crown 8vo. 3s. 6d.*

George Gissing. THE TOWN TRAVELLER. By GEORGE GISSING, Author of 'Demos,' 'In the Year of Jubilee,' etc. *Second Edition. Cr. 8vo. 6s.*
'It is a bright and witty book above all things. Polly Sparkes is a splendid bit of work.'—*Pall Mall Gazette.*
'The spirit of Dickens is in it.'—*Bookman.*

George Gissing. THE CROWN OF LIFE. By GEORGE GISSING, Author of 'Demos,' 'The Town Traveller,' etc. *Crown 8vo. 6s.*

Henry James. THE SOFT SIDE. By HENRY JAMES, Author of 'What Maisie Knew.' *Second Edition. Crown 8vo. 6s.*
'The amazing cleverness marks the great worker.'—*Speaker.*

H. James. THE SACRED FOUNT. By HENRY JAMES, Author of 'What Maisie Knew.' *Crown 8vo. 6s.*
'"The Sacred Fount" is only for the few, but they will prize it highly, for it is worthy of its illustrious author.'—*Pall Mall Gazette.*

S. R. Crockett. LOCHINVAR. By S. R. CROCKETT, Author of 'The Raiders,' etc. Illustrated. *Second Edition. Crown 8vo. 6s.*
'Full of gallantry and pathos, of the clash of arms, and brightened by episodes of humour and love.'—*Westminster Gazette.*

S. R. Crockett. THE STANDARD BEARER. By S. R. CROCKETT. *Crown 8vo. 6s.*
'A delightful tale.'—*Speaker.*
'Mr. Crockett at his best.'—*Literature.*

Arthur Morrison. TALES OF MEAN STREETS. By ARTHUR MORRISON. *Fifth Edition. Cr. 8vo. 6s.*
'Told with consummate art and extraordinary detail. In the true humanity of the book lies its justification, the permanence of its interest, and its indubitable triumph.'—*Athenæum.*
'A great book. The author's method is amazingly effective, and produces a thrilling sense of reality. The writer lays upon us a master hand. The book is simply appalling and irresistible in its interest. It is humorous also; without humour it would not make the mark it is certain to make.'—*World.*

Arthur Morrison. A CHILD OF THE JAGO. By ARTHUR MORRISON. *Third Edition. Cr. 8vo. 6s.*
'The book is a masterpiece.'—*Pall Mall Gazette.*
'Told with great vigour and powerful simplicity.'—*Athenæum.*

Arthur Morrison. TO LONDON TOWN. By ARTHUR MORRISON, Author of 'Tales of Mean Streets,' etc. *Second Edition. Crown 8vo. 6s.*
'We have idyllic pictures, woodland scenes full of tenderness and grace. . . . This is the new Mr. Arthur Morrison gracious and tender, sympathetic and human.'—*Daily Telegraph.*

Arthur Morrison. CUNNING MURRELL. By ARTHUR MORRISON, Author of 'A Child of the Jago,' etc. *Crown 8vo. 6s.*
'The plot hangs admirably. The dialogue is perfect.'—*Daily Mail.*
'Admirable. . . . Delightful humorous relief . . . a most artistic and satisfactory achievement.'—*Spectator.*

Max Pemberton. THE FOOTSTEPS OF A THRONE. By MAX PEMBERTON. Illustrated. *Second Edition. Crown 8vo. 6s.*
'A story of pure adventure, with a sensation on every page.'—*Daily Mail.*

M. Sutherland. ONE HOUR AND THE NEXT. By THE DUCHESS OF SUTHERLAND. *Third Edition. Crown 8vo. 6s.*
'Passionate, vivid, dramatic.'—*Literature.*

Mrs. Clifford. A FLASH OF SUMMER. By Mrs. W. K. CLIFFORD, Author of 'Aunt Anne,' etc. *Second Edition. Crown 8vo. 6s.*
'The story is a very beautiful one, exquisitely told.'—*Speaker.*

Emily Lawless. HURRISH. By the Honble. EMILY LAWLESS, Author of 'Maelcho,' etc. *Fifth Edition. Cr. 8vo. 6s.*

Emily Lawless. MAELCHO: a Sixteenth Century Romance. By the Honble. EMILY LAWLESS. *Second Edition. Crown 8vo. 6s.*
'A really great book.'—*Spectator.*

Emily Lawless. TRAITS AND CONFIDENCES. By the Honble. EMILY LAWLESS. *Crown 8vo. 6s.*

Eden Phillpotts. LYING PROPHETS. By EDEN PHILLPOTTS. *Crown 8vo. 6s.*

Eden Phillpotts. CHILDREN OF THE MIST. By EDEN PHILLPOTTS. *Crown 8vo. 6s.*

Eden Phillpotts. THE HUMAN BOY. By EDEN PHILLPOTTS, Author of 'Children of the Mist.' With a Frontispiece. *Fourth Edition. Crown 8vo. 6s.*
'Mr. Phillpotts knows exactly what schoolboys do, and can lay bare their inmost thoughts; likewise he shows an all-pervading sense of humour.'—*Academy.*

Eden Phillpotts. SONS OF THE MORNING. By EDEN PHILLPOTTS, Author of 'The Children of the Mist.' *Second Edition. Crown 8vo. 6s.*
'A book of strange power and fascination.' —*Morning Post.*
'Inimitable humour.'—*Daily Graphic.*

Jane Barlow. A CREEL OF IRISH STORIES. By JANE BARLOW, Author of 'Irish Idylls.' *Second Edition. Crown 8vo. 6s.*
'Vivid and singularly real.'—*Scotsman.*

Jane Barlow. FROM THE EAST UNTO THE WEST. By JANE BARLOW. *Crown 8vo. 6s.*

J. H. Findlater. THE GREEN GRAVES OF BALGOWRIE. By JANE H. FINDLATER. *Fourth Edition. Crown 8vo. 6s.*
'A powerful and vivid story.'—*Standard.*
'A beautiful story, sad and strange as truth itself.'—*Vanity Fair.*
'A singularly original, clever, and beautiful story.'—*Guardian.*
'Reveals to us a new writer of undoubted faculty and reserve force.'—*Spectator.*
'An exquisite idyll, delicate, affecting, and beautiful.'—*Black and White.*

J. H. Findlater. A DAUGHTER OF STRIFE. By JANE H. FINDLATER. *Crown 8vo. 6s.*

J. H. Findlater. RACHEL. By JANE H. FINDLATER. *Second Edition. Crown 8vo. 6s.*
'A not unworthy successor to "The Green Graves of Balgowrie."'—*Critic.*

J. H. and Mary Findlater. TALES THAT ARE TOLD. By JANE H. FINDLATER, and MARY FINDLATER. *Crown 8vo. 6s.*
'Delightful and graceful stories for which we have the warmest welcome.'—*Literature.*

Mary Findlater. A NARROW WAY. By MARY FINDLATER, Author of 'Over the Hills.' *Third Edition. Crown 8vo. 6s.*
'A wholesome, thoughtful, and interesting novel.'—*Morning Post.*
'Singularly pleasant, full of quiet humour and tender sympathy.'—*Manchester Guardian.*

Mary Findlater. OVER THE HILLS. By MARY FINDLATER. *Second Edition. Cr. 8vo. 6s.*
'A strong and wise book of deep insight and unflinching truth.'—*Birmingham Post.*

Mary Findlater. BETTY MUSGRAVE. By MARY FINDLATER. *Second Edition. Crown 8vo. 6s.*
'Handled with dignity and delicacy. . . . A most touching story.'—*Spectator.*

Alfred Ollivant. OWD BOB, THE GREY DOG OF KENMUIR. By ALFRED OLLIVANT. *Fourth Edition. Cr. 8vo. 6s.*
'Weird, thrilling, strikingly graphic.'—*Punch.*
'We admire this book. . . . It is one to read with admiration and to praise with enthusiasm.'—*Bookman.*
'It is a fine, open-air, blood-stirring book, to be enjoyed by every man and woman to whom a dog is dear.'—*Literature.*

B. M. Croker. PEGGY OF THE BARTONS. By B. M. CROKER, Author of 'Diana Barrington.' *Fifth Edition. Crown 8vo. 6s.*
'Mrs. Croker excels in the admirably simple, easy, and direct flow of her narrative, the briskness of her dialogue, and the geniality of her portraiture.'—*Spectator.*

B. M. Croker. A STATE SECRET. By B. M. CROKER, Author of 'Peggy of the Bartons,' etc. *Second Edition. Crown 8vo. 3s. 6d.*
'Full of humour, and always fresh and pleasing.'—*Daily Express.*
'Ingenious, humorous, pretty, pathetic.'—*World.*

H. G. Wells. THE STOLEN BACILLUS, and other Stories. By H. G. WELLS. *Second Edition. Crown 8vo. 6s.*
'The impressions of a very striking imagination.'—*Saturday Review.*

H. G. Wells. THE PLATTNER STORY AND OTHERS. By H. G. WELLS. *Second Edition. Cr. 8vo. 6s.*
'Weird and mysterious, they seem to hold the reader as by a magic spell.'—*Scotsman.*

Sara Jeannette Duncan. A VOYAGE OF CONSOLATION. By SARA JEANNETTE DUNCAN, Author of 'An American Girl in London.' Illustrated. *Third Edition. Cr. 8vo. 6s.*
'The dialogue is full of wit.'—*Globe.*

Sara Jeannette Duncan. THE PATH OF A STAR. By SARA JEANNETTE DUNCAN, Author of 'A Voyage of Consolation.' Illustrated. *Second Edition. Crown 8vo. 6s.*

C. F. Keary. THE JOURNALIST. By C. F. KEARY. *Cr. 8vo. 6s.*

W. E. Norris. MATTHEW AUSTIN. By W. E. NORRIS, Author of 'Mademoiselle de Mersac,' etc. *Fourth Edition. Crown 8vo. 6s.*
'An intellectually satisfactory and morally bracing novel.'—*Daily Telegraph.*

W. E. Norris. HIS GRACE. By W. E. NORRIS. *Third Edition. Cr. 8vo. 6s.*

W. E. Norris. THE DESPOTIC LADY AND OTHERS. By W. E. NORRIS. *Crown 8vo. 6s.*

W. E. Norris. CLARISSA FURIOSA. By W. E. NORRIS. *Cr. 8vo. 6s.*
'As a story it is admirable, as a *jeu d'esprit* it is capital, as a lay sermon studded with gems of wit and wisdom it is a model.'—*The World.*

W. E. Norris. GILES INGILBY. By W. E. NORRIS. Illustrated. *Second Edition. Crown 8vo. 6s.*
'Interesting, wholesome, and charmingly written.'—*Glasgow Herald.*

W. E. Norris. AN OCTAVE. By W. E. NORRIS. *Second Edition. Crown 8vo. 6s.*

W. Clark Russell. MY DANISH SWEETHEART. By W. CLARK RUSSELL. Illustrated. *Fourth Edition. Crown 8vo. 6s.*

Robert Barr. IN THE MIDST OF ALARMS. By ROBERT BARR. *Third Edition. Cr. 8vo. 6s.*
'A book which has abundantly satisfied us by its capital humour.'—*Daily Chronicle.*

Robert Barr. THE MUTABLE MANY. By ROBERT BARR. *Second Edition. Crown 8vo. 6s.*
'Very much the best novel that Mr. Barr has yet given us. There is much insight in it, and much excellent humour.'—*Daily Chronicle.*

Robert Barr. THE COUNTESS TEKLA. By ROBERT BARR. *Third Edition. Crown 8vo. 6s.*
'Of these mediæval romances, which are now gaining ground, "The Countess Tekla" is the very best we have seen. The story is written in clear English, and a picturesque, moving style.'—*Pall Mall Gazette.*

Robert Barr. THE STRONG ARM. By ROBERT BARR, Author of 'The Countess Tekla.' Illustrated. *Second Edition. 8vo. 6s.*

C. J. Cutcliffe Hyne. PRINCE RUPERT THE BUCCANEER. By C. J. CUTCLIFFE HYNE, Author of 'Captain Kettle.' With 8 Illustrations by G. GRENVILLE MANTON. *Second Edition. Crown 8vo. 6s.*
A narrative of the romantic adventures of the famous Prince Rupert, and of his exploits in the Spanish Indies after the Cromwellian wars.

Mrs. Dudeney. THE THIRD FLOOR. By Mrs. DUDENEY, Author of 'Folly Corner.' *Second Edition. Crown 8vo. 6s.*
'One of the brightest, wittiest, and most entertaining novels published this spring.'—*Sketch.*

Andrew Balfour. BY STROKE OF SWORD. By A. BALFOUR. Illustrated. *Fourth Edition. Cr. 8vo. 6s.*
'A recital of thrilling interest, told with unflagging vigour.'—*Globe.*

Andrew Balfour. TO ARMS! By ANDREW BALFOUR. Illustrated. *Second Edition. Crown 8vo. 6s.*
'The marvellous perils through which Allan passes are told in powerful and lively fashion.'—*Pall Mall Gazette.*

Andrew Balfour. VENGEANCE IS MINE. By ANDREW BALFOUR, Author of 'By Stroke of Sword.' Illustrated. *Crown 8vo. 6s.*
'A vigorous piece of work, well written, and abounding in stirring incidents.'—*Glasgow Herald.*

R. Hichens. BYEWAYS. By ROBERT HICHENS. Author of 'Flames,' etc. *Second Edition. Cr. 8vo. 6s.*
'The work is undeniably that of a man of striking imagination.'—*Daily News.*

R. Hichens. TONGUES OF CONSCIENCE. By ROBERT HICHENS, Author of 'Flames.' *Second Edition. Crown 8vo. 6s.*
'Of a strange, haunting quality.'—*Glasgow Herald.*

Stephen Crane. WOUNDS IN THE RAIN. WAR STORIES. By STEPHEN CRANE, Author of 'The Red Badge of Courage.' *Second Edition. Crown 8vo. 6s.*
'A fascinating volume.'—*Spectator.*

38   MESSRS. METHUEN'S CATALOGUE

Dorothea Gerard. THE CONQUEST OF LONDON. By DOROTHEA GERARD, Author of 'Lady Baby.' *Second Edition.* Crown 8vo. 6s.
'Bright and entertaining.'—*Spectator.*
'Highly entertaining and enjoyable.'—*Scotsman.*

Dorothea Gerard. THE SUPREME CRIME. By DOROTHEA GERARD. *Crown 8vo.* 6s.
'One of the very best plots we have met with in recent fiction, and handled with that quiet unerring realism which always distinguishes the author's best work.'—*Academy.*

C. F. Goss. THE REDEMPTION OF DAVID CORSON. By C. F. GOSS. *Third Edition. Crown 8vo.* 6s.
'Dramatic instinct and a vigorous imagination mark this soul history of a Quaker mystic.'—*Athenæum.*
'A really fine book.'—*Public Opinion.*
'A powerful and original book, and unusually striking.'—*Pilot.*
'Worthy to stand high in the ranks of modern fiction.'—*Literature.*

OTHER SIX-SHILLING NOVELS
Crown 8vo.

A SECRETARY OF LEGATION. By HOPE DAWLISH.
THE SALVATION SEEKERS. By NOEL AINSLIE.
STRANGE HAPPENINGS. By W. CLARK RUSSELL and other Authors.
THE BLACK WOLF'S BREED. By HARRIS DICKSON. Illustrated. *Second Edition.*
BELINDA FITZWARREN. By the EARL OF IDDESLEIGH.
DERWENT'S HORSE. By VICTOR ROUSSEAU.
ANNE MAULEVERER. By Mrs. CAFFYN (Iota).
SIREN CITY. By BENJAMIN SWIFT.
AN ENGLISHMAN. By MARY L. PENDERED.
THE PLUNDERERS. By MORLEY ROBERTS.
THE HUMAN INTEREST. By VIOLET HUNT.
THE KING OF ANDAMAN: A Saviour of Society. By J. MACLAREN COBBAN.
THE ANGEL OF THE COVENANT. By J. MACLAREN COBBAN.
IN THE DAY OF ADVERSITY. By J. BLOUNDELLE-BURTON.
DENOUNCED. By J. BLOUNDELLE-BURTON.
THE CLASH OF ARMS. By J. BLOUNDELLE-BURTON.
ACROSS THE SALT SEAS. By J. BLOUNDELLE-BURTON.
SERVANTS OF SIN. By J. BLOUNDELLE-BURTON.
PATH AND GOAL. *Second Edition.* By ADA CAMBRIDGE.
THE SEEN AND THE UNSEEN. By RICHARD MARSH.
MARVELS AND MYSTERIES. By RICHARD MARSH.
ELMSLIE'S DRAG-NET. By E. H. STRAIN.
A FOREST OFFICER. By Mrs. PENNY.
THE WHITE HECATOMB. By W. C. SCULLY.
BETWEEN SUN AND SAND. By W. C. SCULLY.
SIR ROBERT'S FORTUNE. By Mrs. OLIPHANT.
THE TWO MARYS. By Mrs. OLIPHANT.
THE LADY'S WALK. By Mrs. OLIPHANT.
MIRRY-ANN. By NORMA LORIMER.
JOSIAH'S WIFE. By NORMA LORIMER.
THE STRONG GOD CIRCUMSTANCE. By HELEN SHIPTON.
CHRISTALLA. By ESMÉ STUART.
THE DESPATCH RIDER. By ERNEST GLANVILLE
AN ENEMY TO THE KING. By R. N. STEPHENS.
A GENTLEMAN PLAYER. By R. N. STEPHENS.

THE PATHS OF THE PRUDENT. By J. S. Fletcher.

THE BUILDERS. By J. S. Fletcher.

DANIEL WHYTE. By A. J. Dawson.

THE CAPSINA. By E. F. Benson.

DODO: A DETAIL OF THE DAY. By E. F. Benson.

THE VINTAGE. By E. F. Benson. Illustrated by G. P. Jacomb-Hood.

ROSE À CHARLITTE. By Marshall Saunders.

WILLOWBRAKE. By R. Murray Gilchrist.

THINGS THAT HAVE HAPPENED. By Dorothea Gerard.

LONE PINE: A ROMANCE OF MEXICAN LIFE. By R. B. Townshend.

WILT THOU HAVE THIS WOMAN? By J. Maclaren Cobban.

A PASSIONATE PILGRIM. By Percy White.

SECRETARY TO BAYNE, M.P. By W. Pett Ridge.

ADRIAN ROME. By E. Dawson and A. Moore.

GALLIA. By Ménie Muriel Dowie.

THE CROOK OF THE BOUGH. By Ménie Muriel Dowie.

A BUSINESS IN GREAT WATERS. By Julian Corbett.

MISS ERIN. By M. E. Francis.

ANANIAS. By the Hon. Mrs. Alan Brodrick.

CORRAGEEN IN '98. By Mrs. Orpen.

THE PLUNDER PIT. By J. Keighley Snowden.

CROSS TRAILS. By Victor Waite.

SUCCESSORS TO THE TITLE. By Mrs. Walford.

KIRKHAM'S FIND. By Mary Gaunt.

DEADMAN'S. By Mary Gaunt.

CAPTAIN JACOBUS: A ROMANCE OF THE ROAD. By L. Cope Cornford.

SONS OF ADVERSITY. By L. Cope Cornford.

THE KING OF ALBERIA. By Laura Daintrey.

THE DAUGHTER OF ALOUETTE. By Mary A. Owen.

CHILDREN OF THIS WORLD. By Ellen F. Pinsent.

AN ELECTRIC SPARK. By G. Manville Fenn.

UNDER SHADOW OF THE MISSION. By L. S. McChesney.

THE SPECULATORS. By J. F. Brewer.

THE SPIRIT OF STORM. By Ronald Ross.

THE QUEENSBERRY CUP. By Clive P. Wolley.

A HOME IN INVERESK. By T. L. Paton.

MISS ARMSTRONG'S AND OTHER CIRCUMSTANCES. By John Davidson.

DR. CONGALTON'S LEGACY. By Henry Johnston.

TIME AND THE WOMAN. By Richard Pryce.

THIS MAN'S DOMINION. By the Author of 'A High Little World.'

DIOGENES OF LONDON. By H. B. Marriott Watson.

THE STONE DRAGON. By R. Murray Gilchrist.

A VICAR'S WIFE. By Evelyn Dickinson.

ELSA. By E. M'Queen Gray.

THE SINGER OF MARLY. By I. Hooper.

THE FALL OF THE SPARROW. By M. C. Balfour.

A SERIOUS COMEDY. By Herbert Morrah.

THE FAITHFUL CITY. By Herbert Morrah.

IN THE GREAT DEEP. By J. A. Barry.

BIJLI, THE DANCER. By James Blythe Patton.

THE PHILANTHROPIST. By Lucy Maynard.

VAUSSORE. By Francis Brune.

THREE-AND-SIXPENNY NOVELS
Crown 8vo.

THE MESS DECK. By W. F. SHANNON.

A SON OF THE STATE. By W. PETT RIDGE.

CEASE FIRE! By J. MACLAREN COBBAN.

THE KLOOF BRIDE. By ERNEST GLANVILLE.

THE LOST REGIMENT. By ERNEST GLANVILLE.

BUNTER'S CRUISE. By CHARLES GLEIG. Illustrated.

THE ADVENTURE OF PRINCESS SYLVIA. By Mrs. C. N. WILLIAMSON.

A VENDETTA OF THE DESERT. By W. C. SCULLY.

SUBJECT TO VANITY. By MARGARET BENSON.

FITZJAMES. By LILIAN STREET.

THE SIGN OF THE SPIDER. *Fifth Edition.* By BERTRAM MITFORD.

THE MOVING FINGER. By MARY GAUNT.

JACO TRELOAR. By J. H. PEARCE.

THE DANCE OF THE HOURS. By 'VERA.'

A WOMAN OF FORTY. By ESMÉ STUART.

A CUMBERER OF THE GROUND. By CONSTANCE SMITH.

THE SIN OF ANGELS. By EVELYN DICKINSON.

AUT DIABOLUS AUT NIHIL. By X. L.

THE COMING OF CUCULAIN. By STANDISH O'GRADY.

THE GODS GIVE MY DONKEY WINGS. By ANGUS EVAN ABBOTT.

THE STAR GAZERS. By G. MANVILLE FENN.

THE POISON OF ASPS. By R. ORTON PROWSE.

THE QUIET MRS. FLEMING. By R. PRYCE.

DISENCHANTMENT. By F. MABEL ROBINSON.

THE SQUIRE OF WANDALES. By A. SHIELD.

A REVEREND GENTLEMAN. By J. M. COBBAN.

A DEPLORABLE AFFAIR. By W. E. NORRIS.

A CAVALIER'S LADYE. By Mrs. DICKER.

THE PRODIGALS. By Mrs. OLIPHANT.

THE SUPPLANTER. By P. NEUMANN.

A MAN WITH BLACK EYELASHES. By H. A. KENNEDY.

A HANDFUL OF EXOTICS. By S. GORDON.

AN ODD EXPERIMENT. By HANNAH LYNCH.

TALES OF NORTHUMBRIA. By HOWARD PEASE.

HALF-CROWN NOVELS
Crown 8vo.

HOVENDEN, V.C. By F. MABEL ROBINSON.

THE PLAN OF CAMPAIGN. By F. MABEL ROBINSON.

MR. BUTLER'S WARD. By F. MABEL ROBINSON.

ELI'S CHILDREN. By G. MANVILLE FENN.

A DOUBLE KNOT. By G. MANVILLE FENN.

DISARMED. By M. BETHAM EDWARDS.

IN TENT AND BUNGALOW. By the Author of 'Indian Idylls.'

MY STEWARDSHIP. By E. M'QUEEN GRAY.

JACK'S FATHER. By W. E. NORRIS.

A LOST ILLUSION. By LESLIE KEITH.

THE TRUE HISTORY OF JOSHUA DAVIDSON, Christian and Communist. By E. LYNN LYNTON. *Eleventh Edition. Post 8vo.* 1s.

The Novelist

Messrs. Methuen are making an interesting experiment which constitutes a fresh departure in publishing. They are issuing under the above general title a Monthly Series of Novels by popular authors at the price of Sixpence. Many of these Novels have never been published before. Each Number is as long as the average Six Shilling Novel. The first numbers of 'THE NOVELIST' are as follows:—

I. DEAD MEN TELL NO TALES. E. W. HORNUNG.
II. JENNIE BAXTER, JOURNALIST. ROBERT BARR.
III. THE INCA'S TREASURE. ERNEST GLANVILLE.
IV. *Out of print.*
V. FURZE BLOOM. S. BARING GOULD.
VI. BUNTER'S CRUISE. C. GLEIG.
VII. THE GAY DECEIVERS. ARTHUR MOORE.
VIII. PRISONERS OF WAR. A. BOYSON WEEKES.
IX. *Out of print.*
X. VELDT AND LAAGER: Tales of the Transvaal. E. S. VALENTINE.
XI. THE NIGGER KNIGHTS. F. NORREYS CONNELL.
XII. A MARRIAGE AT SEA. W. CLARK RUSSELL.
XIII. THE POMP OF THE LAVILETTES. GILBERT PARKER.
XIV. A MAN OF MARK. ANTHONY HOPE.
XV. THE CARISSIMA. LUCAS MALET.
XVI. THE LADY'S WALK. Mrs. OLIPHANT.
XVII. DERRICK VAUGHAN. EDNA LYALL.
XVIII. IN THE MIDST OF ALARMS. ROBERT BARR.
XIX. HIS GRACE. W. E. NORRIS.
XX. DODO. E. F. BENSON.
XXI. CHEAP JACK ZITA. S. BARING GOULD.
XXII. WHEN VALMOND CAME TO PONTIAC. GILBERT PARKER.

Methuen's Sixpenny Library

A New Series of Copyright Books

I. THE MATABELE CAMPAIGN. By Major-General BADEN-POWELL.
II. THE DOWNFALL OF PREMPEH. By Major-General BADEN-POWELL.
III. MY DANISH SWEETHEART. By W. CLARK RUSSELL.
IV. IN THE ROAR OF THE SEA. By S. BARING-GOULD.
V. PEGGY OF THE BARTONS. By B. M. CROKER.
VI. BADEN-POWELL OF MAFEKING: A Biography. By J. S. FLETCHER.
VIII. ROBERTS OF PRETORIA. By J. S. FLETCHER.
IX. THE GREEN GRAVES OF BALGOWRIE. By JANE H. FINDLATER.
X. THE STOLEN BACILLUS. By H. G. WELLS.
XI. MATTHEW AUSTIN. By W. E. NORRIS.

Books for Boys and Girls

A Series of Books by well-known Authors, well illustrated.

THREE-AND-SIXPENCE EACH

THE ICELANDER'S SWORD. By S. BARING GOULD.

TWO LITTLE CHILDREN AND CHING. By EDITH E. CUTHELL.

TODDLEBEN'S HERO. By M. M. BLAKE.

ONLY A GUARD-ROOM DOG. By EDITH E. CUTHELL.

THE DOCTOR OF THE JULIET. By HARRY COLLINGWOOD.

MASTER ROCKAFELLAR'S VOYAGE. By W. CLARK RUSSELL.

SYD BELTON: Or, The Boy who would not go to Sea. By G. MANVILLE FENN.

The Peacock Library

A Series of Books for Girls by well-known Authors, handsomely bound, and well illustrated.

THREE-AND-SIXPENCE EACH

THE RED GRANGE. By Mrs. MOLESWORTH.

THE SECRET OF MADAME DE MONLUC. By the Author of 'Mdle. Mori.'

OUT OF THE FASHION. By L. T. MEADE.

DUMPS. By Mrs. PARR.

A GIRL OF THE PEOPLE. By L. T. MEADE.

HEPSY GIPSY. By L. T. MEADE. 2s. 6d.

THE HONOURABLE MISS. By L. T. MEADE.

University Extension Series

A series of books on historical, literary, and scientific subjects, suitable for extension students and home-reading circles. Each volume is complete in itself, and the subjects are treated by competent writers in a broad and philosophic spirit.

Edited by J. E. SYMES, M.A.,
Principal of University College, Nottingham.

Crown 8vo. Price (with some exceptions) 2s. 6d.

The following volumes are ready:—

THE INDUSTRIAL HISTORY OF ENGLAND. By H. DE B. GIBBINS, Litt.D., M.A., late Scholar of Wadham College, Oxon., Cobden Prizeman. *Seventh Edition*, Revised. With Maps and Plans. 3s.

A HISTORY OF ENGLISH POLITICAL ECONOMY. By L. L. PRICE, M.A., Fellow of Oriel College, Oxon. *Third Edition.*

PROBLEMS OF POVERTY: An Inquiry into the Industrial Conditions of the Poor. By J. A. HOBSON, M.A. *Fourth Edition.*

VICTORIAN POETS. By A. SHARP.

THE FRENCH REVOLUTION. By J. E. SYMES, M.A.
PSYCHOLOGY. By F. S. GRANGER, M.A. *Second Edition.*
THE EVOLUTION OF PLANT LIFE: Lower Forms. By G. MASSEE. With Illustrations.
AIR AND WATER. By V. B. LEWES, M.A. Illustrated.
THE CHEMISTRY OF LIFE AND HEALTH. By C. W. KIMMINS, M.A. Illustrated.
THE MECHANICS OF DAILY LIFE. By V. P. SELLS, M.A. Illustrated.
ENGLISH SOCIAL REFORMERS. By H. DE B. GIBBINS, Litt.D., M.A.
ENGLISH TRADE AND FINANCE IN THE SEVENTEENTH CENTURY. By W. A. S. HEWINS, B.A.
THE CHEMISTRY OF FIRE. The Elementary Principles of Chemistry. By M. M. PATTISON MUIR, M.A. Illustrated.
A TEXT-BOOK OF AGRICULTURAL BOTANY. By M. C. POTTER, M.A., F.L.S. Illustrated. 3s. 6d.

THE VAULT OF HEAVEN. A Popular Introduction to Astronomy. By R. A. GREGORY. With numerous Illustrations.
METEOROLOGY. The Elements of Weather and Climate. By H. N. DICKSON, F.R.S.E., F.R. Met. Soc. Illustrated.
A MANUAL OF ELECTRICAL SCIENCE. By GEORGE J. BURCH, M.A., F.R.S. With numerous Illustrations. 3s.
THE EARTH. An Introduction to Physiography. By EVAN SMALL, M.A. Illustrated.
INSECT LIFE. By F. W. THEOBALD, M.A. Illustrated.
ENGLISH POETRY FROM BLAKE TO BROWNING. By W. M. DIXON, M.A.
ENGLISH LOCAL GOVERNMENT. By E. JENKS, M.A., Professor of Law at University College, Liverpool.
THE GREEK VIEW OF LIFE. By G. L. DICKINSON, Fellow of King's College, Cambridge. *Second Edition.*

Social Questions of To-day

Edited by H. DE B. GIBBINS, Litt.D., M.A.

Crown 8vo. 2s. 6d.

The following Volumes of the Series are ready:—

TRADE UNIONISM—NEW AND OLD. By G. HOWELL. *Third Edition.*
THE CO-OPERATIVE MOVEMENT TO-DAY. By G. J. HOLYOAKE. *Second Edition.*
MUTUAL THRIFT. By Rev. J. FROME WILKINSON, M.A.
PROBLEMS OF POVERTY. By J. A. HOBSON, M.A. *Fourth Edition.*
THE COMMERCE OF NATIONS. By C. F. BASTABLE, M.A., Professor of Economics at Trinity College, Dublin. *Second Edition.*
THE ALIEN INVASION. By W. H. WILKINS, B.A.

THE RURAL EXODUS. By P. ANDERSON GRAHAM.
LAND NATIONALIZATION. By HAROLD COX, B.A.
A SHORTER WORKING DAY. By H. DE B. GIBBINS, D.Litt., M.A., and R. A. HADFIELD, of the Hecla Works, Sheffield.
BACK TO THE LAND: An Inquiry into the Cure for Rural Depopulation. By H. E. MOORE.
TRUSTS, POOLS AND CORNERS. By J. STEPHEN JEANS.
THE FACTORY SYSTEM. By R. W. COOKE-TAYLOR.

THE STATE AND ITS CHILDREN. By GERTRUDE TUCKWELL.

WOMEN'S WORK. By LADY DILKE, Miss BULLEY, and Miss WHITLEY.

SOCIALISM AND MODERN THOUGHT. By M. KAUFMANN.

THE HOUSING OF THE WORKING CLASSES. By E. BOWMAKER.

MODERN CIVILIZATION IN SOME OF ITS ECONOMIC ASPECTS. By W. CUNNINGHAM, D.D., Fellow of Trinity College, Cambridge.

THE PROBLEM OF THE UNEMPLOYED. By J. A. HOBSON, B.A.

LIFE IN WEST LONDON. By ARTHUR SHERWELL, M.A. *Third Edition.*

RAILWAY NATIONALIZATION. By CLEMENT EDWARDS.

WORKHOUSES AND PAUPERISM. By LOUISA TWINING.

UNIVERSITY AND SOCIAL SETTLEMENTS. By W. REASON, M.A.

Classical Translations

Edited by H. F. FOX, M.A., Fellow and Tutor of Brasenose College, Oxford.

ÆSCHYLUS — Agamemnon, Chöcphoroe, Eumenides. Translated by LEWIS CAMPBELL, LL.D., late Professor of Greek at St. Andrews. 5s.

CICERO—De Oratore I. Translated by E. N. P. MOOR, M.A. 3s. 6d.

CICERO—Select Orations (Pro Milone, Pro Murena, Philippic II., In Catilinam). Translated by H. E. D. BLAKISTON, M.A., Fellow and Tutor of Trinity College, Oxford. 5s.

CICERO—De Natura Deorum. Translated by F. BROOKS, M.A., late Scholar of Balliol College, Oxford. 3s. 6d.

CICERO DE OFFICIIS. Translated by G. B. GARDINER, M.A. *Crown 8vo.* 2s. 6d.

HORACE: THE ODES AND EPODES. Translated by A. GODLEY, M.A., Fellow of Magdalen College, Oxford. 2s.

LUCIAN—Six Dialogues (Nigrinus, Icaro-Menippus, The Cock, The Ship, The Parasite, The Lover of Falsehood). Translated by S. T. IRWIN, M.A., Assistant Master at Clifton; late Scholar of Exeter College, Oxford. 3s. 6d.

SOPHOCLES — Electra and Ajax. Translated by E. D. A. MORSHEAD, M.A., Assistant Master at Winchester. 2s. 6d.

TACITUS—Agricola and Germania. Translated by R. B. TOWNSHEND, late Scholar of Trinity College, Cambridge. 2s. 6d.

Educational Books

CLASSICAL

THE NICOMACHEAN ETHICS OF ARISTOTLE. Edited with an Introduction and Notes by JOHN BURNET, M.A., Professor of Greek at St. Andrews. *Demy 8vo.* 15s. net.

'We must content ourselves with saying, in conclusion, that we have seldom, if ever, seen an edition of any classical author in which what is held in common with other commentators is so clearly and shortly put, and what is original is (with equal brevity) of such value and interest.'
—*Pilot.*

THE CAPTIVI OF PLAUTUS. Edited, with an Introduction, Textual Notes, and a Commentary, by W. M. LINDSAY, Fellow of Jesus College, Oxford. *Demy 8vo.* 10s. 6d. net.

For this edition all the important MSS. have been re-collated. An appendix deals with the accentual element in early Latin verse. The Commentary is very full.

'A work of great erudition and fine scholarship.'—*Scotsman.*

MESSRS. METHUEN'S CATALOGUE   45

A GREEK ANTHOLOGY. Selected by E. C. MARCHANT, M.A., Fellow of Peterhouse, Cambridge, and Assistant Master at St. Paul's School. *Crown 8vo. 3s. 6d.*

PASSAGES FOR UNSEEN TRANSLATION. By E. C. MARCHANT, M.A., Fellow of Peterhouse, Cambridge; and A. M. COOK, M.A., late Scholar of Wadham College, Oxford; Assistant Masters at St. Paul's School. *Crown 8vo. 3s. 6d.*
'We know no book of this class better fitted for use in the higher forms of schools.'—*Guardian.*

TACITI AGRICOLA. With Introduction, Notes, Map, etc. By R. F. DAVIS, M.A., Assistant Master at Weymouth College. *Crown 8vo. 2s.*

TACITI GERMANIA. By the same Editor. *Crown 8vo. 2s.*

HERODOTUS: EASY SELECTIONS. With Vocabulary. By A. C. LIDDELL, M.A. *Fcap. 8vo. 1s. 6d.*

SELECTIONS FROM THE ODYSSEY. By E. D. STONE, M.A., late Assistant Master at Eton. *Fcap. 8vo. 1s. 6d.*

PLAUTUS: THE CAPTIVI. Adapted for Lower Forms by J. H.

FREESE, M.A., late Fellow of St. John's, Cambridge. *1s. 6d.*

DEMOSTHENES AGAINST CONON AND CALLICLES. Edited with Notes and Vocabulary, by F. DARWIN SWIFT, M.A. *Fcap. 8vo. 2s.*

EXERCISES IN LATIN ACCIDENCE. By S. E. WINBOLT, Assistant Master in Christ's Hospital. *Crown 8vo. 1s. 6d.*
An elementary book adapted for Lower Forms to accompany the shorter Latin primer.

NOTES ON GREEK AND LATIN SYNTAX. By G. BUCKLAND GREEN, M.A., Assistant Master at Edinburgh Academy, late Fellow of St. John's College, Oxon. *Crown 8vo. 3s. 6d.*
Notes and explanations on the chief difficulties of Greek and Latin Syntax, with numerous passages for exercise.

NEW TESTAMENT GREEK. A Course for Beginners. By G. RODWELL, B.A. With a Preface by WALTER LOCK, D.D., Warden of Keble College. *Fcap. 8vo. 3s. 6d.*

THE FROGS OF ARISTOPHANES. Translated by E. W. HUNTINGFORD, M.A., Professor of Classics in Trinity College, Toronto. *Cr. 8vo. 2s. 6d.*

GERMAN

A COMPANION GERMAN GRAMMAR. By H. DE B. GIBBINS, D. Litt., M.A., Headmaster at Kidderminster Grammar School. *Crown 8vo. 1s. 6d.*

GERMAN PASSAGES FOR UNSEEN TRANSLATION. By E. M'QUEEN GRAY. *Crown 8vo. 2s. 6d.*

SCIENCE

GENERAL ELEMENTARY SCIENCE. By J. T. DUNN, D.Sc., and V. A. MUNDELLA. With 114 Illustrations. *Crown 8vo. 3s. 6d.*
[*Methuen's Science Primers.*

THE WORLD OF SCIENCE. Including Chemistry, Heat, Light, Sound, Magnetism, Electricity, Botany, Zoology, Physiology, Astronomy, and Geology. By R.

ELLIOTT STEEL, M.A., F.C.S. 147 Illustrations. *Second Edition. Cr. 8vo. 2s. 6d.*

THE PRINCIPLES OF MAGNETISM AND ELECTRICITY: an Elementary Text-Book. By P. L. GRAY, B.Sc., formerly Lecturer in Physics in Mason University College, Birmingham. With 181 Diagrams. *Crown 8vo. 3s. 6d.*

Textbooks of Technology

Edited by Professors GARNETT and WERTHEIMER.

HOW TO MAKE A DRESS. By J. A. E. WOOD. *Illustrated. Second Edition. Cr. 8vo. 1s. 6d.*

CARPENTRY AND JOINERY. By F. C. WEBBER. With many Illustrations. *Second Edition. Cr. 8vo. 3s. 6d.*
'An admirable elementary text-book on the subject.'—*Builder.*

PRACTICAL MECHANICS. By SIDNEY H. WELLS. With 75 Illustrations and Diagrams. *Cr. 8vo. 3s. 6d.*

PRACTICAL PHYSICS. By H. STROUD, D.Sc., M.A., Professor of Physics in the Durham College of Science, Newcastle-on-Tyne. Fully illustrated. *Crown 8vo. 3s. 6d.*

MILLINERY, THEORETICAL, AND PRACTICAL. By CLARE HILL, Registered Teacher to the City and Guilds of London Institute. With numerous Diagrams. *Crown 8vo. 2s.*

PRACTICAL CHEMISTRY. By W. FRENCH, M.A., Principal of the Storey Institute, Lancaster. Part I. With numerous diagrams. *Crown 8vo. 1s. 6d.*
'An excellent and eminently practical little book.'—*Schoolmaster.*

ENGLISH

ENGLISH RECORDS. A Companion to the History of England. By H. E. MALDEN, M.A. *Crown 8vo. 3s. 6d.*

THE ENGLISH CITIZEN: HIS RIGHTS AND DUTIES. By H. E. MALDEN, M.A. *1s. 6d.*

A DIGEST OF DEDUCTIVE LOGIC. By JOHNSON BARKER, B.A. *Crown 8vo. 2s. 6d.*

A CLASS-BOOK OF DICTATION PASSAGES. By W. WILLIAMSON, B.A. *Fourth Edition. Cr. 8vo. 1s. 6d.*

A SHORT STORY OF ENGLISH LITERATURE. By EMMA S. MELLOWS. *Crown 8vo. 3s. 6d.*
'A lucid and well-arranged account of the growth of English literature.'—*Pall Mall Gazette.*

TEST CARDS IN EUCLID AND ALGEBRA. By D. S. CALDERWOOD, Headmaster of the Normal School, Edinburgh. In three packets of 40, with Answers. *1s.* Or in three Books, price *2d., 2d., and 3d.*

THE METRIC SYSTEM. By LEON DELBOS. *Crown 8vo. 2s.*
A theoretical and practical guide, for use in elementary schools and by the general reader.

METHUEN'S COMMERCIAL SERIES

Edited by H. DE B. GIBBINS, Litt.D., M.A.

BRITISH COMMERCE AND COLONIES FROM ELIZABETH TO VICTORIA. By H. DE B. GIBBINS, Litt.D., M.A. *Third Edition. 2s.*

COMMERCIAL EXAMINATION PAPERS. By H. DE B. GIBBINS, Litt.D., M.A. *1s. 6d.*

THE ECONOMICS OF COMMERCE. By H. DE B. GIBBINS, Litt.D., M.A. *1s. 6d.*

FRENCH COMMERCIAL CORRESPONDENCE. By S. E. BALLY, Master at the Manchester Grammar School. *Second Edition. 2s.*

GERMAN COMMERCIAL CORRESPONDENCE. By S. E. BALLY. With Vocabulary. *2s. 6d.*

A FRENCH COMMERCIAL READER. By S. E. BALLY. *Second Edition. 2s.*

A GERMAN COMMERCIAL READER. By S. E. BALLY. With Vocabulary. 2s.

COMMERCIAL GEOGRAPHY, with special reference to the British Empire. By L. W. LYDE, M.A. *Third Edition.* 2s.

A PRIMER OF BUSINESS. By S. JACKSON, M.A. *Third Ed.* 1s. 6d.

COMMERCIAL ARITHMETIC. By F. G. TAYLOR, M.A. *Third Edition.* 1s. 6d.

PRÉCIS WRITING AND OFFICE CORRESPONDENCE. By E. E. WHITFIELD, M.A. 2s.

A GUIDE TO PROFESSIONS AND BUSINESS. By H. JONES. 1s. 6d.

THE PRINCIPLES OF BOOK-KEEPING BY DOUBLE ENTRY. By J. E. B. M'ALLEN, M.A. *Cr. 8vo.* 2s.

COMMERCIAL LAW. By W. DOUGLAS EDWARDS. 2s.

WORKS BY A. M. M. STEDMAN, M.A.

INITIA LATINA: Easy Lessons on Elementary Accidence. *Fourth Edition. Fcap. 8vo.* 1s.

FIRST LATIN LESSONS. *Sixth Edition. Crown 8vo.* 2s.

FIRST LATIN READER. With Notes adapted to the Shorter Latin Primer and Vocabulary. *Fifth Edition revised.* 18mo. 1s. 6d.

EASY SELECTIONS FROM CÆSAR. Part I. The Helvetian War. *Second Edition.* 18mo. 1s.

EASY SELECTIONS FROM LIVY. Part I. The Kings of Rome. 18mo. *Second Edition.* 1s. 6d.

EASY LATIN PASSAGES FOR UNSEEN TRANSLATION. *Seventh Edition. Fcap. 8vo.* 1s. 6d.

EXEMPLA LATINA. First Lessons in Latin Accidence. With Vocabulary. *Crown 8vo.* 1s.

EASY LATIN EXERCISES ON THE SYNTAX OF THE SHORTER AND REVISED LATIN PRIMER. With Vocabulary. *Eighth and cheaper Edition, re-written. Crown 8vo.* 1s. 6d. Issued with the consent of Dr. Kennedy. KEY 3s. *net.*

THE LATIN COMPOUND SENTENCE: Rules and Exercises. *Second Edition. Cr. 8vo.* 1s. 6d. With Vocabulary. 2s.

NOTANDA QUAEDAM: Miscellaneous Latin Exercises on Common Rules and Idioms. *Fourth Edition. Fcap. 8vo.* 1s. 6d. With Vocabulary. 2s. Key, 2s. *net.*

LATIN VOCABULARIES FOR REPETITION: Arranged according to Subjects. *Ninth Edition. Fcap. 8vo.* 1s. 6d.

A VOCABULARY OF LATIN IDIOMS. 18mo. *Second Edition.* 1s.

STEPS TO GREEK. *Second Edition, Revised.* 18mo. 1s.

A SHORTER GREEK PRIMER. *Crown 8vo.* 1s. 6d.

EASY GREEK PASSAGES FOR UNSEEN TRANSLATION. *Third Edition Revised. Fcap. 8vo.* 1s. 6d.

GREEK VOCABULARIES FOR REPETITION. Arranged according to Subjects. *Second Edition. Fcap. 8vo.* 1s. 6d.

GREEK TESTAMENT SELECTIONS. For the use of Schools. *Third Edition.* With Introduction, Notes, and Vocabulary. *Fcap. 8vo.* 2s. 6d.

STEPS TO FRENCH. *Fifth Edition.* 18mo. 8d.

FIRST FRENCH LESSONS. *Fifth Edition Revised. Crown 8vo.* 1s.

EASY FRENCH PASSAGES FOR UNSEEN TRANSLATION. *Fourth Edition revised. Fcap. 8vo.* 1s. 6d.

EASY FRENCH EXERCISES ON ELEMENTARY SYNTAX. With Vocabulary. *Second Edition. Crown 8vo.* 2s. 6d. KEY 3s. *net.*

FRENCH VOCABULARIES FOR REPETITION: Arranged according to Subjects. *Ninth Edition. Fcap. 8vo.* 1s.

SCHOOL EXAMINATION SERIES

EDITED BY A. M. M. STEDMAN, M.A. *Crown 8vo.* 2s. 6d.

FRENCH EXAMINATION PAPERS IN MISCELLANEOUS GRAMMAR AND IDIOMS. By A. M. M. STEDMAN, M.A. *Eleventh Edition.*

A KEY, issued to Tutors and Private Students only, to be had on application to the Publishers. *Fourth Edition. Crown 8vo.* 6s. *net.*

LATIN EXAMINATION PAPERS IN MISCELLANEOUS GRAMMAR AND IDIOMS. By A. M. M. STEDMAN, M.A. *Tenth Edition.*

KEY (*Fourth Edition*) issued as above. 6s. *net.*

GREEK EXAMINATION PAPERS IN MISCELLANEOUS GRAMMAR AND IDIOMS. By A. M. M. STEDMAN, M.A. *Sixth Edition.*

KEY (*Second Edition*) issued as above. 6s. *net.*

GERMAN EXAMINATION PAPERS IN MISCELLANEOUS GRAMMAR AND IDIOMS. By R. J. MORICH, Clifton College. *Fifth Edition.*

KEY (*Second Edition*) issued as above. 6s. *net.*

HISTORY AND GEOGRAPHY EXAMINATION PAPERS. By C. H. SPENCE, M.A., Clifton College. *Second Edition.*

PHYSICS EXAMINATION PAPERS. By R. E. STEEL, M.A., F.C.S.

GENERAL KNOWLEDGE EXAMINATION PAPERS. By A. M. M. STEDMAN, M.A. *Third Edition.*

KEY (*Second Edition*) issued as above. 7s. *net.*

EXAMINATION PAPERS IN ENGLISH HISTORY. By J. TAIT PLOWDEN-WARDLAW, B.A., King's College, Cambridge. *Crown 8vo.* 2s. 6d.

www.ingramcontent.com/pod-product-compliance
Lightning Source LLC
Chambersburg PA
CBHW051242300426
44114CB00011B/858